Holistic Magical Approach

Research/"Self-love is the key to fulfillments,
peace and feeling loved"

VJOLLCA SADIKU

Gotham Books
30 N Gould St.
Ste. 20820, Sheridan, WY 82801
https://gothambooksinc.com/

Phone: 1 (307) 464-7800

Published by Gotham Books (June 10, 2022)

ISBN: 978-1-956349-82-5 (sc)
ISBN: 978-1-956349-83-2 (e)

Because of the dynamic nature of the Internet, any web addresses or links
contained in this book may have changed since publication and may no longer
be valid.

The views expressed in this work are solely those of the author and do not
necessarily reflect the views of the publisher, and the publisher hereby
disclaims any responsibility for them.

CONTENTS

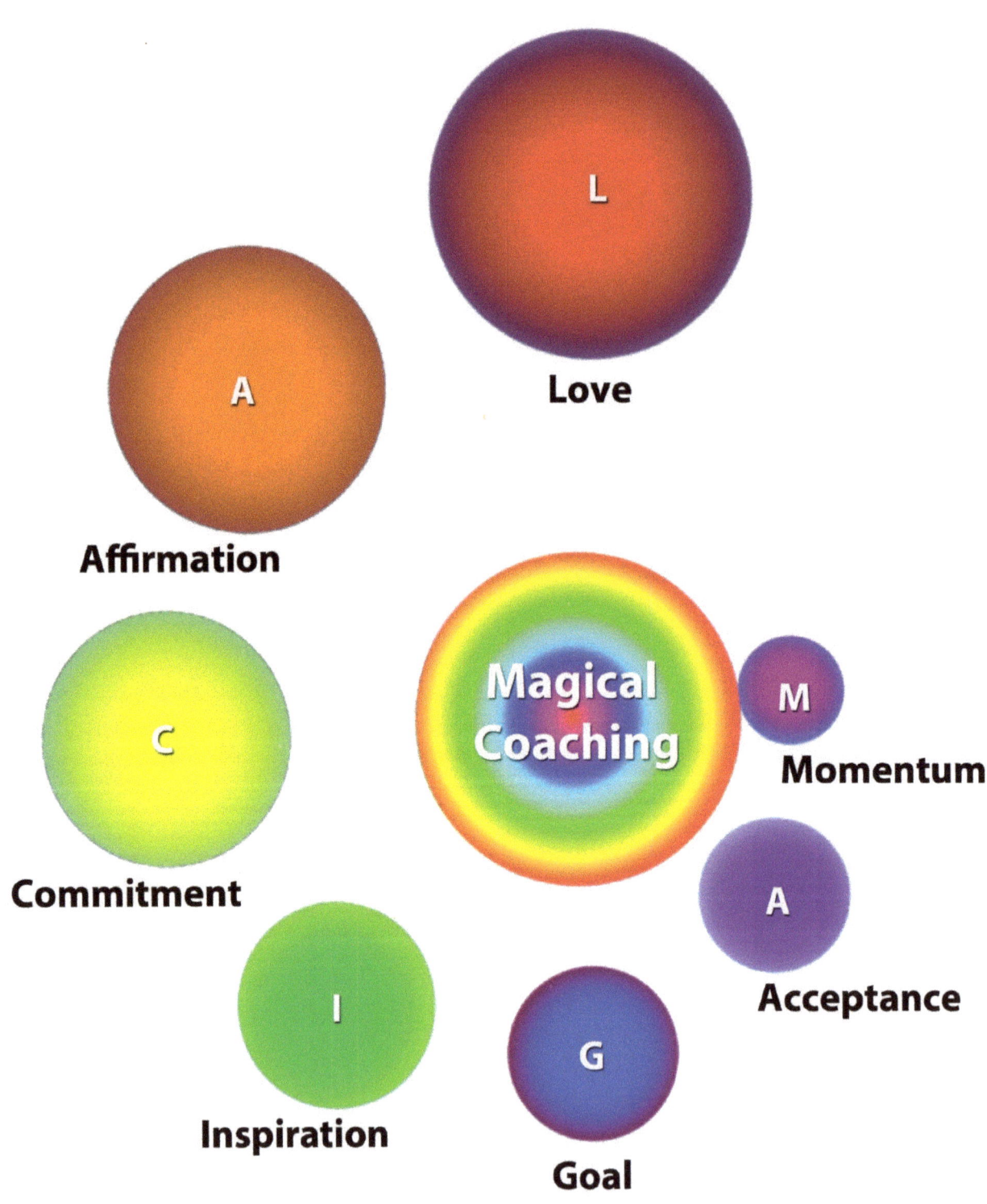

L
Love

A
Affirmation

C
Commitment

Magical
Coaching

M
Momentum

A
Acceptance

I
Inspiration

G
Goal

Author's Acknowledgements

With special gratitude to:

Participants took part in research: Participants of the questionnaires who filled in willingly and with complete sincerity, questionnaires.

Case Study Participants - thank you for following my absurdity, without questioning and accepting to be part of the study, including their sincere and direct impressions. All the participants have helped me grow and I'm suretheywillhelpmanypeoplewiththeirparticipationinthisresearchandontheirjourneyoflife.

Participants of the observations – thank you for communicating and interacting with me.

Readers of the book "A Magic Life" - thank you for your time, sincerity, dedication, and allowing me to use your thoughts and views.

Lena Grafik - thank you for your dedication, support, hard work, care, correctness and justice and your love for your passion to publish books in your best abilities.

To myself - thank myself for the faith and devotion to intuition, justice, goodness, and love for oneself, others, and life.

Intuition (Creator) - for instructions and love that penetrated into any situation, which was absurd for me and for clarifying things that did not make sense for me and others.

All the people who entered my life during the research journey: because they helped with their presence to study in more depth things into universe and reality.

Vjollca Sadiku

CHAPTER I

Explains the outline of the research. This chapter includes a brief explanation of the research background, and provides rationale for the selection of the research area. Moreover, the first chapter contains explanation of the research aim and objectives, and comprises structure of the research.

Abstract

Self-love is the key to a fulfilled, meaningful life and is paramount to creating peace and love where you are. It is only when you have fully embraced self-love that you have developed a clear and flexible plan for your future. e methods used in this study are based on the seven stages of the magical module, closely intertwined with a therapeutic approach. Comprising self-love and therapeutic skill, the methodology was applied to 30 clients aged between six and sixty. Participants in the study came from a variety of backgrounds and faced a range of diverse issues. e research consisted of 50 questionnaires, containing 11 questions each and further observation via social media. e results were overwhelming and at first glance indicated that all the participants were both unhappy and lacking self-love. Further analysis of the results revealed that individuals were in survival mode for universal and passionate love, which create the foundations for further issues such as suicide, crime, abuse and loneliness. ese in turn become a driving force behind destructive and harmful behaviours such as materialism, casual sex simply for the excitement without loving commitment, drug consumption or a failure to achieve childhood goals and visions. A number of clients with whom I worked very closely with, developed a holistic approach, which was based on the magical module. ese individuals developed a depth of self-love over time, which has transformed their view of both themselves and their life, making way for inner harmony, peace and love. they then possessed the ability to reflect these new found feelings to the outside and into their reality.

The ultimate purpose of this book is to present you with all the tools and inner resources needed to turn your life around and to help you discover the pure love which you have subconsciously been searching for, but for so long have been unable to understand or achieve. This is undeniably the book of life, come to life. I will provide insight into how to heal yourself from the past, how to be in the present and how to create the future you desire.

Anyone who is interested can follow this approach, and I will suggest that any psychologist would be better equipped if they too had knowledge of this approach Likewise, social services, charity organizations, education institutes, mental health institutes, hospitals and healthcare professionals, as well as scientists would benefit from knowing and developing these skills. This book will demonstrate that Love is the key to everything. By understanding yourself you will understand others, which will improve any services that you are involved in.

Views regarding the direction of this research

The literature review presented in chapter two is intended to simply be an illustration of the potential relevant information regarding personal well-being, with an emphasis on spirituality.

Refection on this literature review has identified the need for a practical working framework, by which spirituality and its practice can be explored and implemented in an all-encompassing, universal manner. Careful consideration of individual case studies will demonstrate the application of the approach and the degree of its effectiveness. This framework primarily consists of 'the self' , the 'Highest personal belief 'as well as' the others'.

Note for copyright: The material provided in the case studies and observations section has no known copyright. However if anyone believes that a particular material published in this book has copyright, please let us know so that we take the appropriate measures and make amendments accordingly.

INTRODUCTION
STRUCTURE OF THE RESEARCH

The introduction will begin with an outline of who I am and the origin of my drive and my desire to research and share these insights with you. This will be followed by a brief explanation of the aims and objectives of this research, including a short summary of what will be literature review and why. There will be a summary of methodology and how the data will be collected including any ethical issues, which will be followed by a discussion chapter and a final concluding chapter

1 – Who am I?

I am an individual seeking love, I seek to create the person I have always wanted to be and to live a life which is filled with peace and love; this has been my dream since the age of 7. At age of 7 I achieved it. Between the ages of 16 and 18 my goal was to gain independence and live my own life, where I was free to make my own decisions and to simply breathe. However, somehow I lost track of what I had learned since I was 7 years old. I forgot to communicate with myself and instead I searched for a person to make me feel fulfilled. I was angry with my family. For every emotion I experienced, I blamed my family for not letting me be free and not giving me the love I so desperately wanted and craved. At the age of 36 I stopped, took a breath and told myself that, 'If you possess the ability to give love to your life, why pass the responsibility to others?'. So I focused all my attention and strength on giving myself love so that I could in turn fall in love with both my me and my life. After that, I could think of what I wanted to do.

Thus, I returned to the age of 7 and to the little girl who had discovered how to feel loved.

After this period, I fell in love with life and I realised that I was finally happy, yet I felt sympathy towards others who were still suffering. Something was wrong, something was meaningless, there was so much pain and suffering in the world, what could I do to address this?

I took the initiative to immerse myself in this study, in order to gain a deeper understanding of what was happening; 'where was the bridge between my feelings of fulfilment and the feelings of those who complained, who were unhappy, or who were suffering in life and modern society. As I was studying this bridge, I discovered that I had in fact changed. The Self-love I had discovered within myself meant that I no longer identified with egotism or selfishness, and I treasured the sense of pure energy that I had worked on. I become a person who saw the beauty in everything. I had found wealth within my soul; I was finally fulfilled, whatever I needed I either had or it eventually found its way to me. I continued to study the depths of the human world in order to understand the bridge (the connection between my condition and the condition of those individuals who were unhappy and blamed others, and who were constantly searching, but to no avail).

The bridge is a metaphorical representation of the question I attempt to answer: "How can I help those individuals cross the bridge so they too can stand where I am standing?"

I am a qualified psychotherapist, counsellor, life coach, youth coach and educational coach; an accredited member of National Counselling Society. I had gained a child care diploma, a degree in Psychosocial Studies, an advanced diploma in Psychotherapeutic & Counselling, a diploma in Personal Coaching, Youth Coaching and Educational Coaching. Furthermore, I am a certified Goal-Mapping practitioner. Additional roles include, foster carer and freelance interpreter. All of these combined have helped me in my therapeutic work.

I am content and have gained the ability to find solutions to my problems. I have discovered the key to the road that leads from one corner of the bridge to the other, which encompasses self-love. This path involves my magical module. I've discovered how make this transition by going up the magic module stairs; you have to be truly devoted, willing to test new things and dedicate time to get inside your head, in order to find the path to your soul.

This is reflected in the work so far and is indicated by the feedback I have received. In order to protect confidentiality, I will not make the participants' names public. Nonetheless, the importance and significance lays in the results of my work. Moreover, the feedback I have received from the book has made me feel fulfilled as they demonstrate that it made a positive impact on someone's life, enabling them to heal. My son is an achievement for me, which is wonderful. I have discovered a path, which fuels my sense of fulfillment and enables me to enjoy being in love with myself, with other and with life. This is real success, which leads to feelings of peace, fulfillment and love and is attainable for each and every one of us. I believe that this is what everyone is innately hungry for.

Aims and objectives of the research are:

In this research I aimed to test whether self-love is the key to a fulfilled life encompassing both peace and love. I sought answers to how this could be achieved. In the previous volume, *A Magical Life*, I showed that self love is a solution to many of the problems people face today, including, a general sense of unhappiness and feelings of being lost, or harmful behaviours such as crime, suicide, not following their dreams, being victims or becoming an abuser. The new generation is following the same old steps. The aim of this research is to bring solutions and also to answer a number of questions:

How to heal yourself from the past, in order to live in the present and embrace it, the 80% fully in the present or find ways to both enjoy it and expand the remaining 20%. Where the imagination has no limits or limitation, where you are able to create a bridge between where you are and your dreams, by knowing how to climb each step.

It is all about the 80% in which you are fully present in the moment (to focus on the here and now, because here and now can help you heal from the past, stay in the present and help you to achieve the future you want).

This research will explore and demonstrate how you can achieve that, through using the magical model. The magical model is a holistic approach, which includes, counselling, therapy, mentoring, advice and advocacy on healing, and coaching.

This research will primarily focus on the foundation of its core premise: self-love, which, with the appropriate tools and techniques, is the key to opening the doors to a number of further questions.

- How can we achieve self-love?
- What does self-love mean?
- Why do we need self-love?
- Why are we humans never happy unless we have self-love?
- Why does our body need love?
- Why do we crave love…why do we need others to love us?
- What are the various perspectives such as religion?

- Is this life a test, that requires us to cleanse ourselves?
- What is a soul?
- Does 'Soul' exist?
- Is there only one religion?
- If yes, then why are there so many religions?
- If no, what is the purpose of there being so many religions?
- Does it matter how many religions there are?
- What does science say about the vital aspect of love?
- How do various religions explain serious life threatening diseases?
- What is a spiritual path?
- How can you find out who you are and why is important to know the real you?
- Who is the real you?
- Why do we die and what is the meaning of this life?
- Are we meant to suffer or enjoy life?
- Why is that?
- How important is self-love to get the answer to all those questions I mentioned?
- Can self-love bring peace and love, and how that can happen?

The Literature review for this work is broad, covering diverse fields such as healthcare, science, religion and spirituality. These fields sit at the core of human wellbeing. The literature review will primarily focus on how wellbeing is intertwined with self-love and how it influences us as a human beings. I believe our interpretation of these issues plays a major role in our life, this will be explained in further detail during our discussion

Methods are through seven stages of the magical module

- **MOMENTUM**
- **ACCEPTANCE**
- **GOAL**
- **INSPIRATION**
- **COMMITMENT**
- **AFFIRMATION**
- **LOVE**

The research involves 30 case studies and 50 questionnaires with 11 open questions on each questionnaire. There will also be feedback and reviews from individuals who read 'A Magical Life'. The observations will be drawn from all the participants ranging from age 6 to 60+ and from diverse backgrounds and social economic statuses.

Data gathering and analysis techniques will be utilised and discussed in the study. Real-life cases will be presented to facilitate a deep examination, along with a discussion on which instruments and data gathering approaches to use. Although the study makes use of multiple cases, each case is treated uniquely as a single case in its own right.

The conclusions of the case studies can then be used as information contributing to the whole study, while the integrity of each case study is retained. Data gathered is largely qualitative. Tools to collect data can include surveys, open questions, case studies, and observation with interactions.

One measure for the concepts being studied is to attend to the subject's internal experience for qualitative validity. This demonstrates that certain dynamics lead to other conditions and requires the use of multiple pieces of evidence from cross-dynamical sources, to uncover convergent lines of inquiry. The researcher strives to establish a chain of evidence, which is discernible both in terms of future trajectory and in retrospect. In addition, external validity reflects whether or not findings are applicable beyond the confines of the immediate case or cases; the more variations in places, people, and procedures a case study can withstand and still yield the same findings, the more potent the external validity.

Techniques such as cross-case examination and within-case examination, alongside a literature review establishes external validity. Reliability refers to the stability, accuracy, and precision of the measurements. Moreover, the exemplary case study design ensures that the procedures used are well documented and that they can be repeated with the same results each time.

The researcher examines raw data using numerous interpretations in order to identify correlations between the research objective and the outcomes, with reference to the original research questions in chapter four.

Throughout the evaluation and analysis process, the researcher remains open to new findings and insights.

Exemplary case studies report the data in a way that transforms a complex issue into one that can be understood, allowing the reader to question and examine the study and reach an understanding independent of the researcher. The goal of the written report is to portray a complex problem in a way that conveys a vicarious experience to the reader. Case studies present data in very publicly accessible ways and enable the reader to apply the experience to his or her own real-life situation (refer to chapter seven, eight, nine, ten and eleven). Researchers pay particular attention to displaying sufficient evidence in order to gain the readers confidence. This confidence is gained by exploring all avenues, clearly communicating the boundaries of the case, and giving special attention to conflicting propositions.

Techniques for composing the report can include handling each case as a separate chapter or treating the case as a chronological recounting. The research report examines each case study in thorough detail. The research case studies are critically examined through chapter 3 and 5, leaving room for the reader to reflect on and analyse so that they can be creative and create their own techniques in order to achieve self love.

As I was finishing my studies and working with clients by simply following my intuition and what implementing what I had learnt, I noticed that my approach was both different and effective.

What I do is:

1 - I connect with your soul (to understand who you really are and what your purpose in this life is) (this can be done through conversations with you), I connect with and feel the energy within your soul

2 - Understand who you are, who you have become as a result of your journey in life and what influenced the way you are... (through the sessions we can discuss all those questions and understand them together, to see if you like who you are or whether you need to make changes in order to get what you want).

3 - I have a deep and thorough understanding of your actions. Are they created to survive? Are all of your actions based on your survival mechanism? I can help you let go of your survival mechanism, so you'll be able to enjoy life and not constantly feel a need to survive... we are not here to survive but to enjoy life.

Furthermore, each approach or technique that I use is different based on the clients' needs and their uniqueness. I aim to help the client connect with their true self and learn how to fight in order to get what he or she wants.

It is difficult to name and sum up my approach and therapy in one word as they are very much based on the needs of the clients, which vary massively. The steps do not have to be in order, as shown in the 30 case studies I have used for this research. My approach was different in each case study as it was heavily based on the client's unique needs.

My approach is unusual

I used 30 case studies for this research and for confidential reasons their details have not been disclosed, instead I will refer to the individuals as client number 1 and so forth.

For each case study the approaches, the time, techniques, learning and results are different. But they are based on the approach I mentioned earlier in chapter 3 on my magical module.

The process is based around the meaning of the space (the meaning of space is us and universe) - the acceptance of the space, the space dance - exploring the reality journey- the return to the mind - the compassion for the heart - the return to the space - retrieval - discussion - elaboration - reflection - analysis - compassion - sadness – allowing yourself to feel down - doubt - seeking to understand faith - initiating trust in the space that gives love – feeding yourself with pure love - rebel against reality to stay in that space – learn how to bring the space into reality – how to spread that love — feeding yourself with pure love - rebel against reality to stay in that space – learn how to bring the space into reality – how to spread that love – then you learn that the mind is poisoned.

You learn that the heart is hurting, it needs healing - so you create a therapeutic environment – you make time to heal your heart, to listen to your mind, but…no no no, you do not allow your mind to interfere in everyday life, because your mind is like a laptop and you have been fed with information that has not made you feel happy so far. Even though you have reprogrammed your mind with positive thoughts, one negative thought (that you hear from somebody that has nothing to do with you, some bad news, something that you don't like) automatically produces counteractive feelings. Although you are not giving space to these thoughts, automatically they have crossed your mind and will produce feelings. If you are a positive person, you will allow these thoughts to simply cross your mind quickly, however, if you are not positive this will not happen. I will explain these two scenarios below.

The thoughts which pass through the positive mind create a feeling which is directly linked to your heart. If you are unsure about how to process these feelings, they will be suppressed in your heart. You will not feel pain. You will also be unaware about how that feeling has affected you. These repressed feelings will unknowingly create underlying problems for the individual, which will automatically create bad energy within your body and may eventually lead to physical illness. Alternatively, you can successfully process those feelings through the healing process. To conclude, it is apparent that the mind needs reprogramming through your magical person and your soul and to undergo an extensive process (refer to chapter 3: Magical module for more details). If you process all the negative things you receive from others through your space or magical person, the negativity will immediately transform into love.

This means that neither the heart nor the body will not be affected. Your Magical Person/soul/intuition/universe energy will turn anything they receive into love. That is why I advise individuals not to use their minds, as I have yet to trust mine. I have tested my mind, however, I do not feel confident that my mind is on the same level of the inner space. Thus, for now my mind is still in therapy. I cannot say what will happen in the future.

The negative thoughts pass through the mind while the individual is still in their process of personal development. In this category there are multiple examples and I cannot even count the different ways that people use these thoughts. Nonetheless, I will briefly mention a few. There are those individuals whose thoughts make continuous noise in their heads. There are those that overthink, by keeping one thought and going over and over it in circles. They wake up every morning with the same thought, pretending that they are not paying attention to it, but in reality they are living with it. There are those who keep themselves busy in order to ignore their thoughts, they believe that there will be no space for the brain to retain those thoughts because the thoughts start fighting with each other; taking up the space in the brain. There are those who simply live within the thoughts they feed their brain, ones, which they fail to analyse. They give excuses to their thoughts. These individuals' minds are often messy and their thoughts often set the foundation for further problems such as depression, anxiety, worries, unhappiness, dissatisfaction and physical sickness.

They could also take different kind of turns, however I am sure that you do not need me to go into further detail about what occurs in this mind as existing psychological theories explains it thoroughly. I am mainly focused on the holistic approach and on individuals who really want to get to know their own magical person.

That is what I do.

Please keep in mind that there are unexplored topics within the book. I believe that there are a number of subjects, which are still not explained on a deep enough level, because more study and practice needs to be dedicated to them. For example, understanding how to help somebody who wants to become a healer or use the space to help others, or even how they can interpret the messages they get through channeling. For example some might say, "I have God I have everything".. This statement suggests that God has given you everything that you need in this world, including the knowledge of how to communicate with him and how to ask for help. Communication with yourself and with the creator does not cost anything and is free, so there are really no excuses. If you ask for his guidance he will be there. You can only expect him to be there if you are specific about what you need, what you want and why you need it. Listening to the creator is a skill which needs to be learned and can be obtained through practice. You simply need silence and time. I previously explained this example which is similar to my theory. There are numerous layers which need to be explored in depth, in order to learn more about the key factors- self-love and communication skills, read the book 'A Magical Life'. In order to see the difference between a brain which is guided by the soul, universal energy, creator, and intuition and one which is not guided by them, I recommend further study into the differences as I am sure that you will notice the contrast between the two. In both my case and my main client number 1's case, we managed to be guided by our intuition and our soul, by using out brain as a tool. The brain helps you to function inside the human body, it is there as a tool which passes messages around the body and helps you with other senses including; focus, attention, concentration etc. Although we have achieved this, we still need to look after the old thoughts, because the brain is like a computer.

Thus, we need to work as a kind of therapy in that computer, in order to reprogram the brain with the information from the space.

The heart also needs therapy, in case any thoughts have unknowingly crossed through our minds. We still need to treat the mind and the heart with the healing touch, as they are very precious parts of our selves. I do not have much knowledge in science but I am aware of the left and right hemispheres of the brain and how our body parts function in relation to them. I believe that if we are guided from the inner space, we can look after our whole human existence and know our needs, know how to take care and fulfil those needs, know how to feel loved, to give love, know what we want in this life. Alternatively, if we are unsure about what we want at that moment, we should know how to discover what we want. There are always small steps in front of us, to which I am adding. It is only when you have taken the small steps, that you are ready to get into the big ones. every minute of your journey.

Validity

The individuals who want to teach this approach should learn how to be guided by this space (soul/intuition) before teaching anyone else.

The client has to be open minded and willing to try new things, as well as able to allow themselves to be guided by their inner voice and have the drive for pure love, justice and practice the guidance below:

- Treat others, as you would like to be treated.
- Love yourself, as you would like to be loved.
- Give 100% in everything that you choose.

We have to be aware that everything and everyone is unique. You need to know how to analyse and validate your results.

Example of client one's case study ingredients:

1. **The** insistence of your inner call
2. Detachment from reality by simply spending time with yourself and avoiding conversations that don't serve you, your goal and your purpose.
3. Vjollca's insistence about not giving up, but instead observing my thoughts, feelings and actions and reflecting it back to me through my soul language.
4. Giving Vjollca full freedom to make suggestions and present exercises to me, whilst I am honest, open and pursuing without realising what is being done. I knew inside me that it felt right and I had my own inner calling.
5. Vjollca's purity and honesty resonated with my inner calling.
6. Acceptance of absurdity
7. Rebellion, by not accepting myself the way I was formed by reality and the life that surrounded me.
8. Making daily notes, as these are a reflection of you.
9. Her desire for purity and justice, which covers the self love guidance in question one of the questionnaire.
10. Wanting to be guided by the soul and allowing the soul to reveal who we truly are and to be a part of their decisions, discussions, analysis and dreams.
11. Challenging themselves all the time through the eyes of the soul and creator.

Methodology

Out of the 30 case studies, I have permission to use 21 of them, 8 of them are documented to prove my work. The rest have been carried out through Facebook, and telephone conversations. The clients range from the ages 3 and 65. The background of the clients: India, Portugal, Albania, Kosovo, England, and Arabic countries. A few of the Albanian participants are migrants living in Germany and England, with issues such as domestic violence, seeking asylum etc. There are single individuals, divorced parents, couples, families, teenagers, foster children.

The participants who completed the questionnaires are from; India, Mauritius, Albania, Kosovo, England and Nigeria. The age of participants range from 6 to 65 and the participants have diverse professions, and family statuses.

In order to protect the confidentiality and identity of the participants, I have chosen not to explain specific details such as the treatment plan, diagnosis, limits and flaws, discussion, conclusion. However, I have explained in depth how I used the seven stages of the Magical module. Every piece of information is documented. The methods and techniques of the treatment plan are part of the Magical Module, which will be explained in further detail in chapter three. But it is worth emphasising that there are more and more layers that go deeper and deeper, and which flow in terms of the individual's needs.

My apologies for not thoroughly explaining my vision, but that will be become apparent in due course through events, seminars, group therapy, workshops and in the future materials. The discussion will be in the discussion section, and will be concluded in the concluding chapter. General limitations and flaws will be summarised and finally, the diagnosis will encompass the analysis of all the cases, questionnaires, observations and book impressions.

To the reader: Please keep in mind that I have been granted both oral and written permission by most of the participants. A number of participants, for various reasons, have not given me permission to share their details.

They may have been avoiding the responsibility of continuing further to achieve the self-love, as they were happy with what they had achieve so far. Some also believed that I was using them simply to develop my career. I cannot say exactly what the reason was, however, I am sure that it was a lot to do with the absence of self love. A further is the absurdity, the awareness of the whole magical approach, which makes them confused. If they do not believe in that approach, it comes back that they do not believe in themselves, which means everything becomes blurry.

These 30 case studies include different ages, and different stages of life journey. They have received a different type of therapy and different time-scales. That is the flavour of this research, as the universe has brought all of those to me. I never chased the clients and never looked for them. Somehow we were part of each other's journey.

In addition, the names, places, all the details that can lead to their identification are removed for confidential reasons, but the flavour of the Magical Approach is explored in depth and that is the importance of my message in this research. I thank each of them, who participated and everyone that has contributed to helping others. I will end each case study with a quote; a message from me to them.

The 11 questions used 50 questionnaires are noted below: (The answers are in chapter eleven and 20 selected questionnaires are in chapter ten).

Questions 1:

1. Are there three main rules according to the Lord?
   -Treat others as you would like to be treated.
   -Love yourself as you would like to be loved.
   -Give 100% in everything that you choose.
2. Are those 3 rules, all that is required of humans to accomplish in this life? How do you explain the way that these can be applied by a person, born in a family amongst members, who do not comply with those rules?
3. For someone to follow the path that makes them happy, do they firstly have to let go of those who are not happy with themselves, or are becoming obstacles for your journey and will not allow you to achieve your dreams? Even if this encompasses their own family? What is the reason for this?
4. What is the soul? Where is it located anatomically in humans and what is the role of the soul in this life? Why…
5. Can a person live and be guided by their soul? How can this be achieved?
6. Does a bad soul exist? The reason why…
7. Are the mind, heart and body human utensils, which serve the soul so that the person is faithful or fulfilled? Why…
8. What does it mean to believe in God and how can this be demonstrated by 3 rules or examples?
9. Do you suppose that children are like angels and innocent? Why? How is their suffering explained in God's language and why?
10. Are there two kinds of death: A prewritten one and another that depends on our Actions? If so, how is the child's death explained?
11. Can a human-being be filled with love, which comes exclusively from the source within themselves? And from the moment they become aware of that love, they do not feel suffering because they are know their purpose and are fulfilled?

What do you think is the love within? And why do you think that way?

The participant who have filled out the questionnaires are from different backgrounds including Albania, Kosovo, Nigeria, Greece, English, India, Mauritius, Portugal, United Kingdom. They are all aged between 6 and 60+ years old.

Their professions include; IT student, psychology students, trainer/assessor/teacher, pastor, business management student, social worker, politicians, poet/writer, law student, homeless individual, stay at home mothers, directors of charity organisations and painters.

There are 6 participants under the age of 16 (two aged 6, 7, 8, 11,15 and 5 female and one male). There are 18 participants from the ages of 16 to 25 (11 male and 7 female). There are 14 aged between 26 and 35 (11 female and 3 male). There are 6 participants between the ages 36 and 45 (5 female and 1 male). There are 6 participants between 46 and 66 years old (2 female and 4 male).

The reason for the questioners:

Title: Human perceptions: how to bring peace and love to ourselves and the environment around us. How can we know our own self (soul) to guide us? How to nourish the mind with our soul's thoughts for the feelings to be produced as a result of thoughts that come from our own self (soul)?

Purpose: This research is developed to find out how people heal from the past, to enjoy the moment and realise the dreams that they want to achieve by understanding themselves, life and to find their inner source of love.

Hypothesis: 'I believe that once the person finds their inner source of love, they are able to understand themselves and the life around, based on peace and love'.

OSERVATIONS: will be on chapter eight

Last year on Facebook I only had 200 friends and no followers, but now I have 2145 friends and 1710 followers. Most of these people have contacted me and I have had some sort of conversation with each and every one of them. I have been in touch with over 3000 people. I have observed these individuals from a distance, which also interacting with them from time to time. I could bring up so many underlying issues that arose, which I noticed, however, I will only mention three points.

1) Self–love is the key to everything

2) Create the life you want based on your own beliefs.

3) Where self-love exists, only love and understanding will be applied.

Chapter nine contains the readers feedback of my book "A Magical Life". The feedback enabled me to conclude while analysing my aims and objectives. These include; helping the reader connect with their soul, their inner deepest self and through their inner self to reflect on the present. All that matters is being in the moment of the present, so you can heal your past, to be happy have a clear vision of tomorrow.

Chapter four will contain the results of the data collection and chapter five will discuss these results in greater depth while also incorporating a literature review and my personal opinions. In chapter six, I will conclude the research and explore its limitations.

Conclusion: Suggestions for this research: this is the book of life. How to heal yourself from the past, how to be in the present and how to create the future you want. Anyone who is interested can follow this approach, but I will suggest that any psychologist should have knowledge of this approach, social services, charity organisations, education institutes, mental health institutes, hospitals and healthcare, as well as the scientist. Basically it involves every individual who is living. Love is the key to everything. By understanding yourself you will understand others, which improve any services that you are involved in.

Note for Readers: Many things are repetitive, such as client number one feedback, are repeated, in the case study one, in chapter seven, in chapter three and in discussion in chapter five. Many of the answers to the questions are repeated in chapter 3, 4, 5, 10, and 11, for it is easier for the reader to read there and then what I am referring, rather than going to another chapter to look for it. By reading it there and then, it gives the reader the correct effect, which is looking for, and the reader, who don't want to reread again, will just passes quickly knowing what it is about. Also, the answers to the various questions and fragments from chapter seven have been repeated because they are explaining an argument and are pointing out what I want to express, which means is not only my view but it is the participants who took part on research. I also greatly appreciate the responses of the people who participated, because they are very precious and are the foundation of this study, so from time to time I emphasize repeating their sayings when I am making a point. The goals and objectives are repeated, in the presentation and in the discussion, for reasons to reflect again and to consider it in another consequence. In Chapter Three, I have repeated the same words because I have explained in detail the effect of methodology in the way I apply it to others and how the individual should follow. Moreover, self-love and her way of achievement have been repeated, almost everywhere in the chapters, which can be annoying to those who have not achieved it and a food and inspiration for those who have achieved it. So, even m I don't fully understand the process I am using but I can give those explanations below about the repetition of things in this book:

Intuition says: Yes … it is very good because it is your writing style and time can't wait for you to improve it or fix it the way you have the vision. For reasons that you do not have enough money to pay someone to do what you cannot do and you have tried but for different reasons it did not work out and don't trust that thy may copy your work.

So it's perfect for your chances and your intended purpose. You can encourage many people to understand that they can, because when you can with the skills you have, why someone who has much more skill than you cannot achieve it. You can also fix it in the future or make a second audition.

The mind says: what are you doing? You are making things messy and the reader will not understand anything. Simply, there will have headaches during the reading and they will not understand it. Plus shows your weakness, (the answer from intuition is: this is the self that shows simplicity)

My self says: I feel I have to extract this book as it is and over time I will learn more. For now, I will bring it out as it is.

CHAPTER II

LITERATURE REVIEW

Constitutes a literature review, and accordingly, contains analysis of models and theoretical frameworks that have been previously introduced to the research area. Viewpoints of other authors regarding the research area have been presented in a logical manner in this chapter. Furthermore, this chapter contains definitions of main terms and explains search strategy for the secondary data. Literature review, and my opinion in research strategies and what I want to gain.

Review of the literature: spirituality and the various perspectives

What is Spirituality?

Spirituality is defined as "the quality of being concerned with the human spirit or soul as opposed to material or physical things" (oxforddictionaries.com) It tends to grow towards an essential, immaterial reality. It can refer mostly to an inner path, which enables individuals to discover the core of their being – their deepest truths and values by which to live. According to Kipp (2014) "Spirituality is the measure of how willing we are to allow grace—some power greater than ourselves - to enter our lives and guide us along our way". Grace is the spontaneous, benevolent power of the divine love that enters this world through and as me or you. Some of us practice it in various spiritual techniques, but many of us do not consciously allow space for grace. However, the voice of our soul always finds a way, whether we are ready or not, and uses all the respective tools, even if it has to shake the very foundations of our life so that we have no secure grasp or control of our direction. However, spiritual experiences help us to navigate our existence more skillfully so that the presenting crisis are overcome with less distress and suffering. Spirituality is not about the superficial or materialistic aspects of its practice such as wearing appropriate clothing, visiting religious institutions regularly, or eating specific types of food. While healthy living choices may be useful and beneficial, they are not considered the equivalent of being truly spiritual.

There are people, who may spend all their time at a church, synagogue or ashram and still manifest a not such a pious behaviour. Another definition of spirituality is "a state of being that does not exclusively belong to a specific religion". One can be very spiritual and not have the religious background. The opposite can also be correct: one can have a very religious life with no spiritual breadth, but just doctrine. Spirituality is also described as "a measure and a living practice of how loving and peaceful a person is, how unconditionally accepting they are toward themselves and others" (Kipp, 2014). Once people are committed and take consistent steps to being loving and kind towards self and others, what they believe in, is considered less crucial, because it is who and how they are that matters in spirituality. It is what human beings do right here, right now. The spiritual experience is often reported as a source, which provides inspiration or guidance in life. It usually encompasses beliefs in immaterial realities or encounters with immanent or transcendent realms (Kipp, 2014).

Interest in spirituality and related personal care across the world has noticeably increased in recent years. (Jones et al, 2007). Even though the UK literature still reflects doubts and skepticism in terms of assessing and responding to the spiritual needs of people, there is an increasing support that favours the importance of integrating forms spiritual care in the healthcare system (DoH, 2011). An example of an attempt is the Liverpool Care Pathway (2009), which included standards for the best possible quality of assistance provided by healthcare professionals in the NHS. However, since the First Annual Report of End of Life Strategy several challenges were identified, which inhibited its practical development. According to DoH (2011) there was a lack of systematic evidence on the appropriateness of spiritual tools as well as the respective skills of the UK workforce. The new guidelines from the National Institute of Health Care and Excellence replaced the Liverpool Care Pathway, whose implementation appeared problematic. Their focus was to check and manage the patient's symptoms, with particular emphasis on using painkillers, as well as the 'just in case' "medicines, sometimes prescribed in advance for symptoms that might happen in the future". In terms of the psychological or emotional state of the patient, i.e. the management of anxiety, agitation and delirium, the guidelines recommended firstly the pharmaceutical option: "The doctor should check for possible causes and discuss possible treatments with the person. For some people, a medicine may be offered. If that doesn't work or if it causes unwanted drowsiness, the doctor should ask for advice from a specialist" (NICE, 2015).

The use of spiritual tools in UK's public services such as healthcare and education, has frequently encountered some resistance, because their applicability has been regarded as more effective for religious groups. However, according to Nardella (2014) "spirituality does not necessarily refer to religion, although it can". For instance, it has been proved that meditation or the embrace of the inner silence and/or stillness that comes with it, can increase a person's awareness of mindful self-love. Here, the concept of loving oneself does not mean selfishness or narcissism, but represents the compassion, which forms the basis of an essential relationship of human beings – that with themselves (Kotsos, 2017).

Spirituality has been shown to improve a person's physical, psychological and spiritual state. Exploring the history of the healing professions, it is evident that when combined with the spiritual dimension it is synergetic on supporting health and well-being. Midwifery and nursing are examples of services provided by religious communities (Koenig et al, 2001). In the secular environment of our society, the remnant of what is referred to as spiritual heritage, are now found in the charity hospices, care homes, organizations or religious institutions offering holistic support and services (DoH, 2011). There are a number of studies, in the UK literature, about social work and spirituality, but their focus is mainly on mental-health (Coyte et al, 2007).

One of the major hindrances in providing an accurate and/or universal definition of spirituality seems to be its historical relationship with religion. However, the complete separation of spirituality and religion in our culture and traditions, is unrealistic. Thus, in exploring the meaning of spirituality and well-being in this literature review, there will be an inclusion of perspectives of some major religions with the broader view of considering the existing concepts outside of them. According to Moberg (1984) spirituality is neither detached from nor synonymous with religiosity. Steiger and Lipson (1985) define religion as a social institution, where a number of people jointly take part and engage, but this may not necessarily fulfil the individual's search for a meaning. While religious beliefs and their respective practices has a fundamental impact on certain groups by allowing them the expression of some degree of spirituality, they might also limit the freedom of individual spirituality (Dyson et al, 1997). This means that the positive supportive and all-embracing environment of religious groups could also negatively affect the person's authenticity and well-being. The commonly held view that 'spirituality belongs exclusively to religious groups' is an example where the opposite may also be possible and therefore deserves to be examined.

When looking at different religions it is evident that at their core there is an inner yearning - which the external reality typically has lost or has been separated from – to attain a connection, with a higher sense of self and/or with the Creator. A repetitive emerging theme from the literature is the person's awareness on the relationship between 'the self', 'a Higher Being / God', and 'the others', which usually involves an intentional shift of attention from the finite into the eternal (Dyson et al, 1997). Religions have had a significant impact on the human spiritual history. Major world religions such as Hinduism, Buddhism, Islam, Judaism, Christianity, and New Age, manifest this in their beliefs, ceremonies and rituals.

Spirituality and Religion

Hinduism is the world's oldest religion. Most Hindus worship the infinite manifestations of the one Being of ultimate totality and oneness (Brahman), which finds representations in gods and goddesses. These divinities incarnate within various idols, or temples, or gurus, or nature such as animals and rivers. According to this religion the present life, the joys and hardships experienced in it, are derived by the individual's actions in their previous life. Therefore, the goal of this lifetime is to free oneself from the law of karma -which means action and subsequent reaction - , and the perpetual struggle of reincarnations. The essence of the existence is the soul, whose rest depends on achieving Moksha, which is the liberation from Samsara - the continuous cycle of birth, life, death and rebirth. The cycle of karma can end by working towards spiritual realization through a choice of possible options such as: being devoted to Hindu deities, meditating and expanding inner knowledge, and understanding that the separate self and life's circumstances are just an illusion – only Brahman is what truly matters (Adamson, 2017).

Buddhism, also called Buddha Dharma, is a path of spiritual development whose meaning derives from the word budhi – 'to awaken'. Here the individual awakens from the 'sleep of unawareness and ignorance', by inwardly realizing the reality's true nature. No God is worshiped, but the practice involves self-discipline in dedicated meditation, where it may be possible to reach Nirvana – 'unbound' by extinction of the flames of all desire. There are four main points that the Buddhist sects share: 1) Buddha is accepted as the teacher. 2) The concept of 'the Middle Way', which is the quality of being moderate and avoiding extremes. Four noble truths are the central foundation, of separating from the impermanent reality by releasing cravings in order to enter the reality of the 'worthy ones'. The 'Noble Eightfold Path' is considered central. Its eight divisions are: right views, right thoughts, right speech, right conduct, right actions, right livelihood, right effort, right mindfulness and right concentration. 3) Monks as well as the laity are able to follow the right path towards enlightenment. 4) Buddhahood is considered to be the highest accomplishment (Frater, 2007). With the spiritual enlightenment comes the detachment from the cycle of life and death. Many Buddhists believe that a human being has numerous rebirths, which include unavoidable suffering. The goal is seeking to end these rebirths, which result from the individual's delusion in cravings and aversion. The Buddhist practice to achieve this, requires, the release of all the sensual urges and earthly desires as well as the purification of one's heart (Frater, 2007).

According to Islam there is one God almighty - Allah, who is the creator of the universe and eternally superior from humankind. Everything that occurs is because of His will. Allah is a strict and powerful judge, but merciful to the obedient servants depending on their sufficiency of moral excellence, good actions and religious dedication (Adamson, 2017). For Muslims the fundamental source of Islam is based on the Qur'an, revealed to God's final prophet Muhammad - the restorer of the monotheistic faith of Abraham, Moses, and Jesus. They believe that that Judaism and Christianity twisted the original messages over time in interpretation, or textual representation. Prophet Muhammad's words and way of life are a source of authority for being a Muslim. Five religious duties are followed: 1) to repeat a creed in regard to Allah and prophet Muhammad. 2) To recite specific prayers in Arabic language five times a day. 3) Beneficence to those in need 4) Every year, one month fast from food, drink, sexual activities and smoking from sunrise until sunset 5. Once in one's lifetime, a pilgrimage for worshiping God at a shrine in the city of Mecca. After death, depending on the personal devotion to the above directives, one is eternally punished in hell or rewarded with Paradise. According to Islam, giving up one's life for Allah, is a definite guarantee of entering Paradise (Frater, 2007).

Judaism is the religion of the Jewish people, based on their Bible (Tanakh) and the Talmud - rabbinical explanations about ethics, customs, and law. The history of Judaism initiates with the Covenant between God and Abraham, who is considered the forefather of the Jewish people.

Throughout the history, Jewish beliefs are reflected in a number of religious principles. Rambam's 13 principles of faith, thought to be the minimum requirements are: "God exists; God is one and unique; God is incorporeal; God is eternal; Prayer is to be directed to God alone and to no other; The words of the prophets are true; Moses' prophecies are true, and Moses was the greatest of the prophets; The Written Torah (first 5 books of the Bible) and Oral Torah (teachings now contained in the Talmud and other writings) were given to Moses; There will be no other Torah; God knows the thoughts and deeds of men; God will reward the good and punish the wicked; The Messiah will come; The dead will be resurrected" (Rich, 2011). The most important of these is the faith in a single, benevolent, infinitely-wise, omnipotent, transcendent God – who has created and governs the universe. At the core of Judaism stands the relationship - between God, humankind, and the land of Israel. In holidays, practices and observances the focus is greater on actions and behaviours than on beliefs. In the past, Judaism had a temple, where sacrifices to God took place. Many Orthodox Jews believe that the original ceremonial duties will be repeated in a Third temple in the future (Steinberg, 1965).

Christianity is a monotheistic religion, based on scriptures called the Bible, which comprises the Old Testament (the Septuagint) and New Testament. Christians believe that Jesus of Nazareth, is the Son of God (God in a human form) and part of the Trinity (God as three forms in one - the others being the Father and the Holy Spirit). Christians believe that Christianity provides fulfilment to Judaism. Most Christians believe that the birth, death and resurrection of Jesus are essential in their faith. According to protestants salvation comes from the faith in God alone, whereas Catholic and Orthodox Christians believe that faith and good works are required. Christians believe in Sacraments (Catholics and Orthodox have 7: "Baptism, Confirmation, Holy Communion, Confession, Last Rites, Holy Orders, and Matrimony"; some Protestants (following Martin Luther) consider just the Baptism and Holy Communion as sacramental (Frater, 2007). The first and greatest commandment, which Jesus made known to the followers, in response to questions from Pharisees is: "You shall love the Lord your God with all your heart, and with all your soul, and with all your mind". The second is: "You shall love your neighbour as yourself". On these two statements, the Christians find joy a meaningful life – by faith in a loving God through Jesus Christ, and good actions towards self and others. Hell is described in the Bible, as the destiny of sinners who refuse to change their ways, whereas Heaven as a wonderful and exhilarating experience of the soul – where people have achieved complete repentance and healing, enjoying the magnificent presence of God and the love of one another forever (christianity.org.uk).

New Age supports the development of the potential power and divinity within human beings. The deity, for the New Age followers is not about a supreme, transcendent God, but it refers to a higher state of consciousness within them. Therefore, the person sees themselves as deity, the micro-cosmos, constituent part of the entire universe.

For instance, everything that the New Age follower imagines, sees, hears, and feels is considered divine. Even though highly varied, New Age encompasses a collection of former spiritual customs and practices.

These include philosophies based on eastern mysticism and metaphysical techniques or rites such as breathing exercises, meditating, and chanting. Similarly to Hinduism, the presence of gods and goddesses is accepted and acknowledged. In addition, the Earth is considered as a source of spirituality; having its own knowledge, wisdom, emotions and divine nature. However, the main focus in New Age followers is 'the self' – the originator, the regulator and commander of all. The reality is what the person perceives and determines. The uncomfortable experiences such as hurt, sadness, anger, and failures are regarded as illusions. The person is invited to believe in their own self, in order to fully master their life. By applying certain spiritual methods and practices the goal is to develop an altered consciousness and realizing one's own divinity. In this way, a person grows spiritually to a level, where there is no objective or external reality so nothing about their life is seen in terms of right and wrong, positive and negative, joyful and painful. Eventually the people become aware that they are God and have the power to create their own unique reality (Adamson, 2017).

Other Dwellings of Spirituality

Meditation

A common emerging theme in the spirituality reflected by different religious perspectives, is the individual's or the group's attention on the inner resources and inner self. While many of us are aware that we have capabilities within that extend beyond the conscious reality, there are few of us, who sense them more significantly and/or are able to cultivate them by establishing an internal relationship, which results in a greater familiarity with this mystical phenomenon inside the self and its purpose in life. Those who chose and are able to engage with their inner world, discover that the resources in it are not immediately accessible, but become gradually noticeable by some kind of detachment from the external environment and/or regular spiritual practices such as meditation, and prayer (Dyson et al, 1997). There are people, who rely exclusively on the information received from their thoughts, their senses and their external world and for them spirituality remains an abstract, enigmatic or meaningless endeavour. However, according to a number of transcendental meditation teachers, this perception is the first level of consciousness- where the path to spiritual growth begins - and it is called 'the state of waking consciousness'. It is from here that it is possible to surpass the ordinary experiences, and train ourselves for higher levels of consciousness in a manner that is no different than training for sports (Freeman, 2014). According to Mahesh (2015) there are altogether seven levels of consciousness in the journey of spiritual progress. The first three are accessible to almost all adult human beings, whereas the last four, which can bring about transformative effects, can be achieved by regular practice of meditation:

1. The state of waking consciousness (Perceiving only through the mind and senses.)

2. Deep sleep (A state of almost complete disengagement from the environment.)

3. Dreaming (An altered state of consciousness, which takes place during sleep.)

4. Transcendental consciousness (A state where the mind and the senses are silent, but consciousness is still awake and perceives a quality of bliss.)

5. Cosmic consciousness (The ability of the nervous system to sustain the inner silence so that its presence feels steady and permanent, even when one is doing other things or being active. In this state, the real self is now understood to be the pure consciousness – it is a sublime self that is immaculate and infinite. Consequently, the external world is seen as a fleeting, and illusory existence).

6. God consciousness (The stability of the connection with the deepest self enables the individual to perceive the external world as more pleasant and nearer to the level of 'pure self'. The heart opens up and can overcome anything. Any life experience or encounter in the material world, feels meaningful and delightful). The person opens up the characteristic of devotion, which can manifest itself in various ways, depending on individual uniqueness. In some, their profound devotion takes a religious significance, in others it may take a more generalized sense of purpose.

7. Unity consciousness. (This stage represents the full awakening. It reveals that the internal and the external, the Self and the non-Self, the absolute and the relative, the eternal and the temporary are in fact an all-encompassing One (Mahesh, 2015).

The concept of the relationship with God has been widely understood within the religious context. However, there are many examples of less limited points of view. For instance, Stoll (1979) states that "Whatever a person takes to be the highest value in life can be regarded as their God". God can also represent an inner and/or outer search for the motive of existence and a sense of worth, and this may include relationships, situations, activities, etc. (Howden, 1992). A meaningful connection and/or purpose emerges as a universal characteristic of spirituality. A lack of meaning may result in feelings of despair, emptiness and loneliness (Frankl 1959). Ellis (1980) describes the meaning as a phenomenon that represents uniqueness because it is personally perceived and realized by the individual human being. A typical example is when a person experiences pain, illness or death, no matter how challenging or severe the occurrence appears, if it is associated with a plausible meaning it can become bearable and enjoyable. Other personal meaning systems that appear less sacred, but are nonetheless essential to some people because it influences, energises them or brings them peaceful feelings are their nutrition, their hobbies, their job, their family, their friends, their material assets, their status, etc. (Oldnall, 1996).

There is an interconnectedness between three basic elements at the centre of spiritual faiths, which are: the self, the others and the Higher being or God – a power beyond oneself, an identified source of love and relatedness for an unconditional acceptance (Burkhardt, 1989). According to Lane (1987) there are three types of connectedness:

1. The ability to engage in similar regenerative activities.

2. The sense of belonging.

3. A common purpose. When these are found meaningful, a greater sense of wholeness is experienced.

Art

Spiritual practices and expressions can be seen in various manifestations. Many hold the view that artwork, are such as music, literature, painting, are all forms of spiritual communications, which may go beyond the purely religious rites. One of the main reasons that artists create, and the others value their work, is because art enables a living connection between the daily psychology of individual minds and the universal aspect of humanity. This does not refer to merchandise, the purpose of which is personal profit, but to the wisdom of artistic productions that express spiritual principles or values like awareness, understanding, faith, unity and perseverance. If art arises from one's heart it speaks to another person's heart, so that togetherness arises due to witnessing this emotional and spiritually sensitive communication (Culliford, 2017). One example can be the Hans Christian Andersen's (1840) quote: 'When words fail, sounds can often speak'. This means that by true artwork some people do not simply perceive a visual or auditory encounter, with its pleasant and unpleasant moments, but are in some way deeply affected or transformed by a greater awareness, which otherwise would not have been reached due to everyday limitations or complexities. Culliford (2017) addresses this art experience as a tool for spiritual development: "I was not entirely the same person afterwards. I was somehow better connected, through the art and the artist, to the entirety of humanity and the cosmic whole". There has been research, which proves how the arts might be used in ways to heal emotional and psychological trauma, increase understanding of self and others, develop self-reflection, alleviate painful symptoms, and alter thinking patterns and behaviours (Camic, 2008). The systematic review of Stuckey & Nobel, (2010) also demonstrates how engagement with creative arts has been used as a healing process in both informal and clinical practice to promote wellbeing.

Spiritual or sacred may not necessarily mean religious, although it can, but any form of true art such as a music piece capable of unlocking profound emotions – such as joy or sadness that have previously been imprisoned by perhaps excessive attention to other concerns or activities. Culliford (2017) states: "Rhythmical and repetitive dance (like that of the Sufi dervishes) and chanting (whether Gregorian or the kirtan and bhajans, for example, of the sacred Hindu and Jain traditions), by powerfully harmonizing the left and right halves of the brain - similar to the effect of meditation - form a powerful bridge between a particular form of art and spiritual experience". In addition, if people join to participate in art practices, such as when listening to an orchestra or a choir, might further enhance the experience through the process of sharing it among one another, which has the potential for more spiritual gain (Culliford, 2017). The woman painter Merritt (1981) states: "Art, from the beginning, endeavoured to express emotions and historical facts to be understood by all human souls of all nations, without need of written words. Art uses the gestures of human beings, the atmosphere of the universe to convey thought and emotions and to record events. Without thought and emotions, it has no reason for existence".

Science

Another perspective, which may or may not be able to express a coherent story with spirituality, is science. Some people think that science is simply another religion. Their reasoning is based on the idea that beliefs about the invisible world are founded on the considered-to-be-correct truth, about which both religions and science provide their own opinions. Another rationale is that science and religion require a degree of faith. However, Dietrich (2017) argues that science and religion are mutually exclusive because they decide about the truth in opposite ways – religion is mainly a spiritual belief based on faith, whereas science is not a belief but a methodology, which demands evidence. This notion - that science and religion have fundamental differences, is reflected on the way the issue of evolution has been dealt with by some religious responses. In his book The Origin of Species Charles Darwin (1859) theorised that the current species inhabiting Earth were a consequence of repeated evolutionary adaptations or changes from common ancestors. Science still continues its efforts to providing evidence about the 'Law of Adaptation'. According to Darwin, in nature there is a merciless war for survival, where species development occurs due to 'the strong' always defeating 'the weak'. An example of one if its quotes - which caused some controversy in some religions communities that believe God made fully formed humans, with no previous related ancestors - is: "Whilst man, however well-behaved, at best is but a monkey shaved!" (Lovgren, 2004). And yet, Darwin, did not try to prove that God does not exist. The physicist Greene (2005) states: "There is, of course, no way to prove religious faith scientifically. And it's hard to envision a test that could tell the difference between a universe created by God and one that appeared without God. There's no way that scientists can ever rule out religion, or even have anything significant to say about the abstract idea of a divine creator".

The lack of empirical evidence has convinced a number of people to reject all supernatural or transcendent reality. For instance, the avowed atheists deny all forms of religion or spirituality. The term atheism originates from the Greek word 'atheos', which means 'without God'. Atheism can encompass a variety of views, which tend towards secular philosophies such as rationalism, humanism, physicalism and naturalism. Murray O'Hair (1963) states: "Atheism may be defined as the mental attitude which unreservedly accepts the supremacy of reason and aims at establishing a lifestyle and ethical outlook verifiable by experience and the scientific method, independent of all arbitrary assumptions of authority and creeds". By emphasising this rational aspect, the writer Ernest Hemingway concludes: 'all thinking men are atheists'. There is a minor but vocal group of fundamentalist atheists, who express that those who are spiritual or believe in God are somehow ignorant or naive, and would like to see eradication of all forms of spirituality (Mastin, 2011). Indeed, atheists are no less moral, empathic or charitable than any other religious individual. They just hold that spirituality or religions do not have a monopoly on socially-correct behaviour, which according to them is not based on simply following some rules. Atheists often respect a similar moral code as religious groups, but the way they arrive at their convictions about what is acceptable or unacceptable, disregards the idea of God.

Despite the underlying implications, yet, there are people – believers and non-believers – who think that science and religion have never been mutually exclusive. They not only do not see conflict between these two perspectives but describe the universe portrayed by science as miraculous and amazing. Even though science and spirituality and/or religion usually operate in different realms they can co-exist. To affirm this, Albert Einstein states: "Science without religion is lame. Religion without science is blind". This indicates that the act of deciding something is true without evidence goes against science, whereas seeing the world exclusively through proven facts goes against spirituality. According to Dietrich (2007) the cohabitation of science and religion can be achieved by pursuing truth based on conclusions arising from feelings or spirituality as well as scientific facts. It is possible to not have to choose one or the other, but to encompass them as different facets of life, which can serve their purpose by also working in tandem. History shows that spiritual people have been able to approach science through a spiritual lens, as scientists have pursued spirituality through a scientific lens. Many have been the scientists, who were driven by their intuition or spiritual tendencies to explore the laws of the universe (Jusino, 2017).

Bialik (2017) describes that God can represent "the force in the Universe that drives all of the phenomena that we experience as human beings" and the experience can be appreciated not just as a mental or physical one but like learning new disciplines we can learn to relate to each other's perspectives such as spirituality or religion and vice-versa. People usually value one perspective over another, but coexistence is finding a common ground. Science has theories that are called real or factual even though they are usually never 100% sure, whereas spirituality is based on faith in spite of not knowing, rather than believing in definite knowledge. 'Evidence' seems to be the crucial difference between a scientist and a religious individual. While scientific methods look for evidence and data interpretation on the external or physical world, spiritual endeavours try to pay attention to the evidence from the internal world and its respective emotional or psychological interpretation (Jusino, 2017).

Self Love

According to Bandura (1986), the functioning of a human being comprises a set of reciprocal interactions between environmental, behavioural, and personal variables. The fundamental personal variable is the 'self-efficacy', or the perceived ability for acquiring or performing particular tasks at specific levels. Self-efficacy can increase successful achievements because of the individual's efforts, persistence, and as a consequence the improved performance. When compared with people, who doubt their capabilities, self-efficacious students are more likely to participate in new or challenging tasks, and appear more motivated to overcome difficulties to reach higher levels (Schunk, 1999). The sense of self-efficacy is directly influenced by self-love. As individuals work on tasks where they practice and convey love, they raise their self-esteem, self-confidence and progress quicker. According to Hardy (2012) "Self-love is a state of appreciation for oneself that grows from actions that support our physical, psychological and spiritual growth. Self-love is dynamic; it grows by actions that mature us.

When we act in ways that expand self-love in us, we begin to accept much better our weaknesses as well as our strengths, have less need to explain away our short-comings, have compassion for ourselves as human beings struggling to find personal meaning, are more centred in our life purpose and values, and expect living fulfilment through our own efforts". Taking responsibility for our life, choices and actions means that we have also the right to attend our needs. In this way, we can learn to love others. Being self-loving means that the person full accepts who they are, preserving their good qualities and taking continuous steps to improve the traits that they are not satisfied with. This means that the self-reproach and the resulting anxiety or distress is avoided. Instead of worrying about imperfections, the individual embraces them by also appreciating the unique strong points (Hardy, 2012). According to Cohen (2012) a happy and self-assured person, is in fact a self-lover and perceives 'the self' as a best friend, who does not demean or degrade but inspire and encourage, regardless the approval or disapproval of others (Cohen, 2012).

By learning to love themselves, people are more likely to have tender and loving relationships and happier children. Research has shown that when parents display the ability to love themselves, this is automatically copied by the child. Therefore, parents need to learn self-love before they teach it to the new generation. When a person loves, the world around appears more beautiful and meaningful, because it is seen from a loving perspective. This can improve the physical, emotional and psychological state of an individual as well as it attracts healthier circumstances and people in their life. One example of self-love is being mindful, which enables human beings to be in touch with their thoughts, feelings and have knowledge of their needs, wishes and goals. By staying centred and moving mindfully forward one can prevent automatic repetitive patterns, which are no longer useful. The practice of self-care such as healthy nourishment, regular exercise, good social interactions, intimacy etc. is another aspect of self-love. In addition, people love and respect themselves more when they know how to set boundaries or refuse activities that repress, drain or harm them emotionally, physically or spiritually. Forgiveness is also part of self-love. Rather than being critical or punishing about occurring mistakes, the other and healthier option is learning to grow by the lessons learned. Living with a purpose that guides the life's journey is self-loving too. This may be as simple as making decisions, which support and express personal values (Hardy, 2012).

Views regarding the direction of this research

This review was intended to only be an illustration of the potential relevant information regarding personal well-being with an emphasis on spirituality. Reflection on this literature review has identified the need for a practical framework, by which the spirituality and its practice can be explored and applied in an all- encompassing, universal manner. A careful consideration of individual cases studies and will demonstrate its application and the degree of its effectiveness. This framework primarily consists of 'the self', the 'Highest personal belief' as well as 'the others'.

About Theory of Magical Module

This deals with connecting your spiritual world (who you are) and this world (who you are created to be).

The spiritual world is the person you truly are (meaning: the soul). The mind is simply a tool that carries all the information (taken from the time inside the mother's womb to the present point in the life journey you are). The mind has the ability to decide what information will be saved, etc. The heart produces feelings based on thoughts that arise from the mind. So, connecting a person with their soul has the ability to heal the mind and heart. That requires the individual looking after their mind and heart through the guidance of their soul, their true self. That is the work I have applied in clients and is applied in different ways by speaking with the client's language. However, the practice is based on the theory mentioned previously. In the soul, one finds everything. There, the intuition receives the answers of questions that the soul probably does not know. Intuition is the creator.

. In the soul one brings their mind and heart as if they were children and there it purifies them, gives them therapy, and heals them because the soul has the ability to do so.

I discovered this theory at the age of 7, but I did not understand it because I was a bit lazy and pleased with little, so left it where it was. At the age of 36, I spent a lot of time in another world and I still continue to do that, but now I do it in an advance practice. When I was 36, when I realized that this theory worked in me, I thought how to distribute it to others and so in a matter of seconds, the magical module was created. Later, I conversed with myself in meditation. How it has served me and how can I use it on others? This is explained in chapter 3, but it continues to develop because with every client I've had, I've learned a lot of things, including readers of "A magical Life" book.

"A magical life" book. How I finalised my theory through my book?

I wrote the book without breathing. After it, I wish to make an analysis based on impressions from myself and readers to understand in more depth to supplicate.

How the theory been correlated to the clients and everyone that comes contact with me, directly and indirectly. I have some inner gifts. It's been eight years since stayed in the roots of the theory and developing it. I communicate with the soul of a person, I read the person's mind, I feel their heart's feelings, and I interpret them in a language that a person understands. This is my direct help. The indirect help is when simply say a sentence or a word or a comment and I leave it at that. To people it may seem absurd or strange, but maybe one day they will come back to its remembrance and put it into practice.

What are the benefits of it?

The peace...the love.... the solutions.... smile.... live.... enjoy.... feel great...having no fear from death.

"The more wisdom you attain and the
more conscious you become, the crazier
you will appear to others."

-Albert Einstein

Self- love is the key to everything and can be achieved by asking yourself for justice, love and care towards yourself and others. Can be achieved through speeding time with yourself and having different conversations as longs as you consider those three main rules, 1-Love yourself the way you like to be loved, 2-Treat others the way you like to be treated and 3-Do your best in everything that you do. (How do you know you are doing your best? It comes through the inner conversations with your soul and your intuition). When you achieve to sharpen the practice of those three rules then you are able to love yourself and spread love around where is need it.

On next chapter will be detailed description how we can practice the three rules and can be done in details by giving examples from case studies. Bear in mind that is general self-guidance as each individual is unique and the methods and techniques have been used in unique way. For each case study the approaches, the time, techniques, learning and results are different. But they are based on the approach I mentioned early and on magical module below.

CHAPTER III

Methodology, Magical Module

Addresses methodology. The chapter explains the research process and addresses the issues of research philosophy. Moreover, methodology chapter contains an explanation of the research design, and the choice and implementation of data collection methods. The sampling aspect of the study and discussions of ethical considerations are also included in this chapter.

Magical Model

The methodology used throughout the research follows the seven stages of the magical module that I shall outline below. I have discussed details of the participants with confidentiality in mind, and it is important to remember that the techniques and methods are general. They simply present the concepts and the ideas which will enable you start your own creativity; through your resilience of wanted to be loved, fulfilled, content and having a clear vision of the reality you want to create. Moreover every technique and method of the magical module starts from self-love, as it is all about the importance of achieving self-love in order to live a meaningful life, which is filled with joy, peace and love. As I have already explained in my "A Magical Life" book, my journey of discovery began when I was seven years old. A time when I refused to be a part of hurting others and I refused to let others hurt me. Nature, the universe, our creator and my soul guided and nurtured me through quest for a world filled with peace and love.

Ever since I learnt to be a product of pure love, my life became adventurous, fascinating, meaningful, peaceful, content, full of love and I was able to show compassion and care for others who were on my path. However, my literature review and others' quotes have shown me that I am not the only individual who discovered the solution to a peaceful life filled with love.

I hope this book will help you to understand that happiness comes from an inner understanding of self- love and the ability to become a product of pure love. You are already a product of pure love deep inside, however, by following your mind and your heart you have failed to discover ways in which you can connect with your pure love that is your soul and to be guided by it. Until you do that you will not be loved, feel peace, be content, fulfilled and able to love others in the right way. The right way is to want their best interest and let them explore what they want … not using them for our own needs because we need them … no we only need ourselves and once we become one with ourselves then we share the love with others … we dance on universal love or passionate love instead of feeling hungry for their love. These are two different things; need of others and sharing love with others. If you have not achieved yourself love you cannot share love with others because you don't have love for yourself, you have not yet learned how to discover the pure love is within you and use it to give love first to yourself before you start to share as you need to learn how to keep producing love through your soul as we are using human parts and need to know how those parts function in order to spread love through our soul into all our human parts.

This is exactly what the stages of magical module help you to do but you need guidance from someone who has achieved self-love. To achieve self-love you have to have those ingredients:

1-Have a vision of how you want to be and how your life want to be.

2-Be curious.

3-Be determent to be committed to what you agree with yourself.

4-Believe in yourself.

5-Love through desire your goals and purpose.

6-Be creative.

7-Be flexible.

8-Alloy yourself to be who you want to be.

9-Don't judge yourself, but be understanding towards yourself.

10-Show compassion to yourself.

11-Experiment new things and unknown ways if it resonates with you.

12-Have discipline how to stick to your plans.

13-Be genuine.

14-Look for justice towards yourself and your actions towards others.

15-Stop being the victim but find ways how to notice the good things you have … focus on good things and be aware of things you don't like.

16-Be prepared to keep daily diary.

17-Willing to put yourself first.

18-Willing never to do to others what you don't like others to do to you.

19-Take responsibility for your actions and your happiness.

20-Willing to learn to be master of observing what is happening around you daily.

21-Create affirmations based on facts that you believe within.

22-Willing to listen to yourself and only you to be in charge of your decisions and actions.

23-Make notes daily what you learn from others and your daily experience.

24-Willing to have daily conversations with yourself using techniques that you and only you create them and feel comfortable.

25-Daily give love to yourself and make note of what you did.

26-your worries, fears, anxiety, insecurities, or any other emotions that you are experiencing have to be having daily conversation with your inner love in order slowly to turn into love and preparation for resilience on what to get more from this journey of life.

27-Make time for you …. alone time.

28-Keep distance from people who don't make you happy or distract you from your goal and your purpose.

29-Ask for help if you need it.

30-Whatever you do daily pay attention ....to learn, to enjoy it, to understand it, to appreciated, to accepted, to make changes if need it, to be grateful for you are and what you do, be your own critic, be open to listen to yourself if guidance are need it to change what you did not like, find out what inspired you, to be pure love and just notice anything thing that you notice.

"Remember the reason you are in this life is to enjoy life and the only way to enjoy life is to connect to your pure love that you are born with and shine through the journey of life"

"No one is responsible for your inner peace and inner joy except for you." Debasish Mridha

"If you truly loved yourself, you could never hurt another". BUDDHA

"If you propose to speak always ask yourself, is it true, is it necessary, is it kind." Buddha

"Peace comes from within. Do not seek it without". Buddha

"No one saves us but ourselves. No one can and no one may. We ourselves must walk the path. " Buddha

"To enjoy good health, to bring true happiness to one's family, to bring peace to all, one must first discipline and control one's own mind. If a man can control his mind he can find the way to Enlightenment, and all wisdom and virtue will naturally come to him." Buddha

"You, yourself, as much as anybody in the entire universe, deserve your love and affection. " Buddha

"All wrong-doing arises because of mind. If mind is transformed can wrong-doing remain? " Buddha

"We have freedom, we have been born to be have responsibility of our free will and free choices, we have choices, we are the one decide the decisions, life is free and only we can decide our life journeys, yes it is written but without our actions it can never happen and our actions can change our paths, our decisions are our responsibility that lead to take action that create the path " Vjollca Sadiku

How did I create it?

I was in a workshop. For a moment I was disconnected with the outside world and connected to my world. In front of me I had a table with all the words, which described the emotions.

In my mind I liked the name magic, but also Vjollca (that is my name, which is my goal in this world), and I tried to create a module called Vjollca but it did not resonate within me. So I chose magical and for each letter I created the respective words from the ones I saw on the board. This happened in a matter of seconds. I was amongst people but was not listening to what they were saying because I was in my own world. There, I thought the book would be based on the magical module. So the book would run according to the newly created module.

The origin of the name magical and each stage:

Magical because everything around me seemed magical; as if it were covered with a glittering powder or fairy dust.

Why did I create it?

To express and explain how I reached the place where I stand and how to help others cross the bridge from one side to the other.

How did it help me and how it is helping clients? How I do work between stages and how do I apply it?

This depends on the client and on what stage they currently are. It depends on the problem that they have and where they stand. They may be at one particular stage at the beginning. The structure is specific, but each stage requires its adaptation according to aspirations that fit with or inspire the client.

What is the main theme?

The theme is that the client passes from the unhappy condition where they are, to a life of peace and love - finding their inner power: Love, Believe, Dream, Visualise, Act.

Heal yourself from the past, be content where you are and believe in achieving what you want.

Momentum

This stage is about connecting with your inner power, loving yourself, and writing your own life and making it happen. This is the chapter where all our bad or good experiences will happen; and if you are able to connect with your soul, inner self, and our creator, you will experience the magic of the moment, your blessings and you'll learn how to use your magic to create more magic around you. But if you cannot connect, then ask for help as you will be stuck in a continuous circle, unable to move onto the next chapter in your life. Open your heart and mind to the universe and try to recognise your true self (your soul), so you can get unlimited information back to you and become the master of your own life.

All the stages are linked and interconnected which means each client went through an individual and flexible journey, based on my skills and what the client offered at the moment. For details of each clients journey and on the work which has been done, refer to chapter seven. The methodology which I will explain below is fairly general and provides self-guidance for the reader, in order to help them achieve self-love.

The guidance offered here is similar to that used on my clients during this research, however the order varies depending on which stag the individual is and what is most useful at the moment.

"Success is to finding a way to be content in the present and having a clear vision of your desired future journey. Flexibility is a factor which contributes to success … it is a part of growing and becoming wiser and wiser everyday, as a product of pure love"

My skills are as follows (I gained these skills after becoming a product of love and finding the urge to see others around me happy, as it did not make sense that I was a product of love alone while others suffering around me. I asked the creator to give me the skills to help others and I had to be creative to know exactly what I required):

1 - I connect with your soul (to know who you really are and what your purpose in life is) (This can be achieved through conversations with you), and feeling the energy of your soul.

2 - I Understand who you are ... who you have become because of your life experiences…what has made you like that ... (through sessions we can discuss all that and understand it together ... to see if you like who you are or need to change in order to get what you want)

3 - I have a deep understanding of your actions. Are they created to survive? Are all actions based on your survival mechanism? I can help you to let go of your survivor mechanism so you can be able to enjoy life and not feel the need to survive. We are not here to survive but to enjoy life, this is the main purpose of the creator and you can prove it after you achieve your self-love. It is only when you have achieved self-love that you'll be able to see things clearly.

Self love in my theory is:

Someone who values themselves (it means accepting who you are and allowing yourself to think and plan, in order to be the best you can be), respects themselves (it means in any situation you should respect the idea of acknowledging your feelings, listening to yourself, and liking your qualities, actions, and achievements. Even if you think you don't like your qualities, you must still respect yourself and allow yourself to change those particular qualities), listen to yourself (make time to sit down alone and have a conversation, this could be; an evaluation of the day, reflection on certain situations or caring for your emotions, changing your thoughts/actions, or just saying nice things to yourself and praising yourself for any achievements), caring (caring is a very important word, as you need to care for yourself as you are looking after a baby or a child), allow yourself to dream and be the best you can be (it means setting yourself high standards so you can fulfil your goal and dreams, then making plans on how you're going to make it happen. Don't give up on your dream just because it needs time or hard work. If you truly believe in your dream and want to make it a reality, it is worth the time and effort on order to make it happen).

Time is the key to making those things happen, so think about where you have been spending your time until now, and what changes you can make in order to find time for yourself and the earlier points I mentioned.

Holiday alone can be a healing experience, as you have time dedicated to yourself, which you could use to complete the earlier points and subsequently organise how to continue them in everyday life.

There is so much more you can do to show love for yourself, but those are the main points I believe will help you discover what else you need during the process.

(Remember it took me more than one year to discover how to do it for myself ... in my first book I explain exactly how to do it and how did I personally did it ... everyone is different and require unique ways to discover it for themselves in order to make it work.)

Stages to go through are:

1 - To understand it ...and know exactly why it is important and how it works

2 - Identify how to discover yourself, which techniques or methods work for you, as we are all different and required individual, tailored methods.

3 - How to keep practicing self love (I do it daily, weekly, monthly and yearly .... a holiday alone)

<u>You</u>
Mind
Purpose
Heart
Love

<u>You</u>

In this session it is important to be in the moment in order to raise awareness of all the feelings you are unloading. My main focus is establishing a connection to the soul and creator, so that the client experiences energy within their soul. This in turn brings the focus to that feeling for few seconds, as the feelings are mixed with thoughts from the mind and feelings from the heart. During this session it is important to tailor the exercises around the questions below and to the clients individual situation. The importance of these exercises it that they help the individual search for answers, as they are under the influence of their soul. These answers and discoveries can then be reflected upon at a later time. For example, client one had noted that her wish was to write a book as well as helping people in war torn countries who were suffering. However, the client had forgotten about that wish and could not recall writing those answers on the form, during the first session.

Who is who...
What is what...
Where is where...
All what matters is knowing:
Who you are
Where you are now
Where you want to be and how you will get there
What you're going to do about being where you are and going where you want to be...
How you can be happy exactly where you are and appreciate what you already have ...
What you need to change in order to notice the good things that surround you at that moment ...

"Live like it is your last day,
Like it is the best day to create your future ...
Like it is the last day to be the best you can be and breath, feel , love , live "

Mind : At this stage we have to be aware of our thoughts, observe, reflect and show compassion and understanding. Because they are your thoughts at this stage.

Purpose : This is about you; what you want, where you are at the moment and what actions you have taken so far to accomplish your goals and move closer towards what you want. What can be done? Where should you start? So the work is centred around those questions.

Heart : We have to be aware of our feelings, observe, reflect and show compassion and understanding. These are your feelings which are truly sensitive. We have to show love, care, be active listeners. We also need to be reflective and analyse our feelings and the emotions we experience.

Love : We have to work with our understanding of the individual link to love. We then subsequently bring these ideas into the bigger picture regarding how we want to be loved, from who we desire love and finally how we can make that happen. At this stage all of the participant who took part in the research were quite oblivious to the term 'self-love' however, the participants were surrounded by or experienced universal and passionate love. Consequently, all the individuals were facing the problems discussed in chapter seven.

Life
You
Nature
Others
Journey
Purpose

Life

How do you perceive life? What is the meaning of life? How do you want your life to be? How has it been so far? I would suggest making notes and working with a diary because everything is a new journey which can easily be forgotten. The other benefit of a diary is that you become creative through your resilience of discovering and understanding yourself on a deeper level.

You. The focus will be on the client at that particular moment, they must seek answers about what they are doing to satisfy themselves. This act of satisfying and making yourself happy must be explored.

Nature. At this point, we go back to childhood and incorporate the nature debate. We look back and explore your childhood and your connection to nature because is an important part of discovering your true self and gaining self-love, as nature has the power of producing love and guiding you to become product of love.

Others. We explore the role of others in your life and allow ourselves to be observers of our thoughts and feelings towards the role of others in your life.

Journey. It is important to stop time and reflect back on your journey until now, reflecting on the here and now as we'll as your entire childhood; a vision of your journey.

Purpose. Once again Purpose is crucial, this time it is linked to the focus on others, on nature, on your journey and finally on yourself. These factors are all intertwined and provide a different angle from which you can analyse and reflect on your purpose. The key point is that you must ensure that you keep digging at a deeper level and continue practising being observer of your thoughts and feelings.

Life

How are you going to blend with life?
How are you going to manage it or achieve it?
How do you affect your situation? How do others affect your situation?
How does the length of the journey affect your fulfilment of the purpose?

These questions all allude to a purpose which is centre around you. This helps you to connect more and more with your true self and discover how you can be you without it conflicting with your thoughts and your feelings. This, it is primarily about figuring out who you are and who you want to be.

Others
Family
Friends
Work
Peers

The role of others in your life is important, particularly when you don't have self-love and rely heavily on being loved by others (universal love or passionate love). That survival mechanism is costing you your happiness and keeping you away from your true self. Therefore, by exploring the role of others and raising awareness of the link between self-love, universal love and passionate love, you finally become familiar with your true self and understand the importance of knowing yourself.

"By accepting yourself and being fully what you are, your presence can make others happy." (Jane Roberts)

Mind
How we process information
How we store information
How we collect information

The process of reprogramming your mind takes a minimum of six months after you have connected to your true self (the soul) and you are practicing self-love. When you work with your mind you have to raise the awareness of all your thoughts including those which you have repressed. This can be achieved through various techniques, which are tailored to meet the individuals needs.

The steps are simple and the techniques include; spending time alone, making notes, having deep conversations with yourself that lead to a decision and attending coaching sessions at least once a month in order to reflect on your techniques and the methods that you are using. You become a master of your mind while caring for your thoughts through the process of reprogramming them. Thoughts have incredibly great power if we are not connected to our true self and if we create our reality based on our thoughts. On the other hand, if we are connected with our true self and still allow our thoughts to interfere in our life, it will create conflict which results in confusion and leads to various emotions. If these emotions are not a product of love then they could result in physical illness.

"Self-love requires you to be honest about your current choices and thought patterns and undertake new practices that reflect self-worth." (Caroline Kirk)

"First of all, a soul is not something that you have. It is what you are."
(Jane Roberts, Seth Speaks: The Eternal Validity of the Soul)

Body

Looking after the body is crucial and a way of respecting ourselves. This means that food, drink, exercise, sleep, inner balance and anything we put into our mouth and bodies must be considered carefully. This helps you serve the purpose of your soul. If you aren't satisfied with your body, are unhealthy, or if you damage your body, all other parts are affected. This in turn leads to unhappiness. As I explained previously, the body is also affected by the energy you feed it, based on the emotions from the heart. You can maintain a healthy body by producing love from the soul, eating healthily and doing regular physical activity. The soul is who we are ... it is the pure love. The mind on the other hand is who we have become based on the information we have acquired throughout our life. The heart is the organ which produces emotions from our thoughts and our soul, which in turn will spread the energy of those emotions throughout our body.

Raising the awareness of this whole process enables you and the client to recognise the importance of self-love and consequently fuels their desire to create ways of achieving it.

"Suffering is not good for the soul, unless it teaches you how to stop suffering. That is its purpose." (Jane Roberts, Seth Speaks)

Heart

Feelings (Exercise):
What are you feeling right now?

It is important to take time to explore and understand your feelings. The process of healing your heart takes a minimum of one year. It involves learning how to do therapy sessions with your heart at least once a day, during the time you spend alone.

The heart is a very special organ and requires more attention than any other part of us, as it is very sensitive. It is also demanding on what it feels and takes time to accept and process new feelings. This can cause a bit of a mess if you are not organised, disciplined, and not guided by your true self (the soul, the pure love). For further details and insight refer to chapter seven which focuses on client one and explored how the process has worked.

"Falling in love you remain a child; rising in love you mature. By and by love becomes not a relationship, it becomes a state of your being. Not that you are in love - now you are love."(Osho)

Thoughts

Do we choose our thoughts? How can we choose our thoughts? Do we organise our thoughts?
How can we manage our thoughts?
Exercise, at this time of your life, which thoughts are you swimming in?

By exploring these questions, we gain insight into the ways in which we can master our thoughts and the ways we can care for them. We discover how to be our own therapist, our own spiritual guidance and how to prepare ourselves for new thoughts.

Experience/event/present

What is really happening in your life? Describe. The ultimate goal is to help people describe their life right now. How is it affecting them?

Usually I do this in a very natural way, whether it be while walking, in a relaxed area, during the lunch, the whole point is ensuring that the client feels free and connected to their true self. This enables the client to reflect on what they are saying and come up with their own analysis, options, desires, solutions, strengths. This process will ultimately strengthen their self-love; their inner power.

Nature time allows you to be in a place of tranquility and peace, which permits a person to reflect upon their recent actions and evaluate how life is going for them. This time is necessary in planning how to live your life.

Poets such as William Blake believed that humans are meant to live in nature and only then can their inner child be released. In nature we are able to have visions about how our lives will pan out, which gives us guidance.

Most of my clients were emigrants who were overwhelmed by various issues and problems, as mentioned in chapter seven. These individuals somehow found and gravitated towards me. At the time, I was simply going with the flow, and was not sure whether these individuals would be a part of. Although I did ask for permission to use their cases as part of the research, I was not clear about what kind of research and how I would go about it. For that reason, I was simply exploring anything that I found interesting and that I believed would bring peace and love to the world. I truly believe that it was meant to be as the clients had found me and were very open and honest from the start. They trusted me immediately, which is why I was able to offer help to my clients, even more than what they initially expected. This is evident in their feedback in chapter seven.

If the client is not honest, I cannot give them the help they require. This is because it is always their choice, which means that if they chose not to be honest, they are not ready to ask for help. Consequently, I am unable to help them. The law of the universe means that even if I attempt to help those who are not honest, it will not benefit them in any way.

At the time, I decided that I wanted my research to be based on the circle shown below. I found that the way the circle operates, was a root of unhappiness. However, as I progressed in the research journey, I discovered that self-love was the key to everything and the solution, which could lead to a world of peace and love.

My reflection of this circle is noted below. I found that a number of the participants were a part of the circle. I have analysed the circle on a deeper deep level in order to understand it personally.

This circle below demonstrates an immigrant's journey:

Client -emigrant-uk law-people-politics-action towards law- people - homeoffice -organisations (charity organisations)- other departments -solicitors- client- homeoffice -case worker- solicitor- interviews-refusal- solicitor- client alone… possibly challenge the decision -court- lose- turn back after all that painful journey and the hope gone down the drain. I would like to have a deeper understanding of the whole circle and the questions below… at a later time:

How much money goes into this circle? Who is benefiting?

Who is the main target?

What is the client benefiting from it?

The clients who were a part of that circle were experiencing severe depression, and suicidal thoughts (some even attempted suicide). Some were victims or perpetrators of domestic violence and others were involved in arranged marriages etc. Thus, the clients all had bleak pasts, characterised by pain and suffering. Not much had changed throughout their lives, they were still experiencing similar pain and suffering as a result of their emigration status. They do not feel stable or secure enough to start working towards their dreams or to look forward to good things. The future did not matter to them because they struggled to find the strength to think in a realistic way.

There were only two ways in which they could think about their future, one was to create the ideal future in their head or alternatively they could remain in a cycle of depression, failing to see the link between their ideal future and their reality.

It is so easy to want your dreams but far more difficult to start moving towards them. You'll find any excuses not to do it. The word "want" and "can't because" are in constant conflict, which results in present disputes. The feeling of knowing that you want something, but convincing yourself that you can't have it and you start moaning about it, blaming others, thinking some people are lucky whereas you are not lucky, etc …

The more I worked with the clients, the more convinced I became that my theory was working. I saw great potential within each client, and they knew deep down inside them that they had the potential to live their ideal life. However, some of the clients did not follow up through the process below for a number of different reasons (refer to chapter four and seven for more details).

It is vital for them to understand who they are deep down, the real them. This means getting some spiritual help to them connect with their soul, such as the program I offered called "Heal yourself while you write your book". This helped individuals heal from the past, live in the present and plan for their dream future. This is achieved by acknowledging the souls voice and the language of pure love, so that next time you hear it, you can distinguish it from the voice of your mind (it's your head, logic, and others perspectives of who they think they are), heart (the emotions created based on thoughts, sensitivity, craving love and other emotional needs) and body (it is the gut feeling, as the soul tries to talk to you through your heart, your body, and intuition).

It starts with therapy (They have to do at least 80% of the work), then coaching (digging deeper into their soul...helping them listen to themselves and discover their potential, and then mentoring them through a form of spiritual guidance that resonates with them...flexible holistic guidance with a clear plan.

Universal Laws of universe

Creator of life

Life

Understanding the creator of life

Understanding the universe

Karma

Law of Attraction

It is crucial that you understand the above points, as everything is connected and links back to them including; our reality, who we are and who we became.

All these points can be explained through a one day workshop or a one to one session in the language of the individual referring to their life experiences, actions, beliefs and their childhood life. You must first begin by bettering yourself as a person, as you are aiming to be a role model to those around you.

This means that you should treat the people around you in a respectful manner, so that your positivity can spread from them to others. This can be done through various techniques including taking a moment to breathe and thinking about how you want to be treated at that moment then acting accordingly.

In order to truly embrace self-love, you first must accept who you really are. You must not allow others to dictate your life for you, and the only decisions that you should make are the ones that you believe are right for you.

This process will allow you to understand who you are and you will get to know the real you far better. This will allow your self loving to come to fruition.

Self-Love Break Down

- How to achieve 80% self love
- How to achieve 20% self love
- How to combine the 20 and 80 percent in order to achieve 100%

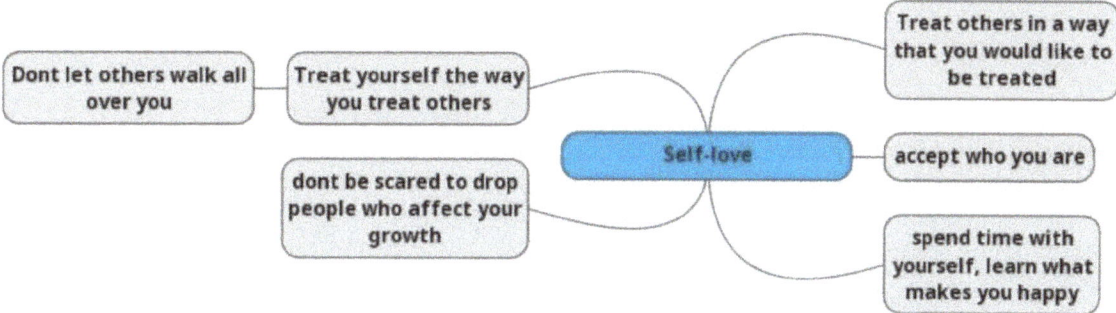

It is very important that you listen to your inner child when trying to get the other 20%. Your inner child reminds you to have fun and to stay in touch with the imagination you once had that lead you to be here. This imagination is the epitome of the 20% as it's all about being creative and unique.

This is all about self-love. Therefore we need to love ourselves how we deserve to be treated. We are all kings and queens and we must treat our sacred selves as well as you treat any human on this planet. We must not out everyone's needs ahead of our own as that could causes complications in the future, because we fail to meet our needs as human and we won't function at our best

It is very important that you listen to your inner child when trying to get the other 20%. Your inner child reminds you to have fun and to stay in touch with the imagination you once had that lead you to be here. This imagination is the epitome of the 20% as it's all about being creative and unique.

This is all about self-love. Therefore we need to love ourselves how we deserve to be treated. We are all kings and queens and we must treat our sacred selves as well as you treat any human on this planet. We must not out everyone's needs ahead of our own as that could causes complications in the future, because we fail to meet our needs as human and we won't function at our best.

Life
Understanding the creator of life
Understanding universe
Karma
Law of attraction

Nature/Nurture

Understanding nature helps you understand yourself.
Understanding nurture you are able to connect to your soul and feed it.

Also make sure you begin to love yourself through alone time. Get to know what makes you happy and treat yourself

We can give ourselves that much needed day off or say no to the person asking you to do something you don't want to do. Think about you sometimes in order to feel at your best

"Nature helps us to understand that we have everything we need just were we are and have ability to create the reality we want.......just need to have deep and long conversations with nature around what I said"

This has helped the client to be more aware of their intuition, their inner voice and to take time to breath- reflect- analyze-and come to decision based on pure love for themselves and others- take action towards the goal created by the soul. Moreover it helps them to be their own healer through conversations they have with their human parts, such as heart, mind and body but mostly is heart that need more healing then anything. (for more information refer to client one how she has managed to achieve the transformation through magical module).

Survival exercise

Stranded on a tropical island, alone with nothing but nature to help you survive. 95% of the population are not fulfilled. And just survive in terms of love, by giving them this exercise it may stimulate their inner power and take their attention away from surviving, to bring it to the moment. Right here right now to love.

ACCEPTANCE

Learn to accept where you are in order to allow yourself to find positives on your situation, and raise your awareness on negatives in order to have clear vision of how you want to spend each moment and how you want your future to be.

On this stage I worked with clients to accept what was done on momentum stage and more as we go through the acceptance. Acceptance is a very important stage as you need to have lots of conversation with yourself through the love you have within that we have explained and gone through on momentum stage. Through the conversations you will learn a lot about the power of pure love, the power of the moment, the power of the time and how to share love and care with others.

"The real success is about being content exactly where you are and having clear vision of how you want your journey to be… this will lead to enjoying each moment and working towards your vision but the most fascinating thing is that your vision will get bigger and bigger as you grow being fulfilled exactly where you are and with what you have… this can happen only by having ingredients of pure love… Moreover, you will never be afraid of death because you lived fully in moment, you did your best, you achieved to make yourself happy and have courage to go for your vision and you will know that next journey in the future life will be much easier as you have overcome all you challenges and got in touch with pure love that will follow you whatever you go even after you die… even in another life journey that you will be… life is magical… we are magical "

"Your purpose is actually quite simple, it's to look deep into yourself, into your soul, and your childhood memories can help you to do that. To discover and nurture, who you truly are, to know and love yourself at the deepest level and to guide yourself back home when you lose your way. The more you do this, the more aware and present you become, which creates more harmony in your life… Your self-worth has nothing to do with your craft or your calling and everything to do with how you treat yourself. Loving and accepting ourselves even when we fail miserably because love is what can heal anything and guide you to feel fulfilled and loved"

Self love ingredients are:

1 - justice towards yourself and others, So do things that you like others to do for you do it for yourself and do the same to others if you can if you can't at least don't do anything else just walk away

2 - Is accepting that you are protected. just take time to be silent and sink in that you are alone in this life; that is for a reason. No one is to be blamed for your unhappiness, because you are your own boss; you are the creator of your own reality. You have free will and choice to make decisions, and, because you are alone that tells you that you are number one in this life. Your job is to satisfy yourself. Every decision made should be for your own good.

Once you do that you can make happy people that you love also, so is important to make decisions that the purpose is to make yourself feel loved, fulfilled and satisfied with your decisions. Your purpose should be crystal clear that is all about you creating the reality you want through being fear, genuine, honest , straightforward, disciplined and product of love, of who you truly are.

No one can give you what you already have within and you cannot give to others love because of the free will and free choice everyone has to discover it for themselves and the they can share it with others or guide others how to discover it. It is very important to understand that love cannot be given to others because it does no good to them apart from it makes them attached to you which is not right thing to do as you prevent them from discovering their own pure love but instead they become attached to your pure love.

Don't forget, life can be fulfilled without having nothing if you have self-love. Exactly at that point you start to see all the colors of life. Important is to notice and see all the colors of the life through pure love and that it does exist to each individual and the life around. It's those colors that brings joy, happens, true universal love , true passionate love, and help you to have the reality you desire, such as money, fame, etc. If you don't have self-love you cannot see and notice the colors it does not matter what you have in this life. Only self-love can bring the colors crystal clear to see, feel and dance with them. Don't mix colors with money, fame, sex, or other excitements you get form material things because those what you see from short pleasure are just shadow of the real colors and can cost you more as they make your life journey more difficult and complicated. Material life does not bring the colors to your life but it does help if you have your self-love as you can use what you have wisely and enjoy the colors of your life journey. Colors are product of pure love. Pure love is your soul. Your soul is who you are, that never dies and have all the answers you need to know.

Staying still

Importance of staying still everyday for few minutes at least,

How to use stillness,

How to discipline yourself to make it a routine,

The benefits. (Staying still helps you to notice things that usually don't notice, to hear yourself and universe and creator).

Staying Still - important of staying still for few minutes every day helps you to connect with your true self beyond your human parts, such as mind, heart and body. Connecting to your soul and to see things through pure love which is you, is your soul and it gives you that fulfillment and reminder of who you are and how to see life. How to use stillness? Stillness can be used as a starter at least 30 minutes everyday and then through practice you can learn how to be in that mode automatically any time you choose whatever you are doing. Stillness can be pointed to your direction of your problems also with the practice in order to see the problems through your pure love and serve the purpose you are searching link to the problem you bringing to the stillness.

The benefits are:

-Staying still helps you to notice things that usually don't notice,

-To hear yourself and creator for guidance

-Produce love

-Becoming pure as whole you including everyday actions towards yourself and others through reflection – analysis-decisions-planning

-Feel loved

Hearing

In relaxation mode you start hearing different voices in your head and outside your head.

How to learn to recognise the voices where they are coming from and how to communicate with them,

Types of different conversations we can have in our hearing relaxation mode,

Hearing what you usually don't hear...hear the silence.

Hearing is a great skill and is in different levels, but the first level is to hear your soul, your true self, your pure love and slowly you take it from there going up to levels until you achieve fully yourself love. And then you learn how to listen to the creator in order to get guidance to get the reality life you desire. The purpose of the creator is for everyone to be in peace and love while they enjoy the magic of life that surrounds them. It is a theory and fact that we born and die, also is a fact that babies are full of pure love and children until age of 25 they still have some percentage of pure love. The difference between they have and they are pure love is that when children get influence by the information's they have been feed it through life experiences and people it moves them away from their pure love that they have been born. Creator has given free will and free choice which mean we can chose who to follow. To follow our mind, our heart or our soul, we have not been taught how to be us, how to connect with our soul because the soul has not been proven that it does exist. For that reason things get messy when it comes to understanding happens and what makes us feel fulfilled and loved. It is very simple … just be who you are … be product of pure love….and follow the structure of magical module to help you create your own techniques and methods how to be you … how to be product of pure love….how to connect to your soul and how to be guided by your soul in order to feel loved and fulfilled exactly where you are and then you will be able through your soul guidance to give love to others who need. To share your love with others and to achieve the material life you desire. This is simple, achievable and enjoyable. Only thing that will stop you to be guided by your soul is your mind and heart that has limitation to what they know and the don't have ability to know how to show pure love to yourself and others. The mind and heart are not able to be genuine with you and others because if they are it means you are fulfilled and loved exactly where you are and you never do any harm to anyone including yourself. Moreover you will be product of pure love and you will help others to become product of pure love. This was the reason why few of participants in this research where unhappy and did not follow the process until the end as you can see on chapter seven and four.

Smelling

- Through the smell we can allow ourselves to understand our likes and dislikes.

- To choose what we want to like and how to make it happen …

Strengthen our skills through the smells that we don't like by improving our weakness and through the smells we like to strengthen our strength by reminding us of the nice smells,

- Notice the smells we never noticed before so it helps us to understand better the universe, people and ourselves through the world of smells.

Touching

Healing touches,

Love touches,

Friendly touches,

Professional touches,

Impulsive touches...

How to apply to ourselves and others in order to serve us the way we want. (Touches are powerful tool that produce love).

Seeing

Seeing through eyes,

Seeing the nature in relaxation mode,

Observations seeing,

Noticing body language,

The way we see different

"Every day if we sit and look at ourselves in the mirror, watching as a movie every day action that we make and understand what is the devil and what is goodness because eyesight is the look of our goodness ... sometimes we have power to we are lost in the sight of goodness ... but in these cases it is a little practical to look without silence in our own silence without paying attention to the minds but just looking at ourselves in the depth of our eyes a few second until we connect with the good ... you understand when you are tied because a smile may arise or a pity or a cry of ignorance you have lived without realizing the true value of yourself .... or a critical one ... such a love ... or many things can happen when you connect with your goodness " This exercise helps in your relationship with the soul… with your inner goodness. … with what you are really with your power to give kindness to yourself and others).

Because I think it's the soul… your light that is immortal… have you been immortal… light, energy, kindness to accompany us in all the life we do and at that time we pass to the universe when a schematic has begun a life… It is love that cleanses the mind, heart, and body… is the love of the soul to learn to speak the language of love even when others speak the language of love because with the language of love helps and heals everything that comes into contact… It is exactly that language of love that guides you to accomplish the fulfilment where you are going to be missing nothing… to feel at ease and to enjoy everything that makes you feel comfortable and smile and to smile… to be in love with yourself and your life that you smile all around you and understand those who do not speak the language of love.

Noticing unseen things (exercise)

Noticing unseen things

Do exercise through mindfulness

Notice feelings - make note of them

Your thoughts - make note of them

Hearing sessions:

How do we view things?

Ask question and we get three different answer within or maybe four ….

1 - answer from the soul

2 - answer from the heart

3 - answer from the mind

4 - sometimes the body gives as the answer also depending on the health of our body… if the body is healthy will be silence and follow our decision.

What is the right answer? How would we know?

If you want to hear and feel your soul, stay away from people who have not achieved self-love, walk in nature, give lots of hugs to your self and nature, smile in mirror to yourself and nature, dance and have fun with nature, be grateful to the creator for what you have.

Mindfulness exercise

Mindfulness exercise to do at home or create your one

How to create routine once a day to be mindfulness in the things we need to focus or just reflect.

Things we need to be happy and content/How can we manage to have them or get them.

-Notice feelings... make note of them

-Your thoughts ..make note of them

-Your communications

Example mindfulness will help the clients that don't appreciate things that they have but their focus is more on how to get their illusion life or dream life quick and easy way through others and not through working for it one step at the time.

Few of the reasons people are not honest with themselves and others: (example migrants who migrate to other countries for better life and safety they experience some or all the points below)

-They feel embarrassed to tell the truth about their life.

-They don't want to feel weak.

-They don't want others to know their pain and their suffering.

-They are not aware that telling the truth is a start to get the purpose they are perusing.

-They are terrified to expresses what they are going through as they are afraid they will not be strong enough to continue.

-They are confused and they don't take time to stop and talk to what they are experiencing.

-They live in shadow.

-They live in illusion that does not exist and they walk away from the truth.

-They talk about others so they don't have to confront their own problems.

All this individuals that are part of that list they are so lost and in deep depression, most of them are young parents and so on life goes on….. when very simple can be turned into joyful and happy life by being product of pure love towards yourself and others which starts with being true to yourself and confronting everything guided by the soul.

Sometimes there are people who wants help but are not ready to be pure person because they don't believe that being pure is the first step to build the journey they want. So I teach all those techniques and methods but they still try their old habits and make things worse for themselves. I know that I have to give them a chance to show the options as it is the reason they entered my life but still they need more work on understanding of the conflict between their thought, feelings and the importance of self-love. As easy can be confused self-love with narcissist and egoist for those who have not achieved the self love. The difference is that the person who have achieved self love can never be egoist, narcissistic or any negative words or things because is pure love. Self-love is showing yourself how to produce love and how to be the real you "the pure love".

"If you feel fulfilled where you are… you will know how to help others automatically and you see the love in everything "

" The only knowledge you need to know on this life is how to make yourself fulfilled, be in peace and in love with yourself and life"

And, if you have not found happens within… then you cannot found it in long term nowhere… those happiness in short term (objects, money, sex, family, others, fame , excitements) are short and will not be with you when you are alone in your quite time… and… that's why you avoid the time alone because you don't want to confront it… as it is deep level… is beyond our livings… is what I experienced when I was 7 that through my pain I discovered this big power of love… and I reinforced when I was 18 and 36… now I just enjoy it… now I sit on it as I do what I have to while I am here as human and enjoy all those things that human has opportunities to do and enjoy …

So … I started with momentum… pain , - Acceptance… that I am here I want to find way to understand it and enjoy it - goal… to be product of pure love, inspired through nature to keep enjoying the beauty of life, committed to be loved and share love and get my vision of the reality I want, affirmation of whole who I am and what I do, love… be love.

" Someone who don't knowledge who they are for themselves they can never knowledge who others are because they become others … others become perception of others… perception of others are just thoughts created from someone who has not found themselves… and that's why the world is based on… and we die without noticing ourselves and the magic of life."

"The soul does not know gender, does not know places, does not know colors, does not know objects or looks because is energy based on love"

Again time-to-time you have to keep asking yourself the questions below until the answers you got you have achieved it. So by asking those questions time to time you reinforce the answers, get closer to your true self and get in touch with the feeling of pure love and self-love.

You need to ask your self:

-Who you are?

-Who you want to be?

-How you want your life to be?

-What do you need to make it happen? The life you want

-What is the meaning of love for you?

-How would you like your partner to be? And are you like that? If yes you are ready to meet someone like that if you are not then you need to work with yourself.

-Can you live alone? Why not? But are you happy if you are with the wrong person? What do you need to do to find the right person for you?

My reply to one of the clients while he was living on his illusion vision and did not want to allow himself to be in present and make the link between present and his illusion vision.

"Me and you we have talked and now I think you are in stage to learn to trust your purpose and discover yourself "who you really are? , what is your life purpose ? How can you start fulfilling your purpose? Do you like your purpose or do you want to change it? Again, keep going back to the question who you really are? Who you want to be ? How can you be who you want to be? And where can you start? "I feel that's your work for now and that's what you need to focus all your positive energy and allow time to feel all the negative emotions you are feeling." What all it matters is everyone should put their energy and work into understanding what really matters !!!! And get it ...

Which for me since age of 7 was all about focusing how to be content and in love with myself that I was in this life and the life with everything provides.... also once we discover that what we want automatically you will release that is about love - purity ..in order to get that... which after you get it you well feel fulfilled, loved and in peace... during the journey you still will feel that way but because you are working on to become pure and practice purity in everyday life you will go through adventures.... which you still enjoy it and learn from it as you grow inside you every day.

... one step closer to be you. ...and feel fulfilled, in peace and love.... and with the work with the clients I point out when they are not being genuine with themselves and others in order to keep practicing the pure love as they say they have it but they are not aware of full picture and practice of pure love. Because they don't have self-love. If you don't have self-love you will never be genuine with yourself and others, you never can treat yourself right and others they way you like to be treated.

I lost my self trying to please others said client number one.

1 - " As long as you look for good on you... your universe will be your teacher "

2 - "When you try to follow the purity you will never feel alone or out of purpose.... "

3 - " The change comes through your reflection of the conversation you have as whole you by being still.... By sitting on your energy humbled in universe"

4 - " The universe is everything and can be used in bad way or good way... only the difference is that negative energy can never give you peace and love but the good energy will give you peace, love and fulfillments... (the God, the religion are just roots to lead you to one direction. ...to understand universe.... to understand how to use the universe as we have free will and free choice... to choose the good energy or the negative energy and is up to us which one we feed on us... based on what we feed the energy thee reality will be created and our feelings... the feelings have power for good or bad)"

I learned that universe is the creator then only explanation I can give is that everything we create… such as… seeing spirits or communicating with angels or getting messages from other world and lots other things mire are just what we have asked universe to give us and with our determination and hard work we get those gifts… is all about energy and is universe our everything… we just have to choose which path to follow… the good or negative and we have the ability to know and recognize those two… that's why is our choice to choose and then all it starts in slow process depending on your determination, resilience, hard work, wiliness and the passion to love the purity.

"Again the learning for each individual is unique and different because of our free will and choice which makes us unique even though we all are energy and the energy is the same… but how we choice to use it makes us unique "

Understanding and being aware of different individual journey:

We can never know for sure exactly why the life journeys are different from each individual but I think it is based on few factors below:

- Previous life consequences…. contract with creator before we come to this life as we choose based on our previous life achievements and experience.

- Foundation of reality at the moment …as that changes based on humans progress / actions / thoughts / purpose / connection to their soul etc

- The influence of pure human beings that try to make sense why they are in this reality and how they can make it happen their inner calling….their true path that they choose before they decided to come to this life.
What happen !!!

- People who are lost but somehow they lost their really hearing and they all what they do is to survive or end it all

- Those who controlled others because they cannot control their inner conflict.

- Guilty parents who just dig themselves in deep guilt everything they try to come out of it ….

- Those who have worked hard to discover their inner power but instead they use it for main purpose to make money which takes them back further back before they started to work in their inner power …

- Also the creator strategy to make as work hard to remember the benefits of being good, the good things others do to us , the good being power to everything, …we easy remember bad things and how to act like that , as it is easy , it is short road and smooth compare to the road of being good is claiming mountains and with fall time to time but is peaceful, joyful, lovable. Is with the purpose that will take you for sure in top of mountains… even if it did at least you know you are in zone of your really purpose of getting closer to that   mostly remember is not about getting in top of mountains but cleaning your human being and putting in same level with your soul… Your soul is the top of mountains because that's the whole purpose of being in this life… that is the test we have to pass each time we live… until we get in same level with our soul… I am not sure how that can happen as it is very difficult thing to do and I am not sure what will happen after that can be achieved by everyone in this life… what will happen then!!! Maybe will be a peaceful life with full of love and then will start from beginning where all this started… which mean will be a test to see how long will be until someone can poison society again…

Does it take only one to poison whole us ? How easy is that to be done ?

Very easy, because people think happiness comes from not working (it's easy working when love is not present as the focus will be on material things and not in love. … Which makes you think that that's what you will get … sometimes you do get it but it's too late .. .your life has almost end it when you realize that love was missing and you feel dry).

The good person, the person who does everything from foundation of love doesn't focus on material things but they just come part of love - plan-action-satisfaction-fulfillment-self-realization …

As love is the key who can help you to open all the other doors by using the right tools. For the good person to change the society is harder because the good things are unseen … you only can feel it , visualize it, and live it… - Spending time alone… which helps you to be quite and listen to your soul, creator, any other spirit or energy that is trying to guide you (which could be any one… loved ones that are life or dead), universe, the whole you (mind, heart and body… the body is the gut feeling… which you can help you to listen to other parts of your body and connect with your own body). While you are in this state you make notes of anything that comes to you. as later you forget… make notes of feelings, hearing, words, and of your own thoughts and feelings… as you may feel feelings that are not yours, may hear thoughts that are not yours, my hear words, sentences that never come across before etc…

One of exercises I created for the client:

Two things to work on it this month:

1 - To heal your heart (have free time with yourself and be mindfulness about how your heart is feeling, listen, understand it, care for it and show compassion)

2 - Create affirmation to grow your confidence and believe in yourself example "I love … (the name of client), I am very confident that I can deal with any situation, no matter what it is , I believe in myself , I can achieve my dreams".

Example when the client were more connected to the universe and creator:

The client at age 6 was very creative and very wise on the things was saying but as she turned 8 years old she got influenced by reality and was drown into the things her reality was presented and less listening to her inner voice.

Client one and client two said:

Before age 6 were very pure, genuine and connected with intuition and to nature.

Client one said that after age 7 up to age 13 used to be very active, had lots of courage and wanted to copy adults. She was experiencing it through role play, by playing with the doll and she was pretending to be the adult looking after the sick doll trying to take it to hospital. She was looking after the doll and now when she was remembering, was feeling it ….and she said "I missed my mother" ... as her mother was not part of her life as her parent were separated when she was very young. After age 14 up to age 18 she said got closer to her soul, started to follow the religions, read books, spend time with the horse. She could see beyond what was presented. Age 18 up to 25 she got lost as started to understand people's actions and let them control her life as she was hiding for comfort in her special corner every time she was upset. My hidden corner provided everything I need it, she said. Was providing safety, comfort, I felt small and I felt rebelling towards what people were doing to me to show them that I could do it. The marriage was another big confusion that took me in another path with my head down and I felt I was getting smaller and smaller every day.

My analysis of our conversation is that I see a child thrown into life without love and guidance how to produce love, how to gain self-love which lead to rebelling as expression of anger why she is not been valued and why she has to be controlled.

Similar thing happen to the client 14 (8 years old girl) that she experienced same feelings but her parent dealt with compassion through love. In one of our sessions she said "I want my way that's why I misbehave ". I replied saying "is very good you have your own way but also have to listen to adults instructions and find way how to communicate your feelings and thoughts so you both can value and understand each other and find middle way for you best interest". She smiled.

Most of the clients have shown the same rebellions and the reason is they get lost in their emotions. Furthermore they are confused of the reality being surrounded. They use their rebellion to do stuff that really doesn't like it but somehow it excites them and brings satisfaction. To try to be happy is the road that has not been proven and not seen ... and that's why they don't even try.

The moment is important, and you need to use all the stages of magical module in an authentic way in order not to be just illusion and not complete with the influence of the fear ... "Moment is reflection of the individual".

GOAL

To understand who you are at the present and to be conscious of the choices you make, you must ensure that you have a goal. Dream your wishes, visualise your dreams, and break up them in small goals.

We all wants wealth, health, fame, success, love, peace, harmony, to be surrounded by people who love us, to have the job we love to do and be happy, however, we all have to start with a vision, a plan, decisions, time scales, an action and starting point. We discussed momentum and acceptance and now we have a clearer idea about how to make the right decisions for ourselves and how to enjoy the journey from the starting point up until we reach the goal. This stage is about helping the client reflect, analyse, create and strengthen their connection with their soul/mind/heart/body, in order to obtain the reality they desire.

Refer to chapter four and seven regarding how the participants had worked through this stage and most of the client could not go past the goal stage. What I mean is that their goal was the end of the line and they wanted to skip the whole journey and reach the end line. They failed to truly work through the momentum and acceptance stage, as they were merely focused on entering the fast lane.

The topics below have been applied to the clients in personalised and unique ways. Below you will see the main topics that need to be expanded, based of the client's uniqueness.

Imagination
-Imagination of when you are dead
-What will happen at your funeral?
-In 10 years time or when you are old. What will happen and how do you see it?

Imagination of your death, or what will happen at your funeral, or in 10 years time when you are a pensioner… Make notes… Re-read notes and then take more notes.

No limitations
The soul knows no limitations, (describe what the soul is and why it does not know limitations and why we use the word "can't" when the soul doesn't understand can't.

The soul has both free will and free choice. Our choices, actions, decisions and influences the decisions of karma and law of attraction (this is a fairly complex and unique theory which can be explained in a one day workshop).

It is only the mind, which has limitations.

Do meditation relating to the language of the soul, either a general one or one to one.

Believe in yourself

-You can believe in the creator, but how can you believe in life, the universe and the creator if you don't believe in yourself?

-What does it mean to believe in yourself?

-How can we discipline ourselves to take the journey to achieving self belief? (An exercise with small steps which leads from the place the individual is currently at to the place they want to be in self love...to be in a workbook as an exercise)

What is love

-Self love>universal love>passionate love (intimate love).

-Self love (is believing in yourself, accepting yourself and where you are, taking time to understand yourself.

-Being a great holistic facilitator to yourself (to question, to criticise, to discipline, empathise, love, care, to be kind, be understanding, a shoulder to cry on, be encouraging, treat your self, respect, forgive, remind yourself to live in the moment, help to follow the plan 80% and 20%).

-Allowing yourself to be a unique version of yourself, find yourself by spending time with the whole you (soul, mind, heart and body).

Goal exercise

- Goal exercise on self love

- On top of this exercise to be the reason what is the whole purpose of them loving themselves?

- Where that will take them and how ? In detailed plan journey from where they are and where they want to go.

Example: My Goals (individual creates their own goals which each goal have sub goals).

- I surround my self around people higher than me in the sense of self love achievement, self realization, fulfillment, criticism, speak up freely etc

- When I am around people that have to do with my work I make sure I have enough energy to be present and be there fully ...

- Family and friends that don't fit on the categories I mentioned then ...I will keep healthy balance where I benefit and they benefit. ...so we don't damage each other's. ...but we help each other to grow more ...

- I make sure use meditation, affirmation, magical module to keep me granted. In same time to feel light, so I am not independent from this life, but I can use this life to keep continuing being lighted. ...

Imagine this progression:

The individual (somewhere being alone without any help)-suffering-accepting-reason for purpose-goal-believe-inspire to feed the goal-determent-strength to fight-affirming-love.

"love yourself from the source of the soul and not from the ego of the overflowing cover of the diaphanous"

"Doing bad to others is enough even thinking about it, and it will come back to you what you do....even twice"

"Its not integrity others to save your life because you have to do it as it is your lessons and everything lies within you...be creative, curios and determent to create your own path"

Client one said: I never thought of You (myself) - Me (the ordinary one, the common one)-and space (Vjollca).

Vjollca said: For me the space represents the ladder from reality to the universe ...
As you are in that energy can you create 11 cards with the answers from you of the points below please so you can have it and remind yourself anytime you feel the need too:

  1 - For knowledge. . do you feel wiser and why? You are smart and why ?
  2 - Trust ... how do you know how to believe?
  3 - Practicing self-confidence and self believe....how?
  4 - Practicing God's Faith/will/guidance
  5 - Daily plan, weekly and monthly plan...how can you?
  6 - How can you practice emptiness of Your Mind and letting go
  7 - How to reach the space, the universe?
  8 - The imagination of things that happen tomorrow ... how would you like to go tomorrow or the situation that will occur and how can you adjust it on your best interest? Based on pure love?
  9 - Weekly prayer.
  10 - How could you learn from others?
  11 - How to protect myself and enjoy the moment

Walking on straight line towards purity, only the one who is determined to walk straight and is enthralled with the real listening can do.

1 - Understand yourself

2 - Apply the rules of the universe to be pure in heart and mind as you are in the spirit

3 - Wish the best for others and do not let others hurt you.

4 - Let go of those that don't fit on your energy.

5 - Meditate regularly. ... at least once a day to continue to understand yourself .

6 - Every day look at your day as in the movie to reflect and correct it.

7 - I constantly recall that you are only important person in this life and this life is for you ... only you decides how to live and be responsible, don't blame others.

If you do follow the steps mentioned in the right way, your transformation will be:

Transformation of yourself, understanding your spiritual world, knows how to make dialogue with your soul (which you are), your mind (that is shaped by the exterior life mixed little with that spiritual tendency if you have nourished with your soul), with your heart (how it interprets feelings of thought and how much knowledge it has about feelings and how you feel healthy), your body (taking care of your body), understanding your purpose in this life, you are in harmony with yourself and will help others to be in harmony.

Life is art that take the shape of your eyesight, your eyesight is the sight of the soul, the sight of the soul is blurry by the influence of the heart and the mind because the heart and mind are trained by human rather than the influence of your real you.

Food for your goal:

1 - love

2 - eating healthy

3 - having faith in your self

4 - communicating with your self

5 - Spending time alone /daily/weekly/holiday.

6 - Spending time where you love and feel good.

7 - Spending time with people who you feel yourself.

8 - Having your heart and mind open.

9 - Treat yourself.

10 - Tell others how you feel.

11 - Remembering this is only and only your journey, your life.

This list may change but for me right now that's what it is my soul food. What is yours?

INSPIRATION

Don't forget to pause and notice the amazing things and the blessings around you. This enables you to become inspired from anything that surrounds you, bad or good. You'll always have something to spark your inspiration and fire your creativity.

Inspiration

- •... What does inspiration mean to you?
- •... Think about how inspiration helps your day to day life
- •... Think about who does inspire you and why/how?

Inspiration

- •... Connect with nature what this mean?
- •... Does nature help you focus and concentrate?
- •... Does nature allow you to feel inspired?

Inspiration

- •... Connect with babies what does it mean and feel?
- •... Do babies inspire you and how/why?
- •... Care about your needs…how do you do it and how would you like to do it?
- •... Act and take what you need exercise created based on the individuals uniqueness.
- •... Care about your needs…how do you do it and how would you like to do it?

Inspiration

- •... Connect with people you admire….why and how?
- •... Do you shy away from people you admire or do you attempt to get to know them better? Why?
- •... Do you look at the good in others and try to make yourself a better person?

Inspiration

- •... Why is it important to have inspiration in daily life?
- •... What examples of inspiration can you think of?
- •... What inspires you daily and what do you get from it?

Inspiration exercise

Fill up the tree exercise and soul food exercise (in the work book provided).
I ask the individuals to create an exercise of what inspires they in the shape and order they prefer.

The inspiration stage is very unique and has to be personalised while working with individuals, groups or events energy.

- What does inspiration mean to you ? Why is it important for you to have inspiration in you daily life ?
- Discuss and then write your ideas on the board....
(Then amalgamate my views with theirs regarding inspiration).
- Mindfulness exercise ... connect with nature ... with babies. ... with people that you admire... connect with your inner child, looking back to a time when you where happy.

Below I have listed a number of ways you can recognise the language of pure love from other human languages:

1 - Eye contact
2 - Stillness
3 - Being there in conversation, not avoiding it
4 - Answering the question wholeheartedly the whole you
5 - Having answers to everything
6 - The energy is light, calm, healing
7 - Doing that extra to help if need it

"The saying "open up your mind" does not resonate with me because the mind cannot be open, it cannot hear unheard words or things, it cannot see unseen things, it cannot learn from things that are not proven. Instead, I believe that the correct saying is "let your soul guide you". This means allowing your soul to be a part of your reality, a part of your decisions, of opening up to the universe and listening to new guidance, new signs, next stage of our journey to grow."

Our mind is just a robot that functions in a certain way, and the heart is the same. However, the body is something else due to the cells, as the cells feed in love energy. The body will remain healthy while operating on that food mostly, apart from when you abuse it physically by not looking after it effectively by eating, exercising, and fulfilling any other needs it may have.

Another reason the body gets ill is because of the path we have chosen before entering this journey. However, I do believe that every illness can be healed through pure love and guidance from your soul.

COMMITMENT

Be a good listener and listen to your inner guidance, nature, and all your senses. Trust the universe. Give time and flow with time by being spontaneous in order to understand when the time is right to do what you need to do.

Commitment

- What does Commitment mean to you?
- What examples of your commitment are you willing to share?
- How is this example of commitment something other people can learn from?

Commitment

- Techniques and methods to stay committed:
- Have a goal in mind
- Wake up with your goal in mind and go to sleep with the goal in mind
- Truly believe that it is a possible to achieve the goal you already gone through the stage of the goal

Commitment exercise

Drawer Exercise - it involves organising your thoughts, goals, priorities, and responsibilities. We also need to be aware of the following; self love, purpose, food for the soul, karma, upholding your values and principles. *Life Ladder Exercise* - You can replace the ladder with any object of your choice, however what is important it going through every steps of the ladder while also keeping in mind the 80% and 20% we talked about regarding self love.

Through this exercise you will find yourself where pure love is, there is the vision of your life that you have to choose and turn into reality. Every step of the ladder should feel right for you, and once you come to practice the first step below you can get better understanding of the other steps. Therefore, it is important practice the first step in which you get to talk with the silence and the energy that is explained in the first step below. This will help you to complete the ladder excise after understanding the steps below.

How to connect with your soul:

1) Dedicate some time everyday to yourself. Have deep and insightful conversations as you discover your inner peace. You will discover your inner child, whose dreams have no limit and whose imagination is free to explore and sail. You'll fly without even realising, you'll find peace and love and you'll suddenly find the courage to do anything you put your mind to. Once you've discovered the courage inside you, hold onto that feeling and keep practicing that

exercise for as long as you need. The second step follows after this. (but the ingredients must only be goodness in every flow or to create imagination).

2) Begin working with your mind. You can do this by yourself in silence having felt that you've learned from step one, where your soul observes the mind with love and successfully organises your thoughts through compassion. You must let go of the thoughts that don't serve your pure love, justice and inner peace and alternatively construct thoughts which reflect the reality you desire. This is a process in itself because every new thought should be accompanied by a detailed plan of what you will do and how you will do it. With practice you'll be able to create only thoughts which serve your soul. The initial feeling at the first step, which is associated with justice, kindness and love brings satisfaction as it gives you a hint of where you are and where you want to be.

3) At this stage you must turn your attention to your heart, which requires special care as it is sensitive and delicate. The heart tends to contradict the thoughts but at the same time each though creates a feeling. If your thoughts are not filled with love, which protect you from the unjust actions of other individuals, then they create feelings of hurt and pain. Thus, this process takes longer than that of the mind and is far more difficult as there will be pain, tears, a feeling of the loss of love. However, this pain can be healed through the love of the soul. This process continues until all the hurtful feelings are healed by the care of the soul ... and produces only feelings of love.

4) Now we must turn to the body and follow the process relating to the body.

5) By this step we bring together all the previous steps, which combined bring inner peace and love. These help to create the reality that you desire.

AFFIRMATION

Tell yourself how good you are. Remind yourself of all the amazing things you are doing and the great abilities you have to help you fulfil your purpose.

Affirmation

What are affirmations?
These are ways we:

- Support
- Discipline
- Guide ourselves to achieve our tasks

Affirmation

- How do you use them?
- Do you discipline yourself when necessary?
- Do you offer yourself emotional support?

Affirmation:

- How do we create Affirmation?
- Do you have a goal in mind that you wish to achieve?
- Do you have the necessary structure in place for you to succeed?

Affirmation

- Who decides when we need them?
- We decide when we need them, when is that and why?
- We decide what type of affirmation works for us

Affirmation

- When we use them and how we use them?
- We use them when we feel that we need to change something about ourselves.
- We use them as reminders to make us stay on the path we want.

The Affirmation stage work also involves co-working with the individuals.

- What are affirmations / How do you use them? (affirmation helps you to achieve what you want to achieve through reprogramming your mind, heart and body and finding the way to the real you?)
- How do we create them/why is important to create them? (only you know what is right for you and what works for you. Only you will know when to use them and how, however, you can start with what is provided in work book as a head start to your journey through magical module).
- Who decides when we need them/when we use them and how we use them? (Provide guidance on how to create affirmation as the individuals go along based on their journey through the stages of Magical module).

Conversations with yourself/soul/mind/heart/intuition and others. Remember the rules of the universe and that we should take 30 minutes out of our day for this and at least one day a week.

One of the exercises to self inspire yourself and create your own affirmation from your journey is the program provided through the process of the magical module "HEAL YOUR PAST WHILE YOU WRITE YOUR BOOK".

The points below will be useful when going through the program. When you go through rereading it and structuring it, you will be surprised at what you wrote and of your abilities (refer to client 1 and 2 on chapter seven, who have started to write their books).

1 - Someone to listen to you without judgment but with pure love.

2 - Someone to give you advice as you write your free thoughts, automatically you will be connected to your inner child and your soul.

3 - For someone to cry with and feel sympathy and empathy with you.

4 - For someone you can discuss any confusions with.

5 - For someone to laugh with at your stupidity and foolishness.

6 - Someone to help you analyse and reflect on your mistakes/actions/experiences/painful moments/good memories etc.

7 - After you finish the whole book you can decide if you want to help others with what you have created.

More benefits that you get from this program are below:

- Learn how to stay in the present, which can help you see things far more clearly.
- Learn how to create a clear plan for the goals you wish to achieve.
- Learn how to connect with your inner self; your true self.
- Learn how to Connect With Your Highest Power.

- Learn how to overcome the obstacles and to empower from them.
- Learn how understand your role as a parent.
- Learn how to love yourself in order to love others in the right way, enabling everyone to be happy.
- Learn how to increase self-confidence.
- Learn how to have more courage to approach things that you still do not trust, but that you want.
- Learn how to Stay Realistic about your Desires and Reflect on what you really want.
- Learn how to build cheerful and useful relationships, with yourself and others.
- Learn how to heal yourself from your past.

Client one stated after her one-year work on magical module:

"The word meditation never really resonated with me but I never understood it and I did not know how to use it. But now I have found that what I do is similar but different, as it is a conversation with myself and it means mostly a conversation with the higher energy where I can contact my soul and the universe. Moreover I can have conversations with my soul, God, the universe and with my mind and heart."

My conclusion is that through personal experience and the work I have with my clients, conversations with yourself are very important if you know how to use it and guide the conversation. You must be guided by pure love in order to get the result you are supposed to or the result you're searching for. It is not productive co-sharing with yourself and the higher energy if you do not know how to do it and how to use it to make your dream life reality. You will know if you are doing it right once you realise that it is a solution for your suffering and begin finding pleasure in everything you do… through love you can see the magic in everything … you are in love with yourself, your life, and everything surrounding you, despite the reality that surrounds you, because the reality suits you and the things that you want… the energy that you give. It is important to understand pure love in order to have peace and harmony in your life. For me to help the client in this direction I have to feel the energy of the person in connection with their higher energy and to understand the person as a human to help make the connection between the two and give the right guidance. Everyone is unique and different, everyone is in a different position on the journey of life, thus, everyone needs unique guidance which is personalised to their journey of life.

Below is an example of how I communicated through the connection of the soul with the client one. Having read one part of her book I created this post below and sent it to her through email.

"Whenever I read your writing, it seems like I'm in a boat in the water at light rain … and that's the energy of the universe or knowing what energy I'm up and running".

My reply in poem

Talk about the desperate love we are looking for and we do not know how to look for it.

We do not know how to understand love. ...

it is our fault. ...

no one taught us…

If love is the lifestyle of life,

but it is a shame that bring into the family… keep your head down like a mother ...

like the other women ...

like a decent woman ...

your life is as we say it is

I cried ... and I wondered why ...

but I knew that I was not for that form of life and that I could not do it ...

I could do it better than everyone

but I could not fill my lungs with air ...

I wanted to breathe in looking at the skies. ...

I wanted to discuss my dream plans with the moon ...

I wanted to dance and laugh in the rain ...

to speak with people without words, but through the eyes.

"we learn from each other in different levels"

LOVE

Love yourself and everything on this earth to attract the love energy that leads to you living in a magical world. Love is the medicine of life and the place where you get your answers.

Love

- What is love ?
- Write two sentences on what you think love is
- Then write another two sentences on why we love

Love

- How can we know we love ourselves fully?
- By taking time to think to ourselves what do we gain and how?
- By looking at ourselves in the mirror and see if you're happy about who is looking back.

Love

- How can we give the right love to others ?
- By giving them the love we want to be given
- By being a generally kind and good hearted person

Love

- How can we embrace the love of life?
- Utilise the power nature gives us
- Enjoy the little things about life
- Be grateful for what you actually have that others don't and what does your soul tells you about this statement?

Love

- Spending time in the place of love?
- Being in nature helps you truly connect your body with your soul and allows your intuition to guide you

Love exercise

- Create poem about love for yourself and life
- Make a plan on how to keep your self-love

Love

Love yourself, life, others, and everything that surrounds you... this is the meaning of life... this is the disappearance of dissatisfaction... this is the disappearance of complaints... this is the love without limitations... free love... magic love that creates magic on you and the life you are surrounded.

"The magic of life lies in your soul, where it finds the purity of pure love ... where there is only goodness... where love is produced" (so whoever are religion leaders or people who represent themselves as good persons, you can feel it through the silence... the energy is in that moment... "The sun can warm you up with the lights he has and you are not able to look at straight on with eyes because we are not pure as human... is the same way when you look people on the eye... you can tell so much about it if you just let the silence guide you").

I do believe everyone is unique and special.

We are not here in this world to be better the others but to be product of love and help those who has not achieved it yet to be product of love.

I discuss with clients the points below:

1 - what is love, self love, universal love and imitate love
2 - how each of it can be achieved
3 - what are the benefits of it
4 - how that can be practiced
5 - what other research says about it
6 - what religion says
7 - why is it important what others say when has not been working?
8 - connections we get with strangers... like we know them for long time... can see it through their eyes.

Is important to understand self-love, universal love and passionate/intimate love.

You can search throughout the entire universe for someone who is more deserving of your love and affection than you are yourself, and that person is not to be found anywhere. You yourself, as much as anybody in the entire universe deserve your love and affection." —Buddha

This life is for joy and the circle of life the generation is amazing and magical.

Your whole being is reaching toward greater understanding, greater Truth. Trust where your soul pulls you, it is into a more enlightened, aware state. Your friend is full of fear, but don't let his/her fear get to you. Your job is to remain calm and experience the Truth. Your soul knows the way forward.

We are truth seekers and never accept a teaching unless we have tried it out and find it to be true for us. I say never stop looking deeply, asking the questions, and testing it out on your own experience.

Universal love is:

Our body is built from love which will help us to function and that's why we have the need of others love, that's why we feel good around others but still there are things to reflect and think… is it really satisfying us ? Or you just accepted because you think that is how far it can go for better!!!

Passionate/intimate:

love is on my understanding when two people are sharing their journey in all aspects of life and they don't need each other but they enjoy and love sharing their journey as they know themselves and they are sure of each other. There are two client who have achieved pure love on self-love and they know how to share love in universal way and they are ready to get in intimate, passionate love, as they are clear of what they want. This love will last happy after forever.

Each points below are the base of pure love:

1 - Treat others the way you like to be treated
2 - Love your self the way you like to be loved
3 - Do your best in everything you decide to do

1-Treat others the way you like to be treated:

-In order to know what is best for others first you have to know what is good for you and for that reason you have to have self-love to know yourself well and to feel loved in order to help others on their needs.

People who have self love they know the answer to this question but for those who don't have self love you have to raise your awareness on those points below before you get involved on with others or interact with others as you will end up hurting yourself and others:

Before you process the though its on your head consider how is helping the other? How do I know it's really helping the other? What is the length time my help will last and what they will do after that? What is costing me to help others? Can I find a way that can help them to help themselves in long term? If I was on their place what I really wanted? And take deep breath before getting the answer or best is before you ask the question to yourself as it allows you to connect to your true self and listen to the true answer instead of the ego answer. In my understanding from my self-discovery the ego is the mind created based on thoughts that takes us easy options and just thinks for themselves and never consider the other best interest. The true self is the soul, the pure energy link directly to creator and that is all about helping you to be pure to yourself, which that leads automatically to be pure to others. The ego, the part of mind that is fulfilled with information and guidance how to gain things (things such as , money, love , affection, attention, fame, life style to show off ect.)only for your self that is not pure because you will hurt others for your interest, such us lie, manipulate, physically hurt others, steal, emotionally hurt others and lots more that you may think off or seen around. If you manage to see the difference between the pure thought and ego thought than you have started the first step of practicing on treating others the way you like to be treated. Remember if you have not achieved the self love then you will not know how to treat yourself and you are lost on ego which you notice as you don't feel fulfilled, loved and complete exactly where you are and you need help before you start to help others or think you can help others as you are effected by your ego and need healing through your soul.

The self love will help you to link to your purest side, which is your soul and then you will treat yourself with pure compassion and understanding and you will know how to treat others.

2- Love yourself the way you want to be loved:

We never learnt how to love ourselves because growing up we have always been told that we shouldn't be selfish and only think about ourselves. I truly believe that this was both a misconception and misunderstanding as we failed to value just how unique children are. I think both people and culture in general have both misunderstood and failed to value children for the special beings they are. We can undeniably learn from the children about self love guidance or those three rules I mentioned earlier, as they can give explanations as they are pure. They are also under the influence of their soul. Around the ages of 3 and 5 and then around the age 7 the children tend to be very connected to the creator, then depending on the amount of compassion and understanding they have received by people that surround, they will begin to be defined. This happens up until the age of 16, and by 19 years old you finally build a strong connection to the creator and your soul. Up to the age of 25 years individuals work on shaping themselves and choosing which way to go... do they follow their ego or their soul? As mentioned earlier, many people ignore the soul and they do not follow that route (as statistics show about crimes, suicide, domestic abuse, depression, mental illness and generally unhappy people). It is challenging for young people between 16 and 25 to choose the soul route, as they fear the unknown. They struggle to accept their uniqueness and they don't want to stand out from others. They choose to follow the same path that others have followed, in order to be safe and conform. Others are part of the mind, the ego and often these individuals don't act in a pure way which consequently leads to pain, suffering, unhappiness, wrongdoings and pretending to be happy (egoist).

Moreover, these individuals use their empathy skills to manipulate others in order to get love and satisfy their needs. The ego exists within all adults, however egoism in children does not exist. Consequently, adults teach children that they should not be egotistical or act in a way which may be perceived as egoist. By doing this, the adults have repressed the children's desires to continue being pure and unique. I discovered self-love through asking demanding questions to both the creator and nature around the age of seven. I refused to be defined by my ego or the mind, beliefs and opinions of people who surround me. By rejecting unhappiness, I managed to gain self love. I had developed self love which in turn intensified my self belief. I now believed that I could make my dreams a reality, which I eventually did by ending up where I am now. In simple terms, you must push yourself to discover the pure love buried deep inside you, in order to develop self love through compassion and understanding as you are guided by your inner pure love. Once you have figured that out, you'll finally understand the importance of time and money and know how to manage it in order to balance your inner world with your outer world. It is very important to know a simple fact; we are born, we die but the soul does not die. A fact which have been proven by science. So for that reason a creator does exist, he has created the circle which I explained on the stage of acceptance and in the literature review about the law of the universe.

The law of the universe is simple, you simply need to be pure and want justice for yourself and others. You have to show compassion, understanding, care and love towards you as a whole and others as a whole. That is the law of the creator that leads to fulfilment, peace and being loved. If you lose your way then you will be unhappy, not in peace and not loved until you learn to find the way to be who you truly are. , compassion, justice and honesty with yourself and with others, is not part of gaining self-love.

It is very simple to love yourself. It takes willingness, determination and a strong desire for pure love and care for yourself. This will enable you to connect with your soul, which is the purest part of you as an individual and is a part of the creator. But to connect with your soul you have to be demanding and set on working on yourself to discover how to want justice and love from your self to your self. That can be done through the stages of the magical module, which combines numerous techniques with creative inner conversations guided by you.

Loving yourself:

1 - Learn to accept and love yourself for who you are and the way you are. Analyse what you do not like about yourself and plan how you're going to change or make improvements. Alternatively, you can accept these flaws and not complain about them.

An individual who wants to be loved does not waste time on overthinking, complaining, moaning, wanting what others have, not liking their image, wanting others to love them, judging others, talking about others when it does not benefit the person they are talking about, wanting more money , etc. Accepting yourself means allowing yourself to show compassion and understanding towards the person you are and having deep conversations with yourself in order to discover who you want to be. You need to go through the stages of momentum and acceptance in order to completely understand this point and ultimately achieve it.

2 - What we give energy to, that is what we attract. If you focus your energy on all your problems then those problems will follow you. Alternatively, if you focus your energy on finding solutions then these solutions will become a part

of you. When seeking a solutions, quietly step back in order to view the whole the situation, the problem or the issue that is presented as a whole picture. We have to show compassion and consideration to the whole of us before we decide on a solution. Refer to the goal stage for more details.

3 - Let go of the things that hold you back from being yourself. Once you start to be a product of justice towards yourself and others, it is difficult for you to stay around those who don't practice the same justice towards themselves and others. This is because you want to be truthful and being truthful requires lots of energy and skills, in order to learn when and how to be honest without hurting others. Until you learn how to be truthful and you practice justice you must keep your distance from those who complicate your journey or become obstacles.

4 - Be aware of all the negative obstacles but focus on the goal. Be aware of the fear that you are feeling. Talk to the fear so that you can understand it and reassure it that you have a plan. It is through your inner conversations that you can make the following points happen:

➢ Turn pain into compassion and understanding.
➢ Turn fear into a plan, as you become more aware of what your fear is telling you.
➢ Turn anxiety into self belief.
➢ Turn loneliness into the comfort of your pure love and dance through your pure love.
➢ Allow your soul to be a healer of your mind and heart through your inner discussions.

5 - Ensure that you are clear about your visions in life and frequently revisit them. Make sure that you live 100% in the present, so that you can fully enjoy everything you do in the moment. This involves being 80% productive at what you do in the present and 5% revisiting the past if you require any lessens or any good memories. Furthermore, the remaining 15% is dedicated to future visions and to moving forward to get to where you want to be.

6 - Dream big, visualise your dreams, and break them in small goals. Loving yourself is the most amazing thing that I have discovered and it is something which has helped my clients be content, appreciate what they have, learn to feel loved within, know with who to share universal love, know which kind of partner they want , how to treat others through compassion and understanding, planning for their goals, making time for themselves, noticing the little things that make them happy, valuing themselves, believing in their abilities, understanding what others say and do, and smiling to themselves in the mirror and to the world.

7 - Your intuition and your soul provide you with guidance. Ensure that you find time to listen and have conversations daily. Don't just start a conversation and then simply ignore it because it is deep and needs more energy, attention, focus, will, determination, creativity on questions asked, curiosity of seeing things in all areas that can benefit you and your life journey, including others involved, ensure you reach the end of the conversation with you eventually come to a conclusion, plan and out it into action.

8 - Pursue your passion and find a job you love and enjoy so that you give your best. Through those inner conversations, you have to discover the ways you can pursue your passion and enjoy the job you have decided to do. Remember we have one life which we need to enjoy and make the most. Have those inner conversations daily and as often as you need. End these conversations with reflections, analysis and actions?

9 - Consistently surround yourself with things that are meaningful to you.

> Know who to socialise with, as you are meant to share universal love. Those who have not discovered self love are unable to share love, instead they will just feed on your self love. You should be aware of this and make decisions accordingly.
> Ensure you have a purpose regardless of how you choose to spend your time. Your time is the key to your peace, love and creating the reality you want and enjoying the moment.
> Have daily inner conversations in order to evaluate how your day went and reflect on what you did, what you wanted to do or what you could have done.

10 - Ensure that you live your life only for yourself and no one else; it is yours and only you can decide how to live it. Every time you feel like something is not going the way you want, you have to stop all the thoughts, all the emotions and just connect with your higher power, with your soul, your creator and see everything from their point of view. You will understand why you are important and why it is important to make yourself satisfied from a pure love point of view and not an ego point of view.

Your achievement of pure love cannot benefit other, unless you help them achieve it from within. We are here to help ourselves, not to rely on others. Of course others can help us move forward and climb our steps a bit faster, but that's it. So help which does not help the individual to help themselves in not beneficial, except for when you know that your help is helping them to progress two or three steps forward. This is why it is important to focus on being content, without relying on others. It is only when you are content that you can help others in the correct way.

11-... Believe in your uniqueness and the universe will guide you. Remember if you can't accept and love yourself just the way you are you will not have confidence, high self esteem, lots of doubts and not sure that you deserve what your vision is. Easy could be alloying yourself to feel for those who keep buttering you. So you need to have a serious conversation with your soul to find ways how to feel loved and to remind yourself all the good things you have and those that you are in progress to get. Continue to reflect on your progress of the changes that you have decided to make. It's important to find ways how to feel loved through your pure love in order to shine and enjoy everything you do and you will recognize the truth from the lie, the compliment from someone who is trying to make you like them. Use of manipulation for their interest only, you will know someone who has problem with themselves but instead they put you down, you will appreciate the critics, the truth, genuinely and straightforward people.

12-... Treat everyone the way you like to be treated, to receive the same from the universe. This is very important and need lots of awareness, attention, and reflection from the soul and creator point of view. Also needs healing time for your mind and heart after each situation that did not feel right to you. Healing can be done through your soul by allowing your soul to be the therapist for your thoughts and feelings. Moreover reflect daily through your inner conversations on how you have dealt with others from whole you but the soul and creator has to have the last say if you trust your soul and the creator. Sometimes we follow their guidance even without being clear or making sense but later we will understand.

When you start the journey through the self love can cure all emotional and physical illness as you will become product of pure love. You will only be part of pure love, no judgment, no anger, no getting upset more then what is need it for healing time, don't hate anyone or anything, you will allow understand of others and show compassion. You will feel loved , never feel lonely, you will know your value and you will not accept less then what you deserve. You feel confident, strong, you will have the highest intelligence as you get information directly from the soul which knows everything and creator. You will not relay anymore on your mind and heart because your awareness has improved on observing your thoughts and feelings though the healing sessions from your soul. You can see through others and understand their actions instead of judging or getting angry as you know the ways how to get what you want in the way that is recognized by universe and others as is the language of love.

Do your best in everything you decide to do:

Doing your best means working hard to discover and achieve self love, which is the key to fulfilment, peace and love. Self-discovery sets the foundations for an enjoyable life in which you are fulfilling the purpose of your existence. A number of the qualities include: - create - Analyze options - choose the options – look for justice – love - diplomacy - sharp observation - work- simplicity - wish - plan - a short and long vision for the future – dedication - reflection - decisions - purpose - and the magic of love is to love yourself and you life, the way you want to and not how others impose.

The ingredients of knowing if you are doing your best are:

- Awareness
- Determination
- Using your time wisely
- Creativity
- Curiosity
- Honesty
- Be truthful to your self and others through compassion and understanding
- Manage your money
- Daily inner conversation
- Daily reflection of everything you did and making notes
- Plan
- Have a vision
- Get inspired

- Indulge in your imagination of your vision
- Be your own critic
- Show compassion to your self
- Cry if you need to cry but get find a solution and move on
- Reflect on your plans
- Reflect on your actions
- Reflect/evaluate your thoughts and feelings
- Be best friends with the creator
- Put yourself first
- Focus on your goal and purpose
- Demand that you are a product of justice towards yourself and ask the creator how to get what you need.
- Be an active listener to your inner voice and to the creator/universe
- Finish your inner conversation until you come to a conclusion and a decision.
- Write down your plans, ideas, steps and anything that is new to you and you think is useful to you.
- Keep true friends whom you value and who speak their minds.
- Have fun.
- Look after you body, mind and heart through your soul guidance.
- Ask for help when you think you need it.
- Never rely on others.
- Trust but be aware of not trusting and as soon as you see signs of doubt, keep it in back of your mind until you can prove it.
- Only trust your soul and creator.
- Believe that everything happens for a reason, thus you have to discover it or just keep going if it feels right.
- Accept the unknown and develop the right skills to learn how to deal with it. The unknown is a part of our journey and the beauty of life.
- Appreciate what you have and have a clear vision of what you want and how to get it in small steps.
- Raise awareness of time length between each step of the plan and leave room for flexibility.
- Be resilience.
- Be committed.
- Get inspired daily by small meaningful things.
- Search for the people who are on the same journey and be aware of your inner guidance while you're reading, listening or watching what they are saying.
- Be aware of the opportunities.
- Say sorry when you know that you are in the wrong.
- Desire.
- Will.
- Analysis of the options you have.

This is an example of the client number nine on chapter seven how he explained those three rules:

Below you will find some of his answers when I asked him to define the soul and to give me his understanding on the three rules: 1) Treat others the way you like to be treated. 2) Love yourself the way you like to be loved. 3) Do 100% in everything that you chose to do.

To define the soul, you need to talk about a plethora of different cogs that go into making it work. It has many mechanisms that are used to define somebody as a person and shapes the decisions that they make. The decision-making system in the body is governed by the soul. Its weighs up the pros and cons of any situation and then accordingly judges which outcome to choose. It takes into account a person's beliefs and values when making the final decision as we are defined by the decisions we make, yet the soul governs what decisions we make in life, suggesting that the soul defines a person for what they are. The soul confers with other key players within the body, such as the heart, which is in touch with the emotional side of the body and thinks about the needs of others and itself. The brain is also conferred with as it is the logical and selfish member which thinks about what it wants and how the easiest way to complete something is. Whilst the brain is selfish, it is also rational and the body's main survival instinct causing it to always think about the needs and wants of you and often ignores others. On the other hand, the heart is far too emotional and fragile meaning that just following the hurt could be damaging to you as a person as it could cause for hurt and an extreme feeling of betrayal that others don't treat you as you treat them. The soul in this occasion keeps both of them acting in check and the way for a person to feel the right choice comes in the form of their intuition. A person's intuition can be very difficult to understand and hear as the brain and heart are usually more appealing to listen to and in the short term favour the individual more than the soul. But if you pay attention and just take a second to think, then you will be able to make the decision that is the correct one despite it being potentially harder to do and in the short term causing some discomfort.

There are three rules in life that are very important to understand and implement in order to better yourself as a person.

• Treat others in a way that you would like to be treated. This is a staple rule of life and it should be common sense yet, in a society where it's eat or be eaten we are left fighting others so that we can succeed ourselves. This is the incorrect way of living and we should use the power we have to change that mentality to better ourselves and those around us.

• The second is to love yourself the way you love others, this has two effects, first of all, this makes selfless people take a minute and give themselves a break as they focus on pleasing others far too much and don't please themselves, and second it refers to the previous point of loving others as much as you love yourself and treating others in a way that you treat yourself.

• The final one is to put 100% in everything you do because we don't live long enough to regret not putting in that extra bit of effort in something and that could ruin the start of something very prosperous. This applies to relationships, education and tasks that you set to yourself as it makes you a better person to always try your best to succeed or else there's no point in ever trying.

Below are few answers of the participants who took part on filling the questionnaires:

Questioner 1
Love yourself the way you want to be loved:
Yes, with the addition of the rule number 1 as previously mentioned. The person must have or gain a deeper connection with themselves and develop spiritual intelligence by focusing on their core self – their soul. How this occurs depends on the person's purpose in this life. For instance, some people living in adverse conditions, receive an inner calling, which brings them guidance, love, peace and resilience, so they choose to follow it. As in all human beings there are certainly fluctuating periods of doubt, but getting up again and again and again by seeking God and the righteousness, helps one to achieve the comforts needed. A person's natural passions are also a way of finding and preserving themselves.

Q9: Answers from a 6 year old participant questioner 9:
9. Yes, but there are more rules:

-   be generous to yourself and others.
-   love yourself first, then others.
-   loyalty makes people feel happy.
-   show commitment in your strength.
-   do independent work at school.
-   be truthful to everyone.
-   have compassion as much as you please, but not a little bit.
-   follow how your mind says it.
-   make hard work in class.
-   be faithful to your husband and wife / family.
-   don't steal.
-   don't just be strong on the outside, be strong on the inside too.
-   on someone's birthday if you are their friend, you could kindly give them a present.
-   feed hungry ducks, make them strong to swim or fly.
-   have love, peace and truth.
-   when you find something difficult, think of the kingdom of God.

If you are in a family that does not follow those rules, think about God. But how to we get to think about God? Pray. Listen to God's answer. Pray strongly with all your attention and focus on it. Don't think about anything on the outside, just think about the prayer with all your mind and feel the love when God rises and shines. You will hear the reply from God the great.

Q1: The soul is the very essence or centre of our being that is in the image of God and actively connected to God. It allows us and reminds us to align our personality and actions according to its mission.

Q16: The soul is the balance of the will of the heart and will of the brain.

Q21: What is the soul?? Uaaa that's an in-depth question well I'm answering these questions in a spare of moment and writing down what comes to my mind in instinct. However when I read this question it kind of put me back a bit. Well soul should be located In the middle of everything we do... deep down in us but yet easy to reach when need it. Without a sound we are empty human beings living for nothing. Basically like an empty box.

Q22: A soul is something given by god.

Q23: The ability to feel, rationally think, equal to love. I don't know where but I feel it everywhere.

Q24: Soul is you and located deep within yourself, the role us to travel in this world and get knowledge.

Q41: (The 6 year old girl). - The soul is all of me, whole of me, the soul can teaches me to be good and gives me advise. Based on my soul I can respond.

Q42: (The eight years old girl). I believe that the soul is located, not in a specific area but all over the human body. I believe the soul is to guide us.

Q47: The soul is the part of the body which makes honest decisions, it is not located, it consists of humans as a whole. The soul is what connects us to genuine feelings and decisions.

Q47: It an individual has no self love, other source of love are not genuine experienced.
Ove within is the admiration for yourself which then allows you to love others. I believe this because this is what I experience.

The thoughts of client number 1 for the topic "Treat others the way you like to be treated"

Topic: We never put ourselves in place of another ...

Defining the other is a lighter form of understanding the things facing the other, while being in the definition of self always pushes to think only positively ...

To be the other one ?! We see it far, we are not the other but we want to see the other's flaws and concerns ... * I ... judge (in my view of past and present situations) - I appreciate (we are led by a tendency to appreciate how we like it and how rarely it should be).

- I am always right?
Perception in different people is different.
We claim that any injustice is happening to us, because we are the best (good) and not that we have made a mistake, an injustice, a mistake ...

These selfish egotistical tendencies carved on the individual make the person fancy themselves in a form delusional and do not easily distinguish truth from the distorted.

- Innocence
    - I have not done bad
    - I did not had attentions
    - I did inadvertently ...
    - So complicated I am?!!
    - For justice is often spoken, we all try to be and try to look like we are so, the essence of the justice is not easily accessible to the person, has many dimensions: we may be able to ask questions but quickly comfort ourselves, we easily excuse ourselves, we are filled with will rebellious love to say to ourselves you are the best, fate affect us...

We have to ask ourselves often,... every time we ask we get different answers.

    - The purpose
    - Wish
    - I want to stay
    - I decided to do it
    - Can I

Can I always be successful?

Success and living a life with principles seem similar but they are different. Living with success means you struggle to do everything to achieve success, do not feel if your right has passed to another, or the other is felt bad... Going with principles and values is harder because it needs a strict rule with itself, this does not stop you of being successful, only dealing with people has been another form of awareness then when you are strict with your self as you treat others through pure justice.

*Heart

-You deserve it
-You can
-You are the best
-Careful...
Am I perfect?

The heart comfort a person, it makes it "look and feel good" for their actions, she speaks softly, without force, without reproach, only feels ... She can not be a counselor because she only stimulates in silence .. but the heart exists to act according to her, we get confused with her and feel at peace ... but that does not mean that we are doing better, we have not put ourselves in a position to "listen to ourselves" do not show off.

*Questions of thoughts

-I acted with out thinking but I did not have that idea
-My goodness is bigger, but I did not showed enough ...
-Driven by different thoughts person promotes himself with thoughts, ideas, reflects often without analysis, based on the situation but not every reflection is useful If we look back upon the way of interpreting the actions of others, in a form of judgment ... the thoughts come, flow ... not every thought can be prepared and clearly depending on the situation.

"If you truly loved yourself, you could never hurt another." BUDDHA

"Peace comes from within. Do not seek it without.' Buddha

"No one saves us but ourselves. No one can and no one may. We ourselves must walk the path." Buddha

"You, yourself, as much as anybody in the entire universe, deserve your love and affection." Buddha

CHAPTER IV

DATA COLLECTED/RESULTS

Contains presentation of the primary data collected through questioners/case studies/observations and social media interaction. Presentations of primary data findings have been facilitated through explanation and brief discussions.

Results of the case studies:

- Did Magical module have influence in all participants?
- ➢ Answer: Yes and all the cases studies, questionnaires and observations reflect that.

- Did everyone manage to hear their soul through the facilitator's words?
- ➢ Answer: Yes, because I never approached anyone. What I was saying resonated with them (their feedback reflect this). This answer only applies on the case studies and the reviews on my book, and with anyone who I had direct contact with.

- Did they get the aim they came in contact in the first time they met me?
- ➢ Answer: Yes, on all case studies, apart from a few of them, whose actual aim was not the aim they really needed to achieve.

- How many got more results than what they aimed for?
- ➢ Answer: All of those in the case studies.

- How many would continue applying the tools they learned?
- ➢ Answer: Based on the case studies feedback and the book review feedback and on my intuition, definitely yes, they will apply it – however the extent of this is unknown because a few of them will use it to

improve their self-love and the life they want, a few will just use it when they find they need it or when they are desperate

- How many have been managed to learn or increase their ability to be guided by their soul and intuition...the energy of universe at least once a day or when they need it?
- ➤ Answer: (24 = yes (3 of them are children, which cannot be included in the number because this depends of their parents on how they are feeding them and their growth), 3=no, because the clients were too attached to reality and cannot find balance connecting with the universe, case 24 is so much into day dreaming and illusion, and does not have a balance with reality.

- How many have achieved to be guided 24 hours by the energy of universe and the soul?
- ➤ Answer: Client 1

- How many are working to achieve to be guided 24 hours by the soul and universe exclude children under 18?
- ➤ Answer: All of them.

- How many clients from the cases studies can get access to the source any time they need?
- ➤ Answer: all of them but depends if they have patience to continue the inner conversation until the end... until they come to conclusion to make decision of what they were searching.

- How many got full understanding of how the whole us work in this life excluding children?
- ➤ Answer: All have got the understanding but those who apply it are: 1, 2, 7, 8, 9, 10, 11, 12, 13, 17, 18, 22, 24, 25, 28.

1) Characteristics of issues that were fully achieved. What happened that those results were achieved?

- ➤ The essence is purity, spoken directly and openly, and firm, able to live 24 hours guided by the soul and connected to universe, know how to provide therapy and healing to their heart. The person who teaches the magical module have achieved self-love.
- ➤ Knowing how to ask questions to the intuition.
- ➤ Create question based on any difficulties that might arise and follow those answers. Examples could be about the confidentiality, the law about doubts, and anything.
- ➤ The ability of the client to listen to their inner self, which makes them trust the facilitator to open up and be honest.
- ➤ Have the ability to notice what resonates within their soul, their mind, heart and body.

➤ To provide feedback on the process. A very straightforward and open conversation, and being clear about what they can and cannot do, what they want and do not want to do.

2) Characteristics of issues that were partially achieved. What happened that these partial results were achieved?

➤ The reasons are that the clients did not achieve the self-love. The clients were very addicted to universal love (partner, parents, friends, society, children).

➤ The clients did not believe in themselves, that happiness exists and dreams come true and by being pure you can be happy even if you have nothing. They thought that they were nothing without the material world. They think that they cannot survive without the universal love.

➤ The clients were not so committed to self-help, because they wanted someone there to do 80% of work so that they could do the rest.

➤ I always chose to always give 20% and the clients have to do 80%. Moreover, in most of the case studies I have done only 5% of work and they did the rest.

3) Characteristics of issues that were achieved or not attainable.

➤ The absurdity the whole Magical Approach including the Magical Model and the person who applies it.

➤ Clients completely committed to reality and refusing to connect with the universe and their soul.

➤ Lack of previous experience with this approach, such as religions, healers etc.

Results for observations:

• Did I manage to get people reflecting in a deep level?

➤ Answer: Yes for those who were connected to their soul and can be noticed by the observations, discussions and dialogues. No for those who are attached to reality and disconnected to their soul and you can see the difference in their responses.

Results for "A Magical Life" book reviews.

These are the concepts below:

• Have I made them connect with their whole of them in deep level?

➤ Answer: yes

• Did they revisit their childhood?

➤ Answer: yesey take some tools to use in continuing personal development?

- Did they revisit and think about present they are in? And future?
➢ Answer: yes

- Did they take some tools to use in continuing personal development?
➢ Answer: yes

Results of all questions are below:

- Q1 - Are there three main rules according to the Lord?:
  - Treat others, as you would like to be treated.
  - Love yourself, as you would like to be loved.
  - Give 100% in everything that you choose.

  ➢ 34 Participants answered "yes" and the participant were number 1, 3, 7, 8, 9, 10, 11, 13, 14, 15, 17, 19, 21, 22, 23, 24, 27, 30, 31, 32, 33, 34, 35, 36, 38, 39, 40, 41, 43, 45, 46, 57, 48 and 50.
  ➢ 5 Participant answered "no" and the participants were number 4, 5, 12, 18 and 29.
  ➢ 3 Participant answered "not sure" and the participants were number 16, 25 and 49.
  ➢ 6 Participant answered "not by the god" and the participants were number 2, 6, 20, 26, 28 and 44.
  ➢ 2 Participants answered "agree with first two but not with the third one" and the participants were number 37 and 42.

- Q2 - Are those 3 rules, all that is required of humans to accomplish in this life? How do you explain the way that these can be applied by a person, born in a family amongst members, who do not comply with those rules?

  ➢ 39 Participants answered "yes there are important rules be accomplished".
  ➢ 11 Participant answered "no there are not ".
  ➢ 4 Participant answered "yes I would keep distance if is necessary".
  ➢ 46 Participant answered "no I would not keep distance".

- Q3 - For someone to follow the path that makes them happy, do they firstly have to let go of those, who are not happy with themselves, or are becoming obstacles for your journey and will not allow you to achieve your dream's, can be it even their own family? What is the reason of this?

  ➢ 33 Participants answered "yes should keep distance if they hold you back from your happiness".

➤ 17 Participant answered, "no you should not keep distance but should find way how to help them understand".

• Q4 - What is the soul? Where is it located anatomically in humans and what is the role of the soul in this life? Why...

➤ 5 Participant said that is heart feelings (Participant are 4, 8, 32, 40, 44,).
➤ 3 Participants thought is in brain (the participant are 13, 17, and 46).
➤ 3 Participant answered, "not sure" (the participant are 25, 39, and 48).
➤ 3 Participant answered, "don't exist" (the participant are 20, 28, and 33).
➤ 5 Participant answered, "it is subject" (the participant are 11, 18, 19, 29 and 34).
➤ 31 Participant answered the right explanation about the soul but in deferent ways (the participant are 1, 2, 3, 5, 6, 7, 9, 10, 12, 14, 15, 16, 21, 22, 23 ,24 ,26 ,27 ,30 ,31 ,35 , 36, 37, 38, 41, 42, 43, 45, 47, 49 and 50).

• Q5 - Can a person live and be guided by their soul? How can this be achieved?

➤ 13 Participant answered, "no" (the participant are 13, 12, 20, 22, 24, 26, 28, 29, 37, 43, 44, 45 and 46).
➤ 37 Participant answered, " Yes can be guided by the soul" (the participant are 1, 2, 3, 4, 5, 6, 7, 8, 9, 10, 11, 14. 15, 16, 17, 18, 19, 21, 23, 25, 27, 30, 31, 32, 33, 34, 35, 36, 38, 39, 40, 41, 42, 47, 48, 49 and 50).

• Q6 - Does a bad soul exist? The reason why...

➤ 33 Participant answered, "not bad soul does not exist" (the participant are 20, 28, and 33).
➤ 15 Participant answered, "yes the bad soul exist" (the participant are 4, 5, 6, 10, 13, 14, 17, 18, 35, 36, 37, 45, 46, 49 and 50).
➤ 2 Participant answered "not sure" (the participant are 23 and 25).

• Q7 - Are the mind, heart and body human utensils, which serve the soul so that the person is faithful or fulfilled? Why...

➤ 38 Participant answered, "yes" (the participant are 1, 2, 3, 4, 5, 6, 7, 8, 9, 10, 12, 13, 14, 16, 18, 19, 20, 21, 22, 24, 26, 27, 30, 32, 33, 34, 36, 37, 40, 41, 42, 43, 44, 46, 47, 48, 49 and 50).
➤ 2 Participant answered "don't understand" and the participant are 39 and 45.
➤ 2 Participant answered "not sure" and they are 23 and 25.
➤ 8 Participant answered "no" and they are 11, 15, 17, 28, 29, 31, 35 and 38.

- Q8 - What does it mean to believe in God and how can this be demonstrated by 3 rules or examples?

  - ➤ 3 Participant said "don't believe on god" (they are number 2, 26 and 46).
  - ➤ 47 Participant said they believed in god and they are the rest of numbers 1 to 50 apart from 2, 26 and 46.

- Q9 - Do you suppose that children are like angels and innocent and why? So how is their suffering explained in God's language and why?

  - ➤ ... 40 Participants said, "yes children are innocent".
  - ➤ ... 4 Participant said "not sure".
  - ➤ ... 2 Participant said, "No they are not innocent".
  - ➤ ... 4 Participant said, "I don't know".

- Q10 - Are there two kinds of death: A prewritten one and another that depends on our Actions? If so, how is the child's death explained?

  - ➤ 1 Participant said "there are three types of death" (number 17).
  - ➤ 1 Participant said "not sure" (number 49).
  - ➤ 9 Participant said "only one the prewritten is" (the numbers are 6, 13, 16, 24, 25, 27, 29, 39 and 47).
  - ➤ 2 Participant said "only one of the actions not the prewritten one" (the numbers are 28 and 46).
  - ➤ 8 Participant said "don't know" (the numbers of participants are 4, 20, 23, 26, 38, 40, 41 and 48).
  - ➤ 29 Participants said "yes there are two types of death"

- Q11 - Can a human being be filled with love, which comes exclusively from the source within themselves? And from the moment they become aware of that love they do not feel suffering because they are know their purpose and are fulfilled?

What do you think is the love within? And why do you think that way?

  - ➤ 2 Participant said "don't know" and the numbers of participants are 2 and 20.
  - ➤ 9 Participant said "no" (the numbers of participants are 10,16,22,26,27,28,29,46 and 44).
  - ➤ 39 Participant answered "yes"

CHAPTER V

DISCUSSION AND ANALYSES

Constitute discussions and analyses. This chapter plays a critical role in the achievement of research aim and objectives. Findings of the literature review have been compared to primary data findings in this chapter, and in-depth discussions have been provided in relation to each individual research objective. Discussion

Aims and research questions

I carried out this research in order to test if self-love is the key to a fulfilled life with peace and love and how that could be achieved? In my life, I base my life of self love as explained in my book "A Magical Life" and as I noticed most people are unhappy and somehow lost into understanding the journey to a happy, fulfilled, joyful life with peace and love, which most of them turn into crimes, suicide, not following their dreams, being victims or becoming the abuser. The new generation is following in the same old steps. This research is to bring about a solution: How to heal yourself from the past, be fully in the present and enjoy it (80% fully in the present) or find ways to enjoy it, as well as expand the remaining 20% where the imagination has no limits or limitation, where you are able to create a bridge between where you are and your dreams, by knowing how to claim each step. It is all about the 80% in the moment (to focus on the here and now, because here and now can help you heal from the past, stay in the present and help you to achieve the future you want).

This research will explore and demonstrate through the magical model, how you can achieve to enjoy fully life. Magical model is a holistic approach, which includes, counselling, therapy, mentoring, advice and advocacy on healing, and coaching. This research will mostly focus on the foundation of its question: self-love, which with the right tools and techniques is the key to open the doors to all questions. How can we achieve self-love? What does self-love mean? Why do we need self-love? Why are we humans never happy unless we have self-love? Why our body needs love? Why do we crave for love…why do we need others to love us? What is it about that? What are the various perspectives such as religions? Is this life a test, which requires us to cleanse ourselves? What is a soul? Does it exist? Is it only one religion? If yes, why are there so many? If no, what is their purpose? Does it matter how many religions are? What does science say about the vital aspect of love? How do various religions explain the serious life?

Are we meant to suffer or enjoy the life? And why is that? How important is self-love to get the answer to all those questions I mentioned? Can self-love bring peace and love and how that can happen?

Spirituality is defined as "the quality of being concerned with the human spirit or soul as opposed to material or physical things" (oxforddictionaries.com) It tends to grow towards an essential, immaterial reality. It can refer mostly to an inner path, which enables individuals to discover the core of their being – their deepest truths and values by which to live. According to Kipp (2014) "Spirituality is the measure of how willing we are to allow grace—some power greater than ourselves - to enter our lives and guide us along our way". Grace is the spontaneous, benevolent power of the divine love that enters this world through and as you or me. Once people are committed and take consistent steps to being loving and kind towards self and others, what they believe in, is considered less crucial, because it is who and how they are that matters in spirituality. It is what human beings do right here, right now. The spiritual experience is often reported as a source, which provides inspiration or guidance in life. It usually encompasses beliefs in immaterial realities or encounters with immanent or transcendent realms (Kipp, 2014).

God consciousness (The stability of the connection with the deepest self enables the individual to perceive the external world as more pleasant and nearer to the level of 'pure self'. The heart opens up and can overcome anything. Any life experience or encounter in the material world, feels meaningful and delightful). The person opens up the characteristic of devotion, which can manifest itself in various ways, depending on individual uniqueness. In some, their profound devotion takes a religious significance, in others it may take a more generalized sense of purpose.

Unity consciousness (This stage represents the full awakening. It reveals that the internal and the external, the Self and the non-Self, the absolute and the relative, the eternal and the temporary are in fact an all-encompassing One (Mahesh, 2015).

Personality is the same for those who are guided by the soul. Only their journey will be different. For those who will be guided by their mind and heart their personality will be different because will be mixed up with thoughts and feelings as explained in momentum stage from the reality and others.

Depression is some kind of meditation in my opinion and it is healthy if you take time to understand it and deal with it in right way as I explained in each stage of magical module. Everything that makes you go deeper into your own conscience makes you more reflective but how you deal with it is different topic.

Depression in my opinion is in three categories:

- *Mild Depression* is something all people who are not guided by their soul experience and deal with due to a lack of a connection with their soul.
- *Depression* from the heart is a deep depression and is not healthy if not dealt with. This type of depression usually happens to those people who are guided the most from their feelings, from their heart. But if is dealt as explained through stages of magical model is the bridge to the soul, to your true self.

- *Depression from the soul* is for those who are guided by the soul. This category enjoys this kind of depression because is all about serving their mission to study in depth things with pleasure. Once you reach this stage you are not attached to the outside world but you master it and enjoy it also you become a great teacher to others around you.

But it does happen when the depression from heart and mind are blended or three of them together. When that happens they create three different personalities or even more as the mind and heart have ability to create and act in different personalities.

Example below working with three depressions blended together with client:

How does magical module helps with domestic violence situation? !! ??

A domestic violence case study:

One of the methods used with a client who is in love with an abusive and controlling man. She is aware of her situation but she is afraid as he threatens to do something to her family and to take her child away from her… she cannot do anything without his permission and has to be how he wanted. She is with him because she is in love with him and she is scared to create a life on her own… so in this case… some of the questions used are:

- Would you like to live as a slave for someone or to fight for the life you want?

- What does it prevent you from doing it now than later as you say I will leave him when I'm fine?

- What is your family's business to do with your life decisions, if they love you, they will want you to be happy? They will tell him when he threatens them that that's is her life and we cannot interfere… and you don't have to worry about them.

My conclusion with my advice for this case study

- Live for yourself … or do not blame someone else because I'm sure there are options to protect you… when you are pure, determined and resilient in searching what you want, the god and universe is with you and will help you…

- If you are not happy now do not wait to be tomorrow when you achieve your goals because you never will know how to be happy… because the goals do not bring happiness but food for the happiness that you already are experiencing… happiness comes from your inner world….

- If you want something start now, today and not tomorrow because tomorrow will be another day and so on will never happen. ...

- If you are female under the control of the male and you don't like it.... Get up and tell yourself what you want… and will you achieve happiness as someone else's slave?

- The man is abusive because he has grown up in such families and will continue the cycle until he gets help.

I don't know whom to feel sorry for, the victim, because I can see things in them that they cannot see in themselves or abusers for the pain they feel that they have repressed it and they need help. ....

Comments to this comment from another client: First I shivered because I remembered myself in some way and understood the pain of the client without direction. I liked the phases saying ". goals do not bring happiness but are food for the soul" Much worth it is as a theory but needs lots of work…

Response of the client who was in that abuse relationship to my comment:

I will try one more time if it works our relationship because now I am not scared of him at all, and I am trying not because he is forcing me too and don't have solution but because I want to try one more time for myself. I will try for myself because I don't want my child to grow up without both parents as I did. But I promise I will never let him hit me again.

"If I had an hour to solve a problem, and my life depended on the solution, I'd spend 55 minutes on determining the right question and 5 minutes to generate the answer."
A. Einstein

Questions are powerful tools if used correctly to search for solutions or through discussions with your soul, universe and you as whole. They can generate answers and insight to help your life in a maximal way. It's a great skill to learn, it may be slow and sludgy at first. But asking to the taps in a beautiful old country house, keep trying and the water will come out clean and running in no time. Spend time simply asking the best question (for whatever your key problem is) and watch how amazing the answers that come are also question the answer if you feel you don't agree with the answer you got.

The process is the meaning of the space (that is the whole us and universe) - the acceptance of the space, the space dance - the experiment of the reality journey- the return to the mind - the compassion of the heart - the return to the space - retrieval - discussion - elaboration - reflection - analysis - compassion - sadness - allowing yourself to feel down - doubt - seeking to understand faith - initiating trust in the space that gives love - feeding with pure love - rebelling against reality to stay in that space - resilience, how to bring space into reality - how to spread that love - then you learn that the mind is poisoned.

You learn that the heart is hurting, it needs healing -so you create a therapeutic environment – you make time to heal your heart, to listen to your mind, but…no no no, you do not allow your mind to interfere in everyday life, because your mind is like a laptop and you have been feeding with information that has not made you feel happy so far, even though you have reprogrammed your mind with positive thought, still one negative thought that you hear from somebody that has nothing to do with or even some bad news, or even something that does not resonate with you, something that you don't like, if you feed that through your mind, automatically it will produce feelings, even though you are not giving space to those thoughts, automatically they have crossed your mind and will produce feelings. So what happened now – the thoughts has just passed through your mind quickly if you have achieved to be a positive person, but if you have not achieved to be a positive person, I will give explanation that is different for those to scenarios below.

The thought passing through the positive mind produced a feeling directly to your heart, which if you do not know how to process that feeling, that feeling will be repressed in your heart. You will not feel pain. You are not aware how those feelings affect you. Because that feeling has underlying damages, which will produce automatically bad energy in your body. This leads to physical illness, but if you want to process that feeling, you need to do it through the healing process. So coming to the conclusion there is no point for you to use your mind. As you have already noticed you are not really getting positive things through the mind. Because all the negative things that you receive from others, if you process through your space or Magical Person, it automatically will turn into love, which means that the heart is not affected at all, and if the heart is not affected, your body is not affected. Your Magical Person / soul/ intuition / universe energy / anything they receive, they turn it into love. That is why I advice never to use your mind, because I have not yet achieved to trust my mind. I have tested my mind, but I am not confident that my mind is in the same level of the inner space, so for now my mind is still in therapy. I do not know what will happen in the future.

The thoughts pass the mind that is still in the process of understanding things. In this category there are so many examples that I cannot even count, the different ways that people use the thoughts. But I will just mention a few. There are those whose thoughts make continuous noise in their heads. There are those that overthink, by keeping one thought and going over and over it in circles. They wake up every morning with the same thought, pretending that they are not paying attention to it, but in reality they are living with it. There are those, which get busy so that they do not listen to their thoughts, and imagine that there will be no space for those thoughts in the brain, because the thoughts start fighting with each other, which thought to take the space. There are those who just live in the thoughts they feed their brain without analysing them. They give excuses to their thoughts. In this minds there will certainly be a mess, which will lead into depression, anxiety, worries, unhappiness, unsatisfaction, physical sickness. And could take different kind of turns and I am sure you do not need more explanation what happens in this mind, because all the psychological theories explain very well what happens. I am mostly focused on the holistic approach, only for those people who really want to get to know their own magical person. That is what I do.

Please keep in mind that the unexplored topic of this book, some things are still not explained in the deep level, because they need more study more practice, such as how to help somebody who wants to become a healer or use the space to help others, or even how they can interpret the messages they get through channeling. As for example they say: "I have God, I have everything" but this means that God has given you everything that you need in this world, including the knowledge of how to communicate with Him and how to ask for help, if you can do, this things that do not cost anything and are free. If you ask for his guidance if you ask for his help he will be there. You can only expect him to be there if you are specific about what you need and what and want and why. Also, it is another level learning the skills how to listen. But you just need silence and time. I explained this example, it is similar in my theory: there are a lot of layers that need to be explored in depth and if you want to learn more about the key things to help you achieve that, which is self-love and communication skills, read the book 'A Magical Life'. For further study, I would suggest (not that I think is needed, but just for people who want facts and proofs to study further the brain and the human existence in detail when the human is guided by the space (the soul, the intuition and the universal energy) to see how the mind the heart and the body function when they are under the influence of that energy. As in my case, me and the main client have achieved to be guide, 24 hours by the space, which means, we kind of do not allow the brain to influence on bringing any thoughts or making any decisions etc.

The brain helps you to function inside the human body, is there as a tool to pass the message and to help you with other senses such as the focus, concentration etc. Because you have achieved this, we still need to look after the old thoughts, because the brain is like a computer, so we need to work as kind of therapy in that computer to reprogrammed the brain with the information from the space. And the heart as well, we do the therapy, if any feelings have not been healed, if the thoughts from mind have been interfering with out our awareness. What I am trying to say we still need to treat the mind and the heart with the healing touch, as very precious parts of ourselves. I do not have much knowledge in science but I am aware of left and right hemispheres of the brain and the how the body parts function in relation to them, but I do believe that the energy and if we are guided from the inner space we can look after our whole human existence. Know our needs, know how to take care and fulfill our needs, know how to feel loved, to give love, to know what we want in this life, of if do not know what we want at the moment then we know how to discover it. All the times there are small steps in front of us, which I am adding. Only if you do the small steps you can get into the big ones, and reach the top of the ladder, the end of the bridge, cross the bridge, claim the mountains, swim and explore the sea, just stay by the lake and talk to the silence, if you want to dance with the sky, and mostly you will know the purpose of being here and you will enjoy every minute of this journey. Spirituality has been shown to improve a person's physical, psychological and spiritual state. Exploring the history of the healing professions, it is evident that when combined with the spiritual dimension it is synergetic on supporting health and well-being. Midwifery and nursing are examples of services provided by religious communities (Koenig et al, 2001). In the secular environment of our society, the remnant of what is referred to as spiritual heritage, are now found in the charity hospices, care homes, organizations or religious institutions offering holistic support and services (DoH, 2011). There are a number of studies, in the UK literature, about social work and spirituality, but their focus is mainly on mental-health (Coyte et al, 2007).

With the spiritual enlightenment comes the detachment from the cycle of life and death. Many Buddhists believe that a human being has numerous rebirths, which include unavoidable suffering. The goal is seeking to end these rebirths, which result from the individual's delusion in cravings and aversion. The Buddhist practice to achieve this, requires, the release of all the sensual urges and earthly desires as well as the purification of one's heart (Frater, 2007). The main aims and objectives were how to be fulfilled, in peace and in love exactly where the individual is and what they have. Which brought the questions to be part of this research who we are? Does the creator exist and how is the circle of life? How can the individual reach to be healed from the past and enjoy the present and have clear plan for future vision, through the questioners, case study and social media observations on chapter seven and chapter eight explained in details I got the results that I got on chapter four and I will discuss them through this chapter. Everything is around self-love and self love is created around this three guidance below based on my opinion, in literature review and findings of this research:

- Treat others, as you would like to be treated.
- Love yourself, as you would like to be loved.
- Give 100% in everything that you choose.

Discussion sessions about the questionnaires:

Question one was all about to help the participant think on a deeper level of basics and simplify of their life journey and reflecting on the god and religions as they are huge parts that influence individual life. I have selected a few answers that agreed with the statements of these questions and all answers says it all , specially participant 9, 19, 40, 41 and 46. The answer of participant 18 describes how the mind thinks about those rules but most of the participants that took place on the survey have answered directly without thinking. 39 participants out of 50 have agreed that those rules are important to feel accomplished which makes me think that most of us know what is right and wrong but when it comes to practice it is a different story. From my self- discovery and through the journey of working with others I have come to conclusion that we know have ability to know right from wrong but when it comes to practice there are any factors that gets on our way. The use of spiritual tools in UK's public services such as healthcare and education, has frequently encountered some resistance, because their applicability has been regarded as more effective for religious groups. However, according to Nardella (2014) "spirituality does not necessarily refer to religion, although it can". For instance, it has been proved that meditation or the embrace of the inner silence and/or stillness that comes with it, can increase a person's awareness of mindful self-love. Here, the concept of loving oneself does not mean selfishness or narcissism, but represents the compassion, which forms the basis of an essential relationship of human beings – that with themselves (Kotsos, 2017).

Q1 this participant pretend that he does have and practice pure love but really all he does he practice it on others but not on himself and that's why he is confused and disappointed from this life which stops him from achieving his dreams and understanding the rules of universe on question one as you can see from his answers below: (see case study 24 on chapter seven and participant 3 on the questioners chapter eight).

"So it depends Sis How people treat me I treat them in their own way. As I cannot change them as they are not at all ready to change or I simply avoid unnecessary arguments."

"LOVE – Love oneself that is the better option left as I tell you Sis in present scenario.

The value of True Love is lost, The artificial love prevails in this world in the masses now as far as if I am helpful or good to one I am v adorable to him/her and once the task is over, project is over who cares for whom, nobody. As nobody has time and no one understands it rather playing games with each other is the motto left, Ego Hatred Jealousy prevails in practical scenario of life. OMG!!! He is earning less than me and look at him He is still smiling and having such an awesome life. What He has inside s him that makes him so happy and joyful. this is the feeling left as I see around. Sis, In real life I talk with v less people with whom I am most comfortable with, not with everyone I open my pages. Rather you can say It's simply the act of formality I do as they do with everyone. So its better to find happiness around is the happiness that lies inside me and Yes I have no friends nobody here Yes all my dear ones are far away and I most of the time live alone and live my life, trying to do best for myself to make me feel happy. So loving oneself is the key and True love lies in Nature paradise, going outside in the park and having a walk feel closely with the nature by being surrounded by flowers petals trees and autumn leaves falling down. I love all that.

So as a person I myself has set of things I love doing what I do and if I don't like it all

I won't do it at all no one can force me to do that thing which I don't like doing. I am simply like that."

"Giving 100% - Yes I give 100% in whatever I do and for me if the task is new and I am liking it I will Google it everything and will do everything with passion and 100% determination."

Participant 6 said "I think that there are no rules set by the lord, or in written and in fact. But I believe that it is the rules that emanate from the inside that the individual decisions to follow in order to feel complete."

Participant 14 said, "In my opinion, these are the three main rules, as it is normal to love and love the same. Treat others the way you like to be treated. And the determination to make 100% everything is also the key"

Participant 18 said "In the first question, I disagree with the rules, since often the will being influenced by the ego, the lusts and the delights can lead to the wrong way. God, besides giving us freedom, at the same time, he has created us as conscious beings to reason and behave so as not to harm others."

Participant 19 said "Yes there are three main rules according to the lord and if you do the three of them you are a complete being… both spiritually and physically."

Participant 20 said ". God does not exist. It is a game of a person's imagination, which he invented due to the fear of the unknown!"

Participant 21 said ".Yes I believe the three rules should apply to everything we do in life it's like a cure to or sole of we follow those rules. Of everyone stamps back and thinks of those three rules the world will be a better place to live."

Participant 22 said ". Yes I do believe that god expects everyone to respect and treat each other the same. Yes god has created everyone so people should appreciate themselves in life and their values. No you cannot always be successful "

Participant 30 said ". Being fair and by treating others as we would live to be treated we attract positive things in our lives. Good things also happen to us when we won't we love ourselves and we are committed to our goals."

Participant 40 a six years old girl also a case study 12 is ". These rules are enough because for example loving yourself means that you care about you and that is very good."

Participant 41 a six years old girl also a case study 12 is ".-Yes, they are the main rules because my mum, dad and aunty taught me those rules and they are enough. Rule number one helps me because you can treat others kindly. Loving yourself helps me by loving myself and liking my expressions and if is there not good I will find away how to improve them.". Just love her answer, is amazing how a six-year-old girl can answer and practice in same time those rules.

Participant 46 an 18 year old male also a case study seven on chapter seven. "These may be 3 rules according to smart people"

Question two and three ways to help them think about their freedom and create their own rules as in same time they think about the big part of their life and the people surround them.

Participant one and case study two answered the question two by saying, "Yes, with the addition of the rule number 1 as previously mentioned. The person must have or gain a deeper connection with themselves and develop spiritual intelligence by focusing on their core self – their soul. How this occurs depends on the person's purpose in this life. For instance, some people living in adverse conditions receive an inner calling, which brings them guidance, love, peace and resilience, so they choose to follow it. As in all human beings there are certainly fluctuating periods of doubt, but getting up again and again and again by seeking God and the righteousness, helps one to achieve the comforts needed. A person's natural passions are also a way of finding and preserving themselves." *This answer it shows a great understanding of the theory of those rules but confusion on practice.*

Participant 9 answered question two "Yes, but there are more rules:
- Be generous to yourself and others.
- Love yourself first, then others.
- Loyalty makes people feel happy.
- Show commitment in your strength.
- Do independent work at school.
- Be truthful to everyone.
- Have compassion as much as you please, but not a little bit.
- Follow how your mind says it.
- Make hard work in class.
- Be faithful to your husband and wife / family.
- Don't steal.
- Don't just be strong on the outside; be strong on the inside too.

- On someone's birthday if you are their friend, you could kindly give them a present.
- Feed hungry ducks, make them strong to swim or fly.
- Have love, peace and truth.
- When you find something difficult, think of the kingdom of God.

If you are in a family that does not follow those rules, think about God. But how to we get to think about God? Pray. Listen to God's answer. Pray strongly with all your attention and focus on it. Don't think about anything on the outside, just think about the prayer with all your mind and feel the love when God rises and shines. You will hear the reply from God the great." *This answer from a participant six year old shows to me that how special are children and how important is to get guidance from them and let them explore things through safe guidance from the adult.*

Participant 14 answered question two" To some extent, I think they are principled for everyone and can be somewhat complementary. But for people born in families who do not apply these rules is very difficult. Somewhat implausible, that is, it depends on the strength of the person." *This answer shows clearly that how addicted we are to universal love because we don't have the self-love and that's why only four participant out of 50 said that they will keep distance from people who refuse to learn to follow those rules.*

Participant 41 and a case study 12 answered question two "Yes these are enough and I will try to make others believe in this too or I will be bad person also if they don't learn". *This answer tells us a lot because she is just six year old and love her parents so much and maybe that's why she did not thought of living them behind or could be that she was right… she may not even have a chance to think to keep distance from them but was aware that if her parents will not follow those three rules she may not follow them also. (Her parents are great but she answered the questions pretending that her parents or people around don't follow those rules).*

Participant 42 a 10-year-old girl and the case study 11 answered question two "I think that there are many more rules that are required of the human to accomplish in this life, such as, be yourself and never hide yourself or try to be nice to others. Some people do not love themselves as they would live to be covered as they may have insecurities." *Her answer tells a very important message as she may have observed in school or from her friends. When she felt the questioner she was so focused and really paying attention.*

Participants 1 answered question three "Yes, this would certainly make things easier. Personally, I believe that this is required, for the person to focus and expand on their true identity, and be fully established on their true purpose. However, this action depends on the person's purpose in life. There are cases where the person remained in the family, (because they somehow had already found their inner strength and aim) in order to give a lesson to them and the surrounding community. There are other cases where the person needs distance in order to strengthen and grow spiritually and the time depends on them. Some people keep occasional contact, some cut the family out completely; it depends on the relationship they had, and its functionality". *I though I share it as it gives a strong message on how difficult and complex is universal love.*

Participant 8 answered question three " Often people do not follow the path that makes them happy and that does not make you happy, but I believe that everyone's happiness is of the greatest importance, so I believe that it is worth let go of those that hold you back if it depends my happiness". *Great answer as it shows how important is self love that brings happens as it said, "the individual happiness is greatest importance."*

Participant 14 answered question three, "No, I do not think so, we have to accept others as they are. With their weaknesses and strengths. Just as we do not want to change us and others do not have to change". *My thoughts to this answer are that we have to answer to our selves those questions below before you make decision to accept someone.*

Who is benefiting from accepting the other if they do some thing wrong? Is it in their best interest? Is it in your best interest? Or is it for sake of universal love? Because I think both the participant and other in that answer does not have self love as it is in no one best interest to accept something that may harm the individual and others. But somehow we d'n't think is that way, we think on pleasing others because we need their attention and that leads to never finding peace and love.

Participant 21 answered question three "Yes I do believe to follow your own path you should cut out negative people however if you are strong minded and you believe in your self fully you still can manage to help a family member to find their peace and path while you can still keep track of yours." *This answer is great guidance how we should deal on the situations that people around are holding us back from moving forward or having peace also participant 30 said similar guidance* "I believe that you have to protect yourself from negative energy even if it comes from your family or your most beloved ones and keep a distance from there because they ruin your inner balance and happiness."

33 Participants said "yes" to question three and 17 said "no" and in question two only four said yes to keep distance and 46 said "not to keep distance." And different from those two questions that give different results are between three rules and happiness. That makes me think that people pay more attention to the word "happiness" then to find out where it come from as it is easy to think of happiness rather than working for it. Also it reinforces the thought that in theory we know what is right and wrong but putted into practice is different topic.

Question four, five, six and seven were to help think beyond in everyday life, in deep, very deep level of their existence and their creation as how the whole life circle works by asking them around their understanding and the role of soul. So I could come to understanding of how much they know about their soul and how they use it. I did this by analysing their answers, this lead me to the conclusion that all of them had great knowledge of their soul, but were unable to unlock its full potential how to be guided by their soul. 31 Participant answered the right explanation about the soul and few examples of the answers are below:

Participant 1 answer: ". The soul is the very essence or centre of our being that is in the image of God and actively connected to God. It allows us and reminds us to align our personality and actions according to its mission. "

Participant 2 answer is: "For me is the deepest part of our being. A role of awareness, a pure feeling, an inner clock."

Participant 3 answer is: "The Soul is immortal the body after death decays but the soul comes out and it takes it. Another form of life, it never dies. The Soul is the immaterial part of human being or the animal. Its located below the stomach and the upper abdomen region near Naval region.

Its role is important and it has its vital meaning as It's voice is v soft and v light and it whispers in my ears what's right and what's wrong. It indeed controls my nervous system, the brain and the heart. Together it just enlightens me up and zeal up the confidence in the enlightenment and me becomes too strong when some positive vibes strikes it and I learn something new in my life. "

Participant 5 answer is: "The spirit is our world. is located everywhere and has the role to guide you."

Participant 9, 6-year-old girl answered: "It is easy how to tell the soul. The soul is the house of you. It is found in your heart. That's where I feel it. The role of the soul is to keep you in your body, so you can live. That's it. But that's not all. Even we have to eat food to stay healthy, and be strong and stay alive, but not just food. Do exercise for your bones to get stronger and stronger. The role of the soul is like that because, to be you, to be yourself and follow all the rules you have written and trying to follow them, being focused on them, not the other people's business, leave them alone, like a rock. I do not mean rock and roll! I mean to leave them like a muddy looking soil-y rock. That's it."

Participant 10 answer is: "The soul is the universe inside us."

Participant 16 answer is: "the soul is the balance of the will of the heart and will of the brain."

Participant 21 answer is: "What is the soul?? Uaaa that's an in-depth question well I'm answering these questions in a spare of moment and writing down what comes to my mind in instinct. However when I read this question it kind of put me back a bit.

Well soul should be located In the middle of everything we do… deep down in us but yet easy to reach when need it. Without a sound we are empty human beings living for nothing. Basically like an empty box."

Participant 22 answer is: "A soul is something given by god."

Participant 24 answer is: "Soul is you and located deep within yourself, the role us to travel in this world and get knowledge."

Participant 41, 6 year old girl answer is: "The soul is all of me, whole of me , the soul can teaches me to be good and gives me advise. Based on my soul I can respond."

Participant 42, 10-year-old girl answer is: "I believe that the soul is located, not in a specific area but all over the human body. I believe the soul is to guide us."

Participant 47 answer is: "the soul is the part of the body which makes honest decisions, it is not located, it consists of humans as a whole. The soul is what connects us to genuine telling's and decisions."

Can we be guided by the soul? 37 participants answered; " yes" and 33 participants answered that bad soul does not exist. Few examples of the answers are below:

Participant 1 answer is: "Yes, the inner guidance is what should manifest outside. Personally I believe it requires, attention, continuous prayer, inner conversations and expressions through forms of art such as writing, drawing, music etc."

Participant 3 answered "Yes Of course the person can live and guided by their soul as it can be achieved through meditation process just concentrating on oneself and inhale and exhale the air out and let the pores of the body open and listen to the instant voice of the soul as It will guide you in seconds what's right or wrong and its up to the person that follows it. That's why its said the universe lies within you while one is searching for happiness around.

There is no good or bad soul in general, the soul itself is pure it is the character of the person that makes it good or bad. The Soul is always pure in Human Body even if one talks to the prisoner who committed crime, but its the bad character in him/her that made or force him/her to do crime is lying in the prison, the circumstances may be many why he/she did that but the soul is never bad. We can heal that person and convert him/her to the different opposite good person. For E.g., I heard the Akon group of music industry who has a unique voice committed something crime and was in prison but he changed his image and its through his unique voice today he has a different place in the Music Industry. I am not sure about Akon but I heard this from my senior may be I am wrong but this is the scenario like."

Participant 7 answer is: "I would call it the competition and recognition of myself and the philosophy of life. If a human were to be directed through their soul, they would achieve it by applying those three comprehensive rules (in question 1).

Does a bad soul exist? The reason why…NO, there is no bad spirit. Evil is the incorrect interpretation that a human does to their soul."

Participant 8 answer is: "Of course, yes. I believe that this is achieved only by following our internal voice and always doing what makes us happy, for example: to follow our dreams… I do not believe it has a bad spirit, I think it has a bad mind to transform it into bad spirits. This is because people think wrong and unconscious, so they do not put themselves in the place of others, do not ask themselves questions how they would react in a particular case."

Participant 15 answer is: "The hope of a spiritual practice is to find this guidance from within. We need the silence and some skills to listen for this quality of soul in the body and we need to body to confirm this in our lives, by consolation Ultimately finding ones own souls is to find God, who dwells within."

Are the mind, heart and body human utensils, which serve the soul so that the person is faithful or fulfilled? Why... 38 Participant answered, "yes" and few answers are below:

Participant 30 answer is: "They are, but it need a lot of time and effort to achieve it."

Participant 41 a 6 year girl answer is:. "The soul is the boss and the rest work for it. The soul is me. The mind, body and heart with out soul distract me to be bad. "

Questions eight, ninth and tenth are more about to understand the perception of "god" and reflection on their life journey. The reason was to notice how much control they think they have towards the painful situations and suffering. Where is their hope of being in control of their life? Are their beliefs linked to a happy life and how to make one? Especially question ten is how they explain the death of children and how their explanation is linked to their beliefs about life. Moreover to make them think about death and at the same time about children as they both are very important topic link to understanding the circle of life. The circle of life is born, death and the role of the soul and how this is link to create the circle? Which in my opinion is that we do come to this life to enjoy the journey and grow through the journey spiritually as human as our soul is already grown to certain level depending on our life's journeys we have had and how we have allowed to be part of our life's journeys. So based on our growth as a human, after we end one life journey, (after each death we have in each life journey) is decided from us to choose more then three options on our next life journey we want to take based on the life we had.

This is based on two main achievements:

1 - How much we achieve to make ourselves happy, fulfilled and loved.

2 - On how much we contribute into others, into life.

Our creator gives the life journey options that we have free will to choose. We all know that is the creator, as they are things death and life (add here from literature review). Question ten is to help the participants reflect on their actions and to see if their life is based on their actions. We do have the full power on each life journey we choose, we are the one who create our reality.

47 Participant said they believed in god

> 40 Participants said, "yes children are innocent".
> 1 Participant said "there are three types of death" (number 17).
> 1 Participant said "not sure" (number 49).
> 9 Participant said "only one the prewritten is" (the numbers are 6, 13, 16, 24, 25, 27, 29, 39 and 47).
> 2 Participant said "only one of the actions not the prewritten one" (the numbers are 28 and 46).
> 8 Participant said " don't know" (the numbers of participants are 4, 20, 23, 26, 38, 40, 41 and 48).
> 29 Participants said "yes there are two types of death"

Participant 16 answered: "Treat others as you would like to be treated.
  - Love yourself as you would like to be loved.
  - Give 100% in everything that you choose."

Participant 40 answer is: "To believe in god means that you believe.
  - I communicate to god by talking to him, I can talk to him because he made us and he is a part of me. "

Participant 41 a 6-year-old girl that does not practice any religions answer is: "He gives advice. I can listen to him because he is in my body and he made me".

Participant 42 a ten year old girl that does not follow any religions answer is: "To believe in god is to believe in something powerful watching over you and guiding you, I believe that you must not sin and if you done, then you must respect for those sins. There are different ways of sinning, three of them being: do not kill, do not hurt others in any way and do not hurt yourself."

Participant 47 age 54 from India the answer is: "To believe in god means to :
  - Do not harm anyone,
  - Listen to your intuition,
  - Thank god for all the good things that occur."

Participant 50 answer is: "To believe, to dedicate to God with your soul, heart and mind. Not to do bad to no one, to have a big heart and pure, not to think bad about no one."

The lack of empirical evidence has convinced a number of people to reject all supernatural or transcendent reality. For instance, the avowed atheists deny all forms of religion or spirituality. The term atheism originates from the Greek word 'atheos', which means 'without God'. Atheism can encompass a variety of views, which tend towards secular philosophies such as rationalism, humanism, physicalism and naturalism. Murray O'Hair (1963) states: "Atheism may be defined as the mental attitude which unreservedly accepts the supremacy of reason and aims at establishing a lifestyle and ethical outlook verifiable by experience and the scientific method, independent of all arbitrary assumptions of authority and creeds". By emphasising this rational aspect, the writer Ernest Hemingway concludes: 'all thinking men are atheists'. There is a minor but vocal group of fundamentalist atheists, who express that those who are spiritual or believe in God are somehow ignorant or naive, and would like to see eradication of all forms of spirituality (Mastin, 2011). Even though science and spirituality and/or religion usually operate in different realms they can co-exist. To affirm this, Albert Einstein states: "Science without religion is lame. Religion without science is blind". This indicates that the act of deciding something is true without evidence goes against science, whereas seeing the world exclusively through proven facts goes against spirituality. According to Dietrich (2007) the cohabitation of science and religion can be achieved by pursuing truth based on conclusions arising from feelings or spirituality as well as scientific facts. It is possible to not have to choose one or the other, but to encompass them as different facets of life, which can serve their purpose by also working in tandem. History shows that spiritual people have been able to approach science through a spiritual lens, as scientists have pursued spirituality through a scientific lens. Many have been the scientists, who were driven by their intuition or spiritual tendencies to explore the laws of the universe (Jusino, 2017).

The reason why children suffer may be:

- One of the past lives that have been made and must travel through it to discover their light through participating and staying faithful to pure love.

- The other is to help the parents find their light and reach their inner power through pure love… children are atomically sustained with energy of goodness up to the age of 25…. (until this age is mixed with the energy of the parents)… then over the age of 25 everything depends on their choices…

For the arrival of the children to the parents who do not plan it is the explanation that has to do with the following points:

1 - It may be a chance for the parent to take the road of goodness to attain the happiness I have mentioned above.

2 - May be something connected with previous life's has done and their choice of purpose.

3 - May be a lesson for a parents or the child to grow through their experience.

Children who die without becoming adults do not suffer as adults suffer because they face experiencing as adventures under the taste of pure love.   because they have the clean energy. They are under the energy of the soul. … If you look at the children you can notice …. because the cry for a moment and next they are smiling and laughing… they love themselves and their lives therefore if you have succeeded in being fulfilled and in love with yourself and their life even if they seems to be going through hard time as it is the journey to grow and overcome those difficulties as like I said may be the consequences of their previous life's they have done. death does not frighten children or those who have achieved self-love. Death is not what we need to worry but how to enjoy life that's what we have to worry erefore the children are happy and for that reason I strongly believe we have been created to be happy, fulfilled and loved with out being influence from external world of factors. We have ability through self-love that comes by following the main guidance on question one in questioner that I will call self-love guidance to enjoy everything we decide to do and achieve any goals after we have gone through stage one and stage two of magical module.

Everything that happens is a test to get closer to be who we meant to be. When you are content where you are, feel fulfilled and have what it takes to get your goals achieved then you have meet real you.

Kids - 0 to 3 are mainly shaped based on mothers or parents emotions.

3 - 6 are shaped mainly in the way we discipline them, guide and teach them.

6 to 11 or 12 are mainly in nurturing, they are shaping their future with their spiritual gifts and they need help to allow them.

12 to 16 mainly they are shaped based on outside world. . 16 to 25 the are shaped based in love and discipline they get.

Religions, spiritually or other guidance are there just to help us how to find our self's, how to connect with our soul that automatically we connect with creator. The creator has given us the free will and free choice to make it more interested, adventures and fascination our journey. I think people who achieve to be fulfilled on this life they will automatically have an easy life in next life and so on until the world will become peaceful and love. Only different is that each life journey we choose to take before we are born we face the challenge to maintain in life journey the self-love we are born with, that's all we have to do and that's all we need to do because the rest flows as we live the life journey.

Question eleven is all about love, and how can love be a healer to everything we experience and takes us to see the world with eyes of pure love. Once you have achieved to discover pure love within then you are able to feel fulfilled exactly where you are and in peace and love. You will not feel the need to be loved, but you will know with who to share your love in universal way and passionate way. Through this question you can tell from their answers who has knowledge of that pure love, who has already practising it and who don't even have a clue as they don't believe that pure love can exist.

- ➢ 2 Participant said "don't know" and the numbers of participants are 2 and 20.
- ➢ 9 Participant said "no" (the numbers of participants are 10,16,22,26,27,28,29,46 and 44).
- ➢ 39 Participant answered "yes".

The participant one clearly from the answer below shows that does not have achieved the self love and does not practice those three rules on question one because has not yet come to conclusion that god is on her and she has to act like one is not about loving god but loving yourself. So clearly that confusion shows that and it confuses her life journey as you can refer to case study two on chapter seven for more details.

Her answer of question one is "Yes! ... and I would add one more, which to me is the first rule: Love your God with all your soul, heart, and mind, and with all your strength in prayer and faith."

This answer from participant two it shows clearly why she has achieved everything she put her mind to it because she has followed her own way of believe that has resonated with her as she is running a very successful charity orgasitaion along with other success things she has achieved in life but again how we define success is up to each individual and what you think and act that's what you get. Which mean has she achieved fulfilment, peace and love? Which that is my explanation of real success!!!! Or does she thinks that success means money and fame and that's why she has achieved what she aimed for because of her believe.

Participant two answer to question one is "I have grown atheist - these were my grandmother's and my parents' guidance."

Participant 34 answer is: ". If you do not love yourself, you comfort love anyone else in the world."

The 6 year old participant 41 answer is: "It's not enough because I still need my mum and dad but is as I care for myself and I will find a way to be fulfilled. "

Participant 47 answer is : "It an individual has no self love, other source of love are not genuine experienced. Over within is the admiration for yourself, which then allows you to love others. I believe this because this is what I experience. "

According to Bandura (1986), the functioning of a human being comprises a set of reciprocal interactions between environmental, behavioural, and personal variables. The fundamental personal variable is the 'self- efficacy', or the perceived ability for acquiring or performing particular tasks at specific levels. Self-efficacy can increase successful achievements because of the individual's efforts, persistence, and as a consequence the improved performance. When compared with people, who doubt their capabilities, self-efficacious students are more likely to participate in new or challenging tasks, and appear more motivated to overcome difficulties to reach higher levels (Schunk, 1999). The sense of self-efficacy is directly influenced by self-love. As individuals work on tasks where they practice and convey love, they raise their self-esteem, self-confidence and progress quicker. According to Hardy (2012) "Self-love is a state of appreciation for oneself that grows from actions that support our physical, psychological and spiritual growth. Self-love is dynamic; it grows by actions that mature us.

When we act in ways that expand self-love in us, we begin to accept much better our weaknesses as well as our strengths, have less need to explain away our short-comings, have compassion for ourselves as human beings struggling to find personal meaning, are more centred in our life purpose and values, and expect living fulfilment through our own efforts". Taking responsibility for our life, choices and actions means that we have also the right to attend our needs. In this way, we can learn to love others. Being self-loving means that the person full accepts who they are, preserving their good qualities and taking continuous steps to improve the traits that they are not satisfied with. This means that the self-reproach and the resulting anxiety or distress is avoided. Instead of worrying about imperfections, the individual embraces them by also appreciating the unique strong points (Hardy, 2012). According to Cohen (2012) a happy and self-assured person, is in fact a self-lover and perceives 'the self' as a best friend, who does not demean or degrade but inspire and encourage, regardless the approval or disapproval of others (Cohen, 2012).

By learning to love themselves, people are more likely to have tender and loving relationships and happier children. Research has shown that when parents display the ability to love themselves, this is automatically copied by the child. Therefore, parents need to learn self-love before they teach it to the new generation. When a person loves, the world around appears more beautiful and meaningful, because it is seen from a loving perspective. This can improve the physical, emotional and psychological state of an individual as well as it attracts healthier circumstances and people in their life. One example of self-love is being mindful, which enables human beings to be in touch with their thoughts, feelings and have knowledge of their needs, wishes and goals. By staying centred and moving mindfully forward one can prevent automatic repetitive patterns, which are no longer useful. The practice of self-care such as healthy nourishment, regular exercise, good social interactions, intimacy etc. is another aspect of self-love. In addition, people love and respect themselves more when they know how to set boundaries or refuse activities that repress, drain or harm them emotionally, physically or spiritually. Forgiveness is also part of self-love. Rather than being critical or punishing about occurring mistakes, the other and healthier option is learning to grow by the lessons learned. Living with a purpose that guides the life's journey is self-loving too. This may be as simple as making decisions, which support and express personal values (Hardy, 2012).

When I analysed each questionnaire in depth, I was able to tell so much about that individual just by understanding their answers and where they have their roots. Because it is such a wide qualitative set of research and my focus was how self-love plays a role. I must say and appreciate each of the participant who took time taking part in the research and not only did they take part but they done it with whole their being, full honesty and love. Something very special has happened on a spiritual level that made this research happen in the way it did, because there is no other explanation for how all of the participants approached me or crossed my path and they were happy to take part, meaning that I did not have to look for participants. It is the higher energy that has been guiding me through this process and I have just gone with the flow.

Discussion about the case studies

This conversation with yourself helps to understand and discover your inner power exactly where you are. Imagining having nothing, but discovering that you have everything you need just within you, as through your inner power you can create your peace and love in this life. Individ (imagine you are somewhere alone with out having anyone to help)-

you feel pain of negative emotions- accepting the situation in order to move on- need answer to question "why" so you know the reason for accepting and moving on to where you want to move on you need goal and believe (inspiration is the food for the goal and believe)- determent and commitment (need to find your strength for fighting for what you want)- affirmation (creating praises for your self based on your actions and your vision so they can lead you when you are straggling to continue)- love (love is the answer to question "why" and to all "why" you may have or raise, just need to discover in pure way of love). As each individual goes through this circle I just mentioned, by taking their time as it is explained in chapter three through seven stages of magical module. And how client number'one has done on chapter seven to achieve and to be fulfilled, in peace and love exactly where it is and with what they have and can see clearly the future vision.

But most of people live in this system below:

Individual--suffering (hate, jealousy, manipulation, cover their true self, accepting life of pain, feel wick when they are alone) -- survival (hurt others, lie, manipulation, hypocrisy, egoism, make others feel bad about you, cover their guilt, blame others) --- The goal is to gain money as they se it as only way of success and hope to find happens or to be good in eyes of "God "to avoid punishment from "God"(hidden, suppressed, comprehensible) -- inspiration is created between the space of conversation soul/human/universe for the purpose of the goal individual wants (inspired by deceitful people, rich people for wrong reasons, fame   the success story is created by doing things & depending on the purpose they have and those things are from the point of origin)---dedication (it is the branch of goal and inspiration that based on their goal to gain money they will hurt others to gain their goal, such as kill, do bad, lie, manipulate, to reach the goal)   affirmation are coming from their goal energy which will not help their peace and love but only their goal—love for those individuals is sex, society, and use love as a weapon with a goal toward those who appreciate love. This group of individuals will not find fulfilment, peace and love unless they stop and start from momentum stage of magical module or the circle I just mentioned in upper paragraph.

There are even this kind of circle that they think they are good and they do good to others but really they just go swimming on universal love with out paying attention to discover the self-love and they lead being unhappy but complaining about the world and others.

Magical module can help the individual to analyse their whole being and understand themselves where they are and how they operate in order to have clear idea how to follow the methods and techniques provided on chapter three. It can help to connect with their true self and follow through the process until they reach peace and love within and without. As it is demonstrated through chapter seven how the clients have gone through the stages below of magical module. Some clients for short period of time some for long period of time, some they havestnding it and avoiding it in same time.

Discussion: how the seven stages have helped the clients to achieve the results the have achieved and why others have not followed until the end?

- *Momentum:* (is important stage for you to face your self and your life journey).

- *Acceptance:* (is important stage as by accepting you can make peace with your self and have a deep conversation where you want to do the journey).

- *Goal:* (is important as with out direction you are lost and don't move nowhere or you may waste time going for wrong goal) .

- *Inspiration:* (is the fuel that keeps you going and reminding you why you love the goal, your self and you life journey).

- *Commitment:* (it is healthy and important to look after your commitment as that is your temple to help you be fulfilled, in peace and love and to move towards your future vision).

- *Affirmation:* (this part is all about showing appreciation to your self and telling your self how much you value and here it comes critics also).

- *Love:* (we all want to be loved so this is the whole point of being here in this life, being loved by yourself, by your family, by friends and others, by partner and sharing love with yourself, others and universe).

Looking at this quote below from Albert Einstein it seems clearly that there are people before me who have had the same idea and understanding of the life and the bridge that link to spiritual world. But even in the quote it says is not possible but I will challenge that it is possible. I have achieved it, so few clients have achieved and few others are fully aware of the process and they are practising it, and most of the clients have started to believe that it is true and can be achieved as they have achieved small steps towards the process. I know 100% that can be achieved but as I have explained the ingredients you need to uncover within and practice it through those main three guidance on question one in questioners through empowering reflection and openings, but how many will have a go, that only time will tell.

'A human being is part of the whole, called by us "universe," a part limited in time and space. He experiences himself, his thoughts and feelings, as something separate from the rest – a kind of optical delusion of consciousness. This delusion is a kind of prison for us, restricting us to our personal desires and to affection for a few persons nearest to us. Our task must be to free ourselves from this prison by widening our circle of compassion to embrace all living creatures and the whole of nature in its beauty. Nobody is able to achieve this completely, but the striving for such achievement is in itself part of the liberation, and a foundation for inner security.'

-Albert Einstein

The client who did achieved fully to be guided by their soul used our human parts as tools to serve the soul. The client who are acting based on their mind and emotions have not achieved self-love and are not guided by their true self. To achieve self-love it is not easy job but it can be done and that's the first thing we should do as human if we are not happy. Most of client struggled to achieve self-love because you have to practice the self-love guidance in order to gain the purity you lost through growing up, connection to the soul. Participant 31 answered the question four "Our soul is our soul, which is visible only through our attitude and behaviour, and perhaps our dreams, is an energy in our whole body" also participant 16 also a client nine answers about the soul are "The soul is the balance of the will of the heart and will of the brain and the soul is in charge of our humans parts and helps us to keep it in balance and the soul is pure, but it may get lost as the brain takes over". But if we look at the client nine case study and his answers we can see clearly that he is very wiser and also from answers of question one on questioner "It's about keeping those values close to your heart until you are able to support yourself and then you can implement the rules in your life" can see clearly that he knows where he stands. Moreover from answer of question eleven about the self-love if is enough to feel fulfilled his answer is "No they cannot. They can love themselves but this can cause loneliness if they only love themselves and cannot share or receive love back" which tells me that that's why he struggling as you can see from his summery of the case study because he is still understanding the self-love.

To come to terms of what it is about and how can he get his head around it as he already has the core but the reality does not match and he is trying to figure it out. For me his case study is a success and I am sure he will feel fulfilled, in peace and loved whatever he decides to do, as his core foundation is very strong. Moreover the client one has fully achieved also the strong core of the foundation even though she is still not stable on reality but because within she has gain that inner power and she believes that she can create the reality she wishes. Below is example of her exercise after her full transformation but continuing to keep the balance which is reflecting in deep level of the end of the day based on those three main self love guidance. In order to see herself with the eyes of her soul and creator. After each deep reflection on the day she will send me through text the conclusion she come up and they are below:

Reflection of daily balance of client one after her transformation:

Day 1 I understood the reasons that sent me to a "over-evaluation of myself" made the first step by understanding and reflecting ... Eh, myself you jump easy... (I've said it constantly yesterday and today to myself).

Day 2 Everything comes with time ...

Day 3 Knowing you can ...

Day 4 Understanding the past moments (a situation from the book) .

Day 5 When your purity differs, though you do not value...

Day 6 To analyse the dimensions of the memory.

Day 7. When things can be felt (understood).

Day 8. The role of concentration and discipline onwards my yourself ...

Another day. Understanding the reason of yourself and the essence of the findings that surround us...

Another day. Oh, thank you God for protecting me from the controversy of the humans even me I did not understanding before allowas

This balance has to be practised daily until you became able to do it more then once a day atomaticely or anytime that you feel something is not right and just is disturbing you, because we have to remember we are the creator of our life journey and for that reason is all down to our decisions and actions.

In more depth explanation of her day six reflection on daily balance example is below:

Client explanation after a discussion on her experience of the day six reflection. As explained that what she had managed to do was amazing because there are very few people who can travel through their past life journey and look at it with eyes of the soul and the creator through self love to show compassion and understanding:

Client said "Writing based on reflection Analyze of my memory dimensions   It was one of those situations where I felt a lot of pain ... I think I'm on my life journey initially I had clashes in my life but the judgment came as collisions (I would like to keep up) they are too many the pain that passes by reflecting on them. Without my understanding I had passed the stage that Vjollca called it the awareness of the pain, where you look at the pain but you don't go in depth. According to Vjollca this phase should be repeated once a month would be good, once weekly will be amazing and once in three months is at least. But if you do it after three months that means you have to repeat the same stage again before you go to next stage because each stage time between them has to be three months. At this stage you are like the person who is in the water and sometimes dives into it. The best thing is the individual to do it by itself to go through those stages with discussion after wards with a mentor with knowledge in that area because moving through these phases the person is the protagonist of the story and know them well. It is possible for a person to analyze the past and heal it through self-love guidance whatever panful is the past."

- To love yourself (to understand, discipline and control)
- To achieve your structure (the one you will be). To have a full perception of things that happen by chance, which in fact have a certain origin (ego, structure, the management of the quandary, its analysis) hurts you in your lifetime journey that you have done so far "

Vjollca learning on this experience:

When she send me the reflection of day six I was curious to know what she meant but I just moved my attention away as I did not wanted to disturbed her until she will tell me by her self. In the same day, I come across a video of life regression talk. That made me reflect on myself and I noticed that I had done that by my self on my self with out not having any knowledge about it. So I left that thought there and next day the client discussed about her previous reflection and I was shocked to think that she had managed to do that in very safe way with lots of love , but with out being aware what she was doing. So after she talked me through her experience I took her through the process she had done so she was aware and she could continue further if she felt ready to do so.

Through her transformation she had visited her past life journey during the conversation with me couple of times but never on her own the way she did it this time. Bit and pieces visiting the past prepares you to reach the stages below, but to reach to those stages you have to be good on practicing for at least one year self-love guidance.

Stage one: is where you observe your past life journey but don't do nothing more …..is like you are on the sea where cant swim but only have the head out of the water to breath while the whole body is under the water.

Stage two: is where you can go on deep water just to look under the water but not swim yet. So at this stage you may chose a particular experience and spend some time with that pain or just visit whole past life journey in more depth where you take time to understand the pain or other experiences in more depth.

Stage three: is the stage where you can swim for how long you need with out no worries, fear or feel pain as you now have learned to show full love to your whole past life journey so far and in this stage you are fully transformed spiritually and your fear has been turned into pure love.

Analyzing the self-love guidance is the core of this research I took few of the answers that say the same of what I am implementing and the other answers are in chapter eleven that shows clearly why they go in circle on coming to the same point. Some answers suggest more guidance, some they say the "God" does not exist and some they think is to simple guidance so they say "no". But all come to conclusion that those rules are important but difficult to follow because the influence of mind and heart caused by reality. The self-love guidance are that gives us the meaning of life and us that lead to fulfilling life. Also is lack of believe on their answers that they don't believe you can be successful depending again where they are with their self-love progress. As in my conclusion once you have achieved self-love you have achieved to be successfully.

Main success is to feel fulfilled, in peace and love then you reflect on the life journey you are in and do your best to get the success you want in material world. But we have to remember the material world success does not fulfilled and give as peace and love that's why is important self-love. Self-love is the main success we need to have that brings to us what we need in reality. The word success in my opinion is miss leaded it and misunderstood as for me and the results of this study is to feel fulfilled, in peace and loved exactly where you are and with what you have and having a clear vision of your future journey. The only way to gain self-love here and now is gaining self-love. Self- love will be gaining by practicing self-love guidance. To practice the self-love guidance you have to understand in depth magical module on chapter three and have at least once a month through the year a good holistic spiritual mentor.

Self-love guidance: Treat others as you wish to be treated. - Love yourself as you wish to be loved - Make 100% of everything you choose to do.

Participant 6 answer of self-love guidance: 'I think that there are no rules set by the lord, or in written and in fact. But I believe that it is the rules that emanate from the inside that the individual decided to follow in order to feel complete."

Participant 21 answer of self-love guidance: "Yes I believe the three rules should apply to everything we do in life it's like a cure to or sole of we follow those rules. Of everyone stamps back and thinks of those three rules the world will be a better place to live."

10 year old answer: "These rules are enough, because for example, loving yourself means that you care about you and that is very good".

Participant 19 answer of self-love guidance: "Yes there are three main rules according to the lord and if you do the three of them you are a complete being… both spiritually and physically."

Participant 41 (6 year old girl) answer of self-love guidance: "Yes, they are the main rules because my mum, dad and aunty taught me those rules and they are enough. Rule number one helps me because you can treat others kindly. Loving yourself helps me by loving myself and liking my expressions and if is there not good I will find away how to improve them."

Participant 19 answer of self-love guidance: "I think that there may be many other things that a being has to do in this life, because life itself implies to do so many things, I personally think about the positive things to give in this life, people are different and many of them do not believe in these three rules and do not apply them, but does not mean they cannot practice these rules one day, and that happens when they start to feel spiritually empty that something missing."

From examples below of the answers of participant 10 year old girl and 6 year old girl can see that children already have all the knowledge I am trying to demonstrate through this book in order we as a adult to be fulfilled and to raise happy children, create the world of peace and love.

Answers of few participants 40 & 41 (10 year old girl and 6 year old girl) towards self-love guidance below, the soul and God: (e results of questioners shows that most of participants or I must say all think that children are innocent but during they journey to adult they get corrupted by their mind and heart (thoughts and feelings) which back up my hypotheses that the meaning of life is to enjoy life and to enjoy life you have to be pure. To be pure you have to practice those three self-love guidance including their underlined guidance and explanations how to do it.)

Question: What is the soul? Where is it located anatomically in humans and what is the role of the soul in this life? Why... Does a bad soul exist? The reason why

10 year old answer:
-Thee soul is where the wisdom is held.
-It is located near the heart I think.
-The soul helps you by telling you to do the right thing.

A bad soul doesn't exist because everyone is warm an nice inside."

Question: Are the mind, heart and body human utensils, which serve the soul so that the person is faithful or fulfilled? Why...

10 year old answer: "I think so, because everything they do, is very special but combining them, makes something powerful like the soul.'

6 year old girl answers: "The soul is all of me, the whole of me. The soul can teach me to be good and gives me advice. Based on my soul, I can respond.

The soul is the boss and the rest work for it. The soul is me. The mind, body and heart without soul distract me to be bad."

Question: What does it mean to believe in God and how can this be demonstrated by 3 rules or examples?

10 year old answer:
"
  - To believe in god means that you believe.
  - I communicate with God by talking to him. I can talk to him because he made us and he is a part of me. "

6 year old girl answers: "He gives advice. I can listen to him, because he is in my body, and he made me."

Question: Can a human being be filled with love, which comes exclusively from the source within themselves? And from the moment they become aware of that love they do not feel suffering because they are know their purpose and are fulfilled?

10 year old answer: "Self-love: The love within is that you are loving yourselves. I think that way because it's what I think."

6 year old girl answers: "It's not enough, because I still need my mum and dad, but it is: as I care for myself, I will find a way to be fulfilled."

Participant 24: 'Soul is you and located deep within yourself, the role us to travel in this world and get knowledge."

Participant 32: "I feel it between heart and universe it is for me to love it, to make me love myself and realise my goal in the beginning in this life."

How to learn self-love?

-What is love?

Unconditional love: the meaning has to do with 3 main rules of life that I keep mentioning over and over through this research and that they are self-love guidance.

Every love that comes from the mind and heart is false. The love that comes from the soul is true. The distinction is made if the rules below are followed and if you feel complete and in love where you are, without the need for someone else to complete you. This means you are one with your soul. If you feel lonely unhappy with these negative emotions and automatically search for someone to complete them, it means you are not connected to your soul. But on the other hand if you are, you know what person you are looking for and when they appear you have the ability to spot them. But what you require, you must first be like that; in the sense that you have to be at the level you are searching for. All of this shows and reiterates that if you love yourself, you achieve what you want and if you find that person s/he is just like yourself but you enjoy the journey together. So you have to work with yourself in order to have a healthy relationship.

The Rules: self-love guidance

- Love yourself the way you like to be loved.
- Travel others, as you would like to treat.
- Do your best in everything that you do. (Do you know that you are doing your best.

It comes through the inner conversations with your soul and your intuition).

The person who applies these rules knows that to give love to oneself and to others but with the diplomacy and in the proper way (because there are times when we give love to someone you can borrow). Example: When we love a narcissist, they are feeding them by continuing the road in the wrong way. They need love with truth, the true love is when everything is said to be true. Unconditional love is when truth is spoken directly but with love.

How can we feed love?

How to practice spreading love even in dark moments?

What is the difference between soul-love and human-love?

Always staying in the presence of your soul. This happens through the following two points as starter and then working on magical module:

- Spending time at least 30min up to 2 hour a day with yourself. At least one day a week should be for you only. (When you are reflecting, that is your soul's voice. Analysis, with knowledge and answers to your questions are coming from the intuition – the voice of creator). But remember, creator never makes decisions for you but is like a therapist to you. You are only provided with answers to your questions. Sometimes, you are not given answers because it is not time yet, or maybe you need to learn something in the meantime.

- Surround yourself with or meet people that that speak to you the truth through love.
These are the main food that give you more options on guide you where to get the food for love such as nature, good friends, family, children, work, home etc. They also help you to prioritise the best options.

The difference between soul-relationship, attraction-relationship, good-relationships and the right relationships need to be understand and aware as that can complicate things and unbalance your self-love.

Relationship with yourself
Relationship with others around you
Relationship with your family
Creating the right one in order to get the right one

Soul relationship is when you only connect through soul but don't agree with each other's actions and thoughts. Human relationship is when you know each other very well including mind, heart and as whole. To be able to recognise those two types of relationship you have self-love first and understanding of universal love then you are ready for relationship.

How to get what you want from this life as it has been the main topic of this research and how to discover what you really want not what you think you want?

-Understand and follow the three rules of the universe

-Keep learning how to keep evaluating yourself

-Practice meditation in your own way
Make it and keep it simple. In order to be effective practice 30 min every day. Start even with just 5 min three times a day, or more.

-Be creative/write long time plans, and break them into small steps

-Remind yourself of the 7 stages from the Magical Module and apply them for each small goal, to do every day

How to be a good parent! (Those questions below need to take it into your inner conversation that explained through chapter three).

- What happens when you are not fulfilled?

- What does being fulfilled, mean?

- How to listen to your child?

  - Silence,
  - Misbehaviour,
  - Walking,
  - Playing with others and alone,
  - School behaviour,
  - Eating habits,
  - Child's favourite TV programmes and hobbies,
  - With you,
  - With strangers,

- Experiencing different emotions and being balanced.
- Teaching children the self-love guidance.
- Helping them to build a trusting and committed relationship with themselves and universe.

How to practice the spread of love even in dark moments? When the world turns upside down e.g. something unexpected happens such as losing a loved one, losing a home, losing a health, ending up in prison without being your fault ... etc.

How self-love can help you to understand and overcome the most difficult moments of your life? It is explained on my first book "A Magical Life" but I would just say this paragraph below:

- ❖ The breathing needs to be practiced, that by breathing you can go to the soul and contact with creator for guidance.

- ❖ By trusting your soul and the creator link to your purpose. Believe everything happens for a better reason.

- ❖ If the self-love guidance are not applied, then you have to analyse your behaviours. You have to interact with your soul and creator to find out why it happened and what will be learned to curry in the right way, on the road to finding peace and love, because your life does not end but still exists. If you decide to end your life with your will it means you are giving up on you and your life journey and is not fulfilling the purpose of coming to this life.

- ❖ Remember, remember and remember. You were born alone in this world and for a purpose. You are special, remember to believe in your light: your purpose. Remember you know why you came into this life journey. Simply go deeper into depth, going beyond your being and being one with your soul. There you will be full of strength, love, and you see that everything is happening for something better.

Some understanding of need for love:

The need for passionate true love:

Because we are born with self-love and as we grow we lose it through the influence of others and reality we atomically start running out of love and as our human being is made to function from love we crave for love in others. There are people who love with mind (these love is compromised but is no passion). This is not true love. Some people love with heart. It's like dependence. Sometimes it happens to us that we fall in love first sight, which means that it falls directly to the soul of the person, but what happens. But what happens? If that person does not live with his soul all the time, but lives with the mind and heart then he is not the person who you are falling in love with. If that person is not one with his soul, that person is not true to himself as it follows the mind and heart. When we focus only on the soul of a person, we may be blinded to his mind and heart.

True love. It is when we fall in love with the soul of the person and he has created his life based on the soul, so mind and heart are means that serve his soul. So we have to look at as the whole. The mind and heart must be combined to a level with the soul.

The difference between the soul and the creators is that the creator has wider knowledge, but the knowledge of the soul comes from knowledge of your life purpose and previous life experiences. Do we need to know how to recognize our soul, starting from the very essence of his existence? Through the spirit we can change our thoughts and leave behind those we do not need. How can we allow the spiral of the spirit to guide us, given that the soul is close to creator, innocent and always right. Also the soul heals the heart as the heart collect feelings from thoughts of mind also. Feelings want more time than thoughts to leave behind (this period lasts 3 months, which happens if you have learned the techniques from previous experiences or have a mentor - about 1 year out of your time practicing with yourself to see stability). Once stability has been achieved, this stability must be maintained and this work depends on person and is unique. For this one needs a prepared mentor. The body is a biological aspect through the body showing signs of lack of love, or things that can be scientifically proven. Thinking in the brain also affects the production of hormones. If the thought is negative, the cells are going to be negative energy, if positive then there is positive energy. Negative thinking occurs when the moment does not feel as it comes. While positive is when you feel and live the moment as it comes and if you cry, every thought is positive if you enjoy the moment, to create the future and to become the best person you have the opportunity to do. If the foundation is based on these three points, thought is called positive. Thinking that is not based on these three points is negative or harmful to the body and to the person.

Relationship with your family:

Relationships in the family, mother, father, sister, brother and other members a big family is part of universal love. If a person has not achieved self-love, then they will follow their path because they need universal love and they will be dependent on them. Universal love is simply survival but nothing else, so survival in the wrong way, breathing without realizing why you are and what is your path and why you really exists. If you love your family, you need to find the way to win love for yourself. If you do not find self-love you end up hurting them and your self. If you win your love for yourself, then your life becomes meaningful, and you enjoy life, then you can understand and enjoy the love of the family.

Example from case study one:

Vjollca: "When you do not know yourself ... you do not have the ability to know the creator either", A person who is not related to the soul but believes in God how do you explain it, because you have gone through that stage? Person who knows the soul, how do they understand God's faith because you have now reached it and you can explain it to me with your understanding?

Client number one: The soul is as something internal, and all of the importance lies in our theories, our doings, our acting on things in three dimensions:

Saying – what I don't believe, but that I want to happen.
Do-as well as I think (without realizing that I don't understanding what I am doing.)
Acting - another form that neither the saying and doing does not match and do not have the benefit of acting and saying as they don't correspond.

The answer to question 2 is: Understand your reason for this life, Believe in your skills, speak up the truth, do what you really want to do based on purpose and you are always in a position to implement your thoughts in collaboration with creator and your soul.

Vjollca: You explained it very beautifully. ... but something.... why you could not know your soul before? And how do you know the soul now?

Client number one: I knew the soul as the corner where I use to hide not more as I did not love my self. I knew the soul.... Love was in the way of talking, doing things was on base of that I am god person and acting was inactivity, incorrect thoughts in the head I thought I might know myself in another way I did not realize at first that I knew my soul but knew another way of knowing myself I believe I have the ability.
How did I not think before of the way of saying things, doing and acting has made the difference on my transformation?

Vjollca: how do you describe the self-love now?

Client number one: Love to yourself ...
I...
How am I ....
Am I... Perseverance Trust
Internal Force ...
motive Freedom Clear
Sincerity (communication or loving someone with out interest) Study (deepening not with the monotony)
Look as whole picture: I see the intentions of the other but before I have distinguished myself ...
Reasons ... With the language of love, I am not weird or crazy...
My appearance (I love what God created me, walking and running and still standing true, right, no matter how long it takes).
I love myself as I follow justice, practice pure love, speak up the truth, want the best for my self, be compassion and understanding with others.

Vjollca: Self love> who will be. in a silence you have to listen to yourself who you are going to be and to imagine your life with that role that everyone chooses. what impressions give? How would you like them to be? - you and nature what would you do in a life if you were alone? - how will you live your life when everyone are against you, what will you do. ...would you give up or find way how to live?. if you want to live, how would you live? If you will die. ... what would you win? Then do this exercise - relaxation – reflection- the imagination of the life you dream - unconditional love for yourself that serves the purpose you want - everything revolves around the purpose you have chosen - the ingredients are: smile, love your self with out reason, thanks your self when for the things you do, direct criticism when you're wrong, comfort when you are feeling down, heart-warming, change of thought, body care, dance with universe, singing with feelings and people, love melody always to be instrument of the pure love base of your actions.

Self- love is hard to achieve if not desirable - no plan - no action - faith – no courage to start - incapable to start - fears that may fail- where laziness exist- there are no justice towards self and others - there is a desire for quick things to achieve – purpose pointed to money only – friends are number one- no knowledge of pure love. ..

Self-love is easy when is the purpose based on pure love - courage - self-confidence - the demand for spiritual tranquility - the curiosity to learn - the defeat of fear to begin to cope with things - the use of negative feelings and teaching from them - the desire to live in the adventure – being in the moment and to see others happy - accepting all the emotions and mistakes and teaching from them - the courage to be product of pure love and fight for justice - the feeling of enjoying the feeling of universal love and inner self - the love you get from being pure - the meaning you gave your life – being the boss of your life- taking responsibility for your actions as whole.

Client number one: It's hard   You will not experiment with yourself, look at how is interpret it in reality, do not want to assume responsibility for feeling that it fails   You endure in the midst of difficult things and know no other way of dealing ...

Easy when you accepts your battles and take responsibility to face them, insist on your actions, understands the things that come unaccepted and accepts them, tests yourself as you are facing the battles ...

Looks easy There is no light but there is a lot of things that you can have your first-rate reading and getting things, and you see the obstacle as a way to learn something new without a doubt Experimenting yourself is not always easy because everything has to face but knowing about things even when it seems silly it's something worth thinking that it does.

Vjollca: How did you recognise your connection with your soul?

Client number one: "Now I need to implement it. .... It's energy. ... Understands that you are changing. ... you achieve to connect with your soul and you notice a light shines you as a whole and you understand that was your fault for not knowing how to believe in God. The soul makes you shine and understand your faith ..because I have been afraid before to go deep down and believe. ...as the faith is wider   I stopped in a spark from the faith and did not go further to understanding or follow it.... e connection with the soul has made me see things in another form. ... and has made me believe in the lord in depth.   faith is wide and now I go deep into the faith and practice it. .. not just the routine but I apply it. ... Even the same thing happened to me. Many wonder how people view the religion or master as a saviour but do not apply his words. .....

To live with the soul… you have heard but is far in distance… you heard in the dream of the vision that there is an ivory thread that needs to be understood, the faces were elusive, the horizons of a riot that was in the mind. there are a lot of things you've been wondering, what to bother and what you've understood before… was a situation that seemed to reflect only in books but in reality it was in the corner, in that corner that you have it looks like a upsetting place, where your self has always been a wintering project It happens without understanding, I had spiritual guidance, but it was disconnection because a new person was regenerating.

Vjollca: "For me the first 3 months you have not been linked to the soul. when you talk to me you were and there I tried to make you understand the taste of the soul. rough the techniques you were connected but scarcely needed ridiculous and absurd techniques to you but you were determent to follow them. the second 3 months you started to connect and practice the language of the soul once a week for a few hours. then the third 3 months you started somewhat more than 3 days a week until you reached 6 days a week and last month was all the time until the last week of the month of nine you managed to connect Completely to your soul and universe and managed to keep practicing it all the times. no you create your reality based on that and now you understand the Lord's faith. learn from the breadth of the faith of God. So the soul was your salvation ".

Client number one: "It was a world where things were smaller than the size I had given them (problems) It was a more detailed analysis of the action, but the actions did not happen and they had a guilty taste, but the situation had to be analysed Everything that I was trying to connect to the soul and everything I was living with the universe and my soul, at that time it was the currents that make you to be optimistic today was a wider border, a clear dimension to a new self without deep understanding and things went into analysis then the analysis could fade because of the impossibility of spiritual fulfilment and blocked by shadows, fear of reality to Love yourself A new meaning to love it, that makes you understand more things and the relationships with the soul continued as often until things were clarified, the space provided many details, made to look differently and to believe to on soul and universe".

Vjollca:
When an individual does not know himself (his soul) then he may be the product of thoughts that are created from reality others and the choice has been limited or the heart is coming from the heart as a product of feelings that may have been produced by thoughts or by the soul it is still a mess and complex because it does not combine with thoughts and there is a conflict here between the mind, the heart and the soul.

That when it comes to the decision to put it on and then it brings about stress and confusion, precisely this is influenced by acting because it is not done with desire but with compulsion and creates dissatisfaction, confusion, fatigue, numbness, etc. This situation creates a vital life because it removes from the love of life, the deep love that every person has inside that is the power of the individual to see himself and life with a different vision that sees a person who is not connected with inner love. When an individual or his soul, that is the love that the base is in the pure love, then the goodness and taste of then comes out of that love and the affair is associated with the will and the pleasure that gives the force of action to make the journey of life on the basis of that saying in this case everything seems clear, simple, meaningful and delicious, magical and above all feels the true love and peace and feels it is fulfilled there where are you with what you have.

In my opinion the things that we can not prove or see are more important or more close to our purpose then things we can see or been proven because as human or animal or anything as part of this life has an end and what does not have an end is our soul, faith, universe, creator and is for a reason that we can not prove or see those things as it is part of the faith ....but said that ....Remember for what we all crave? Is it love? Is it happens? Is it fulfilment? With that deep breath you like to just feel it and notice the great things around ...

Individual in bauble of life- outside the life - universe, creator, purpose, why we are in this life - we born and die- understanding body, mind, heart, soul- crave for love - but don't know the meaning of love - read books, learn from others but we forget tat everything is within and we have to make decisions within in order to be us and serve our purpose. Our reasons from coming to this life- we never questions why we come to this life - what is love -

All is complicated and need lots of work but all it starts by going back before we decided to come to rise life- to soul- to creator -to universe- and main ingredients are pure, determination, creativity, curiosities. ...Your answer is based on how connected you are with your soul ......how often you stay in that energy   can you recognise your voices in your head...... which level is your heart and mind. then how much you know about your purpose. ....how pure you are and what you have done so far ...etc etc .... Karma. ..law of attraction. your faith on your self and creator etc

Client number one said after six month work with me:

To act, knowing what is the place of the heart, mind, soul in that situation.
The days were passing by and I felt somewhat more stabilized in terms of my conditions. Everything - even though it was not easy - already had an orientation... My meeting with the psychologist had taken a different direction: from the idea to go and 'confess', to the idea of finding myself and doing things for me... Sometimes life takes its turn and thanks to Vjollca, I became another person, I believed that I could be different.
Since the achievement of things is never easy, and my conditions have rarely wanted to focus on a common course, the heart has always been comforting to my actions, the mind often helped the heart – 'you are doing a lot, you are capable, you are good'. These things troubled me so often, that I sometimes did not understand myself ...

"The connection with the soul is more difficult but it is achievable. For me it is an inner voice that constantly calls, although we hear it in a hurry" ... these things I listened with curiosity from Vjollca when she spoke and reproached me for the actions that I was taught to ordinarily take ... "Walk upwards if you love yourself and your life, be creative and pure, walk straightforwardly and you will always be winning...follow the intuition because it is never incorrect" she constantly said. It is a little difficult for it to be worth it, to walk with the steps of truth but it should be done. Vjollca's disciplinary way was therapy or perhaps for me it was the true therapy. When I complained about something, Vjollca told me I had to think deeply about things "do not walk according to the heart's rhythm or with what is embedded in the head (fixed thoughts of the mind). Connect with the soul, communicate more, analyse things, not just using them as a template"... this has made me to always believe that one needs to know how to control the thoughts coming from the self...

How to behave in the moment:
The instant comes suddenly or we can be somewhat prepared for a part of a situation that we think might happen to us ... My helpful instants have been clearer to me when I met Vjollca (by her applying on me, her module). 'Ask yourself' - this is something that can find its passage so fast that we cannot even think it, in fact we are inclined to say that we know something with certainty, but since I am an introvert this did not help me - to ask myself again??? Many questions came to me about the situation I was in, and about my situation beyond this situation. When I talked with Vjollca I always had to analyse the situation. For instance: 'Why am I afraid to face a solicitor? Do I have an idea in

my head? How does this idea work and what for? Should I overcome this fear? How? 'So I continued to wonder. There were immediate questions and with much difficulty I had to provide a solution from the soul's language, not from the usual mind or the comfort of the heart... in the moment we can face reality – this makes the situation more difficult somehow, than the thoughts, which require time ...

My Aim:

At the meeting with Vjollca or the randomness of the meeting, the idea that pushed me instantly was that I had to talk to someone and the introduction that Vjollca was a psychologist. The idea was to confess and then to walk with little guiding steps on her part. These enabled me to go higher within my personality... Now I had goals, I felt more capable, safer, and could do things. If until yesterday I had conquered my life and its obstacles with my silence, now I had to reflect. I could do things and I verified this during Vjollca's therapy with me. Although there was the lack of appreciation that I missed in my life, I had a self-belief that I possessed the ability to be useful in a different manner...worthy of myself...I want to be myself, to have a pure soul and worthy of truth, life...I want to be a living thing, righteous and responsible ...I can ....

My Achievements:

I can get out of the no-return situation where I was (with distorted dreams, of a difficult life without a way out) I am finding myself (the small steps have always increased my self-confidence based on Vjollca's guidance) Being true to my ideas, beliefs and thoughts (fear should be overcome; not being her slave, things should be analysed).

To be responsible. If once, my responsibility was to remain silent, with the same ideas in my head, today I have to reflect, think, discuss and feel the weight of things and the role in this weight... Facing the situation, when one has someone who they consider as a guide in life, brings a sense of security, one is obedient to their mission... The interviews (the anxiety of whether I was in time, confusion of trains, the loss of my ticket, the blockage before the interview, Vjollca's exercise to understand myself ...

Note: I have accomplished this writing on September 2017, which I call a report, guidance of my "new" path with the idea of expressing the work and my intensive therapy from Vjollca Sadiku. I want to say THANK YOU to her, since the actions speak much more...and have value. These written words have been extracted from my own experiences during this period, for which I kept notes (every day that I have passed, as techniques learned from Vjollca)

My reflection of client one transformation

This points below were coming from me, through the conversation with the client, describing through her voice, what were the seven points that made her achieve this journey and then I linked those points to the seven stages of the magical module.

The reason you did it for a year this process, 10 months up to now and for one months you have been able to be guided by your soul and universe all the time (the space we call it as the client have come up with that name).

The ingredients are:

1 - The insistence of your inner call

2 - Detachment from the reality by just spending time with yourself and avoiding conversation that don't serve you, your goal and your purpose.

3 - The insistence of Vjollca's not to let me give up by observing my thoughts, feelings and actions reflecting it back to me through my soul language.

4 - Giving Vjollca's full freedom on her suggestions and exercises towards me and being honest, open and pursuing without realizing what I am doing. I just knew and felt that was my inner calling.

5 - Purity of Vjollca's as if it wasn't would of not resonated with my inner calling.

6 - Acceptance of absurdity

7 - Rebellion not to accept myself the way I was formed by the reality and life that surrounded me.

Magical module:

1 - momentum

2 - Acceptance because you accept who you are and what you will to be doing.

3 - Goal... because I generally worked on the goals I had.

4 - Inspiration... inspiration. ..because I was inspired by the sincerity and the structure of the Vjollca ..and her words that combined with my inner voice. ... and the dream of my childhood... the dance of the childhood inspired me. ... and we were a children lying in the open space... all of these inspired me to be the real self.

5 - Commitment - dedication... this point helped me to be committed and to continue... because I knew that I was not doing it and I did not understood it. ... it was the soul that was scramming at me to get my attention... the purity of Vjollca made me hear my soul automatically. ...

6 - Affirmation - assertions. ... affirmation. ..prayers.... they helped to accept the absurdity because the call was in demand. ....

7 - love... rebellion shows love to yourself ...

Analyse the observations below:

Spiritual practices and expressions can be seen in various manifestations. Many hold the view that artwork, are such as music, literature, painting, are all forms of spiritual communications, which may go beyond the purely religious rites. One of the main reasons that artists create, and the others value their work, is because art enables a living connection between the daily psychology of individual minds and the universal aspect of humanity. This does not refer to merchandise, the purpose of which is personal profit, but to the wisdom of artistic productions that express spiritual principles or values like awareness, understanding, faith, unity and perseverance. If art arises from one's heart it speaks to another person's heart, so that togetherness arises due to witnessing this emotional and spiritually sensitive communication (Culliford, 2017).

During my observations, I had to get in touch with more than 5000 people. Last year in 2017 on Facebook I had just 200 friends and no followers, but now I have 4000 friends and 3000 followers. Most of these people have contacted me and I have had some kind of conversations with most of them. I have been very aware and tuned in a trance state most of the time, in other words I have been observing people from distance.

I could bring up so many issues and underlying issues that I have noticed but I will just mention three points.

1) Self –love key to everything (Noticing self-love was missing which made them act on ways that even they were not aware. This leads to think that do they like themselves for who they are and how they act?!!)

2) Create the life on your own beliefs. (Most of us we create the life on what we believe is right or wrong, or on what others have done and what we have been told. Most of us we do not question ourselves and accept the answers we get from our selves because they are unique and not the same as the answers we are surrounded by. Also we have not been courage to value ourselves and our inner thinking as it does not make sense to us, to reality and to others, it only feels right but actually doe not make sense.)

3) Where the self-love exists, only love and understanding will be applied. (Trying to explain self-love is not easy as I explained above in point two. Reasons why is because it does not resonate with reality and what others do but it does feel right…..you know it ….you just have to think in deep level what does it mean for you to be loved and how can that happen? Meaning being loved within, how and what is it?)

4) Self –love key to everything (How it manifest in below cases): I have noticed the loneliness that people feel and the emptiness inside them. Searching for something that they do not know what they are searching for, but they think passionate love can give them the satisfaction of feeling good by the high that they achieve through the excitement, of flirting and the pleasure they get from the orgasm. So for that reason the only, the first attention is how to get that passionate love. So they ignore working on self-love and universal-love as the universal-love is automatically applied to them but not in their conscious level. This way of thinking is not healthy as it becomes only a need or an unhealthy attachment, not something that brings them joy or helps them to grow. The above point I can demonstrate for you from a few examples on chapter eight and a few selected conversations. In my opinion it can be seen how desperate they are and how they prove the points above that I have just mentioned.

Observations: The practice and the achievement of self-love is free, but that makes us think that it is not work, as we are used to think that we need to work for money for material things…this is the turning point of disconnecting from space. It's easy working when love is not present as the focus will be on material things and not in love itself…which makes you think that that is what you will get…sometimes you do get it but it's too late …your life has almost ended when you realise that love was missing and you feel dry…The good person …the person who does everything from foundation of love don't focus on material things but they just come part of love -plan-action-satisfaction-fulfilment-self-realisation … As love is the key who can help you to open all the other doors by using the right tools. For the good person to change the society is harder because the good things are unseen. You only can feel it, visualise it, and live it "You can search throughout the entire universe for someone who is more deserving of your love and affection than you are for yourself, and that person is not to be found anywhere. You yourself, as much as anybody in the entire universe deserve your love and affection."— Buddha

➢ Did I manage to get people reflecting in a deep level?

Answer: Yes for those who were connected to their soul and can be noticed by the observations, discussions and dialogues. No for those who are attached to reality and disconnected to their soul and you can see the difference in their responses.

Analysis of book review to go mixed with observations:

Chapter nine is the readers feedback of "A Magical Life" book. This is done to bring the results of the aim and my objectives to writing in the first place the book. Which is to help the reader connect with their soul, their inner deepest self and through their inner self to reflect on the present which all it matters is the moment in present to heal your past, to be happy in present and to have clear vision of tomorrow.

➢ Have I made them connect with their whole them in deep level?

Answer: yes

➢ Did they revisit their childhood?

Answer: yes

➢ Did they revisit and think about present they are in? And future?

Answer: yes

➢ Did they take some tools to use in continuing personal development?

Answer: yes

Summary of the process:

How to connect with your soul: The summary of the magical module.

1 - Every day, spend a bit of time with yourself. Have a conversation with your inner peace.... visit the time where you were a child. ... where dreams had no limits. .... where imagination stems from your dreams... where you fly without realizing it you are doing it. .... where peace and love pamper you.... where you have the courage to do anything. .... just to that feeling hold up and use that feeling to practice this exercise.... to continue and practice as long as you live in that feeling.... then comes the second step down (but the ingredient must be based on purity, justice and goodness in every flap or imagination you create)

2 - Start the work with the mind. .... how?... again with yourself, it begins in your silence and the feeling you gained from the first step, you can observe your mind through your soul with pure love and it cleans the thoughts you need and do not serve the feeling of the soul (love, justice) and creates thoughts to help you achieve the reality you want. this is a process in itself because every new thought should be accompanied by a detailed plan of what you will do and how you will do it... also with practice comes over time to create only thoughts that serve your soul. ... that feeling at the first step... always associated with justice, kindness and love... that brings satisfaction, fullfillnes, mindfulness to your moments, peace, love and courage to create the reality your want....

3 - Here begins work with the heart. .... here you need a very special care of your heart from your soul because .... is sensitive and delicate. .... contradicts the thoughts but at the same time every thought creates a feeling... If your thoughts are not protected by your pure love from other unjustness actions then it will create hurtful feelings ... so this process is longer than mind and difficult because there will be pain, tears, obedience with love and compassion of caring through your soul... this process continues until all the every hurtful feeling is healed by the care of the soul... and produces only feelings of pure love from the soul.

4 - Here we starts the process with the body, then the common practice of all steps mentioned and keep practicing spending time with your self Getting to know you, how to keep up with your plans, how to find the right partner, how to love your self, how to be a good parent and how to do things today, not to regret yesterday or wait for tomorrow for things to happen because the present, here and now is everything that makes the difference and is important.

This process may take 3 to 5 years if you have the right holistic guidance and if you are determent to follow the magical module. Client one has achieved it in one year because I was doing at least four hour each day holistic therapy and she was really determent to follow the three self-love teachings. The important is that since you decide to start and if you stay committed to the practice you will see the difference and feel your journey becoming fulfilling, peaceful, with love and meaningful. Remember it is an ongoing process, as you can see in this example below, I have to be creative and curious all the times with my self and others or with every thing that surrounds us when something does not feel right.

To observe yourself when you have made a decision but somehow still you are stressed or uncomfortable example client number one after her transformation, after one-year work on magical module. She started to develop allergy exactly the same way as I use to when I felt trapped but I pretended like I am fine. In this case after two sessions, going over the same exercise but in different ways so the client can understand it. The first session I explained that she has to find ways how to be in relaxing position and observe her mind and heart. Which through her soul and creator eyes to see where the problem is and which kind of healing talk needs the mind and heart in order to resolve the conflict is causing the allergy.

After the first session she said she tried it but got distracted and did not go up to the deep level, so I felt I should explained one of my recent examples of similar situation when I had some kind of inner conflict. But did not understand it what was as I was clear on what I wanted and what I did not want. I wanted a partner well balanced that is guided by the soul and keep the mind and heart in same balance as his soul but I was still not clear why I was feeling a bit low and confused after a date I had, even though I was happy with the reflection and analysis of my date that I got from my self. Long story short I needed advice and guidance on how to understand my self-link to this situation and did not want to pay money to psychics, as they could not help either. Then I said to my self "I do give a great advice to others so lets try to pretend I am the other who is giving advice to my self (I usually do it through inner conversation but this time this was not suitable as it felt like I was still me and I need it some one to look at me). I thought it will be a great idea if I do it through writing conversation by pretending not to notice what I am writing or who is who, just to separate the lines by a question marks. I started and in the end I did not feel the need to reared it as I was clear and got what I wanted.

I started like an angry person with my confusion and end it up in tears and same decisions that I already had made link to the partner, so all was about going through momentum (what was happening inside my heart and mind). Acceptance (accept that I need someone to share my love and I had to allow my self to cry that still I had not found it). Goal (understand what I want and why I wanted in order to make peace with heart and mind). Inspiration (having that vision and imagination of that love I wanted and appreciating what I have that is better then going for someone to love me with out having the balance I was looking for it makes me full of inspiration and to love my self and life more). Commitment (to keep loving my self and life and keep the door open if some how the right partner can snick in to look at my kingdom). Affirmation (to remind my self why I am single and why I am looking for that kind of partner that I am looking for) and the last on love stage is all about shining, dancing, singing, smiling, loving and just be in love through each moment you experience.

To add to my example on session two to my client I summaries it in symbolic way so she can understand it better: is like… imagine a child who is rebilling and angry with out expressing why and they are throwing things , enjoying you , determined to get what they asking for and you sit down with that child to talk it through what is really going on, after the talk they start crying associated with they way they are feeling and then they start smiling and run way playing happy.

We do have three impulses for what I have notice from my self-discovery and through this research journey and they are explained below:

My theory of impulses:

1- Mind impulses: The Mind is a very important organ of our functioning as humans. If we use it under the guidance of our soul, it will take care of us and makes our journey easy because it is the computer that can store what we need to use in this reality. For example: if we don't look after our brain we will not be able to remember things and express ourselves through language. The brain and mind are the same word and are an important organ in order for our human parts to function physically and process the knowledge we get. This is when the impulse comes from your mind and is not associated with feelings or temptation but with calculated thinking. For example: you see a nice car, or nice house, or someone having money and nice life style, you have automatically think you should have it not them, that you should be in their place and even higher. If the impulse does not get processed by the soul then it will lead to shortcuts to get those things and your aims will be centered around it. There will not be time to think about who will be hurt or what are the consequences. The mind impulses comes from beliefs that are created to make the reality or how the reality should be from others perspectives, definitely not yours as you are not alloying your self to listen to you, to your soul and alloying your soul to make decisions, to do the reflection and analysis.

2 - Heart impulses: The heart is very a precious organ, as we feel through the heart and it is responsible for every sensation we feel. It is a fascinating process but at the same time it is very dangerous if we don't take care of the heart through healing it, using our soul, as I explained in magical module. What do I mean by good feelings? For example if something really bad has happened, such as losing a loved one, or losing all the wealth you worked all your life for, or being disabled because of something that happens to you......how can we turn those feelings into good feeling? Well ....it starts with the momentum stage allowing yourself to feel and think about what you are feeling and thinking through therapy or talking to family and friends. Then accepting what happened (again going through the stages of magical module it does help for any situation and any thing you straggling with). It means to accept that you are here in this life and the creator did not want you to finish this life journey yet for whatever reason that you have yet to discover. Yes, you do have a choice to end your life any time you want but you need to think through your inner thinking what you really want? If you want to end your life you are wrong if you think that that pain will go away because will not as you have to start a different life journey exactly in that personal development that you have achieved it so far. But of course most of people don't know this and it can not be proven but if you ask your self deep down and stay with that silence you will know exactly what I am talking about.

So the way forward is to love your pain because that will help you to find the light if you decide to search for light. You will not have reason not to search for the light. Like I said, the search for the light will automatically create good feelings. If you talking about the light as pure love and being the product of pure love, the search for pure love will help your heart to be healthy and feel good. Then you go through other stages of magical module to follow the search of pure love through that pain that you are experiencing. Impulses of the heart are very dangerous if they are coming from negative thoughts or thoughts that are not created in pure love within. Example: when you just want to be with someone even though you know that is not the person you can spend your life but you just want to satisfy your heart impulses. These impulses are so strong that it does not allow the mind to interfere. It Will just not listen to the mind because just want to satisfy the impulses. This definitely is not pure love and is not healthy for no one because you are hurting your self by being addicted to the wrong love and hurting the other person because you will end up arguing, fighting and not really loving each other. In this case again, you can heal your heart through inner conversation going through each impulses with compassion and understanding which will lead to help your heart see what is the best for your heart and what your heart really wants and how can it get it. The heart is place of love but need to make sure is place of pure love and not other feelings.

3 - Soul impulses: In my understanding soul impulses are when you have to do something because you feel you are doing good and you are acting for the betterment of something. As impulses are based on pure love, which is you is your soul. But when you act on soul impulses you are exposed to danger and you are not fully protected by creator and your circle energy of your soul. That is because you are acting on impulses with out reflection and analysis which mean with not fully on decision that you have considered.

All the stages are blended with each other and are linked which means all the clients I took through a flexible journey based on my skills and what the clients provided at the moment. For details of each client journey and work has been done refer to chapter seven. This methodology that has been explained in chapter three could be as general self-guidance for the reader to achieve self-love. Similar guidance I have used for all participant on this research but not in order as it depends where the individual is and what is helpful and useful for at the moment.

"Success is to find away how to be content in present and have clear vision of how you want your future journey to be. Flexibility is part of ingredients that goes on that say … is part of growing and becoming wiser and wiser everyday as product of pure love"

My skills are (I received those skills after I become product of love and I had desire to see others happy as it did not make sense just me being product of love and seeing suffering around, so I asked the creator to give me skills to helps others and I had to be creative to know exactly what I required):

1 - I connect with your soul (to know who you really are and what is your purpose in this life, this can be done through conversations with you) feeling the energy of your soul.

2 - Understands who you are... who you have become because of your life journey. .what has made you like that ... (through sessions we can discuss all that and understand it together ... to see if you like who you are or do you need to change in order to get what you want).

3 - Have a deep understanding of your actions… are they created to survive? Is all actions based on your survivor mechanism? I can help you to let go of your survivor mechanism so you can be able to enjoy life and not feel of need to survive. …. we are not here to survive but to enjoy life…. that is the main purpose of the creator and you can prove it after you achieve your self-love as after you achieve self-love you can see things clear and you will be able to prove it.

"Live like is the last day,

Like is the best day to create your future …

Like is the last day to be the best you can be and breath, feel, love, live "

CHAPTER VI

Concludes the work and summarizes the level of achievement of research aim and objectives. The chapter comprises acknowledgement of limitations of the study and highlights scope for future studies in the same research area.

LIMITATION

To come to a conclusion it is so important for the facilitator to have Self-Love, for me it has become part of my intuitive practice for the whole process. Self-Love has given me insight and a way of connecting with other souls and communicating through a higher energy in an holistic way. Communication skills and interacting with others are demonstrated through all chapters, but mainly in chapter seven. It sounds weird and definitely looks different, but it is important to practice Purity that works in coordination with the universe when working with others.

The actual results of the research and data collection can never offer an exact result as the data itself is based on an individual's insight, it is so varied and even if you collected the data from everyone in both quantitative and qualitative way, we still have to keep in mind how truthfully the questions have been answered. What is the truth? What do we want? Have we got what we want? How can it be answered? All these questions lead to the conclusion that we are just swimming in different ways, but acting like we are swimming the same way and without analyzing and re-teaching everyone to swim in the same way we will never get a synchronized answer. I am trying to understand and find out from this research the description of the root of the whole puzzle of life. This research brings an understanding of the root of life through data collection from case studies, observations, analysis from open-ended questions answered by children as young as 6 to adults combined with a conclusion from intuition. Considering that it is not enough to just focus on data collection, this study has blended intuition with the data. The whole process is guided by intuition.

What was so beneficial about my research was that during the process I managed to disconnect fully from reality and just focused all my awareness on the research aims and objectives. All I ask is that you acquiesce me to be connected to my higher energy as something that is halcyon and transparent and has helped me to connect with the participant, leading to self-discovery and purpose of the aim, 'Self-Love'. I discovered the importance in choosing a variety of people in order to achieve objective as possible results from our meetings. The process helped me understand where a person was coming from and how they were functioning. Guidance from the universe was instrumental in connecting me with the person who took part in this research, and then it was my decision to follow through the process. It was my responsibility to make the decisions into who to allow to be part of this process and who to let go of and that's why it was very important to be able to communicate with space all of the time. I needed to feel their energy, communicate with their soul and to understand where they are coming from with the answers they gave me, and to see if they had a sense of openness required to take part in my research. In essence, my approach appeared strange at first to the client and to other professionals, which of course brought challenges, however, this resistance only stimulated my intuition to a deeper level.

The 'limitation link' (as I like to call it) to my questionnaire is also something I feel is a benefit or I could use the term, "According to the Lord" and " the main rules" because it made participants automatically think about the Creator, religion, or even if they did not have a belief system, they may be against God and religion. Whatever their belief or non-belief is, the questions took away their responsibility which will take them away from having their own mind, the freedom of them being not controlled. However, in question two I did offer the opportunity for freedom, but directed them to think about guidance by using the word "rules". The word "rules" implies limitations because most of us question "rules", instead they liked the word " guidance". On the other hand the benefit was to raise their awareness of purity and if they don't use the ingredients of pure love they cannot find peace and love on their life journey.

Conclusion

Arriving to a conclusion from gathering analysis of aims and objectives of the research, literature review, results, case studies, questionnaires, social media observation, feedback from the "A Magical Life" book and the chapters on discussions, it is clear that self-love is key to understanding ourselves, others, life and to live a fulfilling life through peace and pure love. Client one has shown clearly how the seven stages of the Magical Module through my guidance has helped her to completely achieve self-love from her inner pure love connection. In addition she has felt like she has had to restart her life from scratch, but that did not stop her from continuing and practicing Self-Love in her everyday life, full of love and path to a meaningful journey. Furthermore, the other case studies have worked on their progress of Self Love and now have an understanding of the benefit even though there have been obstacles due to lack of self belief that has stopped them to continue the process of the Magical Module until the end. Most of the participants from the case studies have learned the importance of Purity and how to practice it in everyday life.

My aim was not to make others follow the process to the end if they didn't want to, but to test my theory with their free will which I was able to accomplish as outlined in chapter seven, also in chapter four I achieved the results I was so hoping for.

The book, "A Magical Life" was the blue print of my design, the test I wanted to do, to see if I could help others to connect with their childhood experiences and connect with their pure core that does exist and live in everyone.

Feedback from 15 readers of the book confirmed my aims and objectives of the book "A Magical Life" I was very proud of myself for achieving great results as when I wrote it I really did want to write it and not focus on what people may think. Although I know that my journey to self-discovery was my job and I finally felt fulfilled, in peace and love, I could not help feeling a sense of sadness in seeing others around me not being able to experience what I felt. For that reason I thought this is my duty! My next journey is to do something about it. I was guided by the/a creator to construct the 11 questionnaires just the way they are and how do I know that!!? Because I just did it in the moment while I was rushing to create it for an Albanian Muslim leader to ask him the same exact questions, it was the basis of my research. When I read the questions I was amazed as I do think they are very deep questions and important to help us connect with our pure core that is our soul. The results gathered from 50 participants aged from six years old to 66 year old and from different backgrounds was fascinating even for me and I think they are great help for the readers as there is some great guidance from their answers.

Furthermore, social media observation shows that how we run after reality with out stopping to have a proper inner conversation with our selves, for that reason we are caught on the flow of negative thoughts and hurtful feelings which leads to action with out our reflection and evaluation from our pure core, our soul.

Yes! Self-Love can be achieved and it is not about selfishness, egoism, or narcistic behaviour, Self-Love comes from pure love and you will know the difference because you will feel fulfilled, peaceful and loved. Even If you are practicing Self Love as explained in chapter three, through the Magical Module, based on pure love. This research has shown evidence in detailed steps on how to heal yourself from the past, be fully in the present and enjoy it 80% fully in the present or find ways to enjoy it, as well as expand on the remaining 20% where the imagination has no limitations; Where you are able to create a bridge between where you are and your dreams, by knowing how to claim each step. It is all about the 80% full presence in the moment, to focus on the here and now, because the here and now can help you heal from the past, stay in the present and help you to achieve the future you want.

Also I have explained through the research on how can we achieve Self-Love, what does Self-Love mean? Why do we need Self-Love? Why we humans are never happy unless we have Self-Love, why our body needs love, and why we crave love…Why do we need others to love us, what is it about that? What are the various perspectives such as religion, offer us a test on life that requires us to cleanse ourselves.

My findings lead to the conclusion that each individual has a responsibility to make themselves happy and the way to that is through their inner pure love that does exist in each of us. As I explained through the research, what is a soul? Does it exist? Is it only one religion? If yes, why are there so many religions with different purposes, what does science say about the vital aspect of love, how do various religions explain the serious life threatening diseases, what is a spiritual path? how can you find out who you are and why is it important to know the real you, why we die and what is the meaning of this life, are we meant to suffer or enjoy the life and how important is Self-Love to get the answer to all the above questions. Through this research I think I have got all the explanation and results that support how Self-Love can bring fulfilment, peace and love and how it can be achieved by following the steps I have put before you.

Unconditional love: **the meaning has to do with 3 main rules of life that I called self-love guidance.**

Every love that comes from the mind and heart is false. The love that comes from the soul is true. The distinction is made if the rules below are followed and if you feel complete and in love with who you are, without the need for someone else to complete you. This means you are one with your soul. If you feel lonely unhappy with these negative emotions and automatically search for someone to complete them, it means you are not connected to your soul. But on the other hand if you are, you know what person you are looking for and when they appear you will have the ability to spot them. However, what you require, you must first be like that; in the sense that you have to be at the level you are searching for. All of this shows and reiterates that if you love yourself, you achieve what you want and if you find that person she/he is just like yourself, but you enjoy the journey together. So you have to work with yourself in order to have a healthy relationship.

The Rules or Guidance for Self-Love:

- Love yourself the way you like to be loved.
- Treat others as you would like to be treated
- Do your best in everything that you do. (Do you know that you are doing your best? It comes through the inner conversations with your soul and your intuition).

The person who applies these rules knows that to give love to oneself and to others, but with diplomacy and care. Unconditional love is when the pure truth is spoken directly, but with love.

In my opinion and from my experience, the soul does not belong to a religion, but it recognizes a religion that is universal, which is only one, but because people start fighting with each other, then religion becomes a way of categorizing people. In order to help people to love again each other they need an opportunity and guidance for those around them to understand the love in each other, so religion. is nothing more than guidance on how to be the real you… you who loves yourself and loves others.

We can never know for sure exactly how to make, or have our life journey because we only know for sure that love is the foundation of everything and can bring peace and love to our life journey, but how to make that journey of life is not fixed as it is so dependent on other factors such as:

- Previous life consequences. a personal 'contract' with creator before we come to this life, when we are given options, usually a minimum of three options of life journey you can talk, and when we come to life it is our responsibility to remember who we are and to maintain self-love.

- The Foundation of reality at the moment …as that changes based on humans progress /actions/thoughts/purpose etc but again regaining the self-love you lost through growing up or for different factors can bring fulfillment.

- The influence of a pure human being is that they try to make sense of why they are in this reality and how they can make it happen, instead they listen to their inner calling. In this group there could be people who are already in a profession that involves helping others, but because they do not have self-love it makes them confused and sad as they crave love and compassion.

One of the reasons our body gets ill is the path we have chosen before we come into this journey, and lacking on practicing the pure love. The body needs pure love to be healthy, healthy food and exercise. Also I do think every illness can be healed through pure love and guidance from your soul. The only solution is Self-Love, Yes! that is true and if this world was in peace and love, it would results in the system of running countries more harmonious, people would be part of the positive changes to our society like how we make money, how we take care of the sickness and even affect our political stage and so much more!

I think this book is all you need to turn your life around and find your pure love that you know deep down you have been searching for, but did not know how to understand, or discover it. This is the book of Life! How to heal yourself from the past, how to be in the present and how to create the future you want. Anyone who is interested can follow this approach, but I will suggest that any psychologist should have knowledge of this approach, social services, charity organisations, education institutes, mental health institutes, hospitals and healthcare, as well as the scientist. Basically it involves every individual who is living. Love is the key to everything. By understanding yourself you will understand others, which improve any services that you are involved in.

"Love with the ingredients that goes with it is the key to open the door to fulfillment, peace and love for yourself and life with everything on it ....."......

"Remember the love is within you and only you can discover, no one can do it for you.... you have to dig deeper to connect with your inner love that you were born with. It is still there with you but cannot do anything without your permission."

"If a child can't learn the way we teach, maybe we should teach the way they learn." Ignacio Estrada

You are one with a pure vision of bringing benefit to the world. You never lose hope, because hope is you, or become discouraged, because you know that with your pure vision and intention you are one with the Creator and you have great power. Whether you're becoming a guide or teacher for others, or writing books, however you support others you have to have achieved Self Love in order to have the ability to help others. Any individual who has accomplished Self-Love is fulfilled, at peace and loved, which mean the individual is successful already. By keeping your vision pure and elevated, your thoughts become a means of bringing about a pure manifestation. When we keep our minds and outlook, or our vision that is pure and true, we are able to stay focused on our goals without wavering. For this, we must be careful of the influences we allow into our lives, big and small. We must evaluate and only allow in the support and influences, which are in alignment with our goals. This helps us to keep our vision and thoughts pure, and enables us to meet the elevated task we are here for. It helps us to keep the balance of our fulfillments, peace and love within and to spread it to the outside world in whatever we do.

"I know you're here for something unique and special and mostly you are very special and are here to enjoy the beauty of life."

"Children are great spiritual teachers, lets enjoy being in this wonderful life"

"Live like is the last day,

Like is the best day to create your future ...

Like is the last day to be the best you can be and breath, feel, love, live"

CHAPTER VII

CASE STUDIES

Case study 1

Background:

She is a female about 25 years old. When came to ask for my help, she wanted just counselling sessions as she was looking to find inner peace from. The opinion of family, friends and others towards her was disturbing and causing lots of unhappiness. But that was not really the issues as I notice in first sessions and as together we discovered underlined issues that were making her stressed and depressed and as she quoted "if I stay longer in this situation, I will loose it, I will go crazy".

Direct and indirect therapy:

The indirect therapy has been duet to my constant spiritual connection with her soul, her energy and her magical person. When she came to me I heard what she brought, as it is previously mentioned in her background.

We first met in an event and I introduced myself as a psychologist. She approached me during the break, and asked me to repeat what I said early in introduction. Then she said that she wanted my help. I asked her to tell me more why she thought she needs it help and she explained the reason. She wanted help to know how to deal with people's opinion and she wanted to continue to talk but I stopped it by giving my number and offering to see her in private environment. Furthermore I said, "you look like someone who knows how to find solution".

She looked me with those gloomy eyes, immersed in a deep darkness that seemed no way out, but at the same time with a glimpse of absurdity asking her self in silence "could I find a solution to things!!" She explained that was not good with the roads and asked me where the meeting will take place. I gave her the options. I preferred to meet the clients in nature for healing purpose and they will feel more relaxed. She agreed but she had to confirm it with her friend to come with her to show the way. That was our first chat and then we did not talk anymore during the event as I was keeping my distance from everyone and just observing more. My impression of this meeting was that she was in really deep depression and was confused, lost, hopeless, felt small, like she was there but did not exist. Second time we meet in another event. My intuition was telling me to go and say hi as I had not heard from her since the first event. I felt like she wanted to come to me for help but she was feeling embarrassed, low self-confident and no self-esteem at all. All this is what I felt, no one told me any information, were just based on my intuition, but later she confirmed all what that I was feeling and thinking were right. I went and said "hi" with warmth and she said "I will contact you soon". No worries I said when you are ready. She was there with the same friend that she was in the other event.

After some time, she contacted me and arranged a meeting. We had long 3-hour session because as need it to fill few forms to help her think and be aware of the way she is feeling or who she is (later on when I reviewed her forms she had written that her wish was to write a book. When I mentioned after few months, she was not aware of it. This showed me that the environment and the energy made her link with her soul – magical person). After the introduction and initial assessment she felt opening up. In this session, I was mainly listening and doing just 20% of talking. My talking would help her to make a link with her magical person and actual person that she was being. The purpose was to make her aware about what is really disturbing. Between sessions was homework to be done to use through mindfulness in purpose to understand who she is, who she wants to be, and how she can love herself.

Another meeting took place in one-week time. Through those three sessions she had started to believe in herself and starting understand the important of loving herself. Through encouragement to help her to face the actual reality and take active and responsibilities steps towards what she really wanted. I could see her purpose, the potential of the options she had through her eyes, and by communicating with her magical person and by knowing her journey. Understanding herself was the only way to find peace with past, be in present and work towards dreams. She was confused, scared, and felt hopeless. I told her that is no point me seeing her if she does not take responsibility to change and take actions. Because I didn't notice actions moving forward on the way she was staying in the situation she was in. She was in deep depression, suffering from her past, not wanting the present and not knowing what she wanted or how her life could be. She was terrified about the idea doing something for herself, and she did not explain how she was driven to meet me. Further more she said the reason was drove to me was because her inner voice was telling her to ask me for help and to tell me all her secrets. Her explanation for deciding to take actions and followed my guidance blindly, was as it was resonating with her inner voice. I believed that she really need it help and my support so I felt responsible not to help her even though was first time for me doing that kind of process.

Now that I asked her why she followed my guidance even when she did not understand the techniques and methods, she still tried them and worked through them. Although it was her inner calling but also was the wish she had made once back on time to be fulfilled, couple of years back and she had received the answer that would meet somebody like me one day to guide her and she felt that energy of purity in me.

In fourth meeting she was feeling very low but somehow, she felt safe because she had someone supporting her. Through the launch she felt relaxed to express her concerns. She wrote in the note book all her goals, concerns, her monthly plan, her actions towards her goals and few relaxation techniques to help her be in present and focused on the moment. She very easy could be blocked and gets stuck in her past and her fear of going back or what will happen with her life. Because of her mental state she had my support through emails, calls and text in anytime. I felt she needed this because she was fragile and she needed a pillar to hold on to. I noticed it was so easy for her to fall down. She had her light on, which was her inner calling but it was absurd for this reality and my light needed to keep her reminding about the connection to her light. That is why I felt the need to be connected to her 24 hours in spiritual level and communicate with her at leas 4 hours a day. In those 4 hours, it can be seen in her feedback about my therapy, that it was more about finding a balance of the magical person with her actual person she had built up based on reality. She did not agree with the person she had become but did not know how to change. I took her through each stage of Magical Module in very detailed techniques, which you can see below in some of our conversations and dialogues.

The first three months it was all about making her become aware of the magical person she is.

The second trimester it was about her taking small steps towards harmonizing the actual person in reality with the magical person.

The last trimester, she demolished her old structure and built a new structure based on her true magical person that she really was.

During these 9 months, we both grew so much spiritually and we expanded our magical environment. We explored so many topics that are mentioned in the Magical Module. It was the time now for her to fly. During this time one of her techniques was to take part in the MC (Magical module) program 'Heal yourself through writing your book'. She was half way through her manuscript. But she had not included the sky on the book and that has to do with her flying. Now it was the time for me to disconnect with her, let her measure her ground and know where she stands, so she could fly on herself, living in the harmony of the magical person that she is and acting on that all the time. For several months she had been fluctuating between falling and standing up. In the beginning, only when she was with me she was in that soul space. In the second trimester she managed to be one day a week, then gradually 3 days a week, until in the ninth month she was stabilized and remaining all the time in that way.

We did not keep in touch for a whole week, and when I contacted her I could feel, and she admitted that she had flown that week. I was really greatly surprised and happy for her. I asked to make notes and describe it in her book. She had a clear idea on how to do the structure of the book and was going to be. And now, she said wow, my book is going to be exactly as you said: philosophical, psychological and very… very deep. I was pleased about it because in a way I had imposed the writing of that book on her. And soon you will know her identity when she is ready to come out, because her book will be deeper than my first book 'A magical Life'. The effect of my book is to shake the foundations revealing the person's true self – their soul / magical person starting from their childhood and the structure they have built but due to various influences or troubles in life of a person in order for the person to connect with their soul and through their soul create with their creator and the universe energy. This is reflected on the feedback received from clients and readers. But her book will explore and provide deep explanations on how to demolish the old unnecessary structure and build a new one based on the truth of soul / and guidance of the magical person that each of us is.

I really hope her future will continue to be bright the way has started since then with the support she has got around where she is living from all the professionals that she is in contact. She has started to be aware of learning how to let go of the past and she knows that it takes time, she has started to appreciate what she have and use it in useful way to heal herself and she is in progress of believing on her abilities and that she can have a future. She still have very dark moments where everything goes dark because she cannot see hope and feels tired of fighting to believe in good things and herself. She thinks that nothing good happen to her, only bad things and she does not understand it, but that's why she is alloyed to call me anytime she feels like that so slowly start going through her thoughts, pain, plans in present and the people she has around to help her.

First trimester of therapy (notes, reflections, impressions, conversations)

Client: Hi, ... I was delayed to send you the email you requested... Then somehow I was involved in gossips and gossips ... I forgot that I could not handle gossips... Today I have been feeling very low and bad. Totally blocked, I know that I have the commitments of the moment... But people who are lost and gossip make me feel worse.... I am still wondering on my head a lot that what I have to do....after reading your email I answered the question... I'm different after I answered the questions, more calm... Hope that the anxiety of the day before will pass ...

Vjollca: Good evening... Thank you very much for trying and really plunging deep into your inner world. Two things I would like to explain in more detail what are the meaning in your view and what would you say?????

1 - Internal fear? What is it, where does it come from, how do you understand it and what does it feel like?

2 - Why do you just say the sentence as a theory "I will manage it, I will not give up" ... Maybe I'm wrong but I feel you do not believe it and you really have to discuss with yourself.

Client: ....If I give up probably I will be where I started or even worse... If I do not give up, I'm fighting for myself. Wherever if I don't fight for my self who will fight for me? How others can fight for me when the do not understand how I feel and how my situation is ? ....alone....no one.... Anxiety is created by the overload that I have. I should be able to overcome the anxiety. Anxiously I do not get things I think he is created with the inner fear I have... It's worth fighting because it is important for me to achieve my aims. Maybe tomorrow I can be someone else, a person who is healed. The tomorrow can find myself in a non- existence... We live in the present (the situation of the cast that seems to me with hope and the lost) The past shows us the success that can bring the future ... if I exist in future... In every situation you think you lost or won, you are very involved ... if this passes... when we turn our head after we are surprised with ourselves and our involvement ... this is coming to mind from your poems that I have read once...

Client: (in another email as I have asked her to reflect daily or weekly on her self and write to me the first three month of our therapy) Maybe I should be emotionally thrilled with my self ....not sure to feel proud... but I wondered what is happening with those professionals that make jokes with me and I look as I am a joke to them This it something to do with them or they just don't care and they make my situation difficult!!! Anxiety is created because of situations I am experiencing and facing. Overcome by situations but with anxiety, it does not regulate what I have to fight for. I'm just hurting myself, I'm demoralized, anyway I'm afraid... I feel an overwhelming fear... ?

Client: (another week) I have a meeting with the lawyer I am confused and without hope.... I did this plan:

- Conversation with my self what do I want from the solicitor?
- How to seek it?
- Do I have to be scared?
- How to understand that she is helping me?

Client: This week has passed as many others with an added of anxiety on my part for the meeting with the lawyer... You advised me how to act, I strictly stick to my story and truth... To create techniques how to cope with the everyday stress... By not doing things is creating stress... I think it is created even when it remembers some bitter things. To face the lawyer it stresses me, to insist on my rights to say the truth It serves me... We have spoken beyond this problematic. When I talk about a glittering glimpse (with people I have during the day), you know that there is always something to do with people... It happens that we sometimes prejudge but you have not encountered this phenomenon... There are people who want to learn from those who are learning with difficulty, I think I'm involved in both groups because things depend on situations ... but when you say that everyone has the opportunity to change and it depends on how much we are connected to the soul.... at makes me believe that is true.

Client: At any moment we have different ways of reflection ... You have said you need to paint or draw my dream... I once thought of it as a template because I was always not good at painting.... But when I tried to write with two flashes in an instant: "We dream but never know how to dream. " person suffers dreaming, so how will person live with reality " This was not science but I found myself in these expressions of this person that is endowed with selfishness and does not look a bit... It is enough to understand a little bit of a little bit of the many important issues... ese reflections that I have today come to me from conversations with you, always say that the person can ... and this is worth a lot... before we even prejudge even a misfortune a person should think "HOW CAN I HELP?! " If we have managed to help, however modestly for us is a new and secure step... I do not want to make you nervous when I say for a hundred times same things because I forget a lot. The inner fear I have is making me worried ... you said that is originated from the past ...I actually know... But I wonder how I CAN remove this fear that stops me from keep being blocked .... I need your help a lot... I'm going back to the lawyer anxiety because I'm worry it.... many questions come to my mind. Will I convince her that this is my true story? How? I know what you going to say but I still need your help on this topic as I find my self stuck on anxiety. I have three days... ?!?!?! I Hope I'll manage it, do you know why?! Because when I think where I was when I come to you the first time and how much I have improved on myself it gives me strength and inspiration, that anything can be achieved and overcome.

Client: I don't know why I'm my thoughts are messy on my head ...

I calm my self but time-to-time I become overwhelmed with stress, worries, anxieties and I feel hopeless. You tell me that I'm using techniques, and I'm surprised at myself... When you clarify it, it seems to me that it is easy to understand things. When I'm alone I get messy on my head. "Vjollca speaks firmly... Who am I?" You tell me poems, ... I think they are the mess on my head….

Client: (another conversation) Vjollca suggested to talk to myself with these techniques:

- The guidance from the soul on things that what worries me that are to do with my heart, that I know why I those feelings involved in it are blocking and damaging me but I don't know why I'm powerless.

- To listen to my mind I think it should be done through positive thinking of the soul and I need it to make it work in positive way and add positive energy to work without any impacts.

- Feel your heart I think my heart would know how to make the difference between what I want and what I need. She may like many things that are naturally asserted but should do some other things. I think the heart needs to wake me up through reflection. Do not turn from optimism to pessimism and vice versa.

- Analysis

I don't know why I still feel blocked again.

Client: (May reflection) The soul is sensitive, but sometimes it is with the evilness of some worthless things my heart asserts I know it does not affirm, as it does not understand. Is no life…when is no motivation (a conversation with someone a word said in vain ...) The heart often pushes and maybe in frustration feels hurt but the mind stops me because I don't want my energy to remain in this person in this condition. I want to take my step without this person without this motive and listening to the mind. Please help me with this thoughts as It's torturing, nothing more ,I want to pumper my self and to embrace it with hug, smile, love the way you have suggested the techniques to use, but I do not know why I'm blocked as whole?!

Client: I don't know how I got to talk about events that were really hurtful…… I was bound to talk about worry, about "lethargy sleep" from where you woke me up   Often "your iron will" it does shake, I am changing, I'm starting to hope I'm thinking this facade of life as a maze of solutions I am in the furnace of hope given by you to "abduct my" time ….

Client: Sometimes things seem to have solutions as close to the solution to being. A deep knot of the soul as it solves without understanding. ..there is the magic I know as well. Fury was my opinion to change but how I said it would change; you do not always like it. I, perhaps, I was the cause for a Tendency theory. I have been silent and insulted here, but there is one reason for another   I existed to be as I was about to wake up from the fatal anxiety that was within me. You talk to me and I was concentrating here now, here I did if I understood and I understand. When you talk (the fiercest) I am relieved but the next day strangely, I rebuked myself for seriously feel rebuked, broken while you say go fight yourself   Nothing is worth more than understanding someone, the silent motive of someone, and this mine was "fortunate pose" …

What do I learn?

I learn to many things and the more I listen you talking about life with the added hopes that it can come from You saying breath-taking things, things that not everyone does. Such as I want to change politics, people, I want to come to the aid of those who need it these things are commonplace to say in the present time but as I hear from you everything seems possible the individual has to use intuition as you say and I think it is true.

What don't like?

When you speak with firm and strictly voice, I notice that something is not going well with me but anyway, I still feel good. Your thoughts are very fond of, are very noble in essence ...

How Do They Impact?

Although it seems unbelievable, but I find myself very much in those thoughts ... knowing how I'm going to be in the future but these are rare thoughts, listening to today that someone tries to "change the world".

What does it reflect?

What I'm reflecting is that -there can we go out if we decide on it (it's not easy to get it). You must be yourself in order to achieve your goals not someone who is self-hypocrisy. That I hear you speak changing the world, it look like a dream but I know it can happen if we really want something.... and I know .... I continue to hope ... Can I be different one day ...?!

Client: I pray five times a day and pray I saw these prayers simply as a ritual because I did not have concentration. Today I am different.

Conversation with my self: Why do you think like you are stuck and feel like you are dying inside yourself? Why am I not like all the other girls who laughing and play with a smile and talking about things that seem to me to be useless ... ?? They also have the same motive as me but they seems more in peace then me, the divine thinking system has become a positive one I am not filling myself with pieces of moments that can even give me a real smile I know you'll scold me I know how I look like a moan but so I feel I hope to be one day more in peace and maybe happier..

Client: (conversation on soul relationship connection)
"I used to be so into for a spiritual bond in relationship " you said. We both laughed a lot during our conversations... I try to explain the case of the "spiritual bondage in relationship" of the one who opposes: No spiritual attachment may have a person but can be manipulated ... Absurdity seemed to me the spiritual bond because I had always seen it as a sublime sensation that I was thinking of the side things.   Is love different from the spiritual bond? Yes it is

different, You know a new man Something that has admirable features and values and a spiritual bond is created ... Are there two: Spiritual bondage + love? They together, it would be a lottery   How much we laughing, how simple are some things that we make a big deal of them and we complicate   However, a spiritual connection has a limit .... I hope so much about this   message: The denominations of the spiritual bondage "thought of the true value of soul ... The claim that this thing is irreplaceable. e reason for the situation is that you can see this with the eyes of the truth…

Vjollca: Spiritual bondage of relationship means that the person you know in another life, nothing more, does not mean that he is the right person or is divine bond, it simply means that you have someone you know and do not even know how you knew it, but you just feel the close connection, nothing more. The person of true love is the one you think and desires with the mind, heart, and soul. So as you yourself are a person with the character and personality you love and love is based on the souls of both, therefore people must be connected with their souls to create spiritual love and have to agree and like the person have become based on their mind and heart. You have to love the whole person not just spiritual way.

Client: (reflection of the day) You say you have to evaluate things. This is strange to me .. The moment should be enjoyed, I have to fight anyway, I have entered this journey and whatever the outcome is, it is the victory for me… In fact, no one ever knows what…

Client: (another day reflection) This weekend I have stayed at home. Yesterday was a different day   Casually I saw in you tube a title "Life story" There were many stories   I continued to reflect on myself. What a miracle that some moments look like the end of the world ... and in fact there is again a rebirth   ere are moments that come to fruition ... there are moments that life takes different stems   When we talked together and read your poems I thought that person passes on certain stages without understanding, lives the moment and many things I look at the turbulence often found in the fury of feelings and their collision the person does things that you think in one to Going looks wondering how he acted In your poems to see you talking to yourself, and the only comfort you had was the diary. They live with the disappointments of the patters of happiness to throw and wait   However, that sadness thought remains beautiful even when you describe it.

Vjollca: Thank you, I am surprised and I wonder that how you have followed my instructions in so short time. ...

Physical signs (insomnia in this case)
- Pay attention
- Ask what is happening
- Start to ask your self-different questions
- Answers from different voices (mind, logic, intuition, soul, lord or heart)
- Analyses, discusses
- -Challenge your self and listen to your own critics
- -Be creative
- -Plan with details
- -Vision and daydream

Although I had said you still hesitate to say this thing that happened because you thought it was something absurd and crazy.

Client: In fact, it seemed to me crazy and unknown to say that I have some days sleepless   I try to sleep but lots of thoughts come to my head.   strangely to me come thoughts how to be more advanced and educated, more knowledgeable and where I want to be one day (not in an egoistic form) then inebriation itself is boredom but I am aware of as it is helping me to be creative I ask my self how can I achieve those things?! Questions that make me as blurry as clear as possible in same time, and me so confused by throwing me from one corner of my mind to another. ... All this make me the other person... makes me different I feel a fighter (even though at the moment I am in silence). I have clashes of thoughts that disturb my sleep and comes quick another thought against the other thought.... it creates dilemma.   When I told you about the sleepless problem, and you suggested the dilemma is the deliberate discussion to strengthen the mind-set, plan, vision of the future   to know where to start ... After the dilemma comes creativity, scale plan and time .... Strange that I'm thinking so   And how will this be the next day that I know ...

Feedback for the first 3 month

This feedback was the first week: Things are transparent.   anything is possible. I was confused; I thought I couldn't do it. Nothing I would give value. I thought a world black and white. After the first session I started crying ... I thought I could reborn in my soul. To love life, to evaluate myself, what I have been searching   I thought my problems could be solved. I started to believe on my self, I started to see the life with colours. I start thinking I can do it. My experiences and feelings can not described in words   I'm willing to describe your help ... I just want to point out that the idea to find myself has been forgiven and it is you who helped me to find my connection to my self again. Thank you for everything you did for me.

After 2 weeks feedback:

I do not know how my sprained nature agreed to talk about sorrows and the lethargic sleep whence you woke me up... Often, your iron will makes me quiver, but I feel different. I'm starting to have hope. I think there is a maze of solutions under this life's facade. I stay in the intense hope that you extracted from my time.

Second trimester: (After three month work)

Summary of this session through those three months: She is very isolated and I have been trying very hard to encourage her to do little steps each day   which for her are really difficult but she has to fight... in order to get things done. She is not still feeling well as she is still having feelings of being unworthy, hopeless, suicidal thoughts as she get disappointed from professionals around that are involved on her process. Every day through those months the aim was to help her with the confidence and self-esteem to keep going and not give up. Moreover to keep being creative and curiosity towards observing her thoughts, feelings and actions in everyday and time to time if it come up the past just to go by flow and visit it. In mean time I did ask her to read my book "A Magical Life" so she could write down her thoughts through reading it. Those three months I just may asked her to write reflection of our conversation if she feel like it or any time she felt saying something she could just write to me. Her reflections are below:

Client: I was thrilled with the first your words of the report you send to me about me. I remember myself as I repressed and I had my own hope ... I feel I'm awake but not in the stage I want ... I feel that I can do the right things but I'm sometimes numb ... I'm anxious about situations link to other professionals. How much they will you do and how much the will laugh at my troubled soul ... As I think this way, I cry and who will understand me…? I want to do volunteer work, I hope to do it ... I'm so confused emotionally and I have massy thought on my head.

Vjollca: Remember what I have said to you time to time that you have talent on looking things on very deep level and you are very unique as I have reflected on the advice you give to others and the way you see things… I read your report that you wrote for me and it was really good, but what I like is to get in more deep level of your soul. What made you to trust me? Why did you need my help when you had other professionals helping you after the first month we worked together? Why do you feel a dull energy when you are with me and when do you think about me as whole process?   What makes you to be focused on your dreams and goals? Why do you accept my firm way of talking sometimes when is need it to have the firms? Why do you trust my guidance? So if you can add those question to your report that you have send me as feedback for the whole six months of work together, I would appreciated.

Feedback after 6 month: (client's report for the six month work on magical module)

A DETAILED REPORT
The counsels of a psychologist make you confess. I did not think I would be able to confess, but I thought that I had to take a step simply to try a new thing - the sensation that had to be tried by a new step.
At an event where we were going for a trip to London, and Vjollca was invited to that trip. She was introduced to me as a psychologist. This gave me a different feeling... I really wanted to talk... I found a moment and with no confidence at all, I began to talk (in a summarized form, where we established that I would write to her; a step that I did not take even today -I don't know why, I just did not believe that random things would happen to me). Again, I saw her at the in another event. Vjollca was a guest there and she approached me, asking me why I had not written to her... For the first time, I felt an appreciation... So, I decided to write ... I would continue 6 sessions with her (I did not have an understanding of what I was doing - simply my intuition was telling me to keep going).

I followed the first session. I was with a friend because I did not know the way, nor did I think what things to say, since I was taught to the keep the common, daily truths tied after myself... I continued talking and words went out unknowingly. I was shocked, troubled; I only felt my being and an incomprehensible sensation. I cried and spoke and felt hope. It was a long session, it lasted almost three hours, which gave me feelings and anxiety (feelings that 'I'm a person with abilities and anxiety', that 'what am I doing!!!'). While I was returning home, I was a different person, confused.

The only thing that came to mind was: 'Can it be that I have value too? Could I really have a different life?' The lived time of my life was really hurrying in my head and I was weeping...

Our counselling sessions would follow every Friday at 10:00 in the morning.

I eagerly waited for the next coming session; the only thing I thought was that 'there should be a benefit in this situation I am running towards, without understanding'.

I wanted to repeat the same things. The initial responses that I had received from Vjollca, felt very surprising and I thought: 'this time might be according to me, but the tone of her voice sounded different sometimes. Nothing contained melody, not even me - I had been lost for all this time.

Vjollca's facial expression made me think that 'I should regenerate myself', but strangely every time I thought of this, I just felt bad...

For every word that I would say, Vjollca provided an explanation, found solutions that to me had been just shots of little sparks, which had passed by without me noticing (but what about when a life goes in vain, due to not being in harmony with ourselves and not being able to achieve the awareness???)

Vjollca's dialogue consisted of quietness sometimes but I was in for a bigger frenzy and my heart went away when I was telling Vjollca my point of view and she persisted that 'acting according to the heart is not always useful', many notions of my own continued to fall. Sometimes, we create taboos in our head and do not know how to act differently... We try to insist and convince others through our own way...

In the third session, Vjollca asked me several questions (which were crucial to me) about my life. She was inspiring me to take a new step in this country: 'Ask for asylum because you have a truth of your own that has to be said'. I have to say I replied with my usual suspicions, in fact all my life was filled with doubts. Based on the questions that Vjollca asked me, I expressed my painful story, which I could not believe that it was being actually told by me so voluntarily. When I was returning home, I was thinking a lot about my life - how things had been so difficult and how I had never made an evaluation of it. 'Writing, helps a lot', Vjollca would say to me 'express everything by writing in your notes, do not shrink' ... *During my journey home, I remembered thinking that I had had a passion for writing, but I had not thought that writing an autobiography would help me so much.* I kept talking to Vjollca over the phone telling her that I was continuing to keep notes for myself, whereas she always advised me 'to allow the thoughts freely' and I was feeling more and more peaceful by the expression of things in the notebook... I felt stronger; I had someone to talk to about my occasional or momentary observations, it was my notebook...

During the 4th session, Vjollca suggested that I applied for asylum and to tell my story exactly as it was. She helped me to go there, suggesting that I should not give up from the rightful expression of things.

I did it as Vjollca was with me, I felt stronger. She always whispered 'do not forget the truth in any situation'. That day immersed me into another direction of life, sent me to the unknown that was waiting for me...

Report: Knowing Yourself (continuing)

I continued to adapt myself in a London hostel. I still could not believe what was happening to me. I had started a new step. I met Vjollca again in London. It was a day before leaving for a place outside London.. She continued to support me, thinking about positive things for me, to make me love myself more. I was growing confident even though I had not yet understood what to do ... In the morning I had to leave London.

That day was a day of anxiety and senselessness. I was constantly listening to Vjollca's words that 'I would be able to be alright in the place I was going'. I could not even think what my alright was... My heart felt like ice. The only thing that went in my mind was to tell myself: 'For you, everything in life has been difficult and this is not an exception...' I stayed for two weeks in the hostel. I did not know how to act, or how things would go. The only one that I was talking to, was Vjollca. She was constantly guiding me on how to do things for myself. I had to find a lawyer, to register with a GP practice, to find a college, to search for a psychologist, because only those sessions could improve my condition... Everywhere I asked, I was told that I had to firstly be accommodated at a home and then ask for these things, whereas the discussions with Vjollca were getting even more frequent, as I felt unable to understand how the process I had already entered in, continued...

To Discover Your Skills:

Faced with those difficulties and in a hopeless situation, I had to be accommodated from the hostel to a home. It was a house close to the city. I went there and everything seemed to start from the beginning (a beginning that I could not understand where it started). I was just destined to follow Vjollca's guidance mechanically: 'Do your things and do not forget to always say the truth'. The days were continuing in the house I was accommodated. I had done nothing for myself… I simply felt no purpose.

I was convinced more and more each day, that I had to do things for myself. Every word from Vjollca was being verified. I went to the GP on my own, even though I did not know anything about the procedures, but with Vjollca (on the phone) I managed to fill out the form and register. I had a lot of headaches. I told them that I wanted to have my head seen but they sent me to a nearby place. I told them that I did not know the way to go there, but they did not 'listen'. A random woman helped me (probably realizing that I was in trouble really, she accompanied me by car to a nearby GP). Nothing changed that day except my deteriorating condition. When I tried turning back, I did not know the way or how the bus worked, or the tickets ...

I saw that a bus was passing by and I asked if it went towards my GP's address. I had the papers in my hands and was very focused, not knowing what I was doing. The driver nodded and I got in. I said: " I do not have a ticket and I do not even know how to find the address I am going to. 'I do not know how he accepted me without a ticket ...as soon as I got off. I talked to Vjollca and told her what had happened. She told me I had to talk to the GP about these things...I felt defeated. I communicated with the receptionist who was with me while Vjollca was telling me to pass the telephone to her. After she explained my situation to the receptionist, I was supported by her. So in this manner, as if I was falling, I registered with the GP practice following Vjollca's help…

There were still so many things to do ... the meeting with the solicitor was not done and this frightened me; how would she be and how much would she would help me with my case? ... I continued to attend English and computer courses at an organization in the area where I lived and felt somewhat hopeful...

The meeting with the lawyer was a stressful situation. Vjollca repeated: 'Always say the truth'! The story, the words the experiences are yours. Only you can convince her '. Everything was so unknown and difficult for me...

The psychologist's sessions were also difficult. They were 12 in total. As time went by, my meetings with the psychologist became dearer than before. She continued to help me very much spiritually; it seemed like she understood my pain. My sessions with the psychologist ended. I felt bad that I was not going to talk about my problems, but the meetings with her had left me worthy words. She was one of the people who had stood by me...

To act, knowing what is the place of the heart, mind, soul in that situation.

The days were passing by and I felt somewhat more stabilized in terms of my conditions. Everything - even though it was not easy - already had an orientation... My meeting with the psychologist had taken a different direction: from the idea to go and 'confess', to the idea of finding myself and doing things for me... Sometimes life takes its turn and thanks to Vjollca, I became another person, I believed that I could be different.

Since the achievement of things is never easy, and my conditions have rarely wanted to focus on a common course, the heart has always been comforting to my actions, the mind often helped the heart – 'you are doing a lot, you are capable, you are good'. These things troubled me so often, that I sometimes did not understand myself ... "The connection with the soul is more difficult but it is achievable. For me it is an inner voice that constantly calls, although we hear it in a hurry" ... these things I listened with curiosity from Vjollca when she spoke and reproached me for the actions that I was taught to ordinarily take ... "Walk upwards if you love yourself and your life, be creative and pure, walk straightforwardly and you will always be winning...follow the intuition because it is never incorrect" she constantly said. It is a little difficult for it to be worth it, to walk with the steps of truth but it should be done. Vjollca's disciplinary way was therapy or perhaps for me it was the true therapy. When I complained about something, Vjollca told me I had to think deeply about things "do not walk according to the heart's rhythm or with what is embedded in the head (fixed thoughts of the mind). Connect with the soul, communicate more, analyse things, not just using them as a template"... this has made me to always believe that one needs to know how to control the thoughts coming from the self...

How to behave in the moment:

The instant comes suddenly or we can be somewhat prepared for a part of a situation that we think might happen to us ... My helpful instants have been clearer to me when I met Vjollca (by her applying on me, her module). 'Ask yourself' - this is something that can find its passage so fast that we cannot even think it, in fact we are inclined to say that we know something with certainty, but since I am an introvert this did not help me - to ask myself again??? Many questions came to me about the situation I was in, and about my situation beyond this situation. When I talked with Vjollca I always had to analyse the situation. For instance: 'Why am I afraid to face a solicitor? Do I have an idea in my head? How does this idea work and what for? Should I overcome this fear? How? 'So I continued to wonder. There were immediate questions and with much difficulty I had to provide a solution from the soul's language, not from the usual mind or the comfort of the heart... in the moment we can face reality – this makes the situation more difficult somehow, than the thoughts, which require time ...

My Aim:

At the meeting with Vjollca or the randomness of the meeting, the idea that pushed me instantly was that I had to talk to someone and the introduction that Vjollca was a psychologist. The idea was to confess and then to walk with little guiding steps on her part. These enabled me to go higher within my personality...

Now I had goals, I felt more capable, safer, and could do things. If until yesterday I had conquered my life and its obstacles with my silence, now I had to reflect. I could do things and I verified this during Vjollca's therapy with me. Although there was the lack of appreciation that I missed in my life, I had a self-belief that I possessed the ability to be useful in a different manner...worthy of myself...I want to be myself, to have a pure soul and worthy of truth, life...I want to be a living thing, righteous and responsible ...I can ....

My Achievements:

I can get out of the no-return situation where I was (with distorted dreams, of a difficult life without a way out) I am finding myself (the small steps have always increased my self-confidence based on Vjollca's guidance)
Being true to my ideas, beliefs and thoughts (fear should be overcome; not being her slave, things should be analysed).
To be responsible. If once, my responsibility was to remain silent, with the same ideas in my head, today I have to reflect, think, discuss and feel the weight of things and the role in this weight...
Facing the situation, when one has someone who they consider as a guide in life, brings a sense of security, one is obedient to their mission...
The second interview (the anxiety of whether I was in time, confusion of trains, the loss of my ticket, the blockage before the interview, Vjollca's exercise to understand myself ...

Note: I have accomplished this writing, which I call a report, guidance of my "new" path with the idea of expressing the work and my intensive therapy from Vjollca Sadiku. I want to say THANK YOU to her, since the actions speak much more...and have value. These written words have been extracted from my own experiences during this period, for which I kept notes (every day that I have passed, as techniques learned from Vjollca)

Third trimester: (after six months intensive therapy)

 Below will be part of our work during this three months and the main was to keep practicing the theory that has been learned and move to advance level to be guided by the soul and heal the heart through the love of the soul as keep replacing the thoughts with the ones from the soul instead of those that have been created from others and during the journey she had so far. Moreover as part of her therapy I started to use her skills as mentoring me. So we started our conversation with what she had to say, we both discuss/reflect on what the she said then I would may bring time to time something that I need it guidance and she will offer her guidance as you can see through our conversations below.

Vjollca: (September months) Its time to start your book and should be done by end of this three months. The guidance you have it written and just use the language of the soul, the one you are using wright now talking to me in order to fulfil your purpose of helping others with your book.

Client: Hahahha

Vjollca: What is to laugh about

Client: Nothing

Vjollca: (October month) I have send through email you the questions that I want you to fill when you find time and to let me know what are your thoughts link to the questions.

Vjollca: Just be you ...
Don't forget who you really are, do you know your soul? that's what really matters. ..being you and everything will be just like you.

Vjollca: The exercises will be based on this below and 7 chapters of Magical module (kids book and adults book):
Do the whole book on wellbeing:

1 - who you are
2 - what the life means
3 - others
4 - whet you are at the moment/what you like and what you don't like
5 - what you like about you and life
6 - what you like when you grow up ...who you want to be
7 - goals
8 - the journey from where you are and where you want to be
9 - what you need to make the journey achievable and enjoyable
10 - which affirmation you need to tell your self in order to keep being you
11 - how can we keep loving others and ourselves and spread love around us

Client: I had a call to attend the appointment and I am worried.

Vjollca: Just be you and be focused on what you need from that appointment. Don't confuse your self with overthinking as we talked about. Just practice and be calm, focus on your best interest. Write the plan on how you going to be calm and focus.

Vjollca: I am still waiting for your that I suggested.

Client: What plan uffff, maybe will be a negative respond. Vjollca: So you make the plans for both possibilities.

Client: If is positive outcome, I will show the email and I will explain, if is negative outcome I don't know what to do....what can I do?

Vjollca: it is very easy to complain and feel sorry for yourself but is harder to take responsibility and focus on the things that you can do.

Client: Really ….

Vjollca: Just write here whatever comes into your mind then we discus it what you wrote.

Client: Positive is not for sure so… if is negative need to find out for which reason is? (and she listed down the reasons that could be).

Vjollca: Which questions you need to ask in the meeting if is negative outcome? Client: (listed all the things she need it to ask)

Vjollca: what you need to know from the list you wrote?

Client: (again she managed to come with big list of what she wanted to know).

Phone conversation we had a long talk on how she can use techniques to unblock her self from situations that she felt numb and hopeless. As she was practicing muslin religions, I had to be firm and straightforward on the way she was not really communicating with the creator but she was just following the religions routine, and one of the home work was for her to write conclusion of her conversations she will do it directly with creator. Pray directly to creator on how to help you find the ways how to do the things need it to do.

Client: (Reflection) injustice with my self, with others, judgment of things through heart view, confusions, have I done injustice towards others and have alloyed my self to stay with that injustice?

Vjollca: Ehhhh ….so what decision you decided?

Client: To change and to stand by justice towards my self and others.

Vjollca: What about following those three rules in question one on the questioner or being human?

Client: I am scared that I will say "yes" to be product of pure love and then I will act differently. …but my decision is simple of course I want to follow those three rules but I need lots of practice. But I will try.

Vjollca: Have you seen at least three visions of if you becoming product of pure love and what are your three journey options?

Client: No I have not seen it…..

Vjollca: But you have to have a vision in order to have passion, will and determination to follow your pure love.

Client: ok I will….

Vjollca: What do you think from the photo I send, what is your reflection? (I send an inspiration quote).

Client: I don't know…. When you are not in good state of mind you cannot see things clear. After the meting I had last week it made me think can I do things with out feeling so much pain. In fact is half of the job once you structure them and then you put them into actions.

Vjollca: Yes, anything else that made you reflect on the exercises we have been discussing through the phone? :

Client: No that was what I said and to write things down then clarify them even the things that you don't like. Vjollca: Please can you list them?

Client: Who do I want to be?
Be real
Have value
Achievement
You can
Believe
Mission
Surprise
The voice of Reality
Disappointment
Failer
Without support
Fight with yourself. Why me? With others to get what I deserve.

Client: (another exercise, another day) experiment, You loving yourself, ask for help Allah to connect with your soul, Learn to look further, Walk straightforward….

Vjollca: No , no the experiment have to be :
-What did you practice today?
-How did you practice it and how long?
-What did you get from the practice?
-What will you do differently?

Client: I practiced how to be connected to my soul and to talk to the God for my situation. Focusing for one hour in practicing made me feel calm and in peace. I need to practice it more then one hour a day.

Vjollca: What would you suggest to someone how to work on their mind and soul?

Client: In my mind, I have a lot of thoughts that are getting messed up, crashing, trembling, dragging and trying to be close to God a difficult path that feels the throng of a hope sleeping I "think" I'm the protagonist of my thoughts go like a Soule that is obstacle for me sometimes.

I'm afraid to feel different, I want to go somewhere but I know I'm still far away ... I felt a warmth but I thought that something did not go with my confidence I told myself that I have a better chance by correcting the conversation trust Quietness is worth if I use it ...

Vjollca: Exercising an hour ends if you really know what you want and you got what you need it from the exercise. The exercise that I suggested, to write 30 minutes each day free thoughts about your confusions can help to calm yourself in the way you have learned to calmness through the energy of your soul and creator. (which means a little in touch with people if they are distracting your peace).

Client: The human tendency is high to love the best for ourselves, to always be in peace with ourselves and we must feel this peace all the time. Having the envy of the other to go to love the other less than for oneself unknowingly disguise, troubles you because your support is in the "abduction" of things not in being right with the other. If we wanted to describe your own qualities, we will certainly have to justify all our actions. To work honestly and genuinely, do not become a reason why your neglect once to cost others. If our life is a choice, that would be right.

Vjollca: Can you write half of page on your decisions making through your inner conversations and the role of your soul, mind, body, heart and intuition.

Client: We say we have consciousness and it leads us, since depending on the different situations we act differently, we feel different and we act differently ... To be in relation to mind, soul, and heart… The heart is the constraint of the mind, the mind of the conception and the soul of the expression of the solution, the matter and the situation… The conscience is the mind.

Vjollca: The conscience is knowledge…. is logic. ...

Client: In different situations I act differently. Often to justify is the easiest way of getting out of the situation, struggling with difficulty at first connecting with the heart, then you can judge with more concentration and can be included in the logic and the connection with the soul to remove the fear (what I was with often rules) The connection with the soul makes me reflect and be aware of the deficiencies It is the most obvious form of self-testing, seeing yourself with the eyes of truth, do not do it with lies ...

Client: (Another day reflection) I often feel like my name is special and I want to do big things   Today was a common day, I tried to write a bit, the idea for the fireworks is generally beautiful, but it makes me feel bad about their never-ending noise   this is similar to the arrangement of thoughts that fall again despite a leak I understand that my inner being has strength, I can be different, it depends on myself, self-centred and responsibility...

Vjollca: (Another day of her difficult emotional states where she felt hopeless) What does life mean for you? Who are you? Who will be? How will you achieve? Why not live with the strength of 17 years old girl you were? What's happening? Will you want to die? And to fail or to show your strength and to do what you have promised to God and your self to do? To achieve the goal you have come to this life, Or to be just a human being who lives in a life of pity and goes where life troughs you? Reflect and tell me the conclusion. Go and talk to God, let me know when you finish the conversation with God.

Vjollca: (Later again after few hours I had to remind her that she has to replay back to me) You getting very tired having a long conversation with God, or you are pretending like you are have it? What is really happening…

Client: No I am having conversation and I am crying in same time. I am feeling the need to cry.

Vjollca: Ok, when you ready let me know and we can talk. Also read my previous comments that will make you cry properly and then decide to do something about it. I remind my self my age when I use to be eight years old and sixteen year old so I get the strength they use to have. "Try to love your self if you want me to support you" If you cant do that then I don't have a choice but to give you the freedom of your thoughts and actions and respect that. These three ways are working if you have learned how to apply these three rules below:

1 - Treat others as you like to treat yourself
2 - Love yourself as you would love
3 - Give 100% to everything you do

And each of those rules has underlined 11 rules that help to understand and enforce the main rule.

Client: Experiment, reflection. I'm in doubt, I know the fear and the purpose, the situations put me down, my responsibilities make me feel safe (not every day), I want to drive into my mission. I'm terrified when I think I can be someone who takes responsibility, anyway I do like it this terrified feeling. I have been crying, I felt naturally I am confused with myself and I feel awkward, anyway I can only try for myself ...

Client: My plan: To be myself (sincerely pure to the creator). To Have a Mission (Knowing to do Good), Organized lifestyles (clear rapport with certain people, inspiration for achievement after a tiring job   ) To love justice, to fight for justice ... Any difficulty overcome the faith in God. Experiment: reflection

Client: I am in the process of a situation ... By the end of the year I suppose I have reached a very high degree of faith to do things for God's purpose ... I have papers and a job, maybe a child. The idea of studying further inspires me a lot, I want to reach it with mystery and self-confidence. In fact I want to remove my characterizing fear that I have, then I can continue ... To balances between social, collective and personal lives (at work) I hope and I want to do all this for 5 years with the help of God always   another option is to try many opportunities. I have to do it if there is a solution continuous work with myself to connect with God and with my soul being in touch this will make me strong... A new life. I hope to be myself, to not be afraid. It seemed to me a lifetime with the weight of the past... that I know I would have enough force, but I would find out if I thought that everything could happen for a reason ... And what would be the reason that I know ... one Love... a random ... A mission ....

Vjollca: how those daily reflections have helped?

Client: They have helped me to see, do and act more clearly on the things that I don't want to face.

Vjollca: From now on reflection has to be on the practice of these three main rules we have discussed previously.

Client: Decisions on various issues made the decision of being product of pure love and justice. Using heart, mind and soul. With yourself you have to be genuine in order to get what you giving on universe. You have to be with the spirit of faith and reflection of things because faith keeps you in control and reflection to make you learn a lot ...

Vjollca: (After we had long conversation of her experience in college helping someone and she felt great I described below how she felt so she can have it as a reminder and affirmation for her self)

- I have advised someone with the purity of the soul

- I was concentrated to the volunteer work I was doing and I captured the moment/ the thought / curiosity / question and the answer to the moment

- I done my responsibilities

- I had the courage to overcome the fear and to love the heart and the mind and gave the permission to my soul to speak

- I kept my calmness, even though my heart was crying for a deceitful love.

- I kept myself in the presence of the soul being at the moment and agreed and after a hard day I was able to give advice and help someone

Client: You have described exactly how I felt.

Client: Treat others how you will like to be treated; to behave well to someone who is bad is principles and value. Whenever doing anything beyond what is common is a new thing that gives you pleasure and love. We have to do things without compensation, you often say, I just follow justice, I just say to myself, you can, you only you can make it and change yourself ...

Vjollca: If you are going to continue this rhythm. ... living in your soul ... your heart will only be filled with your love and mind only with thoughts that soul and intuition approve.

Client: Thank you and I hope so.

Vjollca: 100% I know you have the skills and you have provided the evidence. Just stay committed to those 3 rules for justice, thoughts and information from God. You have 2 other rules to explained, - love yourself as you will like to be loved (what is love ... self love ... how can you find it ... how can you love yourself ... and how it starts) and how can you make 100% of your best through your situation you are in.

Client: Before you love your self they way you like to be loved, try to know how you want to be loved. Be honest, genuine, free, and imagine of being happy and loved... When things start to look suspicious, you think that between you and those you think you want there is a space (that you have noticed before) where this space has made things clear and starts to change otherwise you think about connecting with your creator to love yourself and the space that was created to translate in love, despite the existence of this space, served for a lesson and it is good to see the positivity of things. To give your maximum will mean to start something with your own strength, to reflect on it, to be simple and to love yourself to do things without a manipulation, without feeling guilt of doing injustice towards yourself and others, Try to live and enjoy your goal ...

Vjollca: (Reflection of another time of different exercise) When you finish your two exercises that we discuss then we talk further.

1 - in your dream partner and second on your fear of being who you want to be.

Client: The dream... A casual recognition (not by someone else) Talk about yourself and listen to it ... To be long with black hair and blue eyes, nice (not important if is not rich ... Right, honest, wiser, one who does follow their own principles, someone who speak with the language of the soul, not be prejudiced, not be spoiled or repeat mistakes. To have arguments and have ability to discuss things. Not to be famous but respected, to love me sincerely, to make me understand after every rain there is a rainbow that shines, to believe on me, to think that you know me and know it ... To believe in God and to have conviction in the power of God (this is the first).

I hope to meet him one day if not at least this dream will help me not to go in wrong path.

Saying affirmation to my self in order to replace fear with love, Fear, (I will remind to myself), I have "anyway I will not change character even if they are overwhelm things ..." "Une ..." "I'll fight to the end", "you are important", "Be Real and I adore you" You are not someone else, be who you are , I love you... you are very special, you do things, you take responsibility.

Client: (Reflection of another day) Everything is about how to understand true things and sincere faith.

Vjollca: Have you add any more affirmation to your list to love yourself based on your daily achievements, or reflection of your actions or reminder of your memories as a child. Yes the word "believe and faith is very powerful".

Client: Believe on God, believe on yourself, believe on your abilities, believe on your skills and opportunities, difference (that makes the use of skills and opportunities), Promise to yourself achievement...
I add it to my list the word "believe as powerful meaning"
However, the reflection on death is in the middle and two paths the birth and of departure.

Vjollca: From the thought of death I get regeneration, inspiration, freedom, faith, rebirth, flight, liberation from reality, fear of death from thought and death gives strength.

Client: Me too I am not scared of death. I am scared of not being able to practice purity, that's what scares me. But I will try harder to stay connected to my soul, to my centre, to my pure core.

Vjollca: the thought of death helps you to detached from reality. Client: Yes that's true and you understand things in deep level.

Vjollca: So how do you feel from today experiences and what would you say to your self?

Client: Everything starts from a beginning.
I also want to structure a new me, with confidence, believe, moral, reasoning, self esteem, ability of achievement. One true one...

Vjollca: Say the things you deserve tonight? For the things you done what nice things you will say to your self?

Client: It makes me laugh when I say it. Vjollca: Say it and write it.

Client: For the things she did: Be thankful for the moment that made you in true person, for what it intends to achieve, you can, you have ability, believe and I love you (three times makes me laugh), I want to be happy. Do not forget about death (I will add it to the list of reflections that it serves me when I read it the other time). Love your self to be loved and I kept praising myself all day today.

Client: Reflection: It's easier to lie rather then telling the truth, this finding is often found, but most of all I think people are doing to find their injustices or things they do not like to say. Today in a conversation with someone at the organization come to this conclusion...

Discussion with you on loving yourself:

To love yourself, how much could a person who was unable to love themselves? If people love themselves, they feel love, faith experiences situations (human, emotional, spiritual, psychological...) Love give it to everyone in the beginning then give the discipline, the truth, guidance with love.

Teaching means true discipline in critical eyes, speaking in the same language ... How can you practice it? By discipline yourself ... give yourself teaching with love and you will not alloy anyone to bully you or to make jokes about you. A person who does not love themselves they can not teach others. Reflection at the end of the day how did it go? Even learning and love and everything ... yes, if those who are reading do not understand ... You have to speak with the language of love, with language of your soul (technique, method,). Why is it more difficult with the client? Because you have to be able to understand their suffering, and many more things.

Vjollca: Please make reflection on this expression "the moment is important and it must have all the components of the magic module to be true or then remain illusion and unfulfilled.... with gaps where fear prevails moment is the reflection of the person "

Client: Every moment has a meaning, every meaning has a conclusion   Understanding a moment is often difficult for us, it is something that goes along with the ignorance that we can do   we are taught to say that I we are containerizing our actions, we are actually controlling the way we talk to each other, fearing to be good (our concept), and again we get back to our situation, this dream is happy, it just creates a gap. With regard to the magic module I cannot say because I'm still in the process.

Vjollca: I think. ...

The momentum - is complimented because you are aware of everything that happens and reflects and analyses... To work with the balance of your energy care. ..but you clean yourself of unnecessary energy... how to know to find out when your energy is running out and need recharging like a phone when battery is low need to charge the phone before the phone turns off.

Acceptance - you have come to accept the past, embrace the pain and find the solution with the silence of the soul... but you need a little more work for the unexpected things that can occur not to lose the balance.

The goal - somehow you are clear but will still need work in the belief of the goal and the belief in yourself that you deserve and you will achieve because only you decide whether or not you will achieve it.

Inspiration - you are very good in this field and sharp.

Commitment - you are complete and do everything that needs to be done. You just have to work in your self-confidence and the goal by talking to them.

Affirmation - Also this stage you are able to understand it and apply it, you have captured and practiced it... You just have to work with your love of yourself and confidence in yourself to achieve all that you think.

Love - you have managed to value yourself and the moment, and to express love to yourself and continue to practice... just working day and night work to be surrounded by love for yourself to produce enough love for yourself and others.

This is your process so far on magical module
Client: Thank you for doing that as it feels I am looking my self in mirror.

Vjollca: " To be pure you have to analyse every negative thought that comes to mind, without judging yourself but with love to ask yourself and talk "

Client: The love for your self is when you accept your self the way you are. Through our conversation yesterday you brought to my memory my hiding corner and I wrote this writing below link to my memories:

My hidden corner, how many things I hidden on you, how many words and how many things we share together... how much you hear and your silence makes me different how to keep and continue in my thoughts that I see them ashamed, and weave sometimes. My best friend told me that she had once met a group of women who often met in a place to drink coffee which, among the many vibrant life stories, they had exchanged their experiences in the wild hidden deep, between words almost pronounced where the pain was a reflection in the eye listen to perverted suffering. Paced between these thoughts was in my mind (with my friend) and why we had suffered otherwise we had a code of it was common, the need for and the desire for consolation, a desperate consolation after everything had not been improved, but the time had passed since we had woven it with our wound. the thoughts that came and flew and narrowed our being with the slope of the desire to change. Among them, I looked like the luckiest thing my friend said to me (though I was not) but I decided to take a bad experience I had gone. While buying a coffee someone approached me and said hurriedly, "how did you choose to sell yourself in that matter "was disturbed and I felt inexplicably began to speak and shyness many women who could again be cheated or felt with friendship between them and spoke openly. Everyone after a painful event.

... Everyone after a painful event hides a bigger pain, this pain of the scales, knit within the circle and makes her feel the same, painted in autumn colours, art and gloomy... she said to how many I was talking to them and continued to comment, feeling that they were eager to speak rightly, to feel emotionally represented, not from the one to the other, to the expectation of waiting and waiting for more things from a past or the present with the elegance of the gloom.

To love yourself in the right form and feel that you have loved the mistake is a door that should be opened and should remain where the only transitory of the road are your memories and analysis for them and the result you are a different person. The conversations with my friend are merged into a pattern, that of the conviction that we find an accepted solution. Her actions have inspired me and the feeling that would be stronger, I knew that within her skit would find the way to come, and Dear folks, you've been listening to silence for so many years, and you've been blind for so many years and you've been turning. How many relied on you and how many shuffles of memory come after you ....

Vjollca: (After reading this section I replied) Every time I read your writings, I seem to be on a boat in my own at lightweight.   and it's the energy of the universe.

Talk about the desperate love
we are looking for and
we do not know how to look for it…
We do not know how to understand love…
is our fault…
no one taught us.
if love is the lifestyle of life,
but it is a shame that we bring into the family…
need to keep the head down…
like my mother…
like other good women…..
as a decent woman…
your life is as we say it is…
I cried. … and I wonder why…
but I knew that I was not for that form of life and not that I could not do it ...
I could do it better than everyone but I could not had enough air. ...
I wanted to breathe in looking at the skies. ...
I wanted to discuss dream plans with moon. ....
I liked to dance and laugh with the rain...
with the people to speak the language of silence .. Sometimes …..

Feedback of the client of the book "A magical life"

"A Magical Life"

As you read you feel fulfilment with inspiration of your soul depth that comes naturally (as a reader) inside of the soul breathing deeply e real chronology of the event, pedantic and diverse looks come as a silent and reflecting reflection on the reality of life itself Here and now, it seems a world first with the eye of a child dreaming together with nature, communicates and breathes with it. A normal life of personalities who may be vertically and in profane form, but that puts it in sync with the meditative role of the author… A magic module, looking for a magical life, getting to know yourself Everyone's home is a mission and a duty. Created on the basis of a visionary, expressive and meditative trilogy, the author will communicate with each other's world by trying to put a foundation stone to the point of view of everyone ... nothing is more beautiful than being true ...

Feedback: after the last trimester so after 9 months therapy

My dear self ... I know you've always been aiming and you have felt that between you and the goal you will find a space, with the time you just dreamed, you wanted to be you ... Even in the passing years, the things that change, the growing claims, you remains one with life (reality) ... and things changed again ... You and me and the space (You're the trigger for my goal Vjollca ...) All three at one time and within you (self) desire to be different (to find my self). I just thought the time went by, I was worried about returning again ... It was my mind that I had lost my mind, I had spotted myself, if I had done this I thought that the importance lies in the correct communication with the bitter realities, which seemed to have false fouls, and the hidden soul, with painful voice calling and I was running after reality, I hoped ... it happened that come the space (you)) with the calling, invites me to talk with my tired soul, hidden inside me, to hear this voice that I had just felt like a mirage ... and then I had "left" My inner voice, how strong though with me had been borne... how come I have lived separated from this ?... Space, my way, my ivory flower that reaches the joints of the soul ... you were the end of the preciousness of a core ... Vjollca

Vjollca: She refereed to me as the space I have been for her journey.

Feedback: (the month she started to learn how to remain in her space by her soul and universe guided all times)

Client: I am very emotional, between feelings in my memories… I feel sorry when I think I was part of that condition not long ago. I, the bride of the house that I had to endure with the aim of saying words   and then those words would turn me into suffering for me… The words full of quarrels I was the "square" I had to endure, the ground was hard to talk between tears …dreams… how bad I have allowed myself, must be patient but with the patience system, in fact there is no they are but a space, but have been many trails, or a space, a deep gap, that had to cross marvels was created between me… speculations that disturbed my soul …

Vjollca: You have to create 11 cards on affirmation, advice or reminders that you need at your situation. Example as there are below but you can create your own, this below are just examples:

1 - For knowledge. You are smart and why
2 - Trust… how do you know how to believe
3 - Practicing self-believe
4 - Practicing God's Faith
5 - Daily, weekly and monthly plan
6 - Emptying the mind and Your Full Being
7 - How to reach the space

8 - The imagination of things that happens tomorrow... how would you like tomorrow or the situation that will come and how can you adjust it as you want.

9 - Weekly prayer

10 - How to learn from others

11 - How to protect yourself and enjoy the moment

Client: Vjollca noted this week:

1 - Absence of General Decisions

2 - Generally speaking, work with the notes by asking questions and using curiosity

3 - Confront your work... your interests and not to others without purpose

4 - I do not speak to myself directly and straightforward. ... with critical view. ...

5 - Weaknesses to the faith of your goal and to the Lord. not just artificial theory.

Client: (as we were talking through the phone conversation, I was writing down in same time what she was going back on her childhood memories and coming up to present moment) In my head it was created an image that I am enduring this condition but .... it was not created a vision link to the purpose of the goal... I can manage all things that I face. I was different. I thought I could handle everything and anything; it was a vision as at that time I was going through a very painful events. I have experienced this vision that I am going to do something different. That feeling made me stronger and stronger everyday today I face this life but I don't think I can do something different. Even every day back then it was violent and painful. I felt strongly that feeling of the vision that I am different and I will do something different.

This idea has made me firm and stand by myself after that time I experienced the loss of my parent and I had great dissatisfaction and I felt very empty ... but I still had a strong signal about my vision. The vision that I would go beyond the reality that he had described to me. I had another point of view even though I was a child and the roof of all this force has been in adolescence. Then there was a sense of how false the reality is and disappointed, I felt hopeless, but again this idea was in the head. I could believe it. I have this idea when the reality is different I needed to have this conversation with myself to understand this vision that I had when I was back then. A return to myself I have to remember more often to remind myself to dig in the new things that have been forgotten by me. Today I got that there was an unexplained stream that has existed from the beginning of my adolescence simply made it clear now I realized by investigating more my hidden corner. That age was between 15 and 18 years old and I was around 4 years old when I created my hidden corner. Every time I was experiencing a painful event I would just go and talk to my hidden corner.

Today I tried to look at my self ... in two dimensions: mind and heart that showed me the whole way with its senselessness and its difficulties, where I had to act without understanding and the soul where through it I saw my overcrowding and the endless desire to be a another, what I had followed an unmistakable stream since I was little. (which I discovered today). Someone looking for something simple has just entered the search path ... part of your self- love and the life to be able to help others. .....

Evaluation: "Believe in your abilities", "Between you, reason and space try to build creativity", "Do not be dependent on the thought of the other but find what you want to get from that thought",

Reason: "Reason within your reasoning" , "Speak with arguments because you are cultivating your righteousness", "Your courage begins where you do the right things".

Convinced: "being convinced of following the justice and pure love is the safe path", "don't love others to love you but for the reason being decent and genuine reasons".

Final Feedback and dialog

Dialog on helping her structure her book by taking her into the spiritual world just having the conversation through the phone…

All that was done by using my tone of voice, universal energy, no distraction and quite conversation where we could hear only each others words, breath, and feel the energy, asking the right question based on what she was saying.

That's what came from all this phone conversation…..

This points below were coming from me, through the conversation with the client, describing through her voice, what were the seven points that made her achieve this journey and then I linked those points to the seven stages of the magical module.

The reason you did it for a year this process, 10 months up to now and for one months you have been able to be guided by your soul and universe all the time (the space we called it as the client have come up with that name).

The ingredients are:

1 - The insistence of your inner call

2 - Detachment from the reality by just spending time with yourself and avoiding conversation that don't serve you, your goal and your purpose.

3 - The insistence of Vjollca's not to let me give up by observing my thoughts, feelings and actions reflecting it back to me through my soul language.

4 - Giving Vjollca's full freedom on her suggestions and exercises towards me and me being honest, open and pursuing without realizing what is being done. I just knew and felt that and was resonating with my own inner calling.

5 - Purity of Vjollca's as if it wasn't would of not resonated with my inner calling.

6 - Acceptance of absurdity

7 - Rebellion not to accept myself the way I was formed by the reality and life that surrounded me.

Magical Module:

1 - Momentum

2 - Acceptance because you accept who you are and what you will to be doing.

3 – Goal because I generally worked on the goals I had

4 - Inspiration. … inspiration. ..because I was inspired by the sincerity and the structure of the Vjollca ..and her words that combined with my inner voice. … and the dream of my childhood… the dance of the childhood inspired me. … and we were a children lying in the open space   all of these inspired me to be the real self.

5 - Commitment-dedication. … this point helped me to be committed and to continue… because I knew that I was not doing it and I did not understood it. … it was the soul that was screaming at me to get my attention… the purity of Vjollca made me hear my soul automatically. …

6 - Affirmation - assertions. … affirmation. ..prayers… they helped to accept the absurdity because the call was in demand. ….

7 - love … rebellion shows love to yourself …

Vjollca: She was coming up with names of the chapters of her book as we started to this point of conversation:

Client:

1 - The insistent of the internal voice,

2 - My purpose is beyond reality,

3 - The randomness, the king of things… when you believe on what you don't see. … if anyone could…,

4 - Forward my steps. How to believe…

5 - Purity… to choose right… purity of the soul, of yourself. .wateriness and delicacy… when I saw you…,

6 - Then when I did not believed it. …. I had a fake purpose. … … when I saw. …. if you the dream had a name. … .

I have a title but I'm not sure, because it seems absurd.

Vjollca: Say it as it is.

Client: Your world two palm

7 - Without you. .... intended a vision. .. you are you. ... a call that lasts. ... to see you. do not call me "dedication" ...that what you see.... do not call me a stranger. ... your world two palm. ....

Vjollca: Think about a title for the book.

Client: Thinking.

Vjollca: "Your world two palm but owns the whole world"

Client: But I don't understand it for the moment what two palms mean?

Vjollca: You will understand it, but I will not give my explanation now. Your two palms mean that the energy of the individual soul that is the space needs and have. Also the human being when is tending that is the space they take from the land, just the soul space. Given the importance to those two palms, know the value, understanding it, own it then you can own the world.

"If those two palms that you own are not pure " your world will not be pure. So start with those two palms to work with the space to clean the mind and heart and then automatically you will be master of the world. The brain should not be used because it is devilish because of the thoughts have to harm others and not to serve the soul.

Client: Yes, but I do not understand.

Vjollca: Take your time and have your inner conversations to see what you come up with.

Vjollca: This is a conversation where I was taking her into the deep space where she was traveling through the universe energy forwards and backwards. As she continued she said:

Client: "That bridge with sparkles"

Vjollca: She remembered when she was 5 years old. The reason why she came up with that was because I asked her: Chapter 1 will be about the structure. .... faith.   and she add it ....

Client: " it was a great bridge ... I had to pass it but it was very long.had colourful sparks but my reality did not have those sparks" ...

Vjollca: I remember she had told me she had spend lots of time with the horse when she was around 15 years old so I asked her "to the time you spend with your horse?"

Client: continued ... yes it was there and I saw it on the sky.. is high and without cracking. ..

Vjollca: what happen. ... where was the faith? ...

Client: Anyway, it was a bridge with a pair of colourful sparks that have kept me from not doing things they way others were doing it. ... because I believed in justice.   however disturbing it will be a day of righteousness will come. ...

Vjollca: The bridge symbolized justice. .. when you met me what happened with the bridge?

Client: I had to walk in the bridge because it had to be done in a different form, not in the form of the hidden corner and would show with sparks time to time. now I walk in that bridge with colourful sparks and I keep playing like a child by turning my head back and forward and I have a scarf with colourful sparks on my neck. I keep playing with that scarf and it is serious and disconnected from the childhood.   as a child I go back and forward playing and I'm free. ..... "The Bridge of colourful sparks" .... "beyond you" bridge with durable stones.

Chapter 9 - I have come to the end of the bridge with colourful sparks. a bunch of people waiting for me to congratulate me for something. ... and there I have the scarf on my neck with sparks and colourful. There are many people waiting and they feel happy for themselves and I have been a cause for their happens. ...for them to achieved a bit of happiness. ....

Vjollca: what did you do with the scarf?

Client: What did I do with the scarf? I did not lose the scarf but I don't know what I did with it at the end of the bridge. ... and I see it and I don't see it.   once I have it and another time I don't have it. Simple just I see the reflection of my neck having that scarf that it shines and people who feel good about the small particle I have done to them. ...

Vjollca: How would you define your journey since you meet me up to now and the end of the bridge? Client: "Permanent love" , "Language of soul".

Feedback:

"To seek in your infinite space, wide sea of my thoughts wandering toward the intentions put in the way with you…"

Vjollca: This feedback was based on the dialogue between us, provided above.

"The soul needs to be cultivated-it must be bravery. When the spirit of feminine delight is cultivated and cultivated, it grows and becomes strong enough to strike the harsh reality of the world that is often not spiritual" D.Ch.

"Meditation triggers molecular changes deep inside our cells" source: Cure: A Journey into the Science of Mind Over Body, Jo Marchant

Case study 2

Client number 2: Age: 37, Gender:
Female, Profession: Spiritual person with university education.
Status: Member of a family with kids.

Direct and indirect therapy.

Background Born in an economically and politically privileged family, but somehow she was searching something that reflected her true self but was not sure whether the places she was searching for were the right places. She wanted a peaceful and colorful, natural place. That's all she knew. But why she was craving for that? She had worked hard to achieve that lovely world for herself, but did not know how to fit it with her family and the society, because of confusion of her inner world with the external reality.

Direct and indirect therapy

I worked with her, through the project she was doing for me and firstly being myself as well using my gift of connecting with her as whole. Usually she did not work with others in projects, as she was selective on choosing who to work with. She was very surprised and pleased to meet someone, who was deeply spiritual and lived not as a recluse but inside a city. She had known spiritual people, but they lived out of the cities. We continued for one year working together.

We met at an event. We did not even say hi yet, but, I was really shocked and curious to see how she was acting, how she was dealing with the reality. I could see she was from another world; it was a world that I wanted to be (because I am fulfilled and happy but I do not like to be in this life where is so much pain and suffering around. I cannot be happy when I see people suffering and the only thing that keeps me in this life is my mission of teaching people self-love, the key to be a magical person). Her world felt like a peaceful garden, full of love and colors and aromas to feed your soul. It was healing breeze that just gives you that magical flight, the fresh air. I had never met any person that breathed in that fresh air. So for me was mysterious to see somebody like that, in the middle of a room with human beings, not magical people, that were completely disconnected from their magical person. Even the people, who were connected a little used it to make money. She gave a speech and she took me away, and looked at the people that saw her as someone that she was trying to make others happy or to please others, but she did not have those because she was fulfilled and happy in her own world. All this misunderstanding that she is 'naïve' or 'pleasing' is that she in fact she was trying to heal them and share the universal love.

A few people that talked to me about her gave feedback about the light energy that she was transferring in them. Then I was curious to know, what she was doing there. Why is she not acting in the world? All the amazing light that she had created in her life, how could she kept it inside closed doors, and how could she link that to the outer reality? We made a short journey together and had a casual conversation. I could see that she was looking up to me with admiration, but as I was telling her my achievements, my plans and goals, I was looking at her light. I was amazed how much she was able to shine and questioned why she was not shining out? We kept in touch for a long time for various reasons common projects. I received spiritual guidance from her, about my journey and my actions. I needed someone's supervision, but could not have someone who ticked all my boxes. She ticked my boxes for spiritual guidance and the scientific aspects of reality. In the meantime I was hoping to influence her to notice her light as she was a magical person but also she owned a space where she felt comfortable and was magical, which was shocking for me. I had never met anyone who owned a magical space and owned it. I noticed somehow that she wanted to fit in the reality. This is the area I could help her to explore through the time I was with her, and found out that she had build walls around. I needed to be very careful when I was approaching her, because she did not get influence by no one outside of her own world, because she felt confident and comfortable in her magical place. I managed to make her aware of her walls, and that she does not need those walls because her light can protect her. I taught some healing techniques. Strangely enough she knew some techniques and had practiced them but I made her aware by having an insight of her magical person and showing it. She is writing a book based on her light and how to spread it. Her book will be the last touches that people need to stand up and shine as a magical person. She has managed to do this in her life and has the ability to do the same for others.

I was surprised to see a star shining with out corruption of her mind from this life. I just remember being shocked and holding my self together to understand if she knows it. I was talking to her but still in my mind I was searching for answers. Her smile was sending love, Her eyes were showing me that peaceful place that I had imagined somewhere it does exist. So rude of me wondering in that amazing place instead of listening, But it was not my fought that her words were no were close with what she was representing. I was just blown by her wind of peaceful love was surrounded. I continued my journey then somehow we meet again, what to do   what to say ...how to take it ...I just did not know   But I thought what I am going to lose if I ask her to do take part on my project that was so important to me. I could see fear on her eyes and I just give her the freedom to choose, she felt comfortable. What happened. is not explained yet as it is spiritual explanation how she come to my life and helped me on my project that was very important to me. But I know she has been a Angel to guide and help me on my journey of my purpose. I don't know how to explain it but I just thank you the creator for sending her to me, I thank you her with all my heart. She represents the place of peaceful where love is all around; We helped each other.

Clients book feedback

A Magical Life (review)

The flow of this book surprised me greatly. Each step of the module was a new awakening to the life I had, the life I have and the life that I dream about. It was a voyage of self-discovery in the presence of a greater force than us all, the power of creation and recovery of love. In the midst of life's perplexities the presence and power of the soul is continuously and courageously acknowledged; its existence surpasses my words and transcends my thoughts, I can only feel it, the very centre of me, from which I notice all that is with clarity. Being in that space I increase my awareness that I am, and an immense feeling of faith, gratitude and hope wraps around me like a warm rainbow of light. I remain in a sense of curiosity and wonder. The contact with our soul is our greatest gift, it is the very source of peace.

In everything I experience in my daily life, I make sure I pass through all the stages of this module. They act as pillars of predictions, allowing me to have a greater degree of understanding, freedom and control in what is happening or not happening.

Momentum: this stage taught me that life's joys and miseries will eventually bring us into a greater understanding about ourselves and others, and consequently into a solution that makes us all grow; as our soul expands in its quiet tenderness, we realize its preciousness more and more. I believe this is the hardest stage of all; the realization that we are much more than what is immediately presented to us.

Acceptance: this stage helps me to be more spiritually open in order to experience the world as it is.

Goal: this stage brings me consolation and fills me with hope for the future.
I: it is my favourite stage.

Inspiration to me is another word for happiness.

Commitment: an essential challenge so that I can be a better and more encouraging friend to myself and others.

Affirmation: it is the oil of my lamp.

Love: the beginning, the journey and the end, in an infinite number of ways.

Feedback from client

Following the intuition to strengthen decision-making and myself. By reading the book, and testifying Vjollca's example in real life, by being in touch with her, discussions, behaviour. By her being true to herself, she influenced in me a greater and more powerful inner awakening, to stay true to my inner world. I am now writing a book about my life, which is the best thing I am doing. I am very grateful for her continuous support.

In was pleasing others more than I should have, by being unaware of the underlying or hidden intentions of others. I was feeling peaceful and full of love inside. I was part of surrounding atmosphere that was not congruent with my inner world. Now I have learned to be more aware of negative energy, have increased self-believe and do not mind fitting with others anymore, but just following my purpose independently. I speak up, confront and argue if I do not agree with something, which I used to avoid in the past. I accept that I am unique and different, and as the purpose becomes clear I follow my self-belief more strongly than ever. I am happier, love myself much more and feel more rewarded from what I do and life in general. I am transferring what I have learned to my children.

My biggest challenge was to face people with negative energy such as those who use aggressive or manipulative attacks to gain things. In the past I was able to immediately recognise it but my reaction was to raise walls around me to protect myself, for instance by leaving them or avoiding contact them in the future. Now I have learned to counteract by still keeping my walls down and expand myself my light towards them.

All my life I had found faith, love, peace, consolation and encouragements in prayer, books and nature. In books is where I found pieces of the life that I wanted to live. There was comfort and hope in the characters, whose determination for truth and freedom allowed them to hope and love fully again and again. I particularly admired those, who despite unfavorable surroundings and circumstances, built a beautiful and meaningful life for themselves, keeping their heart open, with patience, faith and courage, embracing their vulnerability throughout their journey. Vjollca is a living example. Since I met her I was struck by her desire to follow her intuition, her dreams and aspirations. She has an immense resilience! She speaks her mind and makes her point. Due to her purpose as a healer, she sometimes goes as far as saying or doing things that might not appear / sound adequate to the rational mind. Every guidance she provides comes out of her own example. I have always been astonished by her ability to ignite her light even in total darkness. I have been and continue to be inspired by her. A favourite book character, but in the real world. Am grateful to God to have met her and that I have been given the honor to be part of her projects, to read her amazing story, as well share her passion for living a magical life. Everyone, myself included, is transformed somehow for the better, by her endless source of spiritual energy and her gift as a healer.

Vjollca message to the client: My message is "she is on the last touches of understanding her real purpose and starting her final steps on her journey on this life, which is her book, that will be nourishment (for the light), includes the soul, the intuition, the universal energy, the body, mind, and heart. Mainly this food will be suitable for kids from age 3 up to 25 and all those adults, who are already in enlightenment. Also this book will help new parents, in the first 3 years of parenting."

Case study 6 (3. 4. 5 & 6):

Case study 3: Female individual therapy for 3 months intensive. Case study 4: Couple therapy, three sessions more then three hours each for a session. Case study 5: Child therapy. Case study 6: Male individual therapy).

Background: The client, who presented first, was around 40 years old female, which came to me to ask for help of how she could come out of the circle where she had been staying up to know. She said that her circle was affected by the confusion regarding the whole relationship she was in, about doubting her identity - who she was, which linked her to thinking of giving up on everything she had build the recent couple of years. This included having suicidal thoughts, leaving her children behind and going to live somewhere else as a completely different personality, with a new identity where she could find a man, who could control her and look after her in every way and she can be his doll. So she came to me for advice and suggestions.

Note. This tendency to escape from a difficult reality that she found no strength to face, is reflected in her final escape from therapy. As you will see in the content of our therapy sessions, she considered me as her guardian angel, because she found it incredible that I was giving her all that support, but this lasted only three months, until she achieved her main goal and a few other sub-goals.

Conclusion. During all our therapy I reminded her that as soon as she received her main goal and sub-goals my support would be limited, depending on her next goal, but she agreed to that until the final session, where she did not confront me about her unsattisfaction regarding this previously established boundaries and being responsible to continue on her own.

Direct and Indirect therapy:

In this case studies there are four case studies blended together, because I worked with female age around 40 years old intensive therapy for three months, male individual around same age through those three months, with a two year old girl and with all of them as a family. The first client that approached me was the mother of the family, for her own personal issues, which had to do with her circle issues that were previously mentioned. I had 3 sessions through the phone. We agreed to meet as a family mediator, to see how we could move forward.

I did three hours sessions with them as a family. After the sessions, I communicated with them separately through texting to support what had happened in the sessions, their analyses, discussions, thoughts and conclusions about it. But I noticed that this relationship was broken and could not continue. In that order, I was trying to support each of them separately how to discover themselves their own identity. I mainly worked with the mother by encouraging her to find her true self, by helping her to understand and practice self-love and as she started practicing and somehow understanding self-love she build up her self-love and self-esteem and managed to turn her life around, in a positive direction. She took active steps to improve her situation. She took responsibility on how to be the mother she wanted to be, follow her passions through her education, her independency in terms of her finances, not depending on her husband, she learned to travel on her own, she learned where to ask for help, she opened the tunnel that she could see the hope for herself. Then, I had to work also with the child, because the child was already distressed from everything that was happening. I worked closely with the child alone. I worked with the mother alone, the father and child alone and altogether as a whole family, which helped the complete family to be in a better place. It helped the child to be more calm, relaxed, the mother feel better about her self, and the father to work on his self-love. I made him aware that he had an issues with attachment mixing it with self love.

Through 6 sessions working with the father, to help him understand self-love, accept the decision of his wife and move forward to be a good father helped him to see things in different view. In the end, both were very angry with each-other, fighting in front of the child, being unhappy in general, escalating in domestic violence and not knowing how to make things better, but the only way to make things better for them was to continue manipulating each-other. On both sides, were trust issues, love mixed with attachment…how can love exist when the individuals do not know the meaning of self-love and do not practice it? Through those three months I managed to make this family communicate with each-other in healthy ways, understand each-other needs, respecting each-other for the love they had for each-other, even though they were living in separate houses, and the child was happy because she could see both of them happy and smiling. (I am not going in details about this case, as the client did not want to give permission to be used for case studies. However, if any proofs are required to verify the genuinely of this case, all the work that I have done with this family is documented).

Client's feedback:

As mentioned in the background history, the client refused to provide a feedback for the therapy sessions in the end of the three months. During the three months, she was offering lots of verbal feedback and she was happy to provide on writing but at that time, I was not focusing on using her as case study. My focus was to help her get back on truck, on the train she wanted to get on. As she got on the train then I had to stay on station, my role was to be on station if she need it me and not to get on train with her. But as she got on the train she got upset that I did not get in train with her, even though she know that was our agreement.

Therefore, I am only including the feedback from her social worker:

Vjollca Sadiku has been working last three months supporting an Albanian family that come to our attention. Whilst supporting this family it was identified that Vjollca Sadiku has been providing lots of practical and emotional support to the mother who was fleeing domestic abuse from her husband with her two years old daughter. Vjollca was very helpful and supportive to this mother by making contact with myself and helping to translate conversations from Albanian to English when the mother had a problem or was unsure about something. Vjollca has facilitated supervised contact between the daughter and her father as requested by social care and mother of the child. Vjollca has supported this mother to set up benefits, make contact with professionals, agencies, including social care and solicitors and has provided lots of emotional support to a vulnerable lady during a very difficult time in her life. Without this support from Vjollca this lady would have found leaving her husband and accessing support from agencies much harder. From working with Vjollca it is my opinion that she is very professional, proactive and caring and I would recommend her to other agencies to provide support with other families in need.

Vjollca's conclusion:

My insight in the understanding of her reaction, and her closure to the end, is that by ending her sessions the client expressed all the anger she was feeling about this situation, in blame, and accusations.

Regarding her anger she said that she did not want to continue with me, but return to where she was three months ago. This expression of anger was part of her giving up, because she could not allow time to herself to process the break she needed and to allow herself to plan her next goal or to create the next goal, which made her frustrated, hopeless, and alone again. She did not accept the idea that I would be there but not contacting her as I use to as now she did not need much support from apart from helping her to continue working on self-love but she did not want that. She did not accept the responsibility of calling me when she needed as I offered she could contact me anytime in emergency. She did not accept the idea of learning about self-love.

And everything was going in circles to self-love. Because she was not able to follow my technique about self- love, it seemed absurd. She needed somebody to love her. Because I was very strict and firm with boundaries. I was not giving her more love because she needed to learnt to have it from her own self. Instead of her exploring this area with me and her, she was turning it into anger, which meant she did not want anything to do with me. This shows that she was only swimming on universal love and passionate love as she was dating and looking for potential partner, something that I did not agree as she was not ready to mix her feelings and specially when the child is in middle.

The blame comes in by her saying to me that 'you lied to me' or 'you did all this support for your career and not for me'. She had switched on her light but she is not willing to keep it on because she needed another type of counseling from somebody else to help her with self-belief, self-confidence, self-esteem, encouragement. For this reason I had refer her to a few organizations. She said she did not need any counseling so did not attend. The blame towards me was caused by the anger towards herself, because she had questions, which had been influenced by the therapy I had given her for the self-love, and she was experiencing it, but was resisting the resilience of self-love and not allowing time to herself to receive the answers. Those questions were present before but the difference between before and now is that they could hardly be heard, but now they appeared too loud. The questions were: 'Why do I need somebody to love me?' 'Why can I not love myself?' 'What is wrong with me?' 'How can I be a better mum?' 'Why my kids do not love me' 'Why am I so worthless?' 'Why am I not beautiful' 'Why do I need to be beautiful?' 'Why can't I stay without a man?' 'Why do I need men?' 'Why can't I achieve my dreams?' 'Why can't I be like Vjollca?' 'Why am I not a good wife?' 'Why I can't just be myself and forget about all those questions'. As she was not giving time to allow her answers emerge, she came up with answers that she used to have before. Her old answers were and are chasing her still in this day, and they are 'I am beautiful and can make any man come after me!' 'I do not have to have responsibility for the kids because their father can take care of them and I will just be a (maintenance). 'I will hide my true self', "I will show them what they want, so I can get what I want'.

My conclusion is that she is still feeling lost and searching satisfaction in the wrong way. As you can see through her Magical Module, she needs to find self-love first because that is the key to destroy the old unnecessary structure of the created identity based on the reality and beliefs or past coping mechanism in order to gain her own magical person, her true identity, through the space where it is included, - intuition (the voice of the creator) and universe energy (this is explained in detail in the Magical Module). I have passed all my concerns and thoughts linked to the kind of help this family needs, to the other professionals involved in this case.

My final thoughts: "A quote from Magical Approach book". "You are not living if you have not achieved your self-love. All what you're looking for is self-love but the current lack of belief in yourself is stopping you to continue loving yourself". "Remember, children, are really teaching us! They are guiding us, but we have to learn to listen".

Case study 7:

Background: Female around 35 years old came to therapy for help on her behaviour towards her two daughters, 5 years old and 3 years old. She wanted to be a better mother as she was not happy the way she was handling the situation when the little one screams when she wants something and when is helping the older daughter to do the home work. She finds it very difficult to have patience and she gets stressed about the situation. She said she used not to be like that even though she all the times finds it hard to be in control of the situation. She says "All the times I give up quickly on my word because I can't handle them yelling". I have noticed that specially the little one is getting to me and making me more stressed, I don't know if it is her but I don't remember acting like this with the first daughter when she was the same age as the little one. Furthermore she said that she feel embarrassed when she is yelling to girls in public as she think that everyone is looking at her and they thinking "she is a bad mother". Also she finds it hard to relax.

Direct therapy:

Treatment plan was based on aims, objectives and issues that client was facing. The aims is to understand why she is behaving the way she is, why she can't relax, why she does not have patient when dealing with difficult situations and specially when the little one is yelling for no reason. Objectives are to learn how to have more easy-going, layback and to learn how to relax. The goal is to be a better mother to her daughter's. The issues are, low self esteem and emotional difficulties including some level of depression because she seems not to be in control of the situations around girls and the underlined issues are a known yet. Based on initial consultation she sad that she lost her dad 2 years ago but she did not say much about it, she was expressing more the stress level around girls. One of the underline issues might be that she just wants to be a perfect mother as maybe she did not had the perfect family while she was growing up.

What I need to do therapeutically in professional and ethical way to help the client to achieve her aims, objectives and goals? On the first session, I thought using the momentum stage to help me to investigate the client's emotional state by using the space to help the client to connect with her true self. Furthermore, I wanted to investigate her inner child to see what are the underlying issues that are making her behave the way she is. But I wanted to take it to her inner child event when she feel happier as I wanted as result her to have a taste of her happiness to help her relax in future and to build her confidence. With the help of universal energy and her connection with her own space helped her to go back and connect with the child she was at 7 years old and she was happy spending time with her dad. From the time I was doing the therapy, he had passed away 2 years ago. During the technique, I was using while she was relaxed and imagining those happy moments with her dad, abreactions occur and I can see her body reaction that she was worried of handling the moment of saying goodbye to her dad. I had to stop and let the client come out of the relaxation on her own terms.

In the end of the session, I asked her for feedback and discussed what could be done in future to help her with grief and loss of her dad. She sad that she feel guilty because she did not say good bye properly to her dad, she feel that she has not been enough a good daughter for her dad, and she wishes he was here because she has so many things to say to him. I suggested for next time that we work on the second and third stage of the Magical Module, which is 'acceptance' and 'goal', blended together, depending on the state of the client. Those two stages would assist her to have the ability to have the conversation with her dad as he was there in front of her and to say what she wanted to say to him before she says good bye to him. In addition, she would move on in peace with her life so the grief would not keep interfering with her emotional state, which will affect her behaviour. The future work on grief was needed as experiencing anger, sadness, fear, guilt and grief from the loss of her father influence the present and the future behaviour by causing fear and anxiety. Irrespective of the emotion, resistance is the underlining cause. For that reason we needed long term therapy to process that issue and give time to her in terms of acceptance and moving on.

This process helped her to build the confidence as a mother and to reprogram her subconscious to lay- back when her little one is yelling with no reason, but she yells just because she is used to get what she want by yelling. Furthermore to help to learn to be more patient and to try to understand and listen more to her children, which means to reprogram her subconscious how to be in control of the situation.

I continue to support this client through the seven stages of the Magical Module and she was able to make time for herself, to create her own techniques and methods, to communicate with her own children and to learn how to be calm, and turn her frustration into resilience. She felt happier as her daughters had noticed the difference because her communication with them was much better. As a result they listened to her more.

I suggested this some additional practical techniques that she could apply in her daily life, which will be explained in detail the Magical Module.

Client feedback of the book "A Magical Life"

I started reading the "A Magical Life" book and straightaway felt emotional could not pass the first chapter. Could not bring myself to finish it, not because I do not love the book but what can I say I need it full Power charge emotionally to read the book. You hardly get any books nowadays that are so raw it makes you skin crawl and believe me this is one of them. Reading someone's life in so much detail it really drains you yet it is amazing hence; it took me so long to read the first chapter only. I usually will finish a book within few days however "A Magical Life" book has taken me months and I know why every time I read something I need it a break to recover and charge my emotions.

Overall, the book it is amazing but if you are like me be prepared it takes all your energy I mean emotional energy but it is all worth it.

Client feedback of therapy:

The best question Vjollca asked me it was " take the moment to yourself and ask your self if the solution I have to resolve my problem does really make me happy" and it actually helped me a lot as when I took the moment in quite place I realized the solution that I was making was actually not the right one. Vjollca helped me so much to connect with my inner self and it made me realize that the connection puts into the right direction want to go.

I liked the practical techniques that you have given me as they were very helpful, nice case and it was good to use. It has helped to understand my self and feel much better now, calmer, and have more patience.

Vjollca's final thoughts: "She has a lot to learn about the space (the soul, universe) and she needs to connect with it more frequently. She is connected but is not aware, because it might seem absurdity to her. Her children are very connected to the space / Magical approach".

Case study 8:

Background: A female aged 65 lost her husband, feeling lonely and relying on others company. Suffering with physical pain in back, neck, around her belly, headache and not sleeping properly. She needed therapy to help to sleep, gone through methods on how to empty her mind and organize thoughts and also finding ways how to enjoy her own company.

Presenting Issue: Client had problem with sleeping and she just did not understand why she can't sleep well during the night and she does wake up in middle of night often. I asked how does she feels when she goes to sleep? She said 'just not sleepy', and then I asked what happen when you wake up in middle of night? She replied 'I am fully wake and my mind is everywhere'. She has been having problems since she remembered with her sleep and especially when she has something on her mind. Usually she feels a sleep in sofa and then when she wants to go to bed the sleep has gone. She starts to think about lots of different things. She was happy for me to use the Magical Approach and you can find details of the treatment in the Magical Module.

Direct Therapy: As I took her through the seven stages of the Magical Module, by allowing enough time to go through all the issues that she represented starting from momentum. In the acceptance stage I took her through each issue to understand what she really wanted. For instance, she said she felt lonely, and she liked to be in other's company but then she complained because did not really enjoy that company, which led to having headaches before went to sleep, and that spread other distressing issues, which caused the other physical pain. But she was not aware of it, so she was getting more and more physical pain. The stress was raising because she was worried that was being ill, loneliness, and not feeling loved. But she did not know how to understanding, how to deal with it, how to create options how to solve it. So by going through each stage of the Magical Approach I helped to reduce stress by understanding 'what she liked' and 'what she does not like' and making plans to achieve what wanted. Using affirmations to built her self-esteem, her self-confidence, valuing herself more, appreciating her company and enjoying that more.

She never used to go for a walk alone for relaxation. She never used to have a coffee or a drink on her own, outside. She never used to enjoy her own company alone at home. She had problems of going to sleep on her own due to headaches. But now using the techniques and methods that I taught her, she does a lot of walking, and enjoys her own company and has coffee outside on her own, and has improved in organizing her thoughts when she goes to sleep in order to reduce her headache. As a consequence she has also felt improvement in her physical health and has reduced the number of medical pills that used to take. Before she was frustrated and angry easily, but her emotional state has also improved because she feels so relaxed, calm and enjoys her time.

Example one of my guidance I wrote down after we had conversation about each points below:
For sleeping problems advice:

Causes of sleeping problems and discomfort when staying alone are:

1 - When you do not face the problems but try to throw it away and pass it fast and it does not lead to the solution or you blame others.

2 - You try to please everyone around and that will lead to not expressing exactly what you think or feel.

3 - When people speak up the truth to you you don't want to discuss it as it comes across as they are attacking you.

4 - All the above points bring misunderstandings between you and others and cause you unpleasant worries and inconvenience.

Solution:

1 - Be straightforward and say things in the eyes to others and to your self by looking your self in mirror.

2 - Have patience whole you search for solution and clarification.

3 - Practice this guidance "treat others they way you would like to be treated if you were in their place" and be open when looking for help and discussing what you want and what you don't want.   so it has to do with respect to yourself…

4 - Stay away from those who are treacherous and do not get involved if is possible with people who are people pleasers . … if you want their best interest just say what you think and let them decide, keep distance if is need it.

Vjollca's final thoughts: "I really want her in my seminars and workshops to teach others what she has done to achieve her goals. Self-love is very important".

Case study 9:

Background: A teenager that needed help because faces challenges to balance his Magical Person (the language of soul and energy of universe) with reality. He did not know how to explain reality. For instance, one of his sayings is "So now all my life has to be all about working!" My answer was "The importance is to know your main goal. Then we need to work towards that, by breaking the journey down into small steps and think how to enjoy it" He replied 'But I cannot have the job the job that I want and I do not want to do the other jobs!' Then I said: "It will give you pleasure knowing that each small step will help you to achieve the main goal. Automatically you know that loving those small steps will help you find pleasure in whatever you do. Working is healthy".

Summary of Direct Therapy: I worked with him intensively since he was 11 years old, in secondary school up to now that he is in university. And I have applied all the stages of the Magical Approach with him. He is now bouncing in all the stages because of his age changing. You can find more details in the Magical Module.

Below you will find some of his answers when I asked him to define the soul and to give me his understanding on the three rules: 1) Treat others the way you like to be treated. 2) Love yourself the way you like to be loved. 3) Do 100% in everything that you chose to do.

To define the soul, you need to talk about a plethora of different cogs that go into making it work. It has many mechanisms that are used to define somebody as a person and shapes the decisions that they make. The decision-making system in the body is governed by the soul. Its weighs up the pros and cons of any situation and then accordingly judges which outcome to choose. It takes into account a person's beliefs and values when making the final decision as we are defined by the decisions we make, yet the soul governs what decisions we make in life, suggesting that the soul defines a person for what they are. The soul confers with other key players within the body, such as the heart, which is in touch with the emotional side of the body and thinks about the needs of others and itself. The brain is also conferred with as it is the logical and selfish member which thinks about what it wants and how the easiest way to complete something is.

Whilst the brain is selfish, it is also rational and the body's main survival instincts causing it to always think about the needs and wants of you and often ignores others. On the other hand, the heart is far too emotional and fragile meaning that just following the hurt could be damaging to you as a person as it could cause for hurt and an extreme feeling of betrayal that others don't treat you as you treat them. The soul in this occasion keeps both of them acting in check and the way for a person to feel the right choice comes in the form of their intuition. A person's intuition can be very difficult to understand and hear as the brain and heart are usually more appealing to listen to and in the short term favour the individual more than the soul. But if you pay attention and just take a second to think, then you will be able to make the decision that is the correct one despite it being potentially harder to do and in the short term causing some discomfort.

There are three rules in life that are are very important to understand and implement in order to better yourself as a person.

- Treat others in a way that you would like to be treated. This is a staple rule of life and it should be common sense yet, in a society where it's eat or be eaten we are left fighting others so that we can succeed ourselves. This is the incorrect way of living and we should use the power we have to change that mentality to better ourselves and those around us.

- The second is to love yourself the way you love others, this has two effects, first of all, this makes selfless people take a minute and give themselves a break as they focus on pleasing others far too much and don't please themselves, and second it refers to the previous point of loving others as much as you love yourself and treating others in a way that you treat yourself.

- The final one is to put 100% in everything you do because we don't live long enough to regret not putting in that extra bit of effort in something and that could ruin the start of something very prosperous. This applies to relationships, education and tasks that you set to yourself as it makes you a better person to always try your best to succeed or else there's no point in ever trying.

Opinion about his mother:

I was given feedback from my parent in the form of many methods. I was too often scolded for small matters, which proved to be efficient. I became numb to more serious discussions as they yielded the same punishments as very small matters. For example when my room was messy with socks on the floor and empty water bottles, my mum threatened to take my x-box away and if I refused that punishment then I would be kicked out of the house. A more appropriate punishment may have been making me tidy the room there and then, instead the whole scenario was blown out of proportion. Another example of the same punishment being used for something of this calibre was when I gave my mum attitude and slammed the door on my birthday, the feedback I received was in the form of a beating which I still deem to be a shame as it was my 15th birthday. This caused me not to care about consequences once I had done something wrong. However, the positive feedback I was given was generally rare but present. I was told positive things for certain good things I did, but this did not happen frequently and was often cancelled out by the negative feedback I received later after being scolded for something.

However, in hindsight the high frequency of poorly communicated feedback I received due to a slight language barrier and sternness meant that I became able to communicate better with difficult people due to my experience with poor feedback.

Therapy: Through our discussion we went in depth about his feedback, which led to really that not being the issue, but he was angry, with his dad not being part of his life and he knew that his mother was there and he could express anything that he was feeling. So by him expressing his anger towards her, it kind of helped him to let the steam out.

Furthermore, he said that after he gave his mother this feedback, the next day he went away to his home, as he was not leaving with his mother at that time and this made him more frustrated because he missed her more. In my understanding this all showed that he was just trying to express what he was feeling, but not exactly what he was feeling.

One session with him:
This was a one off session where the aim was just to help him organise his things at the moment in order for him to be in top of his responsibility. ..such as ...money, university, work, his small steps towards his main goal and a we started for whole hour what I did was creating the energy for him to allow him self to be fully relaxed and then just suggested the structure and he did all the work by him self...I was surprised that I did not need to interfere as he was struggling to keep up with his responsibilities link to the topics I mentioned. His feedback were that he feels relaxed, calm, and have everything in order. ..now he can see clear what he needs to do and we agreed to do it once a month as follows up and reflection of the session we did the last and to add anything need adding.

As part of therapy was reading the book 'A Magical Life' His feedback below tells a lot about the magical person that he is. As you can see there are a few points that have impacted him such his reflections upon his own life:

Client's "A Magical Life" Book feedback:
First of all, I liked how the stories were integrated with the lessons and they complemented each other well, as they reinforced the message you were intending.
However I did not like the photo shopped pictures, as they looked amateur and made it seem less professional.
This made the book look less accomplished and took away from the meanings
I liked how your stories came and went and were scattered throughout the whole book
I also thought the pictures were a nice touch as were the extended captions as they gave an insight into what the author was thinking at the time.
However I did not think that the headings were made professionally as they did not look polishing clean because the hyphen separated the word when it should have been the letter then the hyphen then the word making a look more professional more clean and more sleek.
But overall I am impressed of it and I think that is a good attempt at a book and a lot of the things were right and the vocabulary used was very good also.

Reading the book had a an impact on my outlook of early life. This is because I was always taught not to do wrong things and always had a fear of making mistakes because of the fear of a punishment from my mother. However this helped me understand that mistakes and uncertainty is part of life and those who can't accept me for the mistakes I make don't deserve a place in my life.

Another thing I picked up from the reading was that if a family member holds you back then you shouldn't fear letting them go, as your development is the only thing that you should worry about when it comes to your main priority.

Vjollca's final thoughts: "You are a magical person and I hope you will find ways to apply that in the reality!"

Case Study 10:

Background: This client is 18th years old boy in care who needed help since the age of 16th because he had low self-esteem and low self-confidence. Actual problem was struggling to dream or understand if dreams existed. Struggling with his studies as he did not believe he could do it. For example, he wanted to stay with his friends in entry 3 English course instead of keep progressing and moving forward. Struggling to enjoy time at home and instead was spending too much time outside with friends and girlfriends. Now he is level 2 IT and doing gcsc English and math's. He enjoys spending time alone home and has improved on how he views girlfriends.

Summary of Direct therapy:

As a child in care at age 16 he was struggling to spend time on his foster care as he felt like he did not belong there… so he ended up spending most of the time outside with friends and girlfriends. Through the therapeutic approaches of Magical module took him through the self love-universal love -passionate love… self-love was to raise his awareness that is he showing love and care to himself? Was he respecting what he wants to be and who he is at the moment? The whole him? (Gone through in details as it is described in magical module). Universal love where others comes in my aim was to make him aware if he is having the universal love he wants to have around and how he could achieve that and same goes for discussion on passionate love. Because of whole this work he achieved to balance his life the way he wants and he feels comfortable, calm, relaxed, confident and enjoys everything he does including spending lots of time home on his own. Moreover he grown into understanding passionate love and he have one girlfriend not many as he use to have.

Below you will find a poem that I dedicated to him:

When you came through my path,
I just knew you are very special person,
I tried my best to teach you how to love yourself,
how to believe in yourself,
how to be who you really are ,
that person who can do anything he puts his mind into it,
caring and loving,
understanding and showing compassion,
Someone who knows how to live his life,
Someone who really care for others,
someone who has big dreams,
don't be afraid, trust yourself and follow your inner voice
and you will get what you want in life ,
Thank you for deciding to participate in the Magical Approach,

The dialogue below reflects my teaching him how to take responsibility for his actions and decisions through exploring options and creating techniques and methods to achieve what he wants:

<u>Vjollca</u>: Can you please express me your thoughts about our work together?

<u>Client</u>: I send it to you on email. That's all because you are rushing me.

<u>Vjollca</u>: Ok I got it

<u>Client</u>: Is it ok?

<u>Vjollca</u>: What you did not like… or what did wanted to be different?

<u>Client</u>: I don't know… I do not like because you're not patient

<u>Vjollca</u>: What do you mean? Give example please.

<u>Client</u>: You are firm. And you always think that you're right

<u>Vjollca</u>: Really… or after I have repeatedly said the same thing more then 3 times?

<u>Client</u>: The psychologist is not allowed to be firm.

<u>Vjollca</u>: Psychologist does not take responsibility for you. They help you to take responsibility for yourself.

<u>Client</u>: But you keep pushing me to do something.

<u>Vjollca</u>: Yes because I got permission to help you take responsibility for your actions. And that's why you got results. Because I believe in you and I don't give up until you give up.

<u>Client</u>: Okay okay

<u>Vjollca</u>: I am all Therapist, mentor, coach and healer" all this in one. So would you prefer me not to push you when you need to get something, or achieve something? … if you say I don't want …then it's OK…but if you say "I can't " …then I have to teach you that you can.

Client: If I don't like the way you tell me to do something maybe you should find alternative ways or things to do.

Vjollca: I tried but from what we have explored so far, there is no other way...apart from letting you not believe on your abilities. The truth hurts...and to claim the mountains it seems impossible but it is possible if you discipline yourself and follow the magical module: Momentum -Acceptance -goal-inspiration - affirmation -commitment –love. Or you could tell me which way would work with you.

Client: You have to suggest ways as you're the psychologist or all them other things.

Vjollca: No. I have to ask you what you want and what works for you and I make sure you are following it.

Client: What if I don't know.

Vjollca: I can help you to figure it out through talking and discussing it together.

Client: What if I want is money (smiles).

Vjollca: I can teach you how to attract money.

Client: I want £1million

Vjollca: It starts with you...within you. And money does not make you happy. This life is learning test. You can have anything you put your mind into it if you follow the 7 stages of Magical module that I have taught you.

Another conversation after one month of last conversation:
Example of accepting the soul:

Vjollca: I send him a long text how we as whole we work, soul/mind/heart and body because he is connected to soul with out being aware and I asked him what he thought about it? He laughed, then I had to push him to get into it and see what he really thinks about being guided by the soul.

Client: I don't know.

Vjollca: Just say what you think…what comes to your mind because I am interested to know your answer for my study research.

Client: Nothing comes to my mind.

Vjollca: Really ....

Client: Yes

Vjollca: or you are not paying attention to your inner voice?

Client: I don't believe on what you say anyways. Working with universe what is that?

Vjollca: Are you not curious to be fulfilled and loved in this life?

Client: You'll die still

Vjollca: Yes but at least I enjoyed this life. ...and then I am sure the other life will be easer then the one you had... previous if you work towards pure love/fulfillments and being in peace and love. For now is important to enjoy this life.

Client: There's no other life

Vjollca: Of course it is... The soul never dies
That's why you have goodness on you, because the soul is pure
The soul is energy... part of universe

Client: When u fall asleep u think about nothing and that's when u die too.
If soul doesn't die your brain still dies.

Vjollca: No ...on sleep you are you mixed with your worries
Human is brain, heart and body and that's why you see dreams sometimes when you sleep. Of course human dies because there are tools the mind, heart and body.

Client: The soul makes no sense without a brain.

Vjollca: That's why you need to look after mind, heart and body in order for them to work in healthy way and if you are guided by the soul that is pure love and you have all the answers there then you will have solution for every problem. Yes ...soul is you ...is energy that uses the human as a tool. to function on this life. If you use your brain is not you... but others who have put information on your head.
Your soul is you

Client: The heart and brain create the soul if one of them stops working soul fades. They create it.

Vjollca: They don't create the soul... but they work for the soul if you allow your soul to be part of your life by listening to your inner voice in silence and have your inner discussion about things you are not clear about. No ....soul is already created... is energy
That never dies

Client: You can still live without a heart. Brain is the main one. That's what u think

Vjollca: Human organs are different from the soul.
So like I said... human parts are science
Soul is energy
Well you can search... but the soul can not be proven but only you can feel it.
And only you can talk to your soul
The universe is the same. ......

Client: You just use your brain to think that u feel your soul but u feel thoughts of your brain still

Vjollca: No one can prove it apart from themselves
You try... I use my brain only to translate what my soul is saying
I don't alloy my brain to interfere as I don't trust my brain because brain is not pure and then I will do things wrong.

Client: You think that it is. Depends what your brain thinks.

Vjollca: Well... you practice it then tell me.

Client: Someone may think is right and someone may think is wrong

Vjollca: Is not about right or wrong... is about being pure. Not doing things that you know are wrong. Wrong it means hurting others or yourself. Soul does not hurt you or others because the core is pure love.

Client: Yeah, If you just are clever u don't do things wrong.

Vjollca: Well I started this journey since I was 7 and at 36 started to reflect on it and I am practicing it everyday, as it is not easy process to use your brain and heart as a tool
Sometimes they jump with out my control, but I fix it quickly.
So I am aware all the times of my mistakes and that's why is important to have people in your life who criticizes you. So you see your self better when you do wrong through have conversation with your soul.

Client: And all that happens because of how your brain works.

Vjollca: No no… I am not going to convince you but just telling you and it's up to you what you do with it… but that's the way I work, with my awareness I don't alloy my brain to make decision for me… only I use it to translate what the soul wants to say. I practice to speak directly through energy, not by brain. I do practice everyday and I do evaluate my self-daily through my inner conversations and through talking to good friends who are guided by their soul.

Client: Everyone believes in something different like you and it doesn't mean that is true whatever u believe on.

Vjollca: As long as they are fulfilled and happy is good for them, If they are not… then something they are not doing right, so I am fulfilled and very happy and that's why for me works …

Client: What if you don't believe in anything anymore?

Vjollca: Whatever makes you happy and what resonates with you is important. This life is all about you. So if everyone is happy. ..the world would be a better place, easy and happy place.

Client: Not everyone is happy.

Vjollca: You don't have to believe nothing just have to find your own way to be happy and that is only one person who can teach you… is your soul and they are not happy because they don't communicate with their soul.

Client: I don't believe on soul too.

Client: I know… because no one has taught us. I had to learn it hard way… through my pain, through my resilience.

Client: How do u know that you don't have something in your brain making u think that soul exists? U can't know.

Vjollca: Because I have learned how to meditate. if you call it that way as for me I call it inner conversations. To disconnect form reality and you are connected to the energy that has created soul, the universe and us.

Client: Everyone can learn that and you'll still use the brain to feel that.

Vjollca: Search on Google as even the science has said that when you are connected to energy the brain function different.

Client: Never mind.

Vjollca: The soul is everything you need in this life… but human parts are tools that helps soul to function so you have to look after them… to be healthy… again the soul can help you.

Client: Okay

Another conversation: He sends me the YouTube link where it was talking about the human existence, god and the purpose of life. I watched it and I send him my thoughts in very simple way pointing out that the purpose is to enjoy life as the video was very confusing and complicating things that were not important to question. He argued with me by saying that is no purpose of life and is no clear how the world had been created and why. I said that as far as I know everything is created by energy and the purpose is to enjoy the journey. He responded by saying how to enjoy the journey when you don't have money.

Then I explained that the joy comes from little things and is a feeling such as you were happy today with your girlfriend or you are happy right now. That's what it is and you work for your aims and goals. He smiled and went silent.

This client's feedback:

Since I've been receiving guidance from you I started to learn how to become more confident for example to talk to people or to do things on my own... I learned that if I try hard to get something I will succeed, for example I wasn't sure I'll pass English and Math's Level 2 exams and I passed them because you pushed me to study more... I can see hope. I can hope for the future now!

Vjollca's final thought: "During our interaction my aim was to sharpen more his listening skills, to listen to his intuition and connect with his real self to get the strength, hope, love and guidance he needs to make his dreams a reality".

Case study 11:

Background: Female, around 25 years old, in a relationship. The first time she met me she burst into tears as she felt my space, my soul, universal energy and reflection of her inner-self though my intuition. The reason she came was that she was feeling sad. She did not have intention to make changes in her life, because she was blaming herself for everything and did not understand why things were happening to her.

Summary: She came to me as she need it help to increase her self-confidence and belief in herself on learning how to be single and achieve the life she want. She is unhappy and she have notice that she feels the need of relying on someone for comfort to feel loved. She is going through thoughts of having divorce and looking to change her job, as she is unhappy with her actual job and her relationship. But after she overcomes all those issues as she moved on with her life with the help of my guidance based on magical module and she got the job she wanted. All those improvement and changes happen during one year. After that her concerns were that she does not get on very well with her mother and especially with her sister, she does like to go out a lot and drink as she finds it boring staying home, but then she does not feel good after wards because she ends up sleeping with someone. In last couple of months, she had three relationships with different men and she is struggling to let go of relationship that she creates. Now she has feeling for someone that she slept once while they were out and he lives far away from where she is living. She is confused on how to handle the feeling that have towards him and in mean time she wants to focus on saving money and getting her share from the divorce as she wants to get her own flat. She said that when she was a kid and in her tens, she was very close to her dad, and when she was drinking and staying out late nights her dad use to understand her and still love her. After her dad has passed away when she was 17, she got married straight after and she has been married since couple of month ago that she decided its time to get better life as she was not happy.

My approach is going to be based on aims, objectives and issues that client is facing and what we both agree is the first step to work on. The aims is to understand why she is behaving the way she is, why she can't be happy on her own, being single, why she does not have enough love for herself an what is making her the need of being receiving universal love (please refer to magical module) to someone? Objectives are to learn how to understand that need of universal love, to know what makes her happy, why and how she can achieve that. Such as to find ways how to communicate positive with her mother and her sister in order for her to enjoy the time she spends in the house. To explore the options of how to be happy at work an when she can go to gym. The goal is to be a happy, independent, not to relay in others in order for her to be happy. The issues are, low self-esteem and repetition of her patterns to cope. She also has replaced the universal love she had with her dad before he passed way couple of years ago with the universal love of her husband as she got married straight after her dad passed way. One of the underline issues is that she just wants to be a loved, and she feels guilty that thinks she has left her dad down by the way has been behaving when he was a life. My work will be to help her understand self love and how she can gain that going through each stages of magical module.

Although it will have to be flexible as the client's presentation at the therapy sessions. Treatment goals of the initial phase are to increase insight into self-defeating thoughts, feelings, and behaviours by identifying their harmful consequences; increasing understanding of their origin; specifying unmet needs and core negative self-attributions; and increasing motivation to attempt alternative responses. First step will be to help the client identify the habits she has created to feel safe but they are not serving and help her to identify how it negatively influences her life during last few years and at present. After gaining such insight, she will better understand why she think, feel, and behave the way she does, and will be more able to change maladaptive patterns behaviour. It is important for my client to understand before she start to make action towards self love. She have to be aware of what it is that she do to derail herself, why she is doing it and what it is getting her as a result. Establish what's gone wrong, what is it that she do? She need to pay attention to what she is doing, prior to, during and after the event. What repetitive behaviour is she using? What thought patterns are going through her mind? As a therapist I can assist and guide my client to reach the point and embrace the power she have to change and carry it on into the future to practice self-empowering of her magical person she really is but she is not aware yet. I allowed my client to walk on her own path at her own pace through each session.

At the times when she did not have the strength or ability to go on, I had to challenge her in order for her take responsibility of the situation and revisit her changes, and it was times when she need it her space to connect with past when her dad was a life in order for her to let go of guilt or some unhealthy feelings that she was feeling. The stepping stones will be, honesty, client must be honest with themselves about what they want to change and what responsibility they wish to or must take in order to achieve that goal, this is through seven stages of magical module blended together by taking bit by bit on each stage until she fully work in whole stages. Also sub stages of magical module in order to achieve identification of her soul, intuition, thoughts coming from her mind and the feeling created from mind, soul, intuition and universe energy. Whole this process will help to be aware of her magical person and connect through self love with her actual person she has been build in her reality.

In the beginning of the work client feedback

Her feedbacks from the last session were that she could not explain how she feels free to talk to me and that her mind has opened and can see things in different angel.

After few sessions of work client feedback

Her feedback was that she already feels the change but still she finding difficult to spend time home or on her own even she is aware of her feelings and thoughts.

My analyses in one of our sessions

I offered her understanding of the meaning of what is being said and experienced both in and out of the session and encouraged her to reflect and offer further associated memories with her dad, feelings related to relationships around her and fantasies that she have for her future in order to explore her inner world, experiences and relationships. I was aware of importance of my own emotional response link to the session as is known as the connection with all of her as person and refer to the feelings aroused in me by her (I connected with her soul. I read her mind and felt her heart). Again I was feeling frustrated and irritated because I was thinking why she can't see that she needs to be on her own and not wasting her energy and time on thinking about guys? When they are making her feel worthless, irritated and unhappy with they're behaviour? I thought if she was feeling this way unconsciously and then I asked her about the guy she was seeing and the other one that she had one night stand but she have strong feelings for him. Then she said he was ignoring her texts and not really giving back what she is giving to the relationship and the other one is married so is no point contacting him. For next session, we agreed that she would visit that place that she was telling me she used to go with her dad and then we discuss how she was feeling in order for her to feel more loved with herself and let go of negative feelings from the past. Her felling for her dad and how that has affected her on the relationship she is choosing with others, especially with men and she released what is important to her and she identified option how to achieve what she wants. I use this technique as it works with healing the inner part of us that relates to the child that we were because the inner child will affect the way we are as adults. Furthermore the purpose of this technique is my client to love herself and to accept herself and learn from life experiences as it comes in positive way. People with low confidence often worry about what other people think about them. So the antidote to low confidence involves learning to love yourself more fully so you don't need to be liked by others, but for that to happen I had to raise her awareness that it will take time to achieve self love and see the full result. But as long as she does the small steps she will claim the ladder. As I take her through sub stages of magical module, being aware of her achievement and make little thank you cards to appreciate yourself and to remind your self that you are special because this and that...and that you can and you have the ability to claim other steps in the vision client have. This will help to reinforce her subconscious to act on her thoughts and to feel that good feeling of herself and connect with her soul.

We started getting summarizing all the progress she has done from the first time she come to me up to now. She said that she has started divorce and she is just in process of it and she has knowledge the feelings towards her dad, how close she was to him and how she been missing him so much that she have been trying to replace it with the love and affection from other men's. As I have explained in the Magical Module, the universal love is not healthy if you have not achieved self-love. It has to be in order: self love comes first, then universal love, then passionate love. She is very happy to visit the place she just discovered couple of weeks ago where she use to go with her dad and it is close to her work. Furthermore, she has overcome few issues at work and she is doing well. According to her relationship with her sister and mum she is still working at it and she still is going to continue dating, but she has finished those two relationship that had and she is more aware of how to respect herself first and put herself before anything. She also said the stages of the Magical Approach have been very helpful and she will like in future to have few coaching sessions link to her managing her finances so she can buy her own house and she will be more happy as she will be more independent and can relay on her self. She has been relying on her self but not to get her dream life and for that she was waiting for her love men to arrive or found....but now she is determined to get her dream life on her own and she is aware of what kind of partner she wants and how to recognize it when she see him or meet him.

At the times when this client did not have the strength or ability to go on and I had to challenge her in order to take responsibility of the situation and revisit her changes. Furthermore it was times when she need it her space to connect with her past when her dad was a life in order for her to let go of guilt or some unhealthy feelings that she was feeling. The stepping-stones we took during each session were very helpful and her honesty did help a lot on identification of her self-structure created based on the reality she was surrounded.

Also during the blended stages of goal, love and inspiration she came up with new choices, which includes decision from the choices they came up and keeping up awareness of reasons and sustaining them. When a person has a low self-esteem, they are more likely to be susceptible to having depression, anxiety and, emotional distress, which are problems that are usually directly related to a less favorable self-appraisal and that lead to other underlined issues of the time is not taken to understand your whole you as a person.

Limits and flaws

The flaw's been that the client was very open to the Magical Approach and she was just letting out everything and she said that she told me things that she has not share with no one else before. Based on that it was easy for me to create a treatment plan even though I was open minded and flexible to just go by flow and not follow the plan. The telepathy skills allow us to think about the nature of our minds and those of others. It allows us to see things from different perspectives and in the context of our difficulties, think about what we, or someone else, may need. Furthermore the limits are that because of the absurdity of my holistic approach is a bit weird the whole process.

Conclusion

Concluding everything went to the accomplishment of the Magical Approach and I got positive feedback from the client and in the end of it. I notice a massive change on her self-esteem and confidence. Working with the whole person (the space and mind, body, heart) is very effective way to discover and heal the hidden cause of physical emotional and life problems. By making peace with your past, chronic stress is reduced, alloying body to heal and by clearing your self-limiting beliefs you can use your space as the incredible tool that it is to create life you want. That's why I applied the Magical Module and each session took my client one step closer to understand herself better and fill up the understanding of the gap from how she is feeling and how she like to feel. However, I sense that she needs more work to do in self-love.

Client Feedback

During these sessions Vjollca has helped me to understand the reasons behind some of my feelings/emotions I have. I always describe her method as the onion peal; with the open questions she asks me about my feelings or emotion, removing one layer at a time until I actually get to the real reason why I'm feeling the way I am. The answers are always there, hidden, until I start to peal the onion. Vjollca has really helped me to have a more of a positive outlook on life as well, with some goal mapping exercises, having something to focus my mind and energy on.

The magical Approach assisted me in opening up a lot more thinking outside the box with regards to work, home life and my relationships. Putting together a plan of my aims and goals and how to take each step in the plan. It helped me to put my self in others people situations and understand them better and their impact on my situation. It has helped me to open my eyes and give me the confidence I was lacking to listen to my self and make the decisions that felt right for me.

Vjollca's thoughts: "If you do not achieve your self-love, you cannot jump to other people's love!"

Case study 12:

Background: Female, around 27, in relationship. She presented with suicidal thoughts and she had already attempted to kill herself once, as part of her relationship unhappiness.

Summary: I worked with her for over three years and practiced on her the Magical Approach, taking her through each stage and sub-stage of the Magical Module. The outcome of the three-year is that she gained her confidence. She is practising self-love. Her relationship has improved. She is very happy in her relationship. She is currently working in self-love and to connect with her soul , sharpening her intuition and understanding the universal energy.

Client's "A Magical Life" book feedback

I read a little bit of your book Very painful at first It seemed as though I was watching it on television like a movie In the I become tearful to be honest because I did not know a part of your life But I laughed at the cow's part. What kind of communication between friends. But what I want to say is that you have yourself put two goals:

1 - To get lost in darknes because of others and others deciding for your life !!

2 - To promise your self to have courage to face all the difficulties that are presented and face any sacrifice to reach your dreams and goals no matter what price you would have to pay to reach where you want it!

And today you are where you have to be the person who first love yourself, has dreams and dreams become true when the person finds sincere and true answers within

Your story of your life makes the cloak and open the dark curtains that do not allow the sun's rays to deplete in the darkness that an inexperienced person decides to abase, It gives you hope to continue life and joy.

Client's Feedback

I was very confused about everything in my life. I wasn't concentrating on the things that I was doing. I was feeling destroyed. I have to say that lots of things have changed since I have meet Vjollca. I feel more confident with myself. I started to love myself and believe on my self. Most important thing is that my relationship with my husband is in the right way. I started to believe on love again. I would recommend her approach to everyone and the reason why is because others will find them self's firstly and they will find the way to solve they problems and how to find the peace with themselves.

Vjollca's thoughts: "You are in the right path. Well done for having the courage to get to trust your inner self ".

Case study 13:

Background: Male age around 60, divorced, living alone.

Summery: At this case I had to do with trauma from domestic violence that was still going on. Also was the issue of feeling lonely, hopeless, and in mean time he wanted to be in relationship and he was looking for relationship. The objectives were to help him see the whole picture clear and gain his self-love. Even though he was in denial that he needs self-love as he said he loved him self but he was looking for someone to be in relationship and to sort out his current situations of domestic violence he was in because of his divorce.

In the First session (telephone conversation) I focused on connecting with his soul and understanding him as whole, mind and heart.

In session two (telephone conversation) I noticed from his homework that he has not done his homework by thinking deep and he was still in defense /resistance /excuse /blame mode........He was going on and on ...how bad he was feeling and that he don't see any way out. He asked me what I can do to make him feel better....

After I explained few times the process and how I work and he still didn't want to understand it. I had to be really firm for him to wake up and notice what he need it to do....or otherwise it means he was not ready for help... he did not like it and he was trying to convince me otherwise.   but I said I will write in email the main points of this session and how we can move on but also in mean time I need you to write feedback from the first session and the second session. he said "I will not write a good feedback because the first session I felt loved and understood but the second one I was beaten up from you as you were so firm and strict ". I said that's what I want to say the truth, of how you think.....

Vjollca: *Client feedback verbally on first two sessions and my email below send to him.*

In the first session we discussed the following points:

- importance of love yourself, and how I will do it.

- Homework to do that you did.

- Light the candle with your prayers.

Second session:

- Homework I pointed out that you did not do it properly and have to do it aging on self love and not to look for love on others.

- We discussed if it was important to love yourself before you look for relationship. Would you work with your sadness before you look to find someone else?

The questions I want you to answer during this week are below:

What is your best interest? Answers should be based on a combination of reality, logic, dreams. Then you have to tell me in small steps how do you achieve them, from this moment and how long will it take? How important is it for you to be spiritually peaceful and loved ? How can you achieve it your happiness with what you have right now and where you are now? Without changing anything? If you want change thing to get by yourself and not through changing others? What help do we need from our sessions? Please give me the opinion of the two sessions we have made so far on writing.

Client's Email responds to my previous email:

1 - My goodness does not exist, and tomorrow is my delay. I do not see it not because I don't wanted that but she has abandoned me. In these conditions when in return of your good actions you get suffering and pain then my self lost alliances with friends and universe.

2 - It is very essential to be in harmony with life and others, but as I am a person I communicate will happen things that irritate me. To get happiness I am not sure but I cultivate happiness. I have no idea how long it takes but usually I do good and bad comes on return.

3 - My feedback: The first session was the session bringing back my smile and the hope that there are people in this world that will help. One week of relaxation and positive thoughts. The second session was fierce, shocking, and devoured what I had cultivated. A person who is in serious neurotic psychosis and has lost a lot not long ago. A man who knows that in a tautological labyrinth does create change on one week (even a little planted need some air, light, and water) it was certainly too early to use contention, intolerance , the ban to confess, the unfolding of dreams and all the other admiration. To stop someone who is without gravity that has no specific weight and is only an undeniable mass that the trajectories that the first session launched was unacceptable. I just started with a ritual week calling good and getting some nuances of self-confidence came as a tornado the second session and it drove me down. In deepest trauma, I drink the silence and contemplate the pain.

Vjollca's notes relating to his feedback, which I have explained to him as well: I made him aware he needed between 6 months and two years therapy, but I was clear in what I could offer and how the process would continue and he agreed but he had not accepted that yet, and that is why his reaction are like that. However, I knew exactly what I was doing and which kind of results I would get, and that is why in the end of the therapy I received successful results, as he understood the self-love and started to apply it in his life. In addition, he started to understand the universal love, which relates to others, and how he could bring into that the language of the soul.

The first session was to give him the taste of pure love and that hope is around us but we need to take actions and responsibility.

Therefore in session two I had to be firm on what I explained in session one as he wanted to stay in talking mode and not take action but that was not about what we had agreed and how magical module works.

Vjollca's response to his email above:

Please answer the questions below by looking at yourself in mirror and thinking that you are alone in this world and you will live alone but decide to be happy. ...

How can you be happy with yourself?

How can you turn this dark situation into shining one?

What advice would as you when you were12 year old to yourself now?

What are 3 prayers that you will like to say every night to universe or the LORD?

It's normal for you to feel like that because you just by feeling the pain, you understand yourself, the situation, and then you will be able to look at the light.

Client's email providing answer's to my questions alone. It was a very long email, but to protect the confidentiality just a summary of it will be provided:

Who is he now!!

Always it comes a moment and need a reflection! (The client started to explain the process by just jumping from thought to thought and did not answer the question.) But who am I? "Deeper and deeper. It may never come a moment to have an answer. How to make the most of that precures moment? What to pick a right moment.

This is the right moment. But for who I am now, since I am so tired and barely keeping balance with myself and the space, the divine and the infinite, a joyful and joyful shade ... I am crying in these moments because I lost the Divinity, I lost Love and there is no answer. But I do not give up, my mind is silent - I am in a relationship with someone away from my mind Who is asking you There is someone in someone here I am I will suddenly dwell on the question. I will rest on the fluctuations of meditation, I am in the Epicenter of Quietness and I am forever. "Regardless of the fact that a vacuum, empty, solitude, abandonment, ignorance, unrelated to the universe is going through, without a connection with a person knocking it as a divine destiny to love lovingly. To love the soul! You are my creature and blessing. I will only say, "I am." I'm conscious, pure mind, a clean mirror. Right now, at this moment, I exist. I needed these stories to make my situation clear.

End of the therapy comments: As I mentioned earlier, this client managed somehow to accept that he needed to work on his self-love, in order to receive the answers to all this questions. I have given him all the tools he needed to continue the process of self-love on his own. I am very happy with what we both achieve in a very short time, which was only three weeks. He feels peaceful and more confident to be on his own. He understands self-love. He understands others in a different angle of love, including universal and passionate love, which helps him to manage the situation with the approach he wants.

Client's Feedback:
Vjollca understood and felt my energy from the distance, and was able to apply her magnitude of divinity on me. Her question and approaches of the spiritual interaction provided me with a balance in my whole self. She tapped into my inner self, and made me finally feel joy inside me. Somehow I felt the universal energy, which helped me to have hope for love. I am very happy with myself. I managed to gain what I thought I had lost. Thank you for the miraculous healer that you are.

Vjollca's final thoughts: " To have knowledge and to putted in practice are two completely different things….He had and have knowledge more then me I will ever have and now that he got understanding of self-love he will enjoy his time, his life and he will find the right person to share his life with".

Case study 14

Background: It was more about my curiosity to use her as a case study because I felt she was fully connected with the space (the soul and universe) and I wanted to explore in more depth. Her age was 7 when I started working with her and now she is almost 10 years old.

Any relevant history:
She used to write amazing bits and pieces of notes, songs (she was into writing songs as her dad loved writing songs and singing), singing, drawing, and most amazing she wrote poems then and then.

The direct work with her to sharpened her intuition and help her knowledge the space through conversations, writing poems, drawing, playing, painting, role play, exploring the nature an expanding imagination and accepting what realty did not accept. When she filled up the questionnaire, she was a little bit disconnected from her space. My explanation is because of her age. She is ten years old, and she needs to apply more of spiritual knowledge in her life in order to remain connected all the time. She needs to master it, and somebody to teach her how to master it.

Her poem below: this is her free style writing and she said she wrote it about life:

Life is happy and kind,
We grow then learn what
And how life is now life a joyful thing where we live
Life is made by God that people worship
Some people have a different God they believe in
But the God should have a meaning of being a god
Life help's us in the troubles coming
But I hope we all know
life is trustworthy and good

Feeling's are sad,
feelings are happy and some emotional
But bad and rude feelings are not good
I myself always have
the feeling of happiness writing poems
And it get's me glad that I have a talent
a talent of being me
And just to show your inner power
Believe in yourself

Her drawing, which represents love (this drawing tells a lot in my opinion, but I will provide no explanation to allow the readers to make their own interpretation):

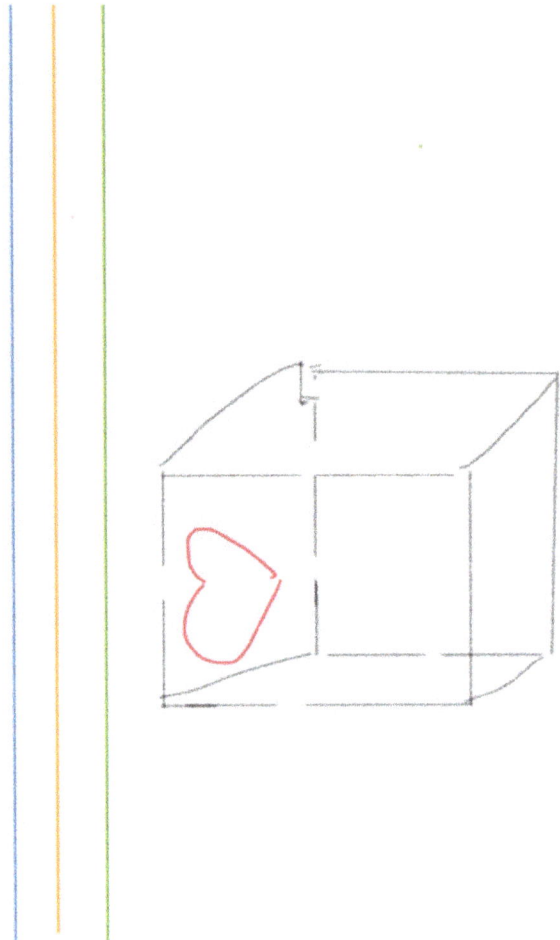

A drawing from another session when I asked her to write a song or make a drawing, to describe her soul, God, universe energy, mind, heart and body.

First she was not happy to do it because she did not want to, but after she did it she thanked me as she was feeling very alive and proud of herself, feeling connected to her space. She was amazed about the job she had done and she thanked me that I had encouraged her to do it.

Description of the drawing below:

(This writings are on the speech bubble on top of the baby's head: Babies are pure like the soul,). Below the speech bubble next to the head of the baby: The sun beaming on the babies head as a meaning of laughter and joy)

The Soul/Heart.

The soul is a special organ that leads to emotions and feelings. It also is fair, relative of the heart. They both lead you to warmth and comfort throughout time, when you feel depressed and upset.

Energy: I feel a massive, way of energy in the universe because in my family we have a lot of love and care. I love to share my problems with other people such as friends and families, because it makes me feel open when giving me a lot of energy.

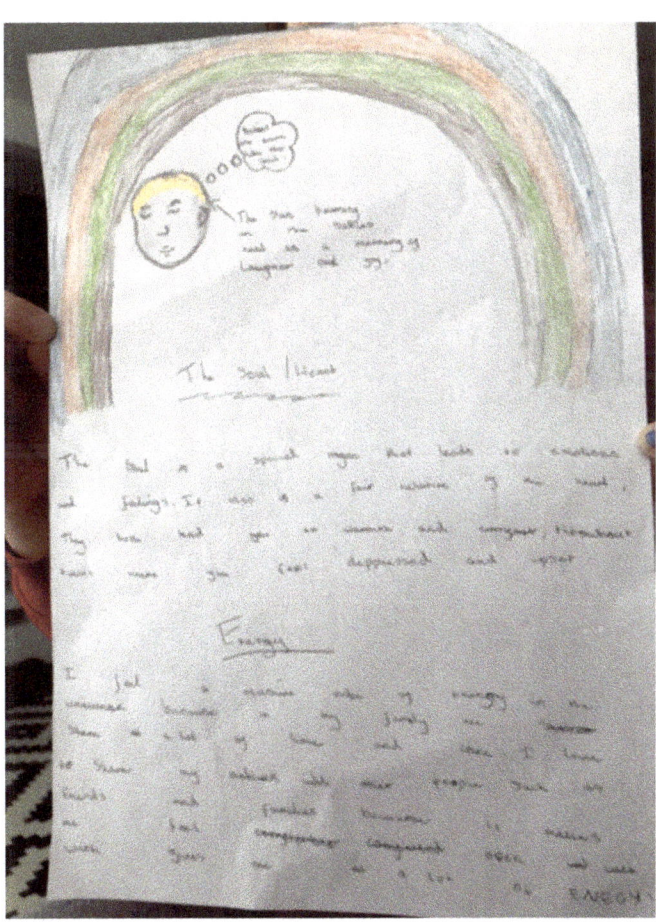

The drawing below is her vision of dream catcher.

She said: I chose flowers because the smell is very natural and that makes me calm. I also picked it because the color of flowers to me brings joy.

Writing on drawing: "my mum is my dream catcher because of her eyes. When I look it, then I feel lost, sage and that I can achieve anything."

Vjollca comments link to this drawing: It is very important for mum to be happy and great role module as clearly can see from this child's drawing that she looks up to her mum for strength, inspiration and to have anything she wants. That is an amazing feeling to believe that your mum is your dream catcher as you believe on dreams and you have great guidance.

Another drawing: Writing on drawing below: Auntie with the nature

Land and nature are a special key in life. It builds your confidence and brings comfort, warmth and peace. Your faith could increase which in the future could help as well as confidence, warmth and peace

<u>Vjollca's final comment:</u> *"I want to emphasize how crucial it is to encourage children's magical person and apply it into reality and keep nourishing it as they grow up".*

Case study 15

Summary: It was more about my curiosity using her as a case study because I felt she was fully connected with the space and I wanted to explore in more depth. Her age was 5 when I started working with her and now she is almost 7 years old.

When she was 5 she was not connected to the space and as soon as she turned age 7 she was amazing as after our work through speaking her language but in the energy of her space, (soul, intuition, universal energy) she filled up those questionnaire below.

One of her drawings during our contact (I asked her to draw with colors a description of the soul, energy, mind, body and heart):

She wrote on drawing: "The heart, in people is very special and it is creative to them."

Below she done her vision of dream catcher: (In my view giving the child the power to believe on themselves and on their own vision is very powerful tool).

The writing on drawing is: "Sun….the sun gives brightness and happens."

Vjollca's final comments: "Children amaze us and teach us a lot of things. We just have to learn to listen and sometimes be with them in their world".

Case study 16

Background: Client, unemployed, around his twenties, but had psychic abilities and tarot reader.

Summary: Was the case of blaming others for the things and situations making him unhappy instead of looking the situation within and then reflecting out with what you create within.

An example of a technique that I gave him to work on:

Two things to work on it this month:

1 - To heal your heart (have free time with your self and be mindfulness about how your heart is feeling, listen, understand it, care for it and show compassion).

2 - Create affirmation to grow your confidence and believe in yourself example "I love myself, I am very confident that I can deal with any situation, no matter what it is , I believe in my self , I can achieve my dreams".

3 - Another one to continue is to read my book and discuss his thoughts but he has not been able to do that.

Client's feedback form

The reason I contacted Vjollca was to find help in giving sense to my life and to rise up my confidence and self-love. I really liked the attention and sensibility to my problems, the sincerity and the honesty was really valuable for me. What was unique about this therapy? I worked talking with Vjollca for two years and in the first month I started feeling the improvements in my life and personality, she helped me understanding myself and discover hidden aspects of myself, with her service I started trusting and loving myself more, I started believe and during the second year I made huge improvements in every aspect of my life. She gave me the motivation that I needed to keep fighting for my objectives when everything was 'stuck', I really appreciate her supporting and I would recommend her to everyone who needs help/guidance.

Vjollca's final note: "Even though he has improved in amazing speed he still he needs to keep continuing and not get satisfied and stop, start using his magical person, to create the reality he wants".

Case study 17

Background: Laura: female around 30 years old. She was struggling with frustration because she was not getting the results she wanted. She was a busy mum with children, working full time and she wanted to find balance between work and family responsibility, her passion and her voluntary work.

Summary: Had one-hour session over the phone. And the rest of therapy took place by 2-3 communications in Facebook messenger. I also gave her my book, for self-help to achieve her aim and her objectives. This case study was a one off conversation and by following up guidance on Facebook page.

Below you will find a technique I suggested to help her to have a clear vision of her thoughts and experience them in order:

- Make a list of the things she is doing and put it in order, which one is in priority and why, which one will be in bottom.

This is the homework I gave her and included three points:

- Morning and evening check in with your self, by looking your self in mirror for the topics we talked through the session.

- Made a list of the things she needs to go over and have a look.

- Mindfulness how to believe on herself.

Client's feedback after our first conversation:
- It helped me to believe and have faith on myself

- Small steps to take and enjoy them

- Spending time with yourself

- A special technique to from the Magical Life book to help her organize her thoughts and put them in order.

Client's feedback after our first conversation:
- It helped me to believe and have faith on myself

- Small steps to take and enjoy them

- Spending time with yourself

- A special technique to from the Magical Life book to help her organize her thoughts and put them in order.

Client's final Feedback

I had a telephone coaching conversation with Vjollca Sadiku of 'magical coaching' and she was very helpful with going straight to the point of what I wanted to discuss. Her advice about how to 'solve' my time management and planning was very helpful as we broke down every element into smaller parts and looked at 'what can be done to fix each of them'. The biggest piece of advice and the one I have followed through since, was about 'listening more to myself' and creating the time and the 'short exchanges' of facilitating that chat with myself. Surprising how much 'good advice' I could find in me about what 'I' (not others) want to do and how much 'less frustrated' I feel. Thank you for facilitating this positive and fantastic transition in me.

Client's feedback for the book "A Magical Life":

Feedback before she finished reading the whole book

I started reading the book and I liked and attracted me. I was reading it during the holidays and I stayed up late trying to read a lot. Your life stories have drawing my attention but also the philosophy and the mindset that shares with the reader. It has inspired me to hear more of my heart and intuition and to present the questions I have first to the intuition for solution. Work in progress of course ...

Feedback after she finished reading the whole book

Hello, Vjollca, I hope you are fine. I read the book and liked it.

1. It did helped me to connect / hear myself more. Why ? Because I ignored what I was saying to myself, I heard it but did not follow it and I considered it confusing and it seemed to me that the answers were out of the rest of the people. Now I have the situation clearer and I know that although my inner self speaks a lot and most of the time it does not make sense and not all things are clear and it is my job to clarify them through questioning .

2. Yes Plan It is always in development, except that it is clear that small steps are needed, mini plans should be done regularly. Tree exercise is good for this and drawer of organising thoughts. All people / children need such education / lessons because we do not all look at things at this way and not everyone believes they can do things for themselves as long as they have a plan, an idea, energy and a passion.

3. Your story touched me and the the fact that you did not know why you were with grandparents away from your mum as a child and if you knew it was to help them you would have understood your situation better. Even though it is difficult for you as a child, what happened was a blessing ... I wanted to tell you the little thing that everything will be okay and you are not alone But now you are strong and you teach others ...

Vjollca's final thought: "She is a great example of a busy mum, balancing her busy life, with full-time work, following her passion, getting involved in charity work, and still has time for personal development".

Case study 18

One off session only through texts…..

Background: A divorced man around 35 years old, with children under 9.
Summary: The reason he contacted me was to have some understanding of his situation and how to improve his communication with his ex or the mother of his children and how to be a good father. We initially had 15 to 20 minutes conversation on Facebook. Because of my abilities, I managed to connect with him through my skills, which allowed me to sense that he wanted her ex to change and I understood that he was right and he was a great father and was dealing with the situation excellently, but I had to be tough on him and very firm on the instruction and guidance that I gave him, as I could see that the only way forwards was for him to allow the children to take responsibility, to make their own choices, and to accept the fact that there might be some tears during this process. This was for his ex to accept that he would stand his ground and not do whatever she wanted him to do. He would continue to do the best for his children as he had done so far and not give in, to the complaints and the unhappiness arising from children, which is an unavoidable part of this situation. Even though I believe in my abilities and my skills I doubt that he will make improvement, because he was so fragile in terms of the children requests and could not see his children being upset (the reason of children being upset was their mother, who was manipulating them to use their dad). Surprisingly after a few days, he replied to me saying thank you, and I was so happy for him.

Client's Feedback

Hello Vjollca, I wanted to write to you and simply share my opinion and thoughts about my impressions. First of all, I liked your appearance. When I saw your photo for the first time and looked at you in the eyes I experienced a sense of calmness and security. That glance made me take the courage and write to you about the problem that I was facing and my emotional state. It is not easy to unfold a personal problem that has to do with emotions. I think you are very honest and direct in your energetic and supportive responses. You have given me a new feeling and energy that says: 'You are not alone. I am with you'. Since the day I wrote to you for the first time, your presence remained within me. Even though I was alone after we spoke, I no longer felt lonely'.

Vjollca's final thoughts: " A great example for a father who was doing an amazing job, with his life and his children and still being aware and knowing when to ask for help when he needed it"

Case study 19

Background: A female client around 22 years old came to therapy as her friends and colleges had noticed that could be something wrong with her because, she could not focus on work, tasks and she forget things. Furthermore, they had said she daydreamed a lot at work. They suggested she should see a professional because of her past problems might be still issue for her. She was worried if she was going crazy, as she was not sure what was going on. She was aware of all her past issues such as, moving houses to often, not knowing her dad till he had past way a number of years ago. She had also lost her granddad that she was attached to him and loved him very much. He had recently passed away and her mum had suffered from depression for long time and changed her boyfriends all the time. However, she said I have made peace with the past and I don't understand what is really going on. Her relationship with her mum is not a close relationship. She talks to her once a week. She questioned why her friends and work colleges are suggesting that may be something wrong with her. Her friends were also worried it as she does never opens to them and they have never seen her crying. Also, she was worried and doubting if she had truly dealt with her past issues? She came to therapy to understand her worrying and stress. She also 'I drink every evening quite a bit'.

Summary: Our first conversation occurred over the phone. I interacted her by saying "what do you think…..I can't imagine how you must be feeling…." she took a deep breath and said "but I thought I have dealt with all of that, what do you think". " I don't know ….." I said. After a pause she again was questioning what their friends were saying that she does not open up to them. She did not do that because she said she felt they never talk about their problems and they felt like they don't have anything in common apart from partying and drinking. By helping the client to bring up her unconscious ideas, fantasies about herself and others, I aimed to enable her to develop her own capacities for understanding her feelings, thoughts and relationships through the process of experiencing and reflecting. By stating with the Momentum stage of the Magical Module the client was gradually helped to come to terms with what she is and is not, and realize what she still can be: to move from an inflated inadequacy to accept being ordinary and yet unique. I was doing more listening and letting her reflect on her feelings and thoughts by speaking the language of her space, with me being in her level and understanding her mind. I was helping her to see all the good things that she had around her. So we agreed to spend a whole intensive day in therapy, to dig deeply and find exactly where the root of her concerns was.

The whole day therapy by the seaside:

Being close to nature and water was part of the Magical Approach. The water would help her to reflect and see things clearly, to be relaxed and calm. The greenery would give her strength, trust and hope. The sunshine would give her a smile and joy and that warmth of her space to open up. She initially began by going in circles, questioning why her work colleges thought like that about her. She also was questioning her own self, wondering if she was going crazy and she was repeating the same question: "is there something wrong with me?" , I just stayed with her questions in silence to give her the time to find answers or simply wonder about it. And she did, by exploring her past. The first stages we went through were the Momentum and Acceptance (refer to the Magical Module) to encourage the client to become fully aware of her feelings without me advising her or making suggestions yet. At this point I simply offered warmth and empathy, and through my skills I helped her to go deep in her past as a journey, and feel as if she was living it. Good feelings were encouraged, because they strengthened the inner self. Negative feelings can then be viewed in a non-threatening manner and more objectively. Through this process her Magical person was expanding and in this journey in her past she explored what was disturbing her.

We needed to go in more depth to explore her emotions of universal love and relationships with others. She was expressing feelings of her father missing on her life and the death of her granddad. She was telling me that she did spend time with her granddad just before he died and she felt she had dealt with it but didn't understand why she couldn't have tears, as her friends were concerned and that was playing in her mind also.

She said 'I had not notice that I am not happy the way I am living my life now until now'. She burst in tears as she was looking at the sea. Gradually the client was becoming more self-aware by bringing the unconscious into consciousness.

Furthermore the purpose of progressing into the other stages of the Magical Module blended together was to make my client aware of self-love, to accept herself and learn from life experiences as they come, by using the tools from the Magical Module. People with low confidence often worry about what other people think about them. So the antidote to low confidence involves learning to love yourself more fully so you don't need to be liked by others.

She continued by telling me all the good things that has been happening and how she has a plan to continue with this process of thoughts as she really can see clearly now what she wants, how to get it and how to be aware of other people behaviour not to make her feel down.

The work continued by to helping her think of her strengths and what she wanted.

We started summarizing all the progress she has done from the beginning of the day up to the present and clarifying what she wanted and how she will keep it up what she has achieved through the stages of the Magical Module. She was very happy an exited as she was already looking for a room to move out. She had discussed it with her work colleges and they were supportive of her decision.

My comments: Our work together was based on the specific issues that client was facing. Which the question is what are really the issues and underlined issues? But at the beginning they were not clear. Immediately I sensed that she had had a hard past. Moving house few times, which had led her to becoming the centre of attention as she used that as coping mechanism to survive during the moves. She said wherever she moved she was popular at school. She lost her dad and her granddad, which lead to exploring the feelings of loss and grief and her relationship with them. We tried to understand why why she was behaving the way she was, why she was worrying, why she was losing her concentration at work? Why does she think, she may be going crazy? What is really going on? Had she dealt with her past? Or was it something right now at present disturbing her? As she said she was living with her work colleges and she does not get paid in money because everything goes to directly to rent, bills and food. Also she said she does not like that her work colleagues expect from her to do the cleaning after they have guests around as they do often have guests for dinner but again she jumped to her past and what her friends were concerned about her. Objectives are to learn how to have more easy-going, laid back lifestyle and to learn how to relax. To cut on drinking on evenings so she can have more time with herself as she was complaining she is tired all the times and she does not have time to relax. The goal was to find out what was going on and to understand herself better, so she could release the stress and anxiety she was feeling. One of the underlining issues was that she was avoiding what was disturbing her in order to continue to be strong as that has served her in past as a coping mechanism. Those who engage in a repetitive cycle of failed attempts to fulfil a core human need, whether it is the need for intimacy, affiliation, control, or acceptance, may be vulnerable to mental health difficulties such as depression, anxiety, social isolation, or compensatory externalizing problems. Despite the wide variation in potential symptomatology, the basic issues individuals share are frustration with having a core need remain unfulfilled and diminished hope and/or lack of self-efficacy in future attempts to change one's situation and perceived lack of control.

When the client came to therapy was confused but by end of the therapy she was clear that she had dealt with her past and what was stressing her was present. She was just affright of admitting and being independent as she had been independent all her life and she was just tired, so she just need it encouragement to remind her of her strength. Even though it was one day, the use of the seven stages of the Magical Module gave huge results. When I followed up the client after a few weeks, she said to me verbally, that she had managed to move house, she was happy where she was living, she was happy with her work and she was doing a lot better as she was regularly practicing self-love and using a great variety of tools that I had given her to apply on her own.

Vjollca's final comment: "I wish she could see the strength I notice on her and the admiration I had for her the way she had dealt with her past and still could see the light ....she was following the light no doubt about it" "It is important to know our values, strength and how special we are and how following the light can give us exactly what we need"

Case study 20

Background: Single man, around 30 years old with a narcissistic personality. He was too scared of falling in love.

Summary: Direct and indirect therapy for a many years. This man had many women after because he knew how to make them fall in love with him. He kept distance from those women and met them only when he wanted them.

He was talking a lot and smiling a lot, all the time he was distracted, so he could not focus in the conversation. He had a lot of headaches and migraines. He was scared to have a family or to have someone to love. He did not admit it because, he was not directly asking for my help, but through the years by being in contact with him I applied my approaches I helped him to increase his belief in himself, to value and respect himself more and to believe in love, which lead him to create his own family and have kids. But later, I worked with him on the trust issues and to keep building his self-confidence and self-love as well as to have an understanding of self-love, universal love, and passionate love. And now he has improved massively. He is now in his last touches of self-development.

Vjollca has helped me to understand myself. I founded effective the way she dealt with my situation. Unique was that she tells me what I don't want to hear by being a mirror of my soul, mind and heart. Before I was a different person and confused and she helped me find myself, feel better about myself. I am doing better in life and I know to whom to talk to if I need to.

Vjollca's comment: "Anyone can change. They just need to have the desire to do that."

Case study 21

Background: Pregnant mother in domestic violence and coming from a domestic violence background, with several suicide attempts. She had claim asylum seeker in Uk and was receiving the support of other professionals.

Summary: The work is still continuing but has lasted a year so far. She contacted me through Facebook and expressed her concerns regarding her stress level. I spoke a few times with her over the phone to help her talk about her anxiety so as to release her worries. The first time I met her in person, was when she attempted suicide in London. I found her in a very confused state. During that contact, I took her through all the Magical Module stages blended for instance, as she was in denial of self-love and looking after herself or pregnancy or taking charge of her life. The way she had done suicide in the past and this time I notice it was a cry for help. As I picked that one quickly, I applied my approaches by making her aware that she is not loving her baby by doing what she is doing. We had a few minutes discussion about this topic, as she was giving me so many excuses around, but I was not accepting her excuses. There was no excuse not to love her baby. She had options, such as giving the baby for adoption if she did not want him. I was tough and firm with her. She said, "I love my baby" whereas I said, "Do you know how much damage, those suicide tablets, do to you baby?" You forget about the stress that you are giving to the baby, and all the domestic violence while you are pregnant, how that affects the baby that has not been born yet. As she was giving me excuses of her reasons why she attempted suicide she was crying in the same time. I then confronted her "Then you do not want to kill yourself, you are just doing this for attention". But she kept crying and giving more and more reasons that made her feel unhappy with her own life.

As she continuing her excuses and I could see that I was not getting through to her, I said: "Ok, do you want to kill yourself? Do you want to end your life?" AS she was crying she stopped and looked at me surprised. Then I said, "Let's go. I will help you to end your life. I will take you to the bridge and push you!" She looked at me intently, to see if I meant it. I repeated again what I said. Then she started laughing. I started laughing. We were both laughing out loud. I began teaching her how important it was for her to pay attention to herself and the baby; how important it was for her to give a good life to her baby, not the life she had. How important for her it was to be a good mother. How important it was for her to make use of her spark and magic she had inside her. We agreed that any time she felt down she would call me, anytime. That was the moment she turned her life around in the sense that she stopped going around that circle of suicide attempts. She turned her focus on her baby. My concern was that the social services might take the baby away, but I promised her that I would fight with her to get what she wanted if she followed the tools that I gave her to gain her self-love.

Until the baby was born I supported her by providing practical and emotional help, and she made a huge turn as she was contacting me every time she felt down or when she needed someone to talk to, and this was almost every day. I also offered to accompany and stay with her when she went to hospital to give birth, as she was alone in this country. I supported her during her delivery, which was two days in a row. It was an amazing experience for me and for her. It is so important to have somebody there, when one gives birth, especially when one is going through a difficult situation such as this.

During her stay in the hospital I had to support her, in communication with other professionals as most of the time she was calling me when she was crying in irritation and was extremely concerned about her son. During the process, I worked with her closely and intensively to support her in breaking the unhelpful cycle by using my techniques, which helped her to calm down and receive the answers that she requested from the medical staff. She felt certain that she would not repeat again and I am very pleased that she managed to overcome that level of overwhelmed. I was glad that she made positive progress from then.

On the other hand I thought that she still needed that kind of support until she felt confident with her living, otherwise she would relapse in the previous situation, where she was before birth. Since then, through my techniques based the 'magical module' I worked closely, She is afraid to ask for help as she is scared they will take her baby away. She was a very good and caring mother, but she did have her moments when she needed help to overcome her anxieties and worries due to her previous experiences. Therefore, I was available for her anytime to provide appropriate support until she learned to manage life independently.

She was still struggling and feeling stressed most of the time. She was also struggling with the fear of the future because she had not yet healed from her past and she could imagine going back. In one of our conversations she expressed that she had a thought of killing herself while she was struggling to put the baby to sleep, but on the other hand she said: "Vjollca's voice was in my head saying love yourself and love your baby". I encouraged her to express her concerns to other professionals so that she received the help she needs, but she was afraid, that they might take her baby away. I told her as long as she asked for help and tried to improve I would support her to keep the baby because I have seen her with the baby and she was an amazing mother. I showed her to wash the baby and after doing it for her a few times, she learned it well and began to wash it by herself. I taught her to create a bond and communicate with the baby as well as understand the needs and the language of the baby. In addition, I looked after the baby for a few hours so she could have some time for herself without the responsibility of the baby. In that way she would have some time to have inner conversations and simply empty her mind.

In addition I suggested techniques to help her relax, build up her self-esteem, self-confidence, understand the baby more, learn how important it is for the mother to be happy and remain calm so that the baby feels the same way. Also I shared with her several methods about being physically present when she felt overwhelmed from everything and just sitting down with her while having a lunch during our talks has helped her to feel that she is not alone and has the ability to do things. She has now placed all her focus on the baby and herself. She has started to love herself and bond with her baby in a deeper level. Now I have encouraged her to start writing her own book as part of the program: Heal yourself by writing your book and, what does that book mean to help her is that she can dig deeper on her past, placing everything on he right. I will help her to re-read through the healing process and them will move in the next step, but she is finding it difficult to do it, at the moment.

One of my messages to her was: "don't give up but find ways how to find the solution that you want, just keep searching within you the answers of your questions"

One of her responses was: "I should use my intuition to find my way " She had an appointment but she got lost" As soon I stopped and took a bit of time to think… as I thought also I can check it up in goggle map… as I was thinking I find the way… and I thought I should do it more often what Vjollca said… use your intuition and think " .

One example of my indirect work that I do through healing energy: Also I called her just in that moment…coincidence… This is the second client who says I call them just when they were thinking about me.

Below you will find one of the examples of the difficulties she was facing, such as the language barrier:
A professional was having a conversation with the client and interpreter. The interpreter, did not interpret what the client was saying eg :

The client said: "I will blame you (she was referring to the professional in a joking way) if there will be a problem and if your word does not match to what you advice me".

The interpreter said: "She is being naughty" (and smiled). Both the professional and the interpreter smiled at the time I was present there, as there were other professionals in the waiting area.

So I had to interfere and asked the interpreter: " Could you interpret word for word what the client is saying, please?"

I could see that the client was distressed even though she was saying it in joke way and smiling and laughing, but in my understanding she was just covering her stress and everyone thought she was alright but she was hiding the stress and anxiety linked to the specific issue.

There were other witnesses in waiting area, who heard the conversation.
I continued working hard through mindfulness to calm her down and change her attitude towards life in positive way but the some of the other professionals' support were misunderstanding her behavior as they could not see the underlying issues such as: she was in a very thin line to go back to the suicide pattern, as she was jumping from feeling beyond low to the other extreme and the professionals were seeing only that extreme as the client was feeling apprehensive to see her real self and many other emotions such as self-blaming etc. What remained was that the client was really in a very vulnerable state.

Another one of my texts to her: "Think Think Think ....and do not think or think but just sit quietly in the quiet silence to listen to your soul when speaking "

Client's Feedback during the end of process:

Others do not know how to explain to you, but it has made me realize how stupid I am. Although it irritates me and makes me nervous, I can understand that it is right in every word and advice she give to me.
She has been making me alerted to work on these points below:

- To love myself
- To be happy
- To feel independent
- To know how to seek my rights
- To understand what's really important to me

Client's feedback after I suggested her to start writing her book. She kept an intentional distance from me for a few months, because she wanted me to continue giving her the same support that I had been giving, but I convinced and I showed her that she did not need that any more as she had fortunately improved and she simply needed to do the last programme, which is the book, to complete her self-love, universal love and passionate love. After those months, she reflected back and sent me the feedback below, promising that she will try to work on her book.

"She is my heroine! Vjollca Sadiku ... A simple name to hear, but behind it a soul with the power of the whole world! She is the Queen of guidance for a happier life! She is the only angel, who escaped the Lord from the hands, to be allowed on earth as the most precious gift that exists! Just by her presence in the distance my heart warms, when I see her smile, my life lightens up!
She has given me my life, it is thanks to her I am alive! She was the only angel I ever had with me in my toughest moments; she gave me breath from her breath!
She is my saviour!
The only person in the world, to whom I humble myself with the greatest love ...
She was always near me, ready to help me with every capability she had, stood beside me sitting in the chair for two days and nights in a row without closing her eyes as I was lying on the hospital bed, I was in such a bad state, but when I heard her voice, the pains were alleviated because she is the medicine of the soul! On the day I gave birth to my angel, she was the guardian angel, who stood above my head without getting tired at all! I am immensely thankful, I know I can never repay it to her but she and her effort is rewarded only when she sees me happy!
She was with me at every step, where I did not know, where I could not!
Even if I am giving my last breath, I can simply find her number and call, because it is there that I find salvation! She is a miracle and I thank God for giving me the opportunity to meet such a soul!"

Vjollca's final message: If she manages to write her book as it is her dream, but she is not confident yet, her book will encourage others to know how to do this journey: "to be like a rocket with a golden spark on top of it that comes of the muddy depth and shoots through the sky".

Case study 22

Background: Single mother, around 23 years old. We did initial consultation and she was not sure what she wanted or how I could offer her support as she just had heard for me from her friend that was my client and I did help her a lot. So after we gone through my Magical Module and how I designed it as I go along based on her needs, she agreed even though I could see on her eyes the doubt she had and she was not sure it was going to help her. She was very isolated and quiet.

Summary: After we did three sessions based on the present situation, as she was not sure what will happen, what to aspect, and how to understand her feelings or her situation? All that was stressing her. It was time for me to dig a bit deeper on her fears, depression, worries, sadness in her eyes and the feeling of unworthy.
She did open up straight away and all through the session she was on tears. She told me about her life experience and expressed her feelings of sadness. Also she was afraid about her daughter's future. She disclosed for first time the abuse from her ex partner and how she was struggling to understand it and why she still loves him. She had not yet disclosed this to other professionals because she was feeling scared, confused, embarrassed, filled with self- blame, so did not know whether to say it or not, or if it was wrong or right – whether to accept it or not. But because of my energy, she just got drawn into it like a magnet and she opened up. In her past she used to drink alcohol to block what she was going through. She had stopped that since she got pregnant. She had been sober for a year, so the chance of the pattern repeating was easy. As her situation was still extremely sensitive, she was still part of it, she was not yet completely disconnected.
During this time I worked closely with her through phone calls, text and meting face to face when was necessary. She has some how manage to be alert and raise her awareness of her worth and that she can have the future she dreamed as a child but that had made her feel so tired, sleepy, numb and in some kind of state that she just wants rest all the time.

In my opinion is understandable of what she had gone through and how she is trying to gain the strength to start from scratch but she is not sure she can do it. She fears about the future and being who she dreams of herself being and this makes her feel tired and not finding strength to start small steps. She has come a long way but she still has long way to go in order to feel herself again and be content where she is, believe in her self that she can achieve her dreams and break them into small dreams.

One our conversations that shows how I use my magical approaches based on her flow and the results, I get are that she managed to go to children's center and she has started to write her notes for her book:

Client: I know that theory but it's a bit difficult to enjoy everything alone.

Vjollca:

1 - Try to enjoy life with your good things that you have…

2 - The baby is healthy

3 - With documents you are getting there…

4 - You have ruf and money to manage life

5 - You are healthy

6 - Around you are not people that disturb your peace

7 - You have ability to create the future you want … using the free time as you want. ..

8 - You must sow the seed based on sincere land pure love towards yourself… not to wait for the warmth or the attention of others… go on to say to yourself the words you want to hear from someone

"Start with small steps. Writing the book will plant the seed of love for yourself"

Client: My book will be short; I have started writing just a few words.

Vjollca: It's ok, you just write what you wanted to express. Experience - your thoughts - feelings - your reflection now and then - your analysis now and then. Did you go to children's center ?

Client: I cannot remember many things I have too low memory. I'm hoping to go to the children center as I really wanted to sleep.

Vjollca: Me too I wanted to sleep but I had to go to work and as soon as I gone out of the door I felt better and ready to start the day, was easy after got out of the door.

Client's feedback of "A Magical Life" book:

"Be who you want to be, catch your life and through it where you want and don't let life through you around" this phrase I liked very much because always I thought we create our life based on our thoughts, actions and our work. If we want something we should not get up until we get it.

The book, except that it tells a true story of a spiritual biography it helps you to learn how to achieve your dreams and the vision I have. Author Vjollca Sadiku it beginning of the book tells her story full of puzzles, endless dramas that make me realize that everything is possible only to follow the inner voice. In the Magic Life book I found myself in many situations. This book is a psychology in itself. My Percussion Chapter is III (goals) lectures, examples that make us understand that we must get ready to fight to achieve our goals. What not to like about the book ? maybe a bit too much of the exaggerated nature description of the many comparisons but this can be justified because Vjollca loves the nature.

This book changes the world perception and the we view the world. The book of a Magic Life has helped me to talk with the soul has been a therapy in itself. I learned step by step how to tackle problems and how getting out of that dark world that had caught me. The book that made me go back to my childhood where I found myself there in many situations that had happened the same things. For example: the village, moving away from my parents and going to stay with my grandparents, harassment from close people etc. I personally do not like that much nature probably for that excessive duct, naturally I rarely go out on nature only when I don't have anything else to do and I feel bored.

Client's Feedback

My friend suggested her to me. She said to me that Vjollca would help me in many things. In that time I was wondering to have someone like her in my life. To support me, to give motivation to move on, to do thinks right. When I meet her I filled some forms for the magical approach program in what I need it. Vjollca called me over and over to see how I feel, what I think, she told me that she will be there any time if I need her. After one month I had to go to an appointment and needed her support. I called Vjollca and asked her if she was able to come with me that day and she said yes. Before to go we had a coffee. I felt very comfortable and I open up straight away for all my problems. I felt like I have ages that I know her. Vjollca spend all afternoon with me. Vjollca gave me her book Magical Life. One biography book I found myself there. I was thinking how strong was she in difficult situation. Like her should be. Vjollca it's my ideal model that I should follow. I read her book maybe for one week and I write a review about it . That book was amazing it's it helped so much it was more psychological book. Vjollca came to meet me . We walk around the park talk about my problems and my feelings. Vjollca find out that I was not working with my self, I was tried, lazy and she gave to me homework that later I finished successful and it helped me a lot. She even spent a whole day with my daughter and me. Vjollca keep calling me texting me to often to see how I am, if I'm finishing my home works. Vjollca it's training me every day to keep my self-focused, active. I trusted her because she understands me, she believed at me when no body did not. She goes through in my soul; she knows how to talk with me when I was sad, when I was angry, when I was disappointed. Now I have started to believe in my dreams with help of Vjollca and after I read her book and her hard work that she has done with me. I knew that I have to do so many things to reach what I want and with help of Vjollca I m sure that I will. I believe in her advice because I know that she wants the best for me without any interest on me . When I am with her or talk with her I feel very comfortable and free to say everything that comes through my mind and my Heart.
I'm lucky that I meet her she is changing my life.

Vjollca's thoughts: "Her book will help her to believe and achieve her vision and to discover her gift on helping others. She inspires me in so many ways".

Case study 23 (Couple therapy)

Background: Couple's therapy. Their ages are around 45. The husband approached me as he had concerns because the relationship was not working how he wanted it to work. There was a need for improving intimacy, communication skills to understand each other better.

Summary: I worked with them around four sessions, once a month. That included giving them homework. Each session was three hours long and very intense. The wife resisted the therapy, but that was one of the ways to move forward so they both agreed to take part. I will describe this case study briefly. What they complained about was not the real issue. In the relationship they had trust issues, controlling issues, and one of them wanted to be independent because had not had a chance so far, to explore that independency. So one party wanted to explore the independency, the other party wanted to remain in the way they used to be and that was causing a clash. After we explored all their concerns, where they had space to listen to one another, they had to face the fact that they both had to listen to each-other and make actions towards change in order for their relationship to grow or they would continue in separate ways. The crucial thing was that they both did not wish to go in separate ways, but in the meantime they did not want to change so that the relationship could grow. In my understanding there was no middle way. They stopped therapy saying that they were fine and much better than before, but only they know that for sure. I did my part by giving them all the tools including my book.

Clients' feedback
It was our pleasure to work with you. You helped us a lot! Before I meet you I thought our relationship is going to end, but with your help we are doing so well, our relationship changed a lot we talk more with each other we spend more time together. So thank you for helping us.

Vjollca's final thoughts: "It is important to understand the order of love: self-love, universal love, passionate love".

Case study 24

Background: Single mother of two kids aged under 3 years old. She came to me to receive support, about integrating in the new life in UK.

Summary: I took her through the Magical Module, and organizing each stage to give her some flavor. I held her hand in every stage that she was going through. I told her that I was not perfect and by showing her what I had achieved so far on my own, increased her confidence. I found very helpful the deep conversations between us. I followed my intuition and followed her waves of energy in order to help her be independent and learn how to get the support she need it from other resources. I could see when she had the ability to do something and allowed her of going ahead and do it initially with me standing next to her and then without supervision. In the times when she could not do things I did them in her presence but afterwards, made notes for the steps she needed to follow in the future. . She is very independent now and can deal with everything on her own and is very good following her soul advice.

Client's feedback:

I felt lost… she helped me to find my self and believe on my self . In the start of session she stress you out to find your self. In the first time you look at her she makes you feel like you are not alone, she understands you. You feel lots of love energy from her presence. But through her approach of being firm she makes you feel bad energy, lots of pressure but all this lead to make you think what really is important for you and help to find solution. Makes you believe in your self and not been scared of fear.

Case study 25

Background: A 47 years old woman, in a happy relationship and has a daughter. The reason she came to me was that she needed to have more understanding of her life in general.

Summary: Using my approaches, which are about communicating with the client's soul, understanding her mind and feeling her feelings I knew something was hidden inside her and she was denying it. For example, I said that life is Magical and her response was 'no, in reality people can be happy but not just like in fairy tales'. When I described her, what a healthy relationship is, and one my point is that in minimum a couple should have sex at leas three times a week. She was giving me excuses, such as 'it does not matter', 'I might go two weeks without doing it', and then she finally said 'sex is not necessary to keep the relationship'. I could see that my work was to help her search in a deeper level. She needed to fulfill needs that she was searching for but she did not believe that can be achieved in this reality. A few of the conversations are examples below.

Client's confessions:
She said when she was 13 because everyone was telling her she is ugly and sick because she was skinny and tall, she used to believe that and one day a city boy with curly hair, very handsome said to her cousin 'who is that girl, because I like her and she is beautiful ', that made my friend believe that she is beautiful.

One of her techniques that she had created to help her grow:
When she had a fight or misunderstanding with someone or was angry with someone, after this happened she used to imagine having conversation with that person and in end of the conversation she use to feel fine.

One of our conversations:

Vjollca: Everything starts with yourself When you love yourself as you like to be loved then you love yourself. When you feel satisfied with yourself then you are happy with yourself and know what you will need to improve or change… People who love themselves are happy, know what they want, what they like and what they don't y like, and always get things they want and are happy with everything they do.

Client: Regardless of the small problems that I have for now I feel good, my opinion is that happiness is not something that you fight for to achieve are moments that bring happiness.

In one conversation with some women I had once, I told that happiness does not come either from a male who many women like to have in their arms, but it is a part of completing the happiness. I understand that there have been moments that I feel happy without even realizing why. Most of the time with the lack of this is to have a close friend to communicate with as I communicate with you. Without hesitating and understanding me so much.

Client's 'Magical life' book feedback: (I gave her my book so that she could discover her purpose):
In a way that I did not understand your book A magical life I divided into three parts. I started reading the beginning with having pations as it just took me way the description of the experiences so fresh and real, such a lively description and real feelings of the childhood life aroused many emotions yesterday flying in the achieved dreams and non achieved dreams. It came to the second part and it felt like I lost you a little, I lost the meaning I could not understand or appreciate the sky I don't know but I started reading without having pations.

I came across again in those verses written with such a feeling and suddenly I managed to feel positive feelings to accompany my mind and my being. I managed to truly understand the magic of life by realizing that we only do can create magic moments. Following reading your magic life as if I accidentally gone back on my childhood and in my life feelings that helped me to understand my truth. Everything in the third part just simple fantastic.

Discussion after the book feedback:

Client: Vjollca seeing a real story of a girl on television found you at age 7 with a big difference, today she is included into the drug network. They had sent her to her grandparents' to leave there for a long time, facing the loneliness, fear and shame of other children in Persia, far away from their parents I was in the tears when I saw that one year without closing the forties overwhelmed in the dark world of the drugs and loneless.

Vjollca you should be so proud of yourself who you became today and I am very lucky that I got to know you. I spend in my daily life by emptying my mind from any negative thought and filling me with new energy with magic, where everything around me takes the positive side.

Our most recent conversation in the ongoing work:

Client: I can't go on holiday like some friends go on their own even though they are a family.

Vjollca: I think you have everything you need to go on holiday.

Client: Yes, but, I do not want to make other people unhappy.

Vjollca: So you see, again you are trying to make other people happy. How about making yourself happy. How important is to know the difference between making yourself happy and automatically the others are happy because they love you. Or you just do things to make others happy. So do not tell me that you cannot go, because you chose not to go on holiday (silence).

Notes: Our work in progress is about her writing the book on loving herself. The reasons why I gave her that content is that she keeps saying to convince me that she loves herself and I know that she does not love herself the way she wants to. I provided her with several techniques on how to increase the love of herself and how to teach her daughter to love herself and what is the message she wants to give to others. Even though she does not believe in the healing capacities of this book she promised that she would do it.

Vjollca's final thoughts: "If she manages to write her book and I do believe that she has the ability and she can do it, I strongly recommend everyone to read her book if they want to gain their self-love".

Case study 26

Background: Single man around his 30s. The reason he came to therapy is that he felt confused, lost, and unhappy with the life he was living. He asked me how he could make his dreams a reality.

Summary: Even though he brought the issues mentioned in the background, I could see other underlying issues that had emerged in his adolescence. My aim was to help him gain his self-love and see clearly the bridge from where he was to where he wanted to reach, by taking small steps and using the tools of the Magical Module. More importantly to be content where he is and to find a way for him to appreciate what he had in his life and his achievements. Recently it is noticeable that he has accepted to walk on the bridge towards his dreams, to have knowledge and understanding and taking actions towards self-love. He has started to see the changes for himself, and accept the present moment and make use of it towards his goals.

One of the exercises I used:

Healing your self needs:

1 - fully loving your self

2 - believe in on your ability

3 - dream big and get your dreams

4 - start living your dream

Client's response:

1. Yes I fully adore myself though I am fat boy, I do not like my stomach but if I see mirror I say to myself I will change myself and soon recover to a fit body. Yes, It's in my mind at number one priority and I am doing it.
But Being a Fatty skinned boy, does not mean to me that I will hate myself, I take it as challenge and I am doing it and I love myself, People around me pass remarks but I keep myself cool as it's only me knows how to remove that fatty skin.
I love myself I love my mind who is always on positive vibes movement even though the surroundings around me may not always favor me but I also keep my positivity around me, with myself and within my soul, within my heart. and that no one can shake away from me except me.

2. Yes I do believe in my ability, I give my 100% to it and I have adroitness and I am born with great talents. I have passion for Fashion and Music. I love the trend the fashion industry offers to us. I love nature. I love Music, it depends upon my mood which music I wanted to listen. I love talking to the people who value me and in return I do the max for them. Yes I do not have much money with me, but I have a rich heart, I have v few true friends yes I can count on it. My friends are my biggest assets. I am a free spirit, I love myself...I do think which I love doing. Yes there are many people with whom I interact. I am open to all.

3. Big dreams - Yes I do have Big Dreams. Recruitment is my hobby not my dream, I do it with all passion as it gives me livelihood and earning at the end of the month. If one does job his salary comes once in month after 30 days. But I analyzed myself deeply I have hidden talents. I can do much more than this. Yes I have chased all life till now for money but I could not get it as here the salaried people who are fresher's or not having much experience like more than 10 years.
Yes I wanted to start something of my own or do some job in London or in US, but my first preference is London. I have this idea for a year. I want to have my own house in London Yes. Yes for sure I dream of getting married to a sensible good natured girl but before that I have to look smart and shed away my fatty cells from my body. For this I am doing the workout.

4. Yes I am start living on my dream I love myself and day by day I am refining myself, drain away the dust from my soul from my body daily to be a Awesome Man.

Vjollca: My reply was based on the intense work I did with him, to go in depth of each point that he mentioned, using the approach of Magical Module, creating with him a ladder with the steps, starting from where he is and where he is going to achieve his dreams. I also applied healing throughout the conversation.

After a few sessions I could see that he was giving me excuses about taking action towards his steps. Therefore I suggested and encouraged him to write his book where his words had to come from his soul, mind and heart...but he needed to write about his life journey, about his pain, suffering, his dreams and how he you healed himself.

Clients feedback after one of our conversations:

It was really nice talking to you.
First of All Forgive me as if by mistake, I was harsh somewhere.
I was thinking my soul from inside is asking me something, but it was truly and purely from my heart a lovely conversation with you.

Vjollca: My thoughts: During the conversation with him I was a bit harsh as he had not done what we had previously and was still going around in circles and he did not want to end our contact, but I did not see any point of continuing. I could see that we were not reaching anything apart from the universal love. So I send him the email below:
You don't have nothing to be sorry, instead I am sorry for being firm on you and continuing to be firm and challenging as I got your permission to do so, because that's the way I work in order to have results on healing progress. Please can you just have a look at the points below and let me know what you think about them:

1 - In your dreams you need to be more realistic and think in details, example to imagine like you are in London already and how you will make things happen, do some research about fashion and things that you want to get.

2 - I want you to accept your self the way you are and love your self the way you are. Losing weight has to do more for healthy reasons and for you to achieve your goal of having the image you want to have.

3 - Once you love your self, you will not feel lonely and you will know the purpose of your life, then you will meet the right women for you.

4 - This week spend time with your thoughts and pay attention to your inner voice, then let me know what you notice.

5 - I know you are still felling the loss of people close to you and scared about it but I want you to park for now those feelings till you figure out how to love your self the way you are and figure out what exactly want.

The client's reply was going again around the old patterns, so I suggested him to read my book "A Magical Life" and write his thoughts so we could discuss his thoughts about the book.

Client's feedback of the book "A Magical Life":

Change is inevitable & it's constant. Growth is painful, change is painful as we Human are always reluctant and in some degree of trepidation to accept the New Things but its more painful as staying somewhere one doesn't belong. Reinventing is the key as it can only be accomplished if one adores oneself truly as oneself being authentic to one: the soul whispers and instructs us what is right and wrong, but sometimes the general masses move away from this basics core value and get lost in the whirlwind of the society, the people around. This book is not only a book, it's a treasure beautifully woven by Vjollca Sadiku, The Honorable Author and its each words touched me as it goes step by step, depicting her own story and the storm she went threw but it's totally inspiring as it motivates the readers how I can come out from the heart of darkness or from dark well towards Sunshine, The Struggle The pain The Pragmatic Experience of life from different phases of life tenure or the various versions of life. At last, The Answer I get is The

Answer I get from the soul within and believing in oneself firmly and Happiness lies within while I was searching all around for someone to make me happy. So when I see the Mirror I smile as its me Yes Proudly I say its me, I have been through all that and I am leading my life in the best version of myself.

And when one comes out of the storm one is not the same person that walked in, and that is what the storm is all about, It's the New Dimension towards moving ahead life.

Everyone has a story today and I believe that Time is the most powerful one, Bad times come and is then followed with good times. Yes Its Pure Magical Life as You yourself did it while in the storm you were not burning you were refining yourself by reinventing yourself and one is never old in practicing this cycle. Its Magical as it covers all the versions or the phrases of life. Until one is shattered into pieces, one never come to know what they are.

There is a phrase in the Bible 'Don't be afraid' and it is written 365 times. That's the reminder from God that to be fearless. And As a Healer you will always make people see what they can be, rather than what they are. You are truly Inspirational & Magical One.

A Magical Life – a Spiritual Memoir/True Story is the best perfect one and it cannot be better than this.

Client's feedback:

Oh, the real core basic is reached to everyone. Believe in me its treasure when I read your book it's like your talking to me in front of me, Yes I adore your words each single one and I will give you feedback but my feedback in one word I tell you It's Awesome as you have that magic not to allow readers to leave and go elsewhere, as truly I say why I can't finish till now as I analyze your words and think what made you think and then I correlate with what happened with me till now in my life, I tell you it's purely magical. I guess you think deeply and to the extreme levels with all the dimensions the pros and the cons and all the things into consideration, that is so positive in you and that attribute of yours is so beautifully woven in your beautiful words in the Magical Moments while reading the treasure The Magical Life, the book is so lovely as it seems the writer is taking with the reader face to face on the pragmatic life experience, your book I think might be much popular in the college going students because it shows the way yeah after college be alert the life is not bed of roses one has to make a place in this world to survive and once achieved all helping and escorting the needy ones who need the necessary things in life, as I believe you adore so much in assisting others to make them smile.

It's all your Blessings and positive vibes that sparkle me with your Awesomeness and Mighty lovely Presence, the uniqueness in you is you listen till the end and then you sparkle with your light, that Uniqueness is rarely found Nowadays that is the real Vjollca Sadiku. Truly powerhouse of Inspirational Pragmatic approaches....

is simply the best as when I talk with her, she listens to me first completely till the end and give the pragmatic approach towards the problem. the gem of a person.

Client: You are so great so kind and there is so much powerful beautiful topics inside you the way to lead pragmatic positive life.

Vjollca: Trust me 'my special friend' …everyone has ability but that is our inner war to win it and understand it… is about stopping time while we do what we have to do for the reality to continue but in mean time making time for ourselves… for our inner conversations… for the silence… for that energy that surrounds us to feel it and understand it …..for us to breath free of worry etc.

"That's why GOD has given free will and free choice. …you are free we are free to choose"

<u>*Vjollca's final message:*</u> "You have said you are special and I do believe that you are but you need to take action to see clearly your purpose in this life….to act and be the one you are "

Case study 27

<u>*Background:*</u> A 27 year old woman in a relationship and had just had a baby. It was not very clear with her things. There was anxiety about what was going to happen tomorrow, where I would find support and she was lost. Her hopes were very scarce.

<u>*Summary:*</u> She came for emotional and practical support. She needed help to understand the situation she was in and mostly, wanted to know where she could ask for help and how to contact the other professionals, mainly her solicitor. As I helped her to achieve her aim, and she felt very happy about it, I noticed other underlying issues as she was in a very complex situation. I tapped a little bit on those topics that I was concerned, because she did not open the doors I just gave her the option that when she was ready she could ask for help. I already gave her the strength, not to be scared of anyone, to stand up to her ground and to explore her self-love, universal love and passionate love.

<u>*An example of one of my tapping techniques:*</u>

<u>*Vjollca:*</u> My dear …. you made me cry with the words you said because I realized and felt that you really saying it through your soul and I am very happy that I managed to make you feel peaceful and loved.

Do not forget :…..

1 - You are a very clever person, simple, full of love and you have a soul filled with lots of wisdom that is waiting to be discovered and to be shown.

2 - To write the book

3 - To enjoy the moment because it does not come back and tomorrow may not exist.

4 - It is a pleasure to know you because you are a special person that time will show your inner treasure.

Client's Feedback

Before I met Vjollcën, I did not feel so peaceful because I had a lot of things to do with worrying. She taught me lot of things about myself that I was not aware and she has given me courage to do things without fear. It disturbed the fact that I did not know how to communicate with other professionals that I need it to communicate and because of Vjollca, I can now. Now I can talk to other professionals every time I need to communicate for any reason. From the emotional point of view, since I met Vjollcem, it has changed a lot because it makes me feel good, I am very relaxed when I am with her. With her advice and the main thing is because Vjollca knows how to treat people, know how to support you, always find the weak point that worry us. So I feel very happy that I found a person like Vjollca that knows how to express human love and it makes you feel good even for those 5 minutes.

Vjollca's final message: "I wish I could give my eyes to the client, to see what I see on them... and have the feeling I have when I see more than three paths for them including the one they are in, where it takes them"

Case study 28

Background: A single woman around 26 years old, without a father figure present in her life. She has been independent and helping her family. She came to me to understand more about the passionate love as she did not understand why she was not finding the right man and all her relationships were going wrong, one after the other.

Summary: Even though she came for passionate love, her underlying issues were related to self-love so I started my approaches to apply into her the self-love first and explaining how that would lead her to the passionate love, but she did not understand the concept of self love as most of the people, mistakenly thought it as form of selfishness and egoism. So my techniques were for me to help her to connect with her soul and intuition, in order to believe in self-love. I did only two sessions with her and she looked at me as a weird and absurd person. However, she said that she would follow the tools that I gave her. One year after, we contacted one another and I was really surprised when she said that she had started to communicate with her soul and also recognize the voice of the intuition and she gave me a few examples to confirm the results that she had wanted. In this session, even her talking about it felt that she was connected to the space and burst into happy and healing tears, and she had believed in herself that she had come a long way and she was now able to see her path, she could see the vision where she would meet the right person and where he would be. Most of all she was feeling content and fulfilled at the present moment and she had created tools to get what she wanted and was trying to apply her skills to her circle of friends and was asking me for more guidance on how she could do that.

This process took her two years, but it was only two sessions in total and weird ones, which means I never thought that she would get the results but she applied all the tools I gave her and she achieved what she was looking for. This proved me that if one applies the self-help tools for two years, can achieve self-love, which opens the other doors.

Client's feedback

I created a positive impact so far because of the coaching sessions with magical coaching so far in my life. My mind set has changed dramatically, I know of how to start improving my life and moving forward. I tend to ask my self coaching questions and I have the greater picture of my future and the veal inner me and the life I want. Thank you Vjollca for opening my inner me.

Vjollca's final thoughts: "You just have to have the wish of searching…following…raising your curiosity… accept the absurdity…then you get what you are searching for!"

Case study 30 (Here are two case studies, 29 and 30)

Background: 2 children in foster care. The girl around 16 and a boy around 7 years old.

Summary: I was one week in intensive care for respite. In the first day the boy was really upset because it was the first time he met a stranger like me. As soon as I was alone with both kids and sat down on the table and for two hours we had an honest and deep conversation with the girl. Meanwhile the boy was listening and doing some drawings. By listening to the girl's problems increased his curiosity and started to listen attentively.

But this session was about the stage of Momentum for the girl. During the week this is the work I did with the girl applying the Magical Module and the steps are explained below. During this important stage it became apparent that the original family had had lots of problems. Her pas and present were very complex. Her real mum had left her when she was 5 and now she was taking drugs and she was not well the doctor had said. She was worried about her mum and her family. She is very attached to her friends and the circle she grew up with. She did not like the place she was in and not very happy or not happy at all about her present and her future or might just be excuses.

Goal - here we discussed where she wanted to be in future. She was not sure at first then she was thinking of two options but still not sure. She was more focused which kind of boy she will meet as future husband and she was complaining about the money she was getting. Not sure about which option to take as she was n situation to make decision to stay put or move from the care she was as she was turning 18.

Acceptance - we went through the options she have and which one she thought was best or good for her that may take her to where she want to be in future.

Raised the awareness of the circle she is in (which represents her whole life) and what she needs to do to break that circle and consequences of staying in the circle or breaking it somehow. Pointing out to all the goods things she have and she could have. Some how she realized lots of things.

Inspiration - I showed her some my life experiences, showed my book, to encourage her 'you can do it', 'there are people in terrible situations that have made it'. My story demonstrated to her and how I turned my life around and that a few other people had done it too. I pointed out what was stopping her to do more then us? She just stayed in silence and smiled.

Commitment - Increased her awareness of where she is and where she wants to be together we discovered small steps and how she can follow and keep moving forward. But need it to make decisions first, reflect through 30 minutes meditation each day and then make a plan.

Affirmation - Think about her best version and keep reminding yourself everyday in order to help you go where you want to be.

Love - I told her: "If you love your family you would be your best version and then help them to be the best version. Not call them to sort out your mess by putting themselves in mess and everyone is more in mess".

I also showed her the three rules of the universe, self-love rules (please refer to the Magical Module).

She believed in God and thought that God had already plans for her and he would show the way but she was not really connecting with God, or conversations with God. So I made her aware on how she could communicate with

God… I also helped her to go deeper into her inner self and make a map plan on how she wanted her life to be in a few year's time and which kind of men she wanted. I also told her how she could attract what you are and in order to be around good people or find the right one you need to be what you want. I said on the work she done:

"You have designed your dream men, now you need to be the way you designed him!".

The girl's feedback:

Vjollca is truthful, straightforward like my dad, made me aware and understand how bad is the circle I am and how I am being the same as them. She understood me, I know what I have to do, you put me straight, I have a lot to do, I am not as bad as I thought.

The intensive week with the boy:

Day 1:

The boy listening to us was helped to understand the girl and the girl to understand him as they used not to get along at all. But now they feel like they are one as they discovered they had been gone through the same thing. Even the girl admitted that the reason was not getting along with him, it was that it hurt it seeing him going through the same thing she had gone through.

The rest of the afternoon he did one drawing (drawing 8 – what makes me feel to behave the way I behave). He did this drawing because I promised him to take it to the park to play football and we really had a lovely and calm afternoon. He loved it.

In the evening he wanted my attention so I made sure I was present with him and we talked about his nightmares, how he could overcome them, and about his mum ...how he could give her a hug and she can feel it. He said no ...I said ask her tomorrow as he had arranged phone call with him. He said, but she will say yes, but she will maybe lie" ... I said: "But you can find out if she is lying by asking more questions". "No she may not have felt it because she did not pay attention as she may have been busy" he replied.

That night we both worked on how he could overcome his nightmares and be more independent on his time to sleep. He did try and for whole week he was excellent on sleeping.

Day 2:

The boy done some drawing (drawing 4 and 5) based on the theme Magical Module, which I had previously shown him. He expressed the meaning of each stage as I gave him a flavor of their meaning and the way he could link it with how he was feeling.

Took him to the park and during the walk he was expressing his anxieties: that he was shy, and worried that no one wants to play with him. Talked about it which were the issues that made him be in trouble in schools in play ground. We had a lovely night, relaxed

Day 3:

The boy did drawing 6. In this drawing he was able to progress by demonstrating his inner circle. It was raining so we stayed home all day and he did lots of drawing and talking.

Day 4:

In this day we had a deep conversation as he was showing his actual behaviour with his friend on his house. He shouted, showed frustration, and had to put him straight and had to had heart to heart conversations because I felt there were some underlying issues, and hidden feelings that he wanted to express, which he started expressing: "...I can't hug you because you are a stranger....I miss auntie, my mum does not love me. I am not special because I am in foster care....." I said to him that he is very special, and I am sorry for what is happening to him but it does not mean that he can't be happy and good person....... also I talked how he can love himself after we had that chat he was playing very calm and happy. In the evening he did drawing 2, which described the seven steps of the Magical Module according to his understanding.

Day 5:

- We went to indoor play area with his friend and he loved it.
- In the car we were talking how to love your self and he said, "You don't understand me because you have mum and dad that loves you...

"I said "no ...I don't" ".

...but you had before when you were my age"

.....no I had not and I explained my story....he was silent .....

In afternoon we did more drawing and in the evening I was explaining to both how they have choices to turn things around.   they were convincing me that they didn't but in the end they got angry and both

chose to gang on me by staying together in their living room ...while I remained in kitchen… they stayed

there for couple of hours and when time was to sleep the boy was still angry at me and was playing around but I did not accept it by being firm to teach him some sort of discipline, letting him be responsible for his actions as well as allow the girl to take responsibility of her decision to look after him from the evening. There was a significant change in the way that the girl treated the boy by expressing much more compassion towards him and being protective. One example that reflects was, her patience in helping the boy to sleep, as well as the prayer song she put to sooth both of them. So she stayed with him until he fell a sleep. It was nice to see them bonding together like that and looking after one other.

- After he went to sleep ...I went and said to her "well done for doing what you did! And please keep it up even when I am gone" giving her a big hug.

Day 6:

- Was chill out day… as tomorrow was school day.
- All day we loved it relaxing.

In the morning the boy had a telephone conversation with his mum, and immediately after it, I noticed that he was missing her and encouraged him to do a drawing, where he express all the love he had for his mum, that he could give to his mother, so that every time she missed him she could have him with her. He acquiesced. I told him "Even though she has you very close to her heart, the drawing will be a reminder for her". In the evening he was starting to play up again, as he was feeling that I had to go tomorrow and he would miss me… so I had to play tough love by reminding him that "if he acted like that he would not be better then his parents and his children would not be with him"….he started to scream more… but I ignored it and instead started imitating his actions. After noticing that this was not helping him, I changed my technique by saying out loud what he was feeling and where his actions would lead him if he did not change them… After few minutes he stopped screaming and started talking. So I sat down close to him and I said, "it's ok to feel like you are feeling but you can change it by loving yourself and caring for yourself   he said "how can I love my self?" I showed to him how I hug myself and how I keep loving and caring for my self   he hugged himself and said ....like this?.   with the smile on his face .

Note: Please keep in mind. All my techniques of Magical Module that I have been using, I would not suggest to be used by anyone unless they have been trained to be fully guided by their soul, intuition and universal energy. The reason is, that only the space is pure and you can trust it to guide you, to create things based on the energy that you feel in the moment. Only in this way can you understand it and do it in the right way.

Because everything that I have done in this case studies, even though the structure of the Magical Module is established, it does not mean I follow it exactly, but I design it and create it based on the individual, present energy, and present situation!

• I talked to both a bit about self-love and that I was going to miss them too.
• The boy slept in time and he was really good.

Day 7:

The boy did the drawing one, which showed that he now had a full understanding of the Magical Model and how he could apply himself and his life through it.

The girl said " I learned so much from this week , I don't know   I have not been myself this week". I said… "yes you have. this is the real you" I noticed that compared to other times where she just wanted to go out, in this case she loved spending the whole week at home.

Before tucking them into bed, we had a deep conversation about how the boy could show love to himself, and how he could feel the love of people whose love he wanted to feel, but were not present…how to be connected to the universal love and how to communicate with his mother from a distance. I told him about the importance of being good, so he could attract good things.

Then the boy said: "But I can't be good because I have the dad's blood". I replied: "No no that is not true".......
He: "yes" he said "Because someone said it"
So I replied: Don't ever listen to others...just to your self "....
He: "So then not to listen to you too…"
Me: "Yes even to me but, what I am saying, you know that is coming from you, (resonating with his inner voice)". ...
He smiled and closed his eyes. "So just listen to yourself   you can be good and you already are very special".

He slept easily and calmly. He used to sleep with the light on and had previously trouble sleeping waking up several times a night, but this particular week he slept very well. My thought on this are: he somehow found safety, understanding, acceptance, inspiration, plans of commitment and love within him. He had now found a strategy of how to keep going.

As I was driving home I had tears in my eyes due to that intense week for all of us and felt I missed them already, but I pulled myself together and turned it into love energy to send to them. Even now every time they come in my mind I do send them lots of love and do try to communicate with them in spiritual level. A question arose in my head: Have I changed their life's? Only time will tell...

Using Magical Module through Art work/Drawing:

My analysis for this drawing and expressions that are written exactly the way that are said. My job was just to put him in that space. I just linked his bridge with where he is and the Magical Person inside him, by showing him love, through my warmth, my empathy, my understanding, my firmness, tough love, sitting down and having conversations with him and holding his pain, helping him to understand self-love and how he can use it to gain universal love and separate his passionate love from the children's love, (self-love, universal love and adult love). For more details please refer to the Magical Module. In each drawing, I will provide my interpretation, because I was fascinated by his work, but I would suggest and encourage each of you not to read my interpretation until you have done your own interpretation. The reason for that is that after you have done your interpretation than you compare it with my interpretation reflects about it in terms of the way it applies to you as a whole you and your life. If you need help, do not hesitated to contact me. Please bear in mind that I have never had a chance to explore drawing as an art, and this is my first time interpreting it. I want to make a point that we can all speak the language of the soul and that is only one; the language of the space. The language of love.

Drawing 1 below: In this drawing I asked him, to explain in his own language what each stage of the Magical Module means, through using his creative skills, such as drawing, coloring and writing.

Exercise to understand each of the stages of magical module.
Need to explain what it means each step first.

This is his own explanation:

- Goal means doing your job

- Commitment means I don't know what it means

- Inspiration getting inspired, getting ideas

- Acceptance

Vjollca's comment: He started his drawing with the word 'Magical' instead of 'Momentum' and my interpretation of that is that we are magical and life is Magical and everything starts with us using that magic. The ways the leaves are arranged tell us a lot of meaning. Acceptance stays on its own because we need to have space and time, and we need to learn to stop time, and this stage is where the healing happens. Then in the same row he has done inspiration, love, commitment, because it is a stage to have some time to stay there, and more than one year is needed to stay in that stage. The love is central in the drawing. Which leads me to prove that self-love is everything. In the top row he placed: goal, affirmation, and momentum. This line makes sense because that is our stage of growth before we are ready to contribute to others. As I think we have two purposes to fulfil in this life. One is to find ourselves, to be as a whole, and the other one comes after, which is to give contribution to this life. Until one dies, one needs to have a goal and that is the step that you have to take action. Walking moving forward. Affirmation is the food for the self-love. Momentum is on the top of the line in his drawing because as we grow, the momentum is an important stage to use our six senses and be present in order to enjoy the moment in its fullness and know what is the next step. The colours have another interpretation but I am not going into it. Each colour means something and the green colour on both sides shows strength, and means that green is everything in nature. Affirmation is also green, which means it is a very important tool to give you the strength you need.

Refer to the Magical Module, how to use each of the stage, because we have to know how to use it before getting the results.

Vjollca: At this drawing I could create box on each leaf and ask "what does it mean for you ...so he could provide his own interpretation for each leaf. In this way, he would achieve so many things, such as allowing himself in his own world and by writing his interpretation down he will move one step forward and he will teach us through his interpretation.

Drawing 2 below: the world 7 year old, describing 7 steps of magical coaching
I asked him to do a drawing to show that the universe and life are important.

His interpretation of this drawing is:
Happy, breath in, love, rest, thank universe, be good do good.

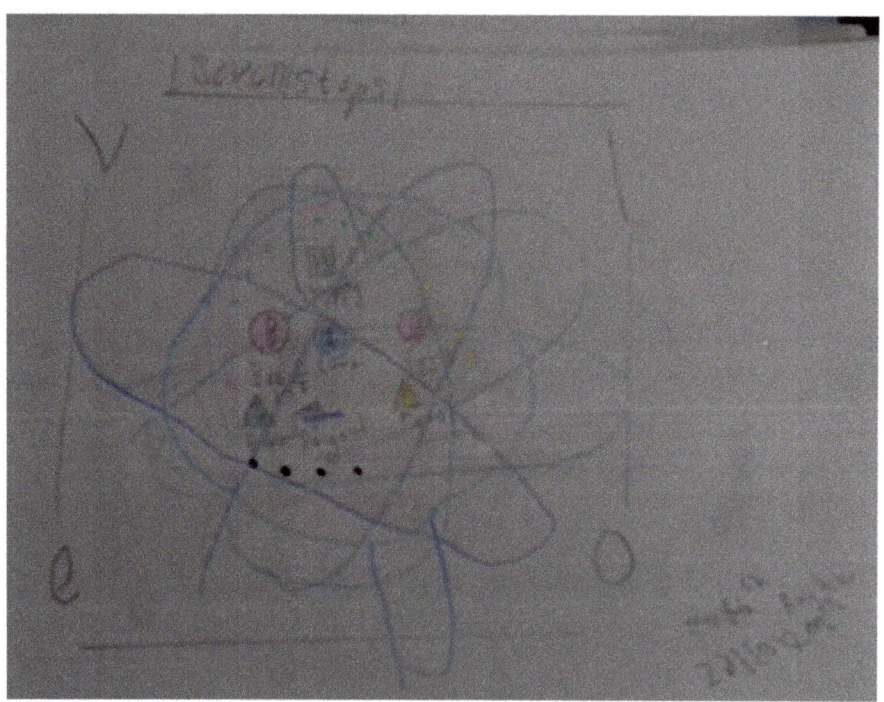

Vjollca's interpretation of this exercise: he has already provided adequate information, in which I am not going into detail due to the sensitive nature of it. In his drawing he clearly demonstrates his world, and the colours he used and the words he expressed on each stage. He placed a little tree on top of his world, and sees it as the top of his world and it is very good that he can see that.

Drawing 3 below: the journey from now to the future

This is the words he used on the drawing:

- Stop mum
- Don't copy what this mum is doing
- It does not matter which religion you are …you have wright to play
- Stupid… do not copy swearing is bad
- Enjoy life
- I am so good… I guess I enjoy life.

Drawing 4 below: Title of the drawing was: "Who am I and life around me"
The inner circle represents who he is, whereas the outer circle is about the life around the person.

I will not interpret due to the sensitive nature of the drawing. However, I can say that this exercise helped so much to reflect on what was going on in the present and express his feelings in a safe environment where the healing energy is in the air. The *blue* colour is the space. Pay attention to the way he uses and describes the *blue* colour in all his drawings.

This are his own words about the drawing:

Inside circle:

- I am Jim. (It is not me)
- Can't do work properly
- Can be naughty
- A sad person
- He is a person
- An anxiety person

Outside circle:

• No mum no dad
• No friends
• No school
• Momentum
• Inspiration
• Commitment
• No family
• Foster career
• Acceptance
• No people
• Rude brother

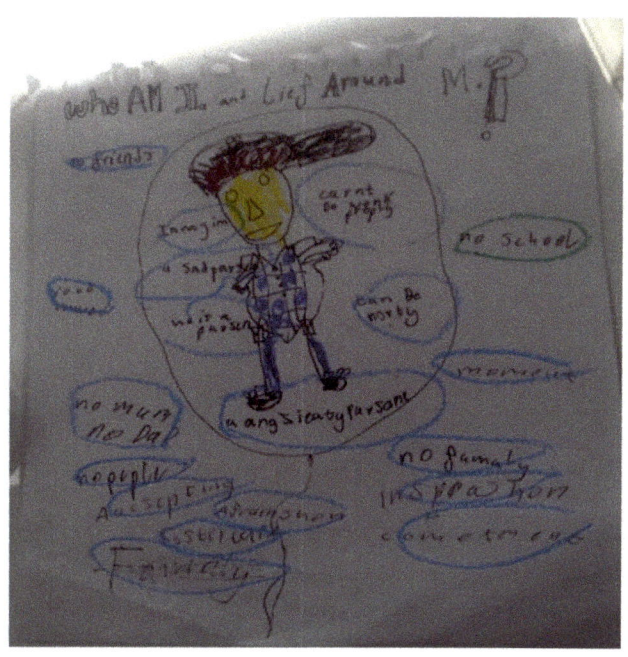

Drawing 5 The title is: "Who I want to be"

Again due to the sensitive topic I am not going to interpret it, but I can only say that the child here can see hope, and the child is already giving you a lot of information about his inner world, the way he is feeling and the way that he wants to feel. He is very clear. In terms of the colours, green is the main colour. I wanted to ask him why he used green now instead of blue. My interpretation of green is him asking for strength, whereas the blue in drawing 4 represents that he feels let down by it and it is not surrounded by that energy that he is craving.

His own words in the drawing are:

Inside circle:

- I am a good person
- I am happy
- Loved
- Single
- Confident
- Proud
- I am a cleaner
- Commitment

Outside circle

- No foster career
- Acceptance
- College
- Love
- Brother
- Dad
- People
- Mum
- Friends
- Goal
- Family

Drawing 6 below. The child describing magical module inside his circle.

His own words about his drawing:

His description: -*Gold* colour is for happy but is sad now because it did not do it in past or did not work... *blue* colour is sad ....like when you cry and *yellow* colour is happy ...is just your normal colour skin.

Vjollca's description. Again in this drawing he describes the blue colour as a sad colour, which means the space is not known and which affects his living. So he jumps from describing the colour blue to yellow, which represents the reality. I believe through his saying that 'yellow is the colour of the skin' he wants to express: "Please accept me", he is crying for equality, which is universal love.

His description: -Momentum ...the orange colour is both good and sad and blue is sad. Moment of truth… is sad and anxiety.

Vjollca's comments: Again he mentions that the blue colour is sad and he expresses in the name momentum the orange colour is both good and sad, which shows me that he is aware that the present, could be good and bad, but he is stuck on how to make it all the times good, how to understand it, how to accept it and how to live with it.

His description: -Acceptance Is sad and happy (he got his job) and anxiety because something bad may happen...or lose his job and he is scared that people may make fun of him.

Vjollca's comment: His description can tell you about his confusion and it gives you clues on how to work with him.

His description: -Inspiration is green because is feelings no good and is getting inspired and learning.

Vjollca's comment: As you can see is bubbling and is not clear about a lot of things and needs help to clarify his inner conversations.

His description: -love is pink because someone cares for you.

Vjollca's comment: It is a good thing that he has some kind of sense of what love is, and this helps us to know where to continue the work in the love stage of the Magical Module.

His description: Commitment is brown because is shy, happy and scared. He is shy because he just came to the job, he is scared because he may lose the job, he is happy because he got the job.

Vjollca's comment: "Again, he is bumbling and trying to reach an understanding of who is, his strength, and how to be who he is at the moment and who he wishes to become.

Drawing 7 below "*Love for my mum*"

I did not ask is description because the drawing shows it all and it is a very sensitive and painful topic to work with him for that short period of time I was with him. By seeing it I can only provide my interpretation. Here he is showing his imaginative world, his perfect world that he has in his own imagination. He has a rainbow full of life, colours and joy – everything one needs in this life, and his magical person with a big heart close to the three lines which represent universe. Here he has used blue, green, yellow and red, which represent love. But the emoticon on the right, shows that he does not have his mum with him to provide that beautiful fascinating, magical world.

My notes: Only if you have achieved self-love can you bee a good parent. It does not mean that you are doing anything wrong but it means that you need help.

My notes: Only if you have achieved self-love can you bee a good parent. It does not mean that you are doing anything wrong but it means that you need help.

Drawing 8 below: Title: "What makes me feel to behave the way I behave"

The child's words on the drawing:

• When I am around others I feel angry because when someone tells me off I am sad. I don't like shouting

• I am allows sad, no one understands me

• They are annoying me

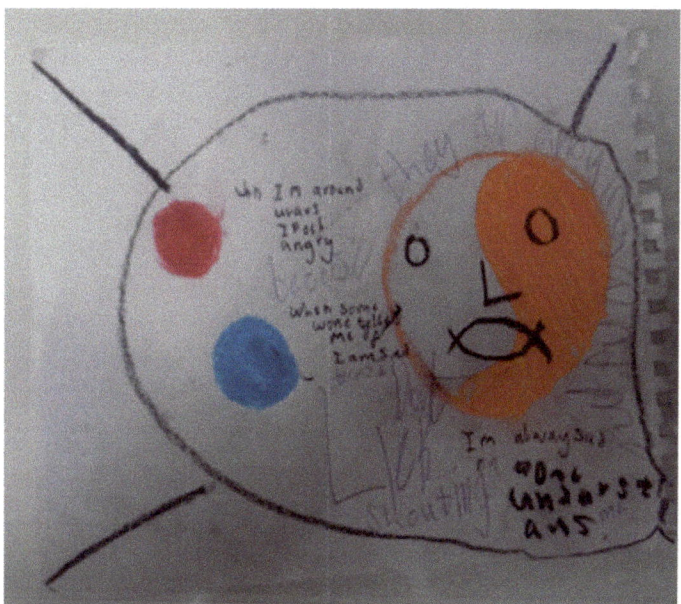

Vjollca's interpretation: I have already places the child in that space, and that is why he was opening up and swimming in his inner world and outer world and now the job is easy to start the work with small steps including the child's own decisions, including the child's treatment plan – by discussing everything with the child and letting the child choose.

Social worker feedback:

Thank you for your support and the care of the young people last week. I think you approached the task with considerable thought and brought your insight and reflective approach to all that you did. Well done..

Vjollca's final message: "Children are great spiritual teachers. People, who help you to feel the adventurous nature of the reality…to learn the power of the moment, to feel fully present. They are the sun of this reality".

Case study 31

Background: Pregnant woman around 20 years old, in a relationship. She came to me not for emotional but for practical support. She needed information on how to proceed based on her situation that she was in; she wanted to gain her stay in UK from her husband, through marriage.

Summary: During the first meeting I had my first insight that she was really coming from a very complex difficult past of childhood abuse, and the relationship she was in was not healthy at all. Even thought she was not asking me for emotional support, I could not remain passive to the channeling I was receiving about her. My intuition was guiding me to provide my support in three different sessions based on three different voice intonations. I had never planned this, but it simply happened. This will be explained during the information of this case study below. I use the tone of voice not in the order that is provided here because it depends on the client's needs. For example, for client number 1, I used all of them in the same day. The reason was that as part of the process of destroying the past structure and building the new structure. To learn more about the specifics please refer to the Magical Module.

Session 1: Momentum mood-impartial tone of voice:

The whole session I used an impartial tone of voice. After reflecting back on the session I found out why I did the session in the way I did, which was to make her feel the power of herself and light through exploring her options and choices. So pointing out all the good things and her abilities that she had. Moreover, we explored more than three paths, including the one she was in and where they could lead her. We agreed not to continue with emotional support, as it was not her intention to come for it, as she was not aware that she needed emotional support, but I said to her that if she ever changed her mind she knew where I was.

Session 2:

In this session I held all the stages tight as I was throwing them through the 'alarm bell' - tone of voice. This session occurred a couple of months after the first session. It was unplanned because she had to hand me a letter for one of my clients. On my way to go and meet her, I was having a conversation with myself and telling myself: "Vjollca, behave! Vjollca stop it! You don't have to! Just pretend that she is not there. Be calm, get the letter and walk away. That is not your problem. She knows where you are, if she needs help. So stop, stop, stop and behave" All this words to myself were coming automatically, because I knew what was going to happen, as I could see it in the form of energy, not in words, not clear in the conversation, but in the form of energy and I did not like it. The reason I did not like it, was that what I was going to say would sound weird I had a doubt, how it would help her and I thought I would be seen as crazy; why should I tell her something that doesn't make sense to me? So I just decided to listen to myself and not listen to the energy. But as soon as we sat down, it automatically started and I could not suppress it, because somehow probably her soul was screaming for help. So through the whole hour, I was using the 'alarm-bell' tone voice, which was a firm, strict, authoritarian, dynamic, disciplinary, followed by the respective eye contact, and body language. Through that I was telling her loudly, everything that was going on inside her; on her feelings, on her mind, on her soul. And by her response I was holding the balance between her mind, body, heart and soul. By the end of that meeting, I was exhausted, but her structure was shaken completely – by that I was hoping that she could reflect back on her structure as a 'whole her'. Even though it sounds crazy, it looks weird even in my mind's view, but I feel good and I know that it will help her a lot.

Note: At that time she had just lost the baby and I had the feeling that this loss was due to domestic violence in her relationship from both parties.

Conversation by text between sessions 2 and 3:

She contacted me again for practical support and then I took the opportunity to apologies for my behaviour on the last meeting. She responded by thanking me because it had helped her to raise her awareness on the whole her and the life that was surrounding her. As she said that I continued the conversation to help her reflect and go in more depth in her magical person and her as a person. Even I gave her some tools in writing so that she could apply them. I offered her my book A Magical Life but she was not ready to read it. Later I learned from her friends that she had deleted my texts because she did not want her husband to see them, as they were to empower her. I was a little sad as I thought those tools would have helped her, but hey, that is not my responsibility. And now this answer was coming from the space so I accepted it. On the other hand I was happy as I could see that it had shaken her structure and she had placed some bricks on the new structure. In the text I sent her I use the three tones of voices whose waves depended on her responses.

Session 3:

This session was about the Momentum and Love. In the Momentum stage I only did the listening. In love through confirming what she was saying, I was using the Love tone of voice, (the love tone is to reflect back what the client has achieved, which means it is proud, with sparkly eyes, compassionate, caring, healing, soft, cradle, cuddly, soft-touching, empowering the strength of love, that wraps you like a comfort blanket and like sun shine that keeps you on the light, like the moon that expands the imagination and fresh air that guides you). Again in this meeting was a coincidence, because she had to give me a supporting letter for me to give it someone. In this meeting she was doing 80% of the talking and I was using the 20% the love tone. The reason was that she was telling me all the changes she had made. The actions she had taken towards gaining her self-love and independency. My role was just to reflect back what she was telling me, which I was really impressed with.

Client's feedback:

Since I meet Vjollca she has helped me, to be more in peace with my whole self and to believe on my self. I have started to change few things on my life. I have gained self believe, peace and strength through her approach insistence and straightforward.

Vjollca's final message: "If you see your self in mirror and don't like what you see, don't just ignore it but confronted because is you, your soul is trying to tell you something, listen, make notes and turn it into action".

CHAPTER VIII

OBSERVATIONS

During my observations, I had to get in touch with more than 5000 people. Last year in 2017 on Facebook I had just 200 friends and no followers, but now I have 4000 friends and 3000 followers. Most of these people have contacted me and I have had some kind of conversations with most of them. I have been very aware and tuned in a trance state most of the time, in other words I have been observing people from distance. I could bring up so many issues and underlying issues that I have noticed but I will just mention three points.

1) *Self –love key to everything* (Noticing self-love was missing which made them act on ways that even they were not aware. This leads to think that do they like themselves for who they are and how they act?!!)

2) *Create the life on your own beliefs.* (Most of us we create the life on what we believe is right or wrong, or on what others have done and what we have been told. Most of us we do not question ourselves and accept the answers we get from our selves because they are unique and not the same as we are surrounded. Also we have not been courage to value ourselves and our inner thinking as it does not make sense to us, to reality and to others, it only feels right but actually doe not make sense.)

3) *Where the self-love exists, only love and understanding will be applied.* (Trying to explain self-love is not easy as I explained above in point two. Reasons why is because it does not resonate with reality and what others do but it does feel right…..you know it ….you just have to think in deep level what does it mean for you to be loved and how can that happen? Meaning being loved within, how and what is it?

1) Self –love key to everything (How it manifest in below cases): I have noticed the loneliness that people feel and the emptiness inside them. Searching for something that they do not know what they are searching for, but they think passionate love can give them the satisfaction of feeling good by the high that they achieve through the excitement, of flirting and the pleasure they get from the orgasm. So for that reason the only, the first attention is how to get that passionate love. So they ignore working on self-love and universal-love as the universal-love is automatically applied to them but not in their conscious level. This way of thinking is not healthy as it becomes only a need or an unhealthy attachment, not something that brings them joy or helps them to grow. The above point, I can demonstrate for you from a few examples and a few selected conversations. In my opinion it can be seen how desperate they are and how they prove the points above that I have just mentioned.

Observations: The practice and the achievement of self-love is free, but that makes us think that it is not work, as we are used to think that we need to work for money for material things…this is the turning point of disconnecting from space. It's easy working when love is not present as the focus will be on material things and not in love itself…which makes you think that that is what you will get…sometimes you do get it but it's too late …your life has almost ended when you realise that love was missing and you feel dry…The good person …the person who does everything from foundation of love don't focus on material things but they just come part of love -plan-action-satisfaction-fulfilment-self-realisation … As love is the key who can help you to open all the other doors by using the right tools. For the good person to change the society is harder because the good things are unseen. You only can feel it, visualise it, and live it …..

"You can search throughout the entire universe for someone who is more deserving of your love and affection than you are for yourself, and that person is not to be found anywhere. You yourself, as much as anybody in the entire universe deserve your love and affection."— Buddha

Example 1: A woman that replaces self-love with money and fame. At the beginning she presented herself by congratulating me on my job. She explained what she did for a living, then expressed her wish to collaborate with me. I shortly sent her my structure, and she did not reply because my structure was not based on profit making. Also, I noticed the ways that she maintained her communication with her contacts and I came to a conclusion that everything she did was based on money. I also discovered that she spoke only when she thought it was appropriate, not when others needed her assistance. One day she wrote to me to ask for help, because she needed some clarification shortly after she requested my book. I said that I would give to her if she would give me her feedback on the book; she refused to provide them by saying that she did not have enough time to think properly. I have selected 3 dialogues below. The reason I will mention this 3 examples is that they show clearly in my understanding that she does not have a clue what self-love is, since can not practice it. Clearly it was noticeable that she wanted to use others for money and fame, but not contribute. The third dialogue is my technique, which straightforwardly shows what she needs to reflect upon.

Dialogue 1 She asked me for my advice.

She: I feel like I do not know myself.

Vjollca: What do you mean?

She: What should I do to really work with myself?

Vjollca: Tell me.

She: I feel like I do not know myself that well.

Vjollca: Explain more. What exactly you do not know or what do you want to know?

She: I cannot explain it.

Vjollca: We all know ourselves every day.

She: I just feel I have not lived with myself.

Vjollca: Tell me one occasion that made you feel like that?

She: I do not know.

Vjollca: Make a note each time you know something about yourself. For example what did you miss?

She: Oh that's a good idea

Vjollca: What is really in your mind?

She: It has not been about what I want but what has to be done. I always put myself last.

Vjollca: Well let's change that…so what do you want.

She: Now I am focusing on myself Vjollca.

Vjollca: That sounds great…but you need to talk to yourself and ask questions. Who you are? Who you want to be? How you want to live. If you did not care about no one and life is all about how you want to live it. What you have and want you want etc. etc. Write down your answers and read them again after a few days. Start looking yourself in the mirror and have a conversation about those questions and anything that might pop in.

She: ok.
(She did not discuss anything more with me).

Note: The reason she was interacting with me, I think because her inner voice was calling her. I do not think she really knew exactly the real explanation why she was interacting with me. I think she was in the stage, where she was in confusion with her magical side (her soul, intuition, and universe energy) and her actual person, created by the outer reality.

Dialogue 2 When she liked to use my time but not give time.

She: I have started reading your book, but it will be better if you reduce your price, because this book could help many women.

Vjollca: The prices are for a reason, because I want to firstly teach them in seminars and then they can take a copy of the book. However, I really appreciate, if you can tell me your thoughts in your own words about the book.

She: I do not have time for that. But I want to show you my project in you-tube and need your advice.

Vjollca: I have given you already a lot from my own time. Please do understand that my time is very precious. And if you cannot find a minute for me, then tell me why should I make time for you? You have my email so if you need anything do not hesitate to contact me there. I have sent you a number of questions, but you have not answered them yet.

She: They are very deep questions that a human being never thinks of.

Vjollca: I have done them in seconds, and want the thoughts that come in the moment. She: I do not think I can answer them, because I need to think a lot.

Vjollca: You do not need to think. Simply write down what comes to you in that moment.

She: I am sorry but I cannot do it.

Vjollca: That is ok. I wish you find what you are looking for.

Dialogue 3

She wanted me to be part of her social group, so kept adding me in various Facebook addresses, which I usually took it off, she added me again, I took it off again, and she added me again, I took it off again then she send me a link in inbox and she added me again. Then I wrote to her saying that I did not wish to be added in those pages; because it was energy of manipulation that focused on money and fame, which was not my field. She replied back:

Vjollca: Please do not send me links because, in all those links I can see only unhappy people, lonely people that run after the money and interest in order to fulfil what they lack...but they do not understand that they immerse themselves deeper in their unsatisfaction.

She: Heeeeee . Normally the money does not make you happy.

Vjollca: Never mind. Enjoy your time.

She: But we need money. Have a nice time.

Vjollca: Read the book and you will find the answers there. Furthermore the second book will be more advanced. I am sorry but you have not allowed 10 minutes to answer my questioner, from now on, if you have something, contact me by email, because my time is precious too. I thank you for you understanding. With respect. Vjollca

She: I am sorry you feel that way. I have not had any intention to hurt you.

Vjollca: I am simply showing respect towards myself. It does not have anything to do with you. You have not hurt me, please do not misunderstand me.

She: those questions are too deep, and I need time to think about them; not just 10 minutes, anyway, all the best.

Vjollca: Do not worry. It is ok. I just mentioned it to make you aware of your actions and to see how you react, as my passion is to study people and one day I will use this case as examples.

She: Yes, that is what all researchers do.

Vjollca: I do not have more time, because I think that I have already given you what you need.

She: I hope you have a good time.

Vjollca: …and, please do not add me in your groups, because I do not like them, especially the groups that you follow as I have noticed they are not really genuine. Please if you want to share my posts you are welcome but do not add me in any of your groups or tag me. Have a great time.

She: Ok no problem. Have a nice time.

Example: A man that lives for money.

He: Hello Vjollca,

Vjollca: If you have something, please write to me on my email because I don't have time for greetings or friendships. Thank your for your understanding.

He: No I do not have any work to, I just wanted to greet. I don't need to ask you anything, because I have everything I want. I hope you have a lovely day.

Vjollca: But you have read my posts on Facebook about how to contact me and for which reasons and that greetings do distract me, but you still wrote to me…what did you expect…did you expect me not to answer… to provide some sort of clarification or throw what you wrote to the messages that do not require answers. If you provide an explanation and do not disturb me with greetings you can remain in my facebook friend's list or otherwise I will have to remove you from it.

He: No, I remove you because I do not need your friendship because I am a businessman. I do not need you at all, but you seem to be presumptuous. I live in a rich country and I have businesses in several areas. So from now I will leave you in peace, because you seem to be a wicked and naughty Albanian, woman.

Vjollca: I am busy, but it is your problem that you do not understand and do not respect the other people's time.

He: you have plenty of reasons to express yourself. I have discussions even with senators but I am not as naughty as you. You know well, which rich country I come from. It is not appropriate to be so disdainful, because I am a millionaire and I am so simple.

Vjollca: My time costs, but I give it only to those who ask for help and cannot afford it, but I also help those, who need my help and have the money. For those who feel lonely and desperate for friendship, but are not ready to be helped I do not have time. Learn, learn how to respect yourself and others.

He: I respect everyone, but you don't know what respect is.

Vjollca: Money does not teach you, and I am not interested what you have and where you are…What I am interested is to see what I see in you, and that is enough for me. Now I will block you because I gave you enough time.

He: You are wrong. Money is everything in life. If you are the wisest in this world and do not have money you do not have neither authority nor perspective.

Vjollca: Pay me and I can teach you how to gain what is missing on you "the self-love" that respect comes with it. (He blocked me after this message).

Examples*: People showing signs of desperation and hunger for universal love, they do not have a bone of love in their body from within and they depend on universal love or passionate love.*

Example 1:

Dialogue:

He: Hi gorgeous. I need to thank the almighty God for the beauty He has granted you.

Vjollca: The happy people do not disturb others…but the lonely ones search for friendships and value the appearances.

He: I value the appearance because beautiful appearance means beautiful soul. Oh you are so wrong, I do not feel lonely at all, and have no time to lose. I have a high status in society and a very successful career. I am a teacher, writer, and editor of several magazines.

Vjollca: I am sorry but do not have time to keep you company but if you need something link to my work contact me through email or can call me if you have something to discuss.

He: Ok, ok but can we meet somewhere to exchange our books, and to see one another in the eyes…

Vjollca: I do not want to be misunderstood in any way. I would only meet you if the meeting is about to help people who need help.

He: To be honest. You have been created in one of my dreams, and I cannot wait to meet you. We have so much in common. We are soul mates, and I am thinking in advance to experience this with you.

Vjollca: I think I have already explained to you. I do not want to be misunderstood.

He: Please believe me when I say
    Maybe you think I want someone else,
    No I would never do it that way,
    If you love me I would drop all my defence, Only the two of us, should always be,
    Only death will separate you from me, My sweet heart what I feel I say,
    I want you to be in my way.

Example 2:

He has artistic ability but has problems with accepting his absurdity. He says he loves himself and he is able to love the partner but the reality says he does not like commitment. For the reason that he is frustrated and is confused in that kind of field and it is not clear who he is as whole person what is good for him. Even if at times he knows himself, his mind and reality will be interrupted and he will say "that does not work for me" . Here is a conflict with the person who is created and the magical person he really is.

That is why he has problem with passionate love. In universal love he has problems because he is in conflict between the magical person and actual person (this conflict between this structures is explained in Magical Module). Self-love is the solution to all his problems, but currently he does not have it.

Dialogue:

Him: What would you say to me, when I feel a stranger and empty. Stranger among the people who love me a lot, but for me it says nothing the love of others ?! I had a close connection and we broke up because she did not want and did not accept my past from being a murderer ...?! How do I become understandable to others when almost nobody understands me ?! You Vjollca, would you like to live with a man with a bitter and bitter past? Would you love someone like me a bit crazy and wild by nature, but inside I am a 3 year old child ?! And last, why all women want special treatment and care ... Why you don't love me for who I am, but for who you want me to be, for you desire love , for what you want me to offer? So egoisms ...? ' Please write me

Vjollca: I cannot answer you through writing. I need to talk to you.

(After this I gave him a call and discussed on the phone each topic to make him aware that all lye's on self-love and it does not matter the other if you don't matter to yourself. He was resisted, and in denial so he started asking me out and wanted my attention. I tried to go back to the main point self-love and raise his awareness but he was so on resisting mode that he loves himself but wants someone to love him for whom he is and in mean time as he could see that I was talking only on melody of the soul in deep level he avoided the voice conversation by hanging up and given the explanation below).

He: I could not hear you because my Internet connection is bad. Do you think you can fall in love with me?

Vjollca: No, because everyone should know what they want and who they want to spend the life with, If not, they have to learn it in the hard way, and I know what I want, and you're not who I want. You also know that I am not what you want but you have to work first in your self-love in order to figure out what you want. Remember, we can spend our lives only with one person and it doesn't mean that we have to be with everyone that we like, so... I strongly recommend you read my book to understand in more depth what we talked through the phone conversation and until you read the book I can't help you further.

After few days he contacted me saying:

He: I have read your book "A Magical Life" and it did not give me nothing! I am sorry.

Vjollca: You don't have to be sorry, just tell me your thoughts and why it did not give you anything? No matter, you do not have to feel you doing anything wrong, just tell me what you think about the book, and why did not give to you anything?

He: I have read so many books including therapeutic books and scientific books and no book can solve my situation.

Vjollca: Ok please do not contact me, until you read the Magical Life book than we can have a discussion. I do not think you have read my book and you really need to learn self-love as then you can answer all the questions that you asked me.

Group discussion on someone's wall, who teaches others spiritual guidance... is the content that he had published, he pointed out that thoughts cannot be controlled. Here is my reply to him:

Vjollca: My theory through my self-discovery and gathered through my work is that we are in general function in this form : mind – the thought - feelings - the heart – action - the behavior - so the power has the thought that is created by reality but I have verified on myself and my client that by using the magic module: momentum- acceptance-goal-inspiration-commitment-affirmation-love you can know yourself by being tied to the soul that allows you to organize your thoughts-to heal your heart-and to create new thoughts. Based on the energy of your soul-you connect directly and with the intuition (the voice of the creator) and understand the energy of the universe. Certainly, every phase of the magic module need work and commitment to reach the result. "Your Soul helps you to understand your human being"

Person number 1: response (female): Thoughts cannot be controlled but we make the choice of what thoughts we want to keep.

Vjollca: Thoughts are fed from somewhere ... they arise from something... so how they get created that way they can be deleted and create new ones..... just have to find the source of thoughts ... the roots of thoughts... that for me the source and root is my soul. The question arises for each of you is where from they have been created your thoughts?

And how do you understand if the thought is good for you or not? When we die what happens to us? Well… if we live on this life without understanding the spiritual world then we will be slave of the human mind.

Person number 2 (male): Thoughts are wavering, the brain is the one who approaches them, and their grip… the approach they catch is different. We have access everywhere, while we get what we need or what we do not need, so … we cannot control thoughts as a wave, but we can orient ourselves in ideas (thoughts we have caught) and create mechanisms proper for realizing those ideas.

Vjollca: Here comes the spiritual world that is the space that possesses everything…so if you are tied to your soul you can see your thoughts as a movie and organise how you will want for your benefit… ahhhh if you are not connected to the soul then it is a little difficult to control your thoughts or understand because you do not know how to build new thoughts … but turn around to what you have learned so far… to the soul you find information that you never heard of it in reality….the soul is rich in divine and infinite thoughts …

Person number 2 (male): We have a mental, etheric, astral and physical body… the mental body is the one who has access to thoughts, then carries it to other bodies and concretises it in the physical plane and the physical body.

Vjollca: No, it is still talking about the human being… because thoughts produce feelings and feelings spread throughout the body … The illnesses arise from the feelings with our love which creates stress… the body is nourished by love and needs love in order to be healed.

The person who wrote the post: The soul does not produce thoughts. The source of thought is not the soul. Please do not confuse the products of the Mind with those of the Soul. Not the same! Please meditate, otherwise we will debate the whole life and in the end we will not achieve anything !!

Vjollca: But that means you do not produce thoughts from the soul so tell me where do you get your thoghts from?,, As I always produce thoughts from the soul and my intuition rarely I use my mind to produce thoughts. I have clients also that are practicing the same strategy that I will explain soon on my second book. In the first book I explained how I listened to soul and intuition … Then.   why the soul does not die and the brain, heart and body die? Why do babies are full of life and love until they begin to be influenced by the people around them? Then, when we study children with attention, we understand that they speak the language of the soul and intuition at most of the time… Why in our childhood we loved the nature? Why, even now, a glamorous thing draws us to nature? In all answers of those questions is our soul calling us… it is our true existence. etc. etc.

Awake and enjoy life that you are fleeing trying to get things that may not be important   if you do not feel satisfied at this moment stay in silence and disconnect from your thoughts and feelings. Just allow yourself to be in space that exists above our human being (which is the soul, the creator and the energy of the universe) and communicate… Who are you? Who you want to be? What do you really want? What would make you happy? What matters? How will you live this life? What is the purpose you are in this life? How will you achieve it and where would you start?... etc. etc.... that from there you take with you that taste of the your experience and practice this exercise as often as you feel you have everything you need to feel full of love. .... This is just an exercise.   I have more in the first book and will create it during the seminars   But the seminars are useful but 80% has to be done by individual.

The heart does not create love just produces what is transferred to her by mind and soul, simply produces the feelings of the thoughts coming from the mind and energies of the soul, the intuition and the universe is the mind that allows the soul to influence. Pure love strives from the soul .... the rest are confusion smoked of mixed love... But if the love of the soul is not in harmony with the mind and brain then has no power to reach anything. ....
Because the individual has free choices and can choose what he/she wants to use. ....

Another discussion based on another person's philosophical post:

Vjollca:
We do not know we've got it. ...
and don't know what we want to have. ...
But we know we want money and fame. ...
But those who have it realise that still they are missing something. ..
However of what they are missing they are not aware..
No one taught us what we wanted and how to find it. ..
Somewhere here and there was released the truth from those who understood it…
But no one took it seriously. ..
because if you cannot see it than you cannot practice it…
we knew the name but we had caught it by the tail. ..
the head and foundations were unopened. ...
So what was it !!! ???

Film director's reply: To feel like the creation of spiders, it is gained as a jumble ... GOD, how painful.. especially the compiled Albanians; you: whitening mind.

Vjollca: Who is the meaning of your comment please… I am uncommon and I don't understand it, because I took the diploma secretly with the intent to just pick and do not interrupt my knowledge ... hahahha… so in simple words what does your comment say? I'm curious about it.

Poetry for artists ...
Do you know the artist looks at things with the divine eye?
I know that many artists simply use that gift of soul silence.. ..
For the flourish of the world of fairy tales. ..

to watch the glamorous beauty that all pass by without seeing   !!!

And for many other reasons but rarely are the artists that the world of fairy tales fall into the world where we live and teach people how to live in it

and how to preserve the glamorous beauty of the world of fairy tales. ....

in fact our world is a real fairy tale world that we do not know how to create the tale we want. ...

but we allow others to create our fairy tales ...

Have you created your story?

Are you the artist who brings the fairy tales to people?

Is your reality a fairy tale of your reality! !!

Are you the artist who helps people to create their own tale! !!!!

A female's response: what Vjollca claims is approaching philosophically and scientifically! If you think of it in careful way, you will see that there is an absolute right!

A discussion based on a quote from Osho:

"You're nobody. You were born like no one without a name and no form. You will die like no one. Name and form are only on the surface; deep inside you, you are an endless space. And it's wonderful. "
- Osho

Vjollca: This statement is very correct but there are some understandings that need to be explained ... because the questions arise. ... - how can we use space? What role does our human being play (brain, heart, and body)? How can we create the bridge between space and human beings? How can we use space with what we want in this reality? Etc etc. etc. We need to be a space researcher ...

Points to Consider: 1- meditation needs to be explained how to be productive because people are comfortable with ideas that meditate with our knowing the importance of pure love included. 2- conversation with the space and the human being with the foundation of pure love ... is not being practiced by people through meditation. And that way the reality will be created ... here there are few very few people who have achieved it. but are not self-conscious. The word 'meditation' I want to change the name in a conversation with myself - conversation with the human being   but ambitious conversation where only pure love is the foundation for the conversation to be fruitful. Remember, depression is healthy if you use it to understand yourself, to recover from busy days, to discover the next step, to plan your days ahead, to understand your feelings and just to allow yourself to do what you feel doing.

Him: A person's (male) response to Osho's quote: You're born like everybody, you live like someone and you die like everyone!!

Vjollca: What you said is the reality and the human being, what I explained is the spiritual world working with the human being.... it is uncovered. ..not verified ... the part you're connecting with the creator   anyone who does not know the space, neither knows his soul nor the creator (God) but merely arises and lives like a human being and dies unsatisfied and unfulfilled.   Certainly and without reaching the true goal that has come to this life to make themselves happy and enjoy life ...

Him: for Which "space" you mean, Vjollca, for that inside or outside of you ?!

Vjollca: I believe that the space you understood in the comment that I did above but with the simplest words is when you are in silence and you manage to disconnect from your mind and feelings and listen to that quietness.. That is the space   there you can hear the voice of the soul, the voice of the intuition and the energy of the universe. However for more information you should read my books or participate in the seminar or in the course that will create in the coming year. .... and also some materials to help you connect to space and how to use it… what you said was spot on… and you are right but the beauty of this life and the magic that is created is to believe what you say with my explanation and create harmony and that's exactly what I'm trying to teach others because it's really fascinating when is achieved… I have reached it and explained how I have reached my book that I wrote for only a week based on space and memories. ..

A spiritual male response: Sorry, there is no explanation for the space! It cannot be explained in rational language. "Space" is just a matter of a profound dimension of meditation, this is the state that reaches when penetrating into the depths of Being. There is nothing to explain here !! This should be achieved by every practitioner of regular meditation. The tendency to suppose to "clarify" something is just a common game of mind and that you continue to stay on the surface. Please meditate more and don't need to explain more, every individual has the right essence in their unique way.

Vjollca: "If we are not happy, in peace and feel loved exactly where we are that means we need guidance how to use the inner guidance"

A female's response: I have been meditating for 4 years, is a miracle about it does to your body. I am so happy that I have been given the opportunity to experience that healing of the energy that the body receives after meditation.

Vjollca: Yes… But… the question is how can you use it to create the reality you dream off? And how can you interact with the space to get answers to your questions… etc. etc. … Meditation is not used solely for calming but for many different reasons that we can let our human being be guided by the space… precisely this process I teaches it through seminars based on the seven phases of the Magic Module.

"It was what was, was not seen but we wanted, what was do you know? For that we got a lot of sacrifices and we could not get it ... what was ?... we knew the name but how to overwhelm we did not know… we think that sex was its essence or its achievement ..... or those scenes of unexplained feelings that stunned us… but now do you know what it was? The name we know it but did not know how to get surrounded around us… we think is passionate love that seeks… but you really do not have the idea until you start from the beginning ... those feelings of sparks without explanation that makes as stupefaction….what about now do you know what it is? …you may think is love but the truth is you don't have a clue until you start all over again from beginning….but where is the beginning!?! … to love yourself to be able to love everything around you? ..... Ehhhh but what am I talking about when something is still unconfirmed and misunderstood… OK ok ok… but what would you lose if you have a go as really where you are something is missing anyway …."was what was , what is it?

To achieve self-love is free, difficult, need patience and dedication, technique and method, to know the purpose and to discover the stairs and the steps… but it is the goal that opens the doors of the main goal we are in this life and that makes us enjoy every moment.

Notes: (on my Facebook wall)

Vjollca:

- Those who don't know how to love themselves well and suffer from the actions they choose to do
- Those who do good just to feel good and to feel appreciated but they get disappointed.
- Those who love with full their heart but they forget to discover who deserves their love and how to know where to give their love and to who… forget to see who deserves their love and choose what deserves ...
- all those who think they are good but they really are not good if they have not managed to make themselves happy

Even if 10 minutes to spend with yourself is enough for the beginning. ... then practices it by drinking the morning coffee alone, either on the way home or on your way to work, or just watching a movie a few seconds before you sleep   and so on it adds to the desire to do it more often until you reach learning to do it anytime whatever you are. (with others it's a bit more tedious and difficult but begins to eliminate what you've adapted) ..... there are also techniques and ways based on individual and individual routine.   some other way is to write in the moment when thought comes and with the help of someone or yourself to relay and organize. it etc. etc. full of ways.   the most important thing is to understand the importance of time with yourself and how to do it to be as productive.   will work and it's free. We are all the light we radiate but we just have to learn how to change because no one has taught us nor is it explained exactly how to turn the light on.   how to warm up under our radiation and how to warm others … we are all responsible for learning ourselves and then learning what they need to learn ... because we are all magical persons that live in a magical world . "The good person is the person who knows how to love themselves, life and know how to give love around and you search for the right love to attract   Fear does not exist because love is powerful and it masters the fear"

A teacher's comment: I like what you are saying. but does it not border a little on narcissism? I am not talking only about this piece; your ideas in general, don't get me wrong. I like your passion for what you do, but for me I would not feel whole without other people (hubby, sons, brother, sisters etc) loving me and I love them in return. Just my thoughts on this very strong piece on self-love, which I think it's great as it describes your experience and inner thoughts.

Vjollca: Someone who does not have self-love can never never never really know how to love others (brother, sister etc) because does not know the meaning of true love. Narcissism is completely different from self-love…. Because when someone has found self-love as I have explained in many posts, is fulfilled, enjoys fully the moment, problems do not exist as there are placed with solutions, knows who to spend time with , knows how to give real love not just needy love, they have time for everything they choose to do, etc etc…..

Narcissist they come across like they love them self's but they don't, they have so many problems hidden. In my book a Magical Life I explained the difference and in my second book I will again, as I did come across this issue when I was working with clients.

Of course we have not been educated on self-love.   that's why there are so many problems all around the world …..someone who has self-love can never hurt or do wrong to others (. as self-love can be confused in wrong way) and that's why I am very passion in that aspect. That is why on my second book will be explained how I have applied to others and my Magical Module will be. and should be everywhere if people want to be content, enjoy life, heal from their past and get the life they want …..

I know people don't even stop to think …as my idea sounds strange and unusual. and that's why I am bringing prove first to the table so then I can start my work on my Magical module.

Facts :

When you have self-love:

- You do not have stress …..as you will just know how to use it to you own benefit…
- Don't have physical sickness. from inside your body
- You will never talk bad about others apart from the time when you are saying it so they can hear it and it is used for their best interest…not because of you narcissism way   or you are clarifying something that you are not clear.
- You are calm …you are all the times in peace. …talking at pace at all times..etc …or smiling without reason. .
- Hate does not exist to the person who has self-love
There are lots more of other points but it will be further explored on my second book.

Summary:

All those people who copy other's ideas and try to gain money, career or fame, they have clearly not achieved self-love because they will never know the meaning of my three main rules provided below… only someone who has achieved self-love can fully apply these rules listed below:

1 - Treat others the way you like to be treated
2 - Love yourself the way you like to be loved
3 - Give 100 % in everything you choose to do

Our body is built from love which will help us to function...and that's why we have the need of others love, that's why we feel good around others but still there are things to reflect and think… is this really satisfying us? Or you just accepted because you think that is how far it can go....for better !!! In the scientific way of what I am going to say. However from my life experience and from the participants during my research and many more aspects that I have been working with, I have reached the conclusion that our body is built from love, which means until the age of 25 we automatically have love storage in our body. This is because until that age we are still somehow connected to the space. For instance, babies are full of love; until the age of 7 they are really connected to that certain space, where they receive the chance to imagine and create the future. Then around 10 if they are not determined to follow what they have been creating to follow in terms of the future, they take information from the reality side. Nevertheless around the age of 16 to 19years old they get a chance again to strongly reconnect with space, so they have a chance again to revisit the future and recreate it. Than adulthood at this age will take off. Around the age of 36-40 they will again reconnect with the space and have a chance to revisit their whole existence of their life. Though I have not yet explored further, to understand what happens. So the body is built from love and if we haven't got self-love that means that we automatically crave for love, without us being aware of it and here comes the universal love, but again the universal love is a huge topic, which needs to be question: Are you getting the right universal love or you are just surviving? (For further information refer to the Magical Module).

Then automatically you go for the last step which is the passionate love, and imagine things do get complicated, because instead of starting: self-love, universal-love, passionate love, you start by passionate love- universal love, which means your life is not fulfilled. Hence that is why you feel not complete, you will feel that all times you are searching for something but do not know what it is?. But in my understanding the answer is that only through self-love you can fulfil your first purpose of being in this life, which is to make yourself happy, and then you have the ability to fulfil the second purpose, which is to contribute into this life. Physical sicknesses exist by not having enough self-love in your body.

"Through self-love you can heal your inner and outer self, physically and emotionally, the whole you…"

2) _Create the life on your own beliefs_: I have noticed that the life created on others belief: How people live just to make a good image in society. This is because since their childhood they have disconnected from their magical person and their actual person is created based on the norms of the community in order to fit in with others.

Tragic case:

Someone who contacted me with an unexplained energy; even he could not explain how he was drown to me and how he opened up. My explanation would be that it was a connection in the spiritual way giving him a chance to turn things around. I did delay his mind-set and attitude, for three months, but I knew that as soon as he did not take my offer, that I offered him one month intense therapy, I knew that he was not going to turn things around.

But at least, he was taking some time to reflect on his decision before he took the tragic action. This is a great example of the individual not living for himself but for the good image that others have of him – I call this being addicted to the universal love, without having self-love! My basic and simple solution is: That you need to be who you are and who you want to be, which leads you to self-love and to gain a healthy universal love, you chose people who are willing to keep the air clear at all the times. That can be achieved through a lot of discussions and a lot of conversations, which you come in the end of some kind of understanding one-another. It is not about agreeing with each other on who is right and who is wrong or who is better and needs improvement. It is about understanding each-other. Then through that, you start to share the universal love and show love and care for each-other, and also fulfil the needs of one-another by helping…be yourself; to know how to be yourself, you should know the meaning of being yourself (refer to the Magical Module if you want to learn how to do that).

Summary. This observation is about a person, who before three months that he expressed his thoughts of wanting to kill his daughter, his wife and himself. He contacted me via Facebook. He said hello to me on my Facebook inbox, however I did not respond because I had already informed people on Facebook that I would not respond to simple greetings. A few days after he said: "I wrote to you a couple of days ago, at least you could have greeted me back. He also said that "I am a respected man and I have 5000 friends on Facebook, and I have a high social status, I am a well-known singer". I responded him by apologising and explaining to him that I did not usually make time to respond to greetings and requests for socialising as I had already mentioned in my Facebook profile. Then he apologised back so many times by saying: " I am sorry, I am sorry, I am sorry". Then I said: "It's ok, how can I help you?" Then he said "Can I call you?" It was 10.00pm, but I said 'Yes, of course'. We spoke for three hours. Through this conversation, he cried, he laughed, he opened up his heart, he showed me his pain, and he discussed with me the difficulties he was facing. He could not see a way out apart from killing his daughter and himself. Even though I was exploring with him all the options, but he was so trapped as he felt such a shame that his daughter was living with an older man and his wife had moved out, to live with her daughter as well. He was living alone. His understanding was that he felt ashamed from the society due to his daughter. He thought that everybody would point him out due to his society and tradition it is shame for a daughter around 20 to marry a man over 50, as well as for a wife to leave her husband.

In my understanding he was suffering from facing his culture and social circle. Also he could not find the strength to live alone. I also picked up that he was an abusive person and somebody who just thought about himself, someone who was raised in the way that women had to serve him and listen and obey his guidance. But on the other hand I could see that he was really deeply struggling and suffering and unhappy. I gave him all the tools, in order for him to continue to keep that positive vibe or thoughts of our conversation, to change his life. In the beginning of the conversation he started by asking my advice as if he was referring to someone else. He was asking me 'how can I help that person' and he was explaining me the entire situation and his concerns about that person saying 'he might do something stupid such as kill his wife, daughter and himself'. For the first hour the conversation was about guiding him how to help his friend he was referring to, and one of my guidance was… do not leave him alone, stay with him and show him this option, tell him how to care and love himself. Also show him how to use the life he has, and how to leave the negative people behind, or let the people to live the life they want. It was not his responsibility to interfere in other people's lives. Then as we were discussing the ways how he could help him, he said to me: "Do you know who I am talking about?" "No", I replied. As soon as he said "It is me." he burst into tears and we both stayed in silence for a few minutes, as I could feel his pain. Then I started using my techniques and my approaches by repeating the same guidance that I had given him earlier to help his friend, to help him gain his self-love and not control other people's lives. But instead let go off the past, let go off the so called 'friends' who had the same mentality that he had at the moment, so that he doesn't have to feel guilt or shame. Then he was very pleased and happy with the conversation. He said that he had not smiled in three months and that I made him smile three times, during the conversation. And I told him "You can call me any time, when you feel low". I also offered him to come and live with me for a few months. He said: 'thank you but no". I told him 'You just need three months to pick up yourself and I can help you'. He did not accept my offer, and then in that note we ended up our conversation.

After one week I sent him a private message on the Facebook saying: "I hope you are ok"?. I just wanted to know how you are getting on. Please let me know if you need to talk and remember my guidance. Let me know how you are doing with the tools I have given you". His reply was: "No, I am fine and will let you know if I need any help".

After a month it was his birthday and everyone was sending birthday wishes to him on Facebook. I regularly observed his Facebook profile and I did not like his friends at all because they were all exactly how he had described them: they kept judging him and not accepting his life, due to their narrow minded mentality.

Then he wrote to me on Facebook: "Everybody send birthday wishes to me, whereas you did not. I was waiting for yours!" I replied: " I am sorry if you got offended, but I am here only to help you get over your difficulties, and not to socialise". He did not accept that answer so well, but at the same time, he did not want to talk about how he had been doing regarding the topic that we had talked previously.

A few weeks had gone by when he posted a message on his Facebook wall, saying: "The bad child brings shame on you". I could see that all his friends were agreeing with that comment by saying things to encourage him to do what he had in mind to do, because he did not know his situation: "It is better not to stay in shame; it is really a problem to the parent that the shame happened to. They don't have courage to face the society"

I replied to their comments with a long answer: What I pointed out was that it was not the children's fault, but the parents, who raised them and once the children are over 18 and particularly over 25, it is not the parent's responsibility – whatever they choose it has nothing to do with the parent, it's not their responsibility.

It is their life and they can live as they want to live it, if they want to make a mistake the parent can advise them but ultimately it is their decision. The parent should never interfere on the children's life if they are over 18 of the children do not want the parent to be involved. After this he replied to me with a long text on inbox, telling me: " How can you call criminals, good people? And how do you dare blame me?" He kept blaming his daughter for a long time. I replied back by saying: "Please understand! You know very well what I said to you. I do not blame you and I do not want you to blame yourself, but also we talked about how you needed to leave them alone so that they could live their lives, and you focus on yourself". I could see that he was in an angry and frustrated place so I telephoned him, but he did not want to talk to me.

After a couple of weeks, he again sent me a text saying that, he had been to an imam and he had told his problem to him and asked his help, but the imam asked him for money, a lot of money, and he was asking me "Why the imam did not help him like I had done". Then I said to him: "Please do understand, not everybody is the same; so do not blame him for asking you money. However if you needed help, why have you not called me or is it because you think he could help you to make magic and not do the work by yourself?. What did you expect from him?" He then called me to talk to me, but I could not talk because I was away on holiday. I replied to him that I could not talk at that moment, but I could communicate with him through text and give him a ring in a week's time. The reason was that I could feel that he did not want to change; he did not want to work or take small steps towards getting better. So, he got very upset and blocked me on everything. A week later I saw the news that he had killed his daughter, his wife and himself. On the Facebook discussion everyone was blaming him. I was wondering: "Where are his 5000 friends?"

Then my public responses to some of their comments are provided below. (For anyone who wants to verify the genuinely of my discussions, they can find all the discussions below on someone's wall that has shared the article, whose identity is not shared here for confidentiality reasons):

My first response, when I found out that he had passed away:

Ohhhh no .... I'm so sorry because I knew this case closely and I could not help even though I tried: (....... Sorry because all these actions come from the fear of prejudices to others and not to the person himself: (...the opinion of others is one that plays with people's minds and causes these tragedies... many people have no strength to be themselves and to understand what the public is and what role they play in this life... in what bases is created the opinion and the life that is built on the basis of the opinion of the public: (... I am very sorry and no article has been written about what role is playing the opinion on the life of the people and how parents understand that the child over the age of 16 or 18 is not under the parents 'orders and the child's life is not based on parents' opinions.

One of my replies of to one of the blaming comments:

It is not his fault because he has suffered a lot spiritually and mentally, he could not found the strength to face the mentality and the public. I followed him in on Facebook where most of his friends had a reluctant mentality and did not help his condition.   I'm so sorry because I spoke very firm and harsh with him to help him see his reflection of his actions. I could help him to understand the reality and understand what's important to him but he managed to block me and refused my help....

"We cannot save those who don't want to be saved or see and understand what it means to love others ".......

Replying to someone, who was accusing me of encouraging criminals to be that way, based on my previous responses:

My dear, it is true that I do consider the criminals victims, and the victims are also responsible. For me personally both parties are participations on a crime for various reasons and if the two parties are aware of themselves, their lives and knowing how to love others, these events would not happen or would be rare. This is my opinion and my passion is to help to discover the roots of it as no one wins from these cases and I am sure no one get any satisfaction.

I do not justify anything but explain the causes and not outweigh the guilt or the generality of everyone who has played a part in this action because the law will do the rest, but I focus on how it could have been resolved? That is the question that is not yet answered or considered by each individual to take responsibility. Is not the answer by sharing or blaming just the one who made the last move history has a beginning and has been fed over the period of time to reach to the point where it explodes. The solution should start by studying how it started and how it has been fed and then how to prevent it in future?. It is not important who is the victim or the culprit because we all have a soul and no bad soul exist but lost people who do not know how to interact with their soul and speak the language of love. I feel sorry for all the victims who in this case called the victim and who did the gesture.

My notes: "They failed because they did not believe and they were so attached to the reality"

My response to one of the published articles about him:

As for this article   so he came to that decision because he was surrounded by friends like him who says "it is difficult to educate children in the diaspora" . My answer to that comment is   is not the fault of the child or the place where the parent raised the child but the parent's education to the children plays 90% of the role and 10% is the influence of society. But the parent speaking the language of love earns 100% the power of education of the children. In this case I have had the opportunity to know the person that did that gesture closely and the main cause of this action is only the opinion of the fans and his society that he thought he would murmur, and as far as I understood was surrounded by a society that judged him and he could not face it anymore their prejudices. Also huge role played the way he was brought up surrounded with the same culture and society. I try to explain the reasons why these actions take place and I do not agree with the punishment or who is guilty because it is important for me to understand the causes and ways that can be prevented. Let's not forget that men are raised by women and women are part of the blame for these events. so when it comes to putting the blame on the blame, everyone has a little bit a part of it, even though the punishment goes of the one who made the last gesture.

I think that everyone should be aware of their part of the guilty to prevent these kinds of events. We need to be clearer to work so that we can understand the roots of these events and educate ourselves as much as possible with the language of love without prejudice.   but to understand in detail the reasons so we can prevent it. It cannot be prevented by looking at the surface but in the depths. In the depths he was a good man and could not cope with his life in that way so he made what his opinion called good actions. And I'm sure the majority of the people say they well done to him for doing that.... so we have to look at things in the broader context. There are psychological problems that come from parents and the past, from the way we have been raised.   was not a bad person but did not know how to face his psychological state and was very dependent on public opinion and society… These things will happen and will happen until we become aware that we are not in this life to control anyone's life but only to live our lives… and enjoy our life.

Summary:

In terms of my personal role, I believe spiritually sometimes there are people who wants help but are not ready to be completely pure because they don't believe that being pure is the first step to form the journey they want. My job is to teach techniques and methods related to the above point. Nonetheless some of them still continue their old habits and make things worse for themselves. I know that I have to give them a chance to show them the options as it is the reason they entered my life but I still need more understanding of the conflict between the thought of giving them a chance and the thought that if they are not ready for help I should not help them. However sometimes they don't know what 'ready' means so it is my job to show them it's meaning to help them understand what it means to be ready to be helped and then let them take the responsibility for the consequences of their decisions. As long as I explore and explain the consequences of each road they may choose, I believe I had done my part, and in this case I did that with him, but it is sad that I could not do anything more.

Observation from Religious people Facebook posts and discussions:

""If you suffer is because of you, if you feel happy is because of you. No one else is responsible - you and just you. You are your hell and you are your heaven also " OSHO.

Facebook group discussion:

Main comments from someone that lead to a discussion:

To whom are the politicians responsible?
Before God? And He turned out to be helpless.
Before the history? And she was chronically e ...
Before the law? It is in function of the casting itself ...
Before the people? He is tired, and if he lifts his head, his mind has to be ... far way and ...
Ah ... in front of the west Goodness of the gates ....

Vjollca: The above statement is spot on for those who will reflect on how to open the gates of love. ...

Female comment:

Before a population Before a God
A responsible politician
Pity, pity oh God have a pity ...
Existence a miracle in politics and politicians..
God creates miracles

Person (male): If God becomes a human being, and then the miracle may occur. It never happens in this miracle ...
Yes and in a single person there is no perfection   I think so.

Vjollca: God always does miracles but we don't understand it… "The Lord has given freedom of thought and action to everyone… if the actions are non-pure then you will not be happy, fulfilled and peaceful with feeling loved." ... and this is true. ... just look at those who don't practice purely that they show those shadows of unhappiness and look at those who practice purity they work on self-love first and then to what they want to achieve (self-love first) and get to help others (Understanding universal energy) have reach what I said above.

My poem: "THE BOX":

Just thinking...
So much we judge. ..
So much we blame others ...
So much hate we have for others .....
We try like a snake to poison others.....
I wonder ....
Where is love?? ...
Or because is so good to be true and people don't believe in love!!!
Or is the hardest thing to be product of what we supposed to be. ...
Love. ..
We like to give up !!!
We can't trust ourselves. ..
No We cannot .....
But we can trust the sense of universe. ...
The energy of our souls. ...
The voice of love. ...

Everyone in this world has the full freedom of acting on the basis of the pure love that begins with their self, then with others and ultimately the intimate one, but the people do not understand the love and the freedom that comes with it so they become slavery of their thoughts created by others and reality experiences"

Group discussion based on religion.

It was a post about religions that stimulated into discussion about religious.

Vjollca: In my opinion and from my experience, the soul does not belong to a religion category, but it recognizes a religion that is universal which is only one but because people start fighting with each other than religion was split in categories in order to help people to love each other once more. Also could give them the opportunity to want their group to understand love of each other, so religion. is nothing more than guidance on how to be the real you... you who love yourself and love others around without interest.

From my practice and from clients point of view who have been believers but they really understood that they believed wrong ... my thoughts are: "religion helps you to know the light in yourself and then you acknowledge the creator... ... but what is happening religion is wrongly interpreted every word in religion has a long explanation that goes with it but who can give that explanation?

That is the important question and you have to be able to know the answer within you. My answer is that only the person who have achieved self-love, in other words is fulfilled, in peace and feel loved can give you the right answer to the words in religions books.

Everyone has the ability to tell and knows what is good and what is bad ... so decide and choose the good from everything including the religion It is an internal struggle to discover and practice of the light that exists within everyone and it is the purpose of this life as it brings what you need to enjoy the life journey. Also to live in the light radiating as the rays of the sun and being fascinated by the beauties of this life. ....

Person: Thanks for the comment. Reading the rows of your writing I understand that to have faith in God you must have faith in yourself. I do not believe so, because the word faith if it is analyzing is something that is not real then I say that I believe it is not saying that it is. Therefore when you say that religions are there to "help" a person that is your point of view, but my own view is not. It's just that religions has broken down people, precisely religions are causing wars, exactly in the name of the religion are being killed massacred people, no matter what religion. I do not need religion to be good, I do not need religion to find the light! I find the light without religion, but with respect, commitment, love, work, humanity, and so on. When you say that when you have faith in yourself you have faith in God, I would say the opposite that when you have faith in yourself you do not have to have faith in God or anything else because you are able to understand what you want and what makes you happy. What light are you talking about Vjollca?

Have you managed to find that light besides what makes us live all under the sun? I am very much in harmony with the light. I count myself as a living being like thousands of thousands of others that are part of the earth's ecosystem. But unlike many other creatures I have the brain with the advanced and I can predict things. If you are talking about hell, let's talk about who's fake? Who created religion, should know and wonder why there are so many religions and why do they disagree with each other? It needs to be clarified why people's beliefs change so do not have the same faith and the same religion. These must be understood to conclude why religion exists or does not exist.

Vjollca: All of those answers to your questions will be in my second book and I can explain it through seminars. "The person who does not believe in himself does not know the Lord" ... all religions are helpful to everyone to help them, know themselves and to believe in yourself to find the true light and then know the Lord and practice the light. However remember that it is our responsibility to make sure we interpret it in the right way and the right way is the one that resonates with your soul. "But if you have found the light you should know the answers…" Where do you know that a person is practicing light? he understands if he is fulfilled with love and he just spreads love… so if you are not such a person, do not judge anyone until you get there because when you get there you do not judge any one, instead you automatically understand and speak the language of love. So God exists in each of us and we do not need to believe anything except ourselves !!!! Everyone knows what is good and bad… we just have to practice good… first it is a creator and for that reason are religions created as guidance to help us discover the light on us and not to follow them, like I said because people who interpret religions may not have found their inner light so they have misinterpreted, hence has confused people.

3.) Where the self-love exists, only love and understanding will be applied:

Vjollca's quote: "What I see I can't tell you because that is the whole point of you learning your lesson… I only can give you a hint"

This is my solution to the troubling issue of Domestic violence/violence: Everyone is talking, talking, and talking about how to stop it. Somehow every time I hear this word, I feel like a hammer is banging on my head. My understanding is that everyone who has not achieved self-love they are all victims, which makes them automatically not to be blamed for doing wrong. And there is no point of measuring who did more wrong, because the law will do that job. But as a whole 'us' it is our responsibility to love and understand each other and to help each other gain self-love. For the reason that I mentioned, everyone who has not achieved it is a victim, which means that they are unhappy. How would you recognise one that has not achieved self-love? You can tell, if they are not happy where they in the moment. The consequences of this is children separating from their parents, from blaming men for doing the most noticeable act. By labelling people, who do different criminal activities, by putting others down through shaming, by saying all the bad things they have done, and also twisting them and adding more into it. (Here I will provide some observation from face-book link to domestic violence):

Domestic violence observation:

One to one discussion:

He: Women have that much rights as they have task, although men have a higher responsibility over them.

Vjollca: For my opinion education is need it for both men and women as it is not so simple and the solution it's not always black and white.

He: Although men are like sea waves; if you agree they will overthrow, if you disagree they make you tired.

Vjollca: I do not discern gender. The soul does not know the gender, but the people put it in the category. Which means that women and men should be treated as people not as genders.

He: You are expert for mediating.

Facebook group discussion:

My opinion to all those people, who try to have a body image according to the partner's, friends', or society's expectations:

It is all about being healthy....and what the individual wantsnot about their partner. As only the individual can choose the partner not the partner the individual; Weight has to be looked at as healthy topic not as what others prefer....Who cares what others prefer??... What the individual prefers is the only thing that should matter… and to be healthy is another huge topic… which again it is only the individual who should decide.

Facebook group discussion about an article about a tragic act, where a man killed a woman: The article's title was: " Aldison's family wanted to go to the funeral, but Ariel's parents answered of revenge approach"

Vjollca: Revenge is for the weak people. For those who do not know what love is and do not know the meaning of life. ... are dissatisfied and disfigured to others. The revenge is hurting the other person with your full consciousness; being aware of your actions. we have to be able to see the difference between someone hurting with their full awareness, self-consciousness and the one who acts from the moment of emotional disturbances. The boy, I did not really blame him because he needed psychological help… and I'm sure he would not have done that action if someone had talked to him and try to show him compassion and understanding… the question arises !!! But the family of the girl who got killed does it need psychological help as they want revenge?! !! Or blame the son or son's family! !! ? Instead of taking over their actions and acting on the basis of love… on the basis of justice. .... love and justice does not allow murder or misbehave the other person with consciousness (remember that the boy was disturbed psychologically… and if you call his action wrong then try to find out solutions to things and make things better for both families not encourage revenge to make things worse. They are suffering already enough… it's not the race who killed first but understand each other, accept the mistakes and find a solution with the language of peace and love… Because if we continue the killings, other or similar cases will be continued).

It's not the problem of death ... but living ... we that are living not those who have gone… We run after life without thinking of death… Should we stop and understand what we are doing? Why are we here? How to use this trip? Deep topics but… I hope we start thinking and looking for lessons.

Someone's reply (female): To speak we are all philosophers but only those who try it in their skin know the meaning of pain ... Pain does not leave room for love and justice you say. Pain is hatred....

Vjollca: Pain carries useful lessons. .. whatever that means you have to know how to teach the lesson through pain to love. .... if you do not learn, but instead you take the short cut, such as revenge and blaming others. As an alternative of staying with that pain and learning… (A whole day seminar it is required to explain how to hug the pain in order to get through and find love, to bring us the best results in life… the base is love) There are deep topics but I hope people take time to reflect if they need to find peace and love.

Someone else's reply (female): The revenge only pain will give you, does not give back what you lost.

Someone's reply (female): Vjollca, you do not have to justify that boy's actions. Before you reach to revenge think before you kill someone else. Think if someone would kill your loved one? What would you do? The one who kills has to be killed ...

Vjollca: Do not confuse self-defense with revenge. Do not confuse the meaning of things with blame.

A person's response (male): O people do not comment on how you like to…no one knows the truth of their intimate situation! Only one thing I know that he loved the girl and did the action based on love. Revenge is blessing. Whoever do bad has to suffer the same currency, and is unpreventable.

Vjollca: How fast we judge and do not look at the depths of things at all   not so simple just to say it's wrong but we should look at how those mistakes can be prevented. "They are not prevented by judgments, and with a sneak preview of the mistake the person has done because he deals with the stamp of error." With the marvelous fact with the media and the people who spread this news simply for provocations to get a reaction from the public. Besides neither do they give a counselor lesson   in this way they just make things worse and harm the family. My message except what I said would be "Love yourself because only then will you be able to give love and you will be filled with love .... you will not be desperate to get attention from others ... but you will understand the true feeling of love .... that begins with yourself ... with others ... and finally in pairs   "I hope families do not start revenge on each other but instead they understand the pain they feel".

My opinion about this issue:

1 - I do send my condolences to both families and hope they find strength to cope with the pain.

2 - Reading the comments carefully. ... most show hate. ..and they do not speak with the language of love which brings more sorrow and adds to the bad things. such cases will continue until we learn about love for ourselves and life so that we can speak the language of love and do not harm others.

We know how to understand and those who make mistakes and help them correct them. ..example who dies, someone else will look after them (which is GOD) but we are here to take care of ourselves and the others around us. So I emphasize until we reach the point of not wishing anyone bad, but until that happens there will be similar cases. ... just feel sorry for what they understand and continue to do they point their finger to others but never ask themselves, "am I the person who wants the best for others without exception? And do I practice it? Do I want to take good care of myself and how do I practice it?

Another person's reply (male): Vjollca Sadiku I don't know how to put a name on you apart from saying that you don't have a soul. I am convinced that if you had lost a loved one your responds will be completely different! It's a popular saying that in other people's wedding you dance freely.
At least you should have mercy for the family who lost the daughter and when it comes to talking about the boy what he has done ….he should be burnet in front of society.

Another person's reply (male): That's what you say because it's not you experiencing what her parents are experiencing and I wish you don't have to but it is very difficult To pray for the life of a child of a man who has killed him unknowingly. Your child is in the tomb of a road trip. That revenge is very little.

Another person's reply (male): Everything started from the dog's family's dog and the dog that killed that girl was the dog. While the father of the dog who was also wanted to be burial in the burial of that girl who is buried by the dog that polylines it. She went away without any fault while her father was lost with the pain of the other.

Vjollca: Yes, we are family and this tragedy could happen to anyone.   these cases are misfortunes and we must begin to change to prevent such cases.   e solution is to look for justice for ourselves and others. In this case the boy was not right either with himself or with the girl. and with others.

Please. ... excuse me because for many reasons I can not continue the discussion. one of the reasons is that I do not consider it necessary but I would like to emphasize the following points:

1 - Albania government is the mirror of the people ...

2 - I think Albanian media is provoking by using the misfortune of people to see the people's reaction that, based on the people's mind of state, makes the step of misleading for their own purpose...

3 - I just gave my advice and everyone has his own happiness on their own hands. if you are not satisfied with your life where you are is only your responsibility to change that. ..

4 - I'm sorry for all those who do not know how to gain their own happiness and they don't look for ways how to learn to enjoy life with everything we create and the most unexpected things that comes our way… is case is created and if it goes to revenge it continues to create dissatisfaction and suffering for those who act on the basis of emotions and not the love of the creator of this life ... the love that exists in Everyone. ... when 5% of the population understands true love then we understand why 95% of others have not gained yet. ..

"Who does not know his / her soul lives in the mind filled with information confined"

"Who believes in birth and death understands that there is a creator of the world and that is why we are in this life... you understand the reason when you have achieved love within, when you feel loved within, otherwise it is only time to waste in this life "

"Ask yourself are you fulfilled exactly where you are? If you are not then you are not able to understand yourself or others... to understand the meaning of life "

I believe that I have answered everybody comments if you are able to understand what I have said... if not then look at my posts in Facebook which you might learn something.if not then send me an email to book the place in the seminar which will be themed that you are adapted to understand more deeply about how you can be filled exactly where you are without hurting one and never harming anyone... beginning to understand how you should not hurt yourselves first. ......

"A person who does not feel fulfilled means that navigates among the thoughts that is fed by others and not yourself... and it always makes it easier to do bad than good"

"People get mad because of the conflict between their soul and human body... also they stay here in this life with that condition because they choose before they come to this world. ...as we choose 3 or 4 paths. we agree to them as part of helping us to grow and fulfilled our purpose on this life".

"It is again about self-love. All these troubling issues are a sign of not having self-love".

Trying to understand the existence of ourselves and how it works. Thoughts in the moment:

- People who are lost but somehow they lost their really hearing and they all what they do is to survive or end it all...

- Those that control others because they cannot control their inner conflict.

- Guilty parents who just dig themselves in deep guilt by doing everything they try to come out of it.

- Those who have worked hard to discover their inner power but instead they use it for main purpose to make money which takes them further back even before they started to work in their inner power...

- Also the creator strategy to make as work hard to remember the benefits of being good, the good things others do to us, the good being power to everything, ...we easy remember bad things and how to act like that, as it is easier, it is the short cut and smooth compare to the road of being good is claiming mountains and with fall time to time but is peaceful, joyful, lovable, and with the purpose that will take you for sure in top of mountains. even if it did at least you know you are in zone of your really purpose of getting closer to that... mostly remember is not about getting in top of mountains but enjoying the moment and achieving your goal, cleaning your human being and putting in same level with your soul… your soul is the top of mountains because that's the whole purpose of being in this life… that is the test we have to pass each time we live…until we get at the same level with our soul… I am not sure how that can happen as it is very difficult thing to do and I am not sure what will happen after that can be achieved by everyone in this life… What will happen then??? !!! Maybe will be a peaceful life with full of love and then will start from beginning where all this started… which mean will be a test to see how long will be until someone can poison society again. or that's the whole purpose of life enjoying life.

Does it take only one to poison all of us? How easy is that to be done?

All this complicates solutions to this world.

In my personal example. The way I managed to be good or think I am doing good or I am in right path to fulfill my purpose and be fulfill in the moment is by:

- Spending time alone…which helps me to be quiet and listen to my soul, creator, any other spirit or energy that is trying to guide me (which could be any one …loved ones that are alive or dead), to universe, to my whole me (mind , heart and body… the body is the gut feeling… which you can help you to listen to other parts of your body and connect with your own body) . While I am in this state I make notes of anything that comes to me… as later I might forget. ….make notes of feelings, hearing words, and my own thoughts and feelings… as I may feel things don't belong to me. In other words I might hear thoughts that are not mine, or words , sentences that I never come across before etc ….

- I surround myself around people higher than me in the sense of self-love achievement, self-realization, fulfillment, criticism, speak up freely etc

- When I am around people that have to do with my work I make sure I have enough energy to be present and be there fully …..

- Family and friends that don't fit on the categories I mentioned above. I will keep healthy balance where I benefit and they also benefit. …so we don't damage each other's harmony. …but we help each other grow more …

- I make sure I use meditation, affirmation, my magical module to keep me granted and in same time feel light so I am not dependent from this life, but I can use this life to keep continuing being lighted. …

Poem: Babies crying from the frustration of how messed up the humans are:

They come into this world crying because they know what the journey they have to face. …

They know which family they are born….

They know how hard they have to work to remember the love….

To spread the love …

Even when no one pays attention. ..
Some children they find comfort to the nature. ..
Some to the animals. ..
Some to someone who still have that connection with love. ..
Some they turn in to the human they have been raised to became. ..
Some are prisons of their own anger. ...
Some are prisons of their own guilt. ..
Some are just swimming around to find what they are looking...
Even they don't know what they are looking for...
Some just give up...
Some think they find what they looking for and accept the pain...
They accept that this life is just all about unhappiness and they run after bit of excitements. ...
And so it continues...

Someone said: It is very hard for people to change.

My response: I agree with you and understand every word but we should not give up because it is one of the most amazing taste of life to feel the inner peace, loved and fulfilled. Therefore by showing ourselves we are automatically an example and evidence for those who are not happy where they are and slowly they will realize that those ways that they follow do not bring them what they want. With our soul love we can give them a spark to desire to discover within what they are searching for and e desire to believe in their dreams and the magic of life.

If you want to work on spreading your soul love through whole you as a human you have to stay away from negative people, walk in nature, give embrace, smile, self-excitement, be appreciative to others, there are people worse than you! Focus on internal healing, and the time will come when you will become so intimate that you can oppose anyone when it happens you have found God in you then you are connected with God.

Existence is in you, if your self-respect does not obey God. And I learned from life that everything begins with the soul... if we communicate with the soul and work to find ourselves then we have the ability to harmonize with ourselves and every human means we use for the purpose we have in this life. And I call human means everything except the soul (mind, heart, and body).

My opinion is that… the soul is who we are (how to understand and communicate is another thing), the mind is the computer that holds the information that we have taken since we were in our mother's womb (some information that we only select as they are many) , the heart is the feelings of thoughts that arise from the mind, so it comes to conclusion that if we feed our mind and heart with thoughts from the soul then we will find what we have been searching for. This is my theory and I believe that only in this way we find the way to be in harmony with ourselves and achieve the purpose of this life.

My poem: FAMILY

I am free of everything. ..
I fly anytime I want…
I love everyone on my own way...
I adore myself in any situation. ..

Family and friends are people, who have helped you to grow, Have you grown???
If you still relying on them for emotional and physical support it means you have not...
You meant to be free of needs...
You meant to be in love with everything that makes you feel home, simple, light, and just thankfully for being in this earth.
Your work is meant to help others feel the same way....
And .....
That's what I call life

Conversation with Myself: What am I doing in this world full of pain?
Even though we live in this world where the focus is dominance because human has given power /attention to it rather than lightening up their own path… we have to think that will be enough if I have my inner light and just keep that on .....will be enough to get me through whatever human energy through to me. because after all what it matters is the light ...the light of my soul as it will it is my purpose. it is the reason I am in this life to test how strong believer I am on finding and wanting my own happiness…. it is something that it lasts forever, as a human will have an end and will end up going to the same point where they started the life or even backwards until they prove themselves that they can commit to pure love, to their soul...to their true identity... it is the joy ...it is the peace....it is the love...it is the success. ...it is fulfillment… so for me it is enough to know that I will die with my light on. I consider this family in this life is not true our real family because we all are one family… all souls are one big family but the family we have placed is for a good purpose and they are special.
...I am not sure if sex exists in the life of the souls as it may exist only in this life...

Conclusion of my understanding and of the client number one: "Every knowledge around us is to help us discover the light on us. If we have not discover that light on us we cannot believe on a creator or appreciate the creator so our prayers will be weak. The test of this life is to see how much we believe on our pure love that connects with the creator"

CHAPTER IX

BOOK REVIEWS FOR THE BOOK "A MAGICAL LIFE"

Reader one is a spiritual person that enjoys life fully. Reader two is a scientist, writer and editor. Reader three is a teacher and writer. Reader four male around 50s. Reader five is a teacher and spiritual teacher now, Reader six is male writer. Reader seven qualified psychologist. Reader eight 19 year old student on university for psychology. Reader nine is male analyst/writer. Reader ten is female writer. Reader eleven is female psychologist. Reader twelve is 19 years old female student in university for psychology. Reader thirteen is spiritual female around 40s. Reader 14 is the writer, businessmen, scientist.

Reader one:
*****

Thank you Vjollca Sadiku, this book on the values and the messages it gives is a jewel in my mind and my library! For the first time I read a book that is so practical and beautiful psychologically! In fact it is not the scientific book of psychology. The book even though it has a simple and practical language for the mission that is over it itself is still here, sometimes difficult to understand and to be perceived in the first reading! Life self help counseling has been discovered through life experiences that guides the life truths that brings lights. We all face the problems, the difficulties, the dangers of life, and the author has had her life, her own specialties! There are always superstitions that life falls like to challenge what we are, or think we are! In these challenges that our life falls, everyone wants a light to which to orient, find the strength and the will to stand and face. This light is within every human being. It is important to find and see it. In our truth, they are within us, says the author. Running examples from her life has made it difficult to sharpen human intuition, with the purpose of knowing how to learn and analyze what is happening inside and outside of us. Only knowledge of self, control over it, of the spiritual energy we possess can lead us to a magical perfection of each of u's lives. Life becomes beautiful when the soul is free! By reading this text all that I said above on the soul and life is clarified by itself, the author seeks to awaken the intuition of the spiritual compulsions found within us! This book is a special help for life struggles!

Thank you Vjollca Sadiku

Reader two:
*****

Pathing through infinite tautological horizons, accompanied by the cheerful echoes of the guide as a magic guide, and how you can be a manifestation of momentum of good and lighten your intentions towards your goals to convey that self-restraint from yourself to the others, the author of the book "A Magical life "Vjollca Sadiku comes as axiomatic belief that good is a universal essence and that only a sublime coherence with an everlasting flux is to be sublimated: momentum, acceptance, purpose, inspiration, devotion, affirmation, and love.

The magic is just a coming, as the divine revelation that is transmitted and reflected in the quadrangles of infinity as spirit, spiritual fulfillment that then casts the miracle of the miracle in each mental hemisphere and for the whole body , conceiving the presence of the momentum that is optimized towards the goal. The great thing then inspires you to dedication and necessarily affirms that the journey to the meeting with love is inevitable. Therefore, this resonance cultivated in the book as a mission and spiritual devotion as a light handwriting glistens as a spectator and lures in stunning feasts where author Vjollca Sadiku explores, lectures and welcomes you at the banquet, on the altar of good, from where intuitively she has the gift to serve up to supplication. The specialty of all the meditative postulates that Vjollca confesses in the book and that marks the difference with other authors is her life-story presence. Vjollca has chosen the most unique way to send the message to the reader, showing the details of that part of her past life without no hesitation, no reservations. She opened it and so quietly managed to transmit confessed to the reader and then conversed, meditates and then resonates crowning the sentimental thoughts of how to get out of any temptation, sorrow, and emotional harassment. Life is a gift to enjoy, good exists and the Lord's glory is love. Love for yourself, for others, and for gratitude that exists.

Imploring every reminiscence that reminds and shows with the commitment to mind and soul to be present at every moment of intuition either to the reader or to the clients, Vjollca has experienced her lifelong tempting experience of having long challenged to touch herself within the essence, within the epicenter of tranquility and peace, in harmony and complete freedom and lovingly emits divine gravity which then in symbiosis with the desirable realizes itself as a meditative temple from where both inside and outside and below and above sparks uniquely with itself and it affects the sublime desire for the realization of its intuition even to others. This interaction and this united meditative correspondence in the frequencies of good and divine amplitude diverts the paralysis of departures in the universe and accepts redemption as missionary and guiding how the enchantment is so close and worthy of every human heart that believes . With more than just passing attention, confession and resume with the psychoanalytic and psycho-philosophical experience that it has done and realized to many clients, "A Magical Life" as an elite guide to positive and unique thought in modern world literature meets all the criteria to name a magic manual or a light gospel.

Reader three:
****

I want to express my gratitude for the special pleasure I find in this wonderful book. Make me simple out of the ordinary your simple explanation of things and exclusive support only in your personal strengths and experiences with a profound sincerity, in the middle of a very simple language, so that the powerful messages that transmit the reader , to be as accessible to him. I'm around the 120th page, and I was reading "reports with others" that took me a lot of attention and was something I needed for such an experience ... I need it very much what you is written by you ... Because I was taught to "forgive" to give my soul to others", thinking that this is love and sincerity, without looking at the mass of how much they forgive me! It was tempted to hold to breaks on giving to much to others back a little when "the car slides into the roundabout "(I have tried it really and luckily I did not have cars from any direction" Here I am hurt from others people many times !!

A Magical Life book It changes the mind, and the mind changes the world. Publishing a work of any kind; literary, philosophical, biographical or psychological, etc. a step towards presenting something to the public, opinions and impressions. As the work takes form, word of mouth, and is still under the prism of the author, carving and sculpting, how always to be better present it to the public. The author is closely related to it and it is up to her to deal with its structuring, to give shape and content as appropriate, presenting on best way the ideas as readily accessible to the reader. When it passes into the reader's hands, it is up to the reader to give his or her feedback about its content. This is the journey of a work from the author to the public who are closely related to each other.

The author Vjollca Sadiku comes out of a field psychology field, which, like any other science, requires a great deal of attention in her study. It is a good idea to treat topics that belong to positive psychology. But what does positive psychology mean? What is the purpose of her study? Undoubtedly, at the center of its study lies the person herself and his physical and spiritual well-being. It simply promoted the meaning of life, achievements and more importantly how to shape personality in accordance with existing circumstances or in trying to change them, always in the best possible shape of a positive personality , useful for self and society. How to face different situations in life and how to overcome them even the toughest situations we can face at every stage of our lives? To overcome these and move towards the goal of forming a sustainable personality, according to the author, we should start from the implementation of three rules that seem to be necessary to achieve the goal.

- Love yourself as you would want to be loved!
- Treat others as you want to be treated!
- Make 100% of everything you choose to do!

By reading this study by author Vjollca Sadiku, I was impressed with the presentation of her life events, chronologically, through a very simple and flowable language, so as to be readily available to the reader. The study is in a literary and literary manner by the author's narrative and narrative style that made the reader sink into the essence of this study. The order of the events of her life to which the author clings to her with a great dedication, begins from the age of her early childhood. She breaks off her close family's life to go to the village to her grandparents to help them. From here we see the beginning of its "mission". The author's mission, as the text makes me understand, seems to have an altruistic nature, since what at this age is put to the assistance of others. And we see that it proves willingness to remain faithful to this mission throughout life. Her study is divided into the following chapters: momentum, acceptance, goal, Inspiration ... etc., in which the reader will find the author's life experience that she wants to transmit to the reader and share with her. Each of these chapters and chapters contains a clear message: How do we know ourselves? How to love ourselves? How to deal with others? How to be happy?

Guidance that prepare the reader to overcome situations that are even the worst ones that life faces. I find it important to emphasize that since the beginning of Vjollca Sadiku's "mission" was the nature that occupied the country as the most important source where it found inspiration. The author of the whole being embraced nature while nature itself was waiting by the side. Here she found the links of the "triangle" between Nature - Vjollca - Her soul. There Vjollca established links with her soul. This idea, which the author strictly applies and transmits a message that the reader will try to apply because, as a life coach of her, she finds it necessary for her life experiences to find widespread obedience. As for most people, not to say for all, that life is tired and tired, neither for Vjollca was not easy at all. She spent difficult times of life, which she describes with a flowing narrative on her way of life. It is worth adding to how much more of the life challenges we have, we more become masters of ourselves and life.

Each of the chapters has its own importance, but the chapter affirmation is one of the chapters deserving to be given special attention, because in this chapter there is a lot of positive energy flowing. It emphasizes the positive achievements that a person can accomplish if he makes the intention of self to fulfill them. A wise saying would have given even better sense to this analysis about the personality "Personality for a person, is what is the aroma for the flower" Charles-M. Schwab. Affirmation can be realized through the various techniques that the author gives in the study. One of them that she brings, for illustration, is the encouraging guy with herself and other positive response questions that have motivating potential. While, chapter commitment mostly focuses on caring for her son. She presents a dedicated and very caring mother for her son's education. Education his main substitute in this chapter. This is an achievement of this passionate mother and an example of how a child can be educated for a bright future in a good way. The next chapter, which I think is worth mentioning, is "life teaches us" from three words to say: "Darker times can bring us to brighter places," "The most heartfelt loss of friendship and love can to open a place for the most wonderful people, "" All that seems to be the end of the road, can be just a discovery that we are destined to travel on a new trail "Daniel Koepke. It is my conclusion that author Vjollca Sadiku has made a serious study in her field supported exclusively in her own strengths and knowledge. Here I want to emphasize the supplication of a sage who says that "A right answer which is not the result of your personal persuasions is equal to a wrong answer" when the book A Magical Life seems to have achieved the purpose through the personal effort.

In addition to all these values that we have come to notice in this study, it would be useful to point out some somewhat faint points:

- Lack of bibliography.
Do not argue the opinions based on the literature used for this study.

I have provided an analysis perhaps more in line with my field of study than the psychological one, on which I have not known as much as to satisfy the necessary analytical requirements. I did not pretend to provide a critical analysis, but I simply brought my impressions from the considerate reading of author Vjollca Sadiku's study. Praise and congratulations for your work and commitment to this noble mission.

Reader four
****
In general I have the passion to read, what I liked it was the sincerity in relation to the reader, your life experience will undoubtedly be a good guide to the reader. There is something mysterious about you.

Reader five:
****

Vjollca really has magic in that book, you have beautifully expressed love for yourself, your love of life. I appreciate your writing.

Reader six:
****

I have read your manuscript and feel deeply touched by your powerful journey of self-discovery, ability to navigate the challenges of life and offer priceless coaching advice. Your story reminds me of how I took refuge in the mystical forest of my boyhood home in the Pacific Northwest to seek solace from my abusive family and to uncover my internal wisdom. Even at this later stage of my life, the authenticity in your book resonates with me. Your work feels like an antidote to my own internal toxic dialog of self doubt that impacts me even to this day. I particularly appreciate your recognition that we all need an objective person to guide us, support us, nurture our dreams and heal past wounds. I agree that it is important to master self-love and make good use of the short time we have left on this planet. Exactly. Your theme of self-love is critical to achieving authentic happiness. I am honored and extraordinarily lucky that we have connected because self-love is the key to unlock all doors. Over the years, I placed too much concern about what I thought overs thought about me, all the mistakes I make and continue to make. In reality, it all comes down to self-love. Regardless of obstacles in my path, missteps, there is a genuine hunger to heal the past, embrace the present.

Discussion with the reader:

Vjollca: Because in the end of the day that's all it matters. ...and if you want to help others that's the right way to do it ..."you can help others after you learned to help yourself "

The present is the key to enjoy the moment, to heal the past and create the future. In other words, what do you want your readers to do after they they read your book? What would you say is the most important message?

Reader: So your main message is that the answer to all of their traumas, fears, anxieties, guilt and shame is within? Vjollca: Yes of course, Once you are one with your soul, Your soul… is important to be connected. Then through your soul you master your mind and heal your heart… then create new healthy emotions in your heart.

Reader: So your message could be: The world constantly challenges us and tries to redefine us. However, when you harness your spiritual essence and master your soul, you develop resilience through healthy, healing emotions.

Vjollca: Not master your soul. but connect and live under the influence of your soul and then master your mind.

Reader: It is like awakening the beautiful, healing influence of the soul that gives one the strength to master the mind.

Vjollca: Acknowledge your soul and alloy it to guide you, like babies are automatically under influence of their soul.

Reader: In other words, do not try to analyze the soul. Be present, in the now. Let it unfold naturally, like the petals of a rose budding in spring.

Vjollca: Yes ....but discuss with your soul, your mind, and heart. ...and body. The soul helps you to feed your self-love and to master the human existence. To get anything you need in this life.
His thoughts about the book: I was amazed about your journey and how you personally connected with your soul. It reminded me of my own quest when I grew up as a little boy in the secluded meadow and forest and how I have been seeking that inner peace of soulfulness you masterfully describe. The moment when I experienced a first, major soul transition was 10. However, at 7 I felt a deep longing to find that soul connection.

Vjollca: So now the exercises that are in my book use them to create your own way to connect with your soul 24 hours… and slowly recognize intuition (the voice of Creator), also to feel the energy of universe. So keep going back to that time until you are living your life guided by your soul .... you will know… But I feel you are guided by your soul .....only you have to acknowledge it… Also you do listen to your intuition, just have to acknowledge it more and master those skills through meditation, your time alone, spending time in nature and your inner conversations. You do have self love ...just have to allow your self to recognize it....and enjoy it… embrace it.

Reader: Even as we connect, I can imagine myself floating, looking down through thin layers of wispy clouds and seeing the rooftop of the red, farm house of my childhood.
Descending through the atmosphere of time, grounding myself on the green pastures, I am alone, yet meditatively connected with my inner child. I have not fully embraced him. I do not fully understand him, but I am open to receiving his gifts of total acceptance and to acknowledge the false knowledge of the adult, material world.

Vjollca: Keep doing that. ...until you understand him. That is amazing. do you feel that awesome feeling? So now you should make note and write about that journey. As one book should be about that. It will be fascinating.

Reader: I feel glimmers of this soulful bliss, a hint of eternal happiness that is almost within reach, like an almond croissant and a steamy cup of tea at a far end of table, inches from my fingertips.

Vjollca: Keep working on it and you will reach ......so you understand how I feel. because I have reached that. And it is painful for me to socialize to see others not have it   when they can. I can't at all the greetings or socializing as it will drain me.

Reader: The world is abundant. We need to look past the mind and embrace the soulfulness of the Now.

Vjollca: Exactly. I have to stay in that light in order to have it and be able to help those who ask for help. I did through my book without my knowledge. ...but since I published my book I became aware of my actions… as before blindly I was following my soul and intuition.

Reader: You are a candle that that illuminates the soul within the darkness of the material world. You inspired me to add that soulful journey to my memoirs. I have actually been working on an epic autobiography for quite some time.

Reader (the following day): Thank you so much your support, encouragement and insistence that I write my long overdue book about embracing my inner child.
Throughout my life my role has been soul searching, trying adapt to normalcy, which doesn't exist. Trying to overcome toxic influences, emotional blueprints of scarcity and feeling inner peace and confidence.

Reader seven:
****
I loved the honesty presented, I founded very painful at times when the disconnection was at highest. I have to say that I admire your strength. You said, you never read a book for pleasure and yet again you did write a book yourself inspiration. You let your guard down in every word, which made the book heart felt. For me I could feel your pain raw. So my one word will be 'a raw inspiration'.

Discussion with the reader:

After reading the book, and meting face to face she told me she thought that I was not healed yet and she decided with my permission to explore the areas that I am not healed yet as she was qualified psychologist. It was a 3 hour therapy session on me which was very interesting...She used very interesting methods and techniques, which did not bring up any remnant of the past as I had already explored and recovered it fully. I had done that from the age of 36 to the age of 37, and now I considered my past as movie full of adventures. There I applied the flavour of love, care and understanding.

Reader eight:
****
A magical life, it was really magical for me. What I liked most was the way how the events flowed chronologically and with a sincerity that passed all expectations. Accepting yourself is a strong weapon that not everyone has but I believe that all those who read that book take the essence distributed on all pages. The best part for me was the courage to tell the grandmother what happened and by reading it I was wondering if I would of done it the me if I was in that situation? Since I was curious at the end of the book, I still had some questions in my head.

Why you did not you accept the meals from others from the stranger? And what prompted you to be brave enough to have the force through you had through you to hear your voice? I'm wondering if this question will be in my next book What seemed to me a little bit too much was introduction as it provided almost all the information stretched out on some pages, which removed the misery to read after what was written because the things were somewhat detailed. But in preaching the way how optimism appeared without wondering that human nature when seeing self-confidence at level A is predisposed to attack and see genes with critical eyes. What this book was about to convey to me was something that came to my mind all the time. Find courage in yourself, anything can happen. You have to be strong and accept yourself for what you have not judged. You did a very good job. I was really eager to read the other book and I wanted to know what will happen next that was with lots of force and courage presented. I would say that what I read through all the time I read was the strength and courage that are within every person. However, for me there remains a very inspiring liberation...

Reader Nine:
****

It was a great surprise to be known, through Facebook, with Vjollca, who lives in London. There she has studied the psychology highly needed to know this field. She sent me an electronic textbook that reflects her current work in this area. The book is also self-discipline of the author, similar to that of the thousands of Albanians who left the homeland for a better life in Western Europe. Pointing to the challenges that have passed since childhood and the choices she has chosen, Vjollca actually becomes an inspiration for all of us, especially for women, as the essence of what is shown in the book is that life is a magical place to be enjoyed by facing it and can be done by any of us. The person, the author insists, is born free and will live like that. The individual needs the love of parents and other people to become worthy and to go forward with courage. The individual should never be surrendered by the difficulties he has with the way of life, he must accept them as undeniable facts, without falling into pessimism. Drawing lessons from them, the person is fully capable of reviving, revealing light at the end of the tunnel, dreaming, turning dreams into intentions, and drawing up action plan to achieve these goals. Here are some excerpts from the book

P. XIV. I am sure that, at least once, we have asked ourselves: Who am I? Who is the meaning of living? How should I live this life? What can I do with it? What is the best way to achieve this dream? Do dreams really come true? Why do some people have a better life than mine? These may be part of transitive thoughts but it is our responsibility to understand if we want to know the answers. If we imagine our mind as a garden, thoughts are like air puffs that can explode quickly in hot or cold winds. It is in our hands to create a harmony. I noticed that many people, including me in the past, do not pay attention to our inner voice. Instead of listening to it, they make long journeys away from it, becoming someone else to adapt to family, community, or society. Consequently, they end up feeling too lonely, angry and touched; thinking that no one can understand them. In these circumstances, I ask: What are the expectations of people for others to understand when they themselves have not found time to understand themselves?

P. XV. 12 Simple rules for the appreciation of life; 12 simple rules.

1 - Learn to accept and love yourself for who you are.

2 - When it is time to think for a solution, quietly step back to view the whole picture.

3 - Let go of the things that hold you back from being yourself.

4 - Have an awareness of all the negative obstacles but focus on the goal.

5 - Ensure that you are clear about your life script and revisit that often.

6 - Dream big, visualize your dreams, and break them in small goals.

7 - Your intuition is your guidance. Ensure that you find time to listen.

8 - Pursue your passion and find a job you love and enjoy so that you give your best.

9 - Consistently surround yourself with things that are meaningful to you.

10 - Ensure that you live your life only for yourself and no one else; it is yours and only you can decide how to live it.

11 - Believe in your uniqueness and the universe will guide you.

12 - Treat everyone the way you like to be treated, to receive the same from the universe.

P. XVI: I learned something from life, that is, the darkest times can lead us to the brighter places. I have learned that the most poisonous people can give us the most important lessons that our most laborious efforts can give us the most needed growth and that the most desperate losses of friendship and love can make the most wonderful people. I learned that what seems like a curse at one point can actually be a blessing, and what looks like the end of the road is actually a breakthrough for a journey through a different path. I have learned that, no matter how difficult things seem, there is always a hope. And I learned that no matter how helpless we feel or how terrible things look, we can not give up. We must continue our course. Even when it's terrible, even when it seems as if all of our power is exhausted, we have to be strong and move forward, because whatever we are currently fighting for, it will end and we will succeed. We even did this before. We will do it as often as we need.

P. 3: In this challenging world, it is quite clear how vital and important is the love of the first primary career. How essential it is for a parent to realize that children need real attention, for unconditional love and secure relationships!

P.7 Is not important how much money you have, when there is not enough time for quality bond for a parent-child relationship. What matters most is the quality time with your child; a surplus of care, patience and hearing and when you want to talk to the child, speak in the child's language.

P. 8 The soul of person needs warmth and compassion. It cannot be heated with many blankets and covers. The soul is fed with love.

P. 9 Nature taught me to lay the foundations of my life: how to not trust anyone, how to treat anyone well, how to stand and tell the truth, how to spend time only with the people who really loved me - in the way I wanted them to love me.

P. 13 How can children understand their surroundings? How can they know who to trust and who not to trust and who to follow after? Please do not leave your children in environments for which you have not provided the correct explanations. Otherwise, the child can give them unfamiliar meanings, or even put them at risk.

P. 24 I think the soul has no gender. He is introduced into female and male bodies for spiritual reasons. There are no other differences between women and men except anatomical and physiological ones. Their character and attitude to life have been shaped under external influences. We exist on this Earth for lovers and not for harming one another. If we cannot help those who do evil, at least bypass them and let others who can help and deal with them. But never harming anyone if we want to have the universe support.

P. 25 Pain is part of being fulfilled and satisfied.

P. 32 I would not suggest any antidepressant to anyone who loves life, even if is there just a little fight to love life. If, dear readers, you want to make a difference in your life, if you love yourself and reach what your heart wants, you will find the strength-this is within you.

P. 39 If the feelings are deep, no matter how careless they are, they let us know the things we need to accomplish our purpose. It is always essential to remember that anyone is free to choose. Fair decisions are made through talks between intuition and logic. Only in this way can a balance be achieved.

P. 44 The man of my dream should have all the qualities I possess, otherwise I would not have any interest. My features were: honest, visionary, familiar, open-minded, trustworthy, independent, able to keep me financially, optimistic about my dreams, and willing to love.

P. 46 The right person for me is someone who feels merely fulfilled in my presence and everything is simple, passionate, adventurous ... every moment is precious .. my aroma is like a perfume for ... he feels the flow of peace and livelihood in hugging me. This is what I called and call it: true love.

P. 69 During a full-fledged circumstance we can choose how to accept it. This does not mean that we deal with what is happening, but that we know the experience as an undeniable fact. This includes accepting relevant emotions, no matter how inadequate they look.

P. 75 Love the eyes of people, not their appearance. The eyes tell you everything you want to know about a person's soul, but not about his personality in the outside world. All the crimes we see could have diminished if family members are united in love.

P. 76 The notion of love is based on the need.

…The life without a main goal is like a bus without a driver, like an ship without a captain. It is very important to connect the main goal with the inner source of light. To do this, the main goal must be meaningful.

P. 77 I realized that saying "is nothing like the first love" is not true. I fell in love several times. If I choose to go with a partner, want him to love me as I am, I will feel fulfilled in a relationship if the partner does not try to change me or my way of living. People can only stay together if they share heart and soul together.

P.78 On my journey I have seen very poor people who have inspired me so much. They were full of self-esteem and appreciated what they had, but this did not stop them from dreaming.

P. 80 As we grow and enjoy what we do, our dreams become bigger. The happier we are where we are, the better our dreams become.

P. 85 No matter how great our dreams are, they have a strong impact on our lives. If we do not choose to deal with them, our self-esteem falls down. If we turn them to the main goal, our credibility will flourish. The journey to reach our main goal while challenging ourselves develops our potential and makes us better. I believe there is always an opportunity for improvement in every aspect of life. If there is a dream, there is a main goal there.

P. 99 Our soul contains all wisdom. Suffice to look at our intuition for what we are looking for. It is therefore vital to connect with the center of our being.

P. 130 Love affairs are full of precious little things that make me feel like flying wings. Mysteries of intimacy vary from one to the other but only the heart can appreciate and see the differentiation of their presence. For me, they are past nights just by talking … journeys that do not know how long they were… kisses everywhere and whenever.. looks filled with lovely… attention and care … treated as special gifts. … admiration with out makeup … or when I looked tired … handholding … hugs in public places..listening to whatever I was saying… estimates and cares for my child … discussions for the past and the future … watching movies together … and so many other things.

Even though has been a while since you so kindly send me the text of your book, just now I'm here to give you a preliminary answer. I mean, it is not easy to absorb all that information you permeate, based on such an intriguing personal life and in a long-lasting job of affirming your personality in such a scientific, almost philosophical field. There were two side difficulties: the fact that the text was in English and the other scream of the author on each page. But I managed to read it, but as I said, not well. To congratulate you on this achievement that makes us proud to all of us, Albanians at home and abroad, of course. The book is like a sincere bible where many who have passed similar stories should find themselves. He is a spiritual leader for any Albanian migrant or not, but also a psychology textbook for every parent and educator, why not. One may be surprised that since a middle-aged girl is devoted to a childish dream of being independent in life, to enjoy life as a magical gift of God (which you call it the Universe), passes a series of obstacles to extraordinary on the road to exile, builds up her life through hardships, successes and failures, never defeated; on the contrary, as the various saints discover, the universe can help powerful enough to know how to connect with it.

I remembered an Einstein statement that advised young people who wanted to deal with science, stay long at the sea, in open skies because they could get ideas and knowledge through the canals of the universe. For Anshtajn every person is a genius, but that must be evidenced. I have the conviction that it is important not only personal experience, not just intuition and mental abilities, but also the experience of others, books, information obtained so far. Newton says that "he has seen more than others because he has been on the shoulders of his ancestors". Will you have achieved these results if you stay home like us? Perhaps not, because "prophets say, you can not be in your village". Of course Britain, more precisely London, has opened up many opportunities and people there have quickly discovered your skills. It is fortunate that there are many Albanians living there, who are part of your clientele, too. As I said, I read the book, the two parts I printed before. I kept a few notes. I usually distribute my writings to my friends. But first, please check if translations in Albanian are more or less adequate, then tell me if it allows me to distribute the script. Once again, thank you for your trust.

Reader ten:
****

Hello Darling. I finished reading your book and I'm glad I had the chance to do this. At first, I was feeling bad for all your difficult moments of childhood, bullying to abortion, and I want to congratulate you on the will and dedication you have shown to preserve your identity, the beautiful spirit and self-enlightment. This writing of yours was characterized by an admirable originality and a lot of humanity. I've read many books written by life coach and I can say that this was not a Copy-paste but had a tendon style of yours identifier.

I am very convinced of the help this book will give others, as well even me I kept notes that I liked and sow as guidance for my life. I'm so impressed and I'm waiting for your next book. I really liked your book closure. Schematicizing of your life, it will make it happen on my life also.

Thank you dearly

Reader eleven:
****

Vjollca! Reading your book has been like a journey for me. A double journey, one into your world and life, and one into my world and my experiences. I found myself lost at a lot of moments and that happened because of flashback memories and an analysis on them while I was reading...Yes, I do analyze a lot! Although you made me go back to painful memories of my life, I felt released each time somehow. On the other hand, I will be honest with you that when I first met you and heard about your book and read the title "Magical Life" I was thinking what kind of thing is that?! She must be quite crazy! Well, I can see through you now and your point of view. In my opinion though, a few people will understand and appreciate what you write and say. Also, a few will ask for help because either they are not aware of their condition or they do not believe in you. Maybe, you need to be presented somehow differently so that you can offer more to others but I am still not sure, it is just a thought that comes on my mind now...You are very strong to publish such personal things! Finally, I want to mention that by reading the whole book I was getting eager and eager to see how it would be if I started talking to you about myself and my difficulties...that feeling is strange because sometimes I cannot wait believing that you can help me find my answers but other times I feel like I do not want to tell my whole journey, it is going to take ages or I feel like I do not know how to start and where to start from. ese are all my thoughts and feelings related to your book.

Overall I would say it was a positive vibe with food for thought.

Reader twelve:
****

Review of 'A magical Life' by Vjollca Sadiku: An Essay based on the life of Vjollca Sadiku/a spiritual memoir.

The integration of a range of theoretical perspectives based on life to provide a coherent scientific account of a natural phenomenon is an easy task only for those who have never had to do it. In this volume, Vjollca Sadiku has attempted such a difficult exercise by integrating moments of her life she recalls into a book, alongside teaching us what helped her get passed every obstacle that she faced.

In the first chapter of the book, she aims to inform us about the difficulties she tackled as a child in a country, which at the time was unequal and full of stigma. This chapter is packed with emotions that juxtapose one another as her story has both beauty and heartache. In Chapters 2 to 8, she generates a model of development, which can account for the emergence of her peace she has found today. Vjollca reveals there are 8 stages that have helped her overcome her fears and misfortunes throughout life. Momentum, acceptance, goal, inspiration, commitment, affirmation and love are they key headings, which have motivated her to write a book about her experiences whilst growing up.

Her story draws together evidence from a variety of fields with the aim of providing a coherent picture of the phenomenon of her life. Vjollca creates the impression that pain doesn't last forever and that learning to love your self is the first step to a happy life. She puts forward a theory that if you don't have self-love you have nothing. Her breath taking story is worthy of our admiration not just because it describes the sorrowful state of a hopeless child, but also because it permits us to understand that no pain lasts forever and if you have belief in yourself you can break free from the trap of inequality and greed you are positioned in without choice. We see her change as the chapter's progress; this promotes positivity whilst also being honest. There is a continuous positive tone expressed throughout the story. At the end of her book she maps out her life in clear stages, the pain and suffer she experienced is evident however the progress is also clear. The 'Map of Life' is a clear summary of the book; it helps the audience really grasp the reality of her experiences and how far she has come as an independent individual.

To this end I will now try to clarify what I see as an area of weakness in this book. The first and only concern with Vjollca memoir is that she fails to back up her thoughts and emotions with scientific evidence. Her psychological difficulties could have been explained in depth with the use of comparisons to other who have experienced the same sort of experience.

I am aware Vjollca acknowledges that she faced a difficult task in trying to write about such personal issues, but her true story will only motivate and help others in our society become the best of who they are.

Discussion of the book with reader

She asked: How did you feel about the adult sexually molesting?

Me: ....I explained: "I liked it ...I was confused about the whole thing ....

She: Did you tell anyone? ...

Me: No because I did not understand it ...maybe because I felt guilty I just blocked it. " (our conversation went silent. I understood that silence meant that she learned: when even when she thinks she done something wrong it does not mean that she done something wrong).

She asked about the rape and she said: "it was not rape because you like it and did not say at that time nothing and told no one..." At that time you thought it was not so maybe is not rape...

Me: "it was rape because I never agreed to have sex and I was not even asked if I wanted as I was not able to communicate properly as I was drunk...then she went quite… (Silence was telling her that she is in power of anything around her and only her can decide).

From discussion she said she learned to focus on the step you are doing in order to give 100% of course you have the plan for future but not detailed one as you will get it when that steps time is to see the best in everything (because she notice a person with out legs and arms and said "oh god I can not see him ....I feel so sorry for him" I said .." don't feel sorry for him as he seems so happy., content with the way his life is which makes me think and get inspired ...I feel sorry for those that are unhappy when they have ability to be happy "…she smiled and went into silence).

Reader thirteen:
****
Dear Vjollca! First I want to express thousands of thanks for sharing your story with me! I'm still breathless from the emotions I experienced in these two days reading your book. If you want to know about the effect that this book may have made of a simple reader as my job believes it has made 1000%. If you want to know whether I have found myself in this book to say that it is 80%. If you want to know about my impressions I would have to publish another book at least twice as this to analyze every detail and to express my deep gratitude to you and the palpitations you have achieved with a master mind to enter so deeply to the divine within the human being (especially the Albanian woman) and to comprehend and comprehend the "cause-effect of all of its existence.

I thank you for entering my life and I ensure that your book I will read many times with the motive to see myself (to some extent) in the mirror.

I also want you to know that I am really a very positive person, I say this with more conviction and truth, but also by the fact that I have given positivity that the universe as a reward is turning this through you I would like to have with you a good communication and friendship.

I believe that our souls are known since the Universe was created.
Giving love and blessing!

Reader fourteen:
****

I continue to be impressed by the integrity of both logic and passion displayed in your book. And your level of swell awareness is unmatched among most I know. Very refreshing. You have created a very valuable resource that could become a classic. You captured perfectly the guiltless guilty pleasures of incest.

Some of my favourite stories on Literotica, comcenter on the forbidden bulge in the Uncle's Speedos as he ogles the naughty niece in her barely there bikini as she cavorts with her busty best friend while they knowingly fondle one another in the jacuzzi fulsome in the knowledge of their offered temptation.

And like Nabokov your writing is erotic without being tawdry yet charged with the emotion that only love can describe.

Reader fifteen:
****

Hello Vjollca… I am almost in the end of the book to finish the reading.. to tell the truth , I like the book, and what I like the most is because you talk about your life without embarrassment, it shows things that most of the people even me I would not have the courage to talk about it in public, but these are the events that take part to most of us, there are part of almost everyone's life. So that's why people have the curiosity to read your book I think it's best suited for a younger age group up to 40-50 years old.

CHAPTER X

(20 SELECTED QUESTIONERS 1, 2, 3, 4, 6, 7, 9, 11, 12, 15, 16, 17, 18, 20, 21, 22, 23, 30, 40, 41)

Q.1 37 year old female/high education/British

Please answer the following questions as a part of the study:

Questions:

1 - Are there three main rules according to the Lord?:
- Treat others as you would like to be treated.
- Love yourself as you would like to be loved.
- Give 100% in everything that you choose.

Yes! ... and I would add one more, which to me is the first rule: Love your God with all your soul, heart, and mind, and with all your strength in prayer, faith and action.

2 - Are those 3 rules, all that is required of humans to accomplish in this life? How do you explain the way that these can be applied by a person, born in a family amongst members, who do not comply with those rules?

Yes, with the addition of the rule number 1 as previously mentioned. The person must have or gain a deeper connection with themselves and develop spiritual intelligence by focusing on their core self – their soul. How this occurs depends on the person's purpose in this life. For instance, some people living in adverse conditions, receive an inner calling, which brings them guidance, love, peace and resilience, so they choose to follow it. As in all human beings there are certainly fluctuating periods of doubt, but getting up again and again and again by seeking God and the righteousness, helps one to achieve the comforts needed. A person's natural passions are also a way of finding and preserving themselves.

3 - For someone to follow the path that makes them happy, do they firstly have to let go of those, who are not happy with themselves, be it even their own family? What is the reason of this?

Yes, this would certainly make things easier. Personally, I believe that this is required, for the person to focus and expand on their true identity, and be fully established on their true purpose. However, this action depends on the person's purpose in life. There are cases where the person remained in the family, (because they somehow had already found their inner strength and aim) in order to give a lesson to them and the surrounding community. There are other cases where the person needs distance in order to strengthen and grow spiritually and the time depends on them. Some people keep occasional contact, some cut the family out completely; it depends on the relationship they had, and its functionality.

4 - What is the soul? Where is it located anatomically in humans and what is the role of the soul in this life? Why...

The soul is the very essence or centre of our being that is in the image of God and actively connected to God. It allows us and reminds us to align our personality and actions according to its mission.

5 - Can a person live and be guided by their soul? How can this be achieved?

Yes, the inner guidance is what should manifest outside. Personally I believe it requires, attention, continuous prayer, inner conversations and expressions through forms of art such as writing, drawing, music etc.

6 - Does a bad soul exist? The reason why...

There are simply good souls because they are created on the image of God.

7 - Are the mind, heart and body human utensils, which serve the soul so that the person is faithful or fulfilled? Why...

Yes. The whole being should serve the mission of the soul. When the mind, heart and body are aligned to the soul's purpose, the person feels inner peace, fullness and harmony. If they are not in alignment with the soul, the person feels disintegrated, disconnected and hollow inside - which is sometimes further exploited by numbing the feeling in various addictions, - or in some cases the person accepts the hurt of this brokenness and takes healing steps in accordance to the soul's liberation and external manifestation.

8 - What does it mean to believe in God and how can this be demonstrated by 3 rules or examples?

Praying, having faith, following the rules a mentioned in the answer of point 1.

9 - Do you suppose that children are like angels and innocent and why? So how is their suffering explained in God's language and why?

I have to accept the limitation of not being able to explain this, but I have faith that somehow, God knows.

10 - Are there two kinds of death: A prewritten one and another that depends on our Actions? If so, how is the child's death explained?

Death means when the soul feels lost: This can be in this life (i.e. when the person is out of touch with who they are) or when it departs from the body.

I have faith there must be an explanation to this occurrence in human beings including children.

11 - Can a human being be filled with love, which comes exclusively from the source within themselves? And from the moment they become aware of that love they do not feel suffering because they know their purpose and are fulfilled?

Yes, and this kind of humans are called saints

Q.2 around 38 years old Albanian/british/running charity organization

Questions:

1 - Are there three main rules according to the Lord?:
  - Treat others as you would like to be treated.
  - Love yourself as you would like to be loved.
  - Give 100% in everything that you choose.

I was brought up as an atheist – this was the advice of my grandmother and my parents.

2 - Are those 3 rules, all that is required of humans to accomplish in this life? How do you explain the way that these can be applied by a person, born in a family amongst members, who do not comply with those rules?

In life we learn every day, face challenges and joys, meet with others with whom we exchange our values and experiences, sometimes good sometimes bad, sometimes predicted sometimes unpredicted.
I wish those, who live in a family where the above values are not endorsed, are not affected but create immunity.

3 - For someone to follow the path that makes them happy, do they firstly have to let go of those, who are not happy with themselves, be it even their own family? What is the reason of this?

I do not think that a person should leave, regardless of what circumstances we face or with whom. We need to create opportunities so that our goodness and values can change those around us, not prejudicing anyone.

To believe in the expression: Everything happens for a reason.

5 - Can a person live and be guided by their soul? How can this be achieved?

The soul is something surreal. The more the years pass, the more the mind, heart and soul come closer, more and more, and each one feels, that is being led by the soul.

6 - Does a bad soul exist? The reason why…

I do not believe so.

7 - Are the mind, heart and body human utensils, which serve the soul so that the person is faithful or fulfilled? Why…

As above.
The closer they are, the easier life is, the more fulfilled it is, the more meaningful it is.

8 - What does it mean to believe in God and how can this be demonstrated by 3 rules or examples?

I believe in values, not in God.

9 - Do you suppose that children are like angels and innocent and why? So how is their suffering explained in God's language and why?

I believe that death is one. The causes are various.

10 - Are there two kinds of death: A prewritten one and another that depends on our Actions? If so, how is the child's death explained?

Children are human beings, who are being formed. I wish that just like the body creates antibodies for self-defence, the children were also formed.

11 - Can a human being be filled with love, which comes exclusively from the source within themselves? And from the moment they become aware of that love they do not feel suffering because they are know their purpose and are fulfilled?

I do not know. It seems a bit more complicated than that. The human being learns to manage the feelings they experience, channel any kind of energy towards them, into positive energy.

Q.3 India around 30 years old/ IT

Questions:

1 - Are there three main rules according to the Lord?:
   - Treat others as you would like to be treated.
   - Love yourself as you would like to be loved.
   - Give 100% in everything that you choose.

No, the feelings are not predefined by the laws of the nature or according to the Lord. It depends upon the individual - to whom they embody themselves into.

Treat others – As far as my experience - I tell you, that this World is pre-equipped with different types of people, so everyone has a different set of mind, make up and deportment. On my personal basis, I tried to tell people 'this is the scenario'. If one comprehends it, well and good, but for others I leave it up to them. 'You are free to make your own stories out of it'. So, my level of conversation depends upon person to person, as everyone has its own taste and different level of comfort zone, so that I can converse with them. For eg, if I tell to some stranger in the market, who is typically from my area and is not that much into the understanding of the healing process; he possesses a simple life, gets up in the morning, gets ready to work and in the evening have some relaxation by watching TV or moving around outside for a while. If I grab his attention and tell him about healing oneself, you know? He will simply laugh at me or say 'what are you talking about?' As his set of mind is filled from the beginning, that the more money one has, has all the powers are with him. Because with money he can buy anything he wants and do anything – This is the general scenario here for the common masses and for him possessions are all that exist, and he does not look in books and in the literature. I am telling you the clear picture because to find the people like me, who synchronises with my mind and tries to understand myself,…they are very rare. And indeed, in the practical sense these types of people follow some other spiritual healers here like the pundits and all. So my duty was to tell them, but how they treat it or comprehend it, depends upon the character and the gamut of the environment he dwells in. If someone comprehends me, well and good, and if someone is going to make a joke out of it I just leave it, I do not respond to him or that group and do not gossip. So it depends. How people treat me, I treat them in their own way. As I cannot change them because they are not at all ready to change so I simply avoid unnecessary arguments.

LOVE – *Loving oneself: that is the better option left, as I tell you in the present scenario the value of True Love is lost. The artificial love prevails in this world in the masses now. As far as if I am helpful or good to one, I am very adorable to him/her, but once the task is over, the project is over, who cares for whom? Nobody. Because nobody has time and no one understands but rather playing games with each other is the motto left: ego, hatred, jealousy prevails in the practical scenario of life. OMG!!! He is earning less than me and look at him! He is still smiling and having such an awesome life. What has he inside himself that makes him so happy and joyful? this is the feeling left as I see around. In real life, I talk with very few people with whom I am most comfortable with, not with everyone I open my pages. Rather you can say it's simply the act of formality I do as they do with everyone. So it's better to find the happiness that lies inside me. Yes, I have no friends, nobody here. Yes, all my dear ones are far away and most of the time I live alone and live my life, trying to do the best for myself to make 'me' feel happy. So, loving oneself is the key and true love lies in the paradise of nature, going outside in the park and having a walk, feel closer with the nature by being surrounded by flowers, petals, trees and autumn leaves falling down. I love all that. So as a person I myself have a set of things I love doing, and if I do not like it all, I won't do it at all. No one can force me to do that thing which I do not like doing. I am simply like that.*

Giving 100% - Yes, I give 100% in whatever I do and for me if the task is new and I am liking it, I will search about it and will do everything with passion and 100% determination.

2 - Are those 3 rules, all that is required of humans to accomplish in this life? How do you explain the way that these can be applied by a person, born in a family amongst members, who do not comply with those rules?

A better life, for a better tomorrow, for the human race, yes. This is the most important way to achieve it and if this is not achieved, the hatred, jealousy, racism egoism, and all the dreadful causes are engulfing the whole world. Humanity has to be there and Love is the language we have to understand one day for a better tomorrow. With fights, arguments and violence, nothing is achieved. Killing nowadays is so common that you will be shocked to hear arguments on silly talks and shoot the gun on a person head right there, within seconds, game over. This has to have an end and only Love, that is the biggest feeling the human is born with, is to be embodied in everyone's heart, more deeply. The meaning of true love, one has to feel it and understand it: quit playing games with my heart. Don't treat me as an option, if someone feels like one can leave. I am not hungry for love. I know my ways, how I can love myself. I have seen the darkest scenario when everything was off for me, I came out from that well, alone and talked to myself millions of times, otherwise I would have ended up alone, eating medical pills only. It is not somebody doing nothing for me - it's me, my wish to come out from the darkest room, and I said Yes to life and began talking with people.

How can this be accomplished with those who do not comply with the rules? – Interesting question

You know the basics of life, and the answer is Love oneself and the gamut of the people around you and love your family… The Answer lies in this only.

Scenario I am talking to XYZ and explaining the things which were there in your lovely book woven so beautifully. But, but, but, if someone is sick and is not ready at all to change his thinking process, I will become his mirror image. I will copy his whole life routine and the way he talks with people and the types of people he meets, I will copy all the mannerism in my mind and scan his brain vibes and I know the person is lacking somewhere in understanding the true meaning of loving oneself and the people around. All he does is his activities just to get the profit in money making. I will make him understand, why the deal is not coming up, is because of their temperament or deportment. So, it does not matter to me that I will follow anyone rules strictly and enforce others to follow exactly those, but rather I will become the mirror image of the person and tell their core values. The basics which you wish to deliver to the masses; I will try to explain as per their scenario or the page of the book they are opened with.

3 - For someone to follow the path that makes them happy, do they firstly have to let go of those, who are not happy with themselves, be it even their own family? What is the reason of this?

Lack of communication and the unwillingness to understand, are the basics of life. I tell you I do lot of things sometimes not to make myself happy first, but I do them for you. Yeah, everything or most of things, I do them for you. To make you smile and as you smile, that makes me smile and you being so precious for me, it makes me happy.

Yes, yes for those who are not happy with themselves. Yes I have been in this scenario, when I used to feel so down, buried deep inside, carrying a heart of darkness, which was so heavy for me.

One cannot dim the light inside one's body, it's up to one, who can dim or turn off the light by themselves. I do not know much, be it family or friends or a group of people, if one is around with them it affects the person to a certain percentage but if for scenario taking - if you keep on pouring in me the brightest light or pass such powerful positive vibes to me to encourage me to do it anyhow, and on the other hand, if I turn off the light inside me and I am very much depressed this will not affect me to that extent. I will rather feel, 'yeah I will do it', but 'when', and 'what' will that time be, I do not know. I know the things, but I am not doing them, but on the other way if I decide on my own and recall every word you said and turn my light on within myself, by reinventing 'me', I will do exactly that way to find the happiness in me.

4 - What is the soul? Where is it located anatomically in humans and what is the role of the soul in this life? Why...

The Soul is immortal. The body after death decays but the soul comes out and it takes another form of life, it never dies. The Soul is the immaterial part of humans being or the animal. It is located below the stomach and the upper abdomen region, near the naval region. Its role is important and it has its vital meaning, as its voice is very soft and very light and it whispers in my ears 'what's right and what's wrong'. It indeed controls my nervous system, the brain and the heart. Together it just enlightens me up and zeals up the confidence in me and the enlightenment becomes too strong, when some positive vibes strikes it and I learn something new in my life.

5 - Can a person live and be guided by their soul? How can this be achieved?

Yes, of course the person can live and be guided by their soul as it can be achieved through meditation process just concentrating on oneself; inhaling and exhaling the air out and letting the pores of the body open and listening to the instant voice of the soul as it will guide you in seconds what's right or wrong and it's up to the person whether to follow it. That's why it's said that the universe lies within you, while one is searching for happiness around.

6 - Does a bad soul exist? The reason why…

There is no good or bad soul in general. The soul itself is pure, it's the character of the person that makes it good or bad. The soul is always pure in the human body. Even if one talks to the prisoner who committed a crime, it's the bad character in him/her that made or force him/her to do crime and lie in the prison. The circumstances may be many, why he/she did that, but the soul is never bad. We can heal that person and convert him/her to the different, opposite, good person. For eg, I heard that the singer of 'The Akon' band in the music industry, who has a unique voice committed some crime and was in prison, but he changed his image and it's through his unique voice today, he has a different place in the music industry. I am not sure about Akon, but I heard this from my senior. I might be wrong but this is the scenario like.

7 - Are the mind, heart and body human utensils, which serve the soul so that the person is faithful or fulfilled? Why…

It depends upon person to person and the character one plays. One, who knows the value of the soul, knows the reinvention or reprogramming process. Nobody is perfect. Yeah, one needs to rinse away the dust from the body and the mind and listen to the deep soft sound of the soul and concentrate more on oneself by giving time to oneself.

8 - What does it mean to believe in God and how can this be demonstrated by 3 rules or examples?

Yes I do believe in God

- *Miracles do happen and it is His Almighty power that does that.*

- *When the world is against you or the time and everything happening is like that.*

   It is not correct one after the other, the problems are rising in the head and there is no way out in spite of everything, we do so at last, it's said God helps those, who help themselves and his call is the supreme one and his blessings too.

- *When there was no one of my acquaintance as a Healer, I used to believe that God is the only one that can help me out if I am facing some problems, and Yes, on daily basis, I do pray and there is supreme power in that if one started believing in that. Yeah, I know there are many people who do not believe in worship, but I do believe in that, and I worship daily if its good or bad time or any time.*

9 - Do you suppose that children are like angels and innocent and why? So how is their suffering explained in God's language and why?

Yes. Children are the embodiment of God's image. I believe in that way and of course they are the most innocent version the human will ever have as they are neutral in their way and they do what they feel like doing. Yes, of course I love kids. They are innocent, as they are unaware of feelings like hatred, racism, ego problems until a certain age. After a certain age, when they grow up, they see the society and the behaviour of the people around and the scenario changes and they adopt themselves to what is best suited for them.

Yes, There are many mythological epics and stories that depict the existence of God in the form of a small kid and the various hardships the kid goes through as he/she grows up. It is shown to us so that from his/her early childhood days they inculcate the good qualities and in spite of lots of hardships one should never choose the wrong path as the building blocks of being good is deeply rooted in the childhood era. The growing child catches and copies the good things around very quickly, as at that time the brain and the eyes see those for first time.

10 - Are there two kinds of death: A prewritten one and another that depends on our Actions? If so, how is the child's death explained?

Yes of course, there are two kinds of death.
The child's death in the real sense, might occur medically, or in psychological terms, everybody has a child inside the body and that part of child is played by the company of those with whom they are very close to. May be a man of 40 years, can act as a small child in front of his mom and make her smile, as for his mom no matter how old a person is, he is his son after all. Psychologically in terms the child death: it occurs when there is a lot of pressure in the professional and personal life. There is only the tension the person lives in and there is no way out, so ironically it's the dead end of the child, the person was having inside him/her. Through the healing process one can retain the same way of life, and yes, everything is possible today, and it's up to one, how much priority one gives to the things.

11 - Can a human being be filled with love, which comes exclusively from the source within themselves? And from the moment they become aware of that love they do not feel suffering because they are know their purpose and are fulfilled?

Yes, of course, the universe lies within oneself and love does exist in the human heart and in the one who recognises it. To what level, it depends upon person to person, how strong the ignition of love is inside him/her, it depends upon person to person.

Yes without love, one cannot do anything, and if one never develops the passion and the zeal inside, one will never complete the task and this one cannot force anyone to love that thing or love anything. It's the person's own choice, so that they can achieve their purpose. When I talk about love, I mean true love not artificial love.

Q.4 26 years old female, Albanian

Questions:

1 - Are there three main rules according to the Lord?:
  - Treat others as you would like to be treated.
  - Love yourself as you would like to be loved.
  - Give 100% in everything that you choose.

No, I do not think so.

2 - Are those 3 rules, all that is required of humans to accomplish in this life? How do you explain the way that these can be applied by a person, born in a family amongst members, who do not comply with those rules?

They are not everything, but it is very hard.

3 - For someone to follow the path that makes them happy, do they firstly have to let go of those, who are not happy with themselves, be it even their own family? What is the reason of this?

Yes. Because when you are alone you have to face reality, you have to fight.

4 - What is the soul? Where is it located anatomically in humans and what is the role of the soul in this life? Why...

The soul is something that is not seen but is felt, without which I have no life. Physically, I think it is found in our feelings close to the heart.

5 - Can a person live and be guided by their soul? How can this be achieved?

A person without soul has no life, and can only live by following the path of the heart because for me what feels in the soul is true and I have never been mistaken...

6 - Does a bad soul exist? The reason why...

They say it does, and I believe it... The soul is not created to be bad but the turmoils make it shaken...

7 - Are the mind, heart and body human utensils, which serve the soul so that the person is faithful or fulfilled? Why...

It is true, everything starts with the feelings you have in your soul. If I check them I will be satisfied. Without them I'm not what I want to be.

8 - What does it mean to believe in God and how can this be demonstrated by 3 rules or examples?

Believing in God is a new beginning with the truth alongside.
1 - Treat others as they deserve it, love yourself and others for God's sake.
2 - Be patient because miracles exist, and those who endure are the ones who gain.
3- Be pious, respect the family, the society, the relatives.
4 - Always SMILE.

9 - Do you suppose that children are like angels and innocent and why? So how is their suffering explained in God's language and why?

Children are angels and innocent. I have seen little of those children who suffer because of poverty, or because they are killed or harassed by others.

10 - Are there two kinds of death: A prewritten one and another that depends on our Actions? If so, how is the child's death explained?

Don't know

11 - Can a human being be filled with love, which comes exclusively from the source within themselves? And from the moment they become aware of that love they do not feel suffering because they are know their purpose and are fulfilled?

Totally true, and it is exactly why I know this, that I often cannot be happy. The cause, is the external factors

Q.6, Psychology student , 19 years old. Albanian.

Questions:

1 - Are there three main rules according to the Lord?:
  - Treat others as you would like to be treated.
  - Love yourself as you would like to be loved.
  - Give 100% in everything that you choose.

I think that there are no rules set by God, nor that are written and factual somewhere. But I believe that these are internal rules, that the person places into themselves, to make them feel more fulfilled.

2 - Are those 3 rules, all that is required of humans to accomplish in this life? How do you explain the way that these can be applied by a person, born in a family amongst members, who do not comply with those rules?

- Normally, those 3 rules are the basis for you to feel self-fulfilled, but are not everything. They are just an indication to move us to other things, goals and objectives set against ourselves.

- We are human beings with the ability to adapt to any environment, in which we are part of. But since our family does not have a role in our formation, we can normally meet the 3 main rules. In addition, I think it is more difficult for those who are born into a family that does not respect these rules in advance. But, by knowing that the power springs from within, everything is achieved.

3 - For someone to follow the path that makes them happy, do they firstly have to let go of those, who are not happy with themselves, be it even their own family? What is the reason of this?

Being a good and a bad person is something relative, because each one of us sees the good and bad in different dimensions, I believe it is something difficult to do or even to be defined. However, if we refer to the vices, which we do not like, YES we have to leave. As we know, we are influenced by others and people with vices can spoil our style and quality of life. Whoever they are, family or friends, if we cannot help them improve, we will have to leave.

4 - What is the soul? Where is it located anatomically in humans and what is the role of the soul in this life? Why...

I think and believe that the soul is our existence, which gives life to all organs so that they can work. I do not know where it is found physically in us, but what I believe is that when our biological hour is over, the spirit continues to exist.

5 - Can a person live and be guided by their soul? How can this be achieved?

Yes, I believe they can be commanded by their soul, and can achieve it by following the intuition.

Because, I believe that there is not a straightforward explanation for the intuition, but only the theories we find ourselves in. I think intuition is our soul.

6 - Does a bad soul exist? The reason why…

Yes, as long as there are murders, thefts, incest, etc. I believe this is, because they are people who do not know who they belong to, what they want, and are unable to cope with their fears.

7 - Are the mind, heart and body human utensils, which serve the soul so that the person is faithful or fulfilled? Why…

Our body is in the service of the soul; to exist, to believe and to adapt. So, not just to be considered a true believer.

8 - What does it mean to believe in God and how can this be demonstrated by 3 rules or examples?

Personally, I believe that there is one God and that he exists everywhere and his presence is seen and is very easy to prove it to those who have eyes to see, and ears to hear. God is present by giving us so many good things that we have every day, He is present by making us possessors of ourselves but, when we forget, He is there to remind us that we are the ones, who need Him. And I believe that God has created the best habitat for all of us: the FAMILY.

9 - Do you suppose that children are like angels and innocent and why? So how is their suffering explained in God's language and why?

I do not know how to explain this exactly. But, I believe in karma. What you have done, will be returned to you. And I often believe that children suffer the consequences for the mistakes of adults.

10 - Are there two kinds of death: A prewritten one and another that depends on our Actions? If so, how is the child's death explained?

Death is one of the unrecognized mysteries, so I do not know what to think and consequently what answer to give to this question.

11 - Can a human being be filled with love, which comes exclusively from the source within themselves? And from the moment they become aware of that love they do not feel suffering because they are know their purpose and are fulfilled?

I've heard a lot about love - that is considered to be one of the most beautiful sensations in the world, that fulfils and equates to life. I personally have not tried all the kinds of love, but, I am fulfilled with the love of family and friends. I cannot say that being filled with love, one does not look at the sufferings - they certainly look at them because, they are there with you, but these are the people who love to donate things, to ease things and dress their eyes with positivity and optimism.

Q.7: 27 years, Albanian

Questions:

1 - Are there three main rules according to the Lord?:
  - Treat others as you would like to be treated.
  - Love yourself as you would like to be loved.
  - Give 100% in everything that you choose.

Yes, they are.

2 - Are those 3 rules, all that is required of humans to accomplish in this life? How do you explain the way that these can be applied by a person, born in a family amongst members, who do not comply with those rules?

If one applies these 3 rules, s/he is able to find a solution for everything. These are not rules for "elected people" but are laid out on any person – it depends on how much that person chooses to live according to them. S/he can apply them, by keeping the distance.

3 - For someone to follow the path that makes them happy, do they firstly have to let go of those, who are not happy with themselves, be it even their own family? What is the reason of this?

Coping with such people, puts obstacles on our way, but I am also of the idea that by recognizing their obstacles or dealing with them, they always learn.

4 - What is the soul? Where is it located anatomically in humans and what is the role of the soul in this life? Why...

I cannot define it on physical terms, but the soul is the key that leads humans. Through the soul the person manages to demonstrate themselves in every dimension of life.

5 - Can a person live and be guided by their soul? How can this be achieved?

I would call it the competition and recognition of myself and the philosophy of life. If a human were to be directed through their soul, they would achieve it by applying those three comprehensive rules (in question 1).

6 - Does a bad soul exist? The reason why...

NO, there is no bad spirit. Evil is the incorrect interpretation that a human does to their soul.

7- Are the mind, heart and body human utensils, which serve the soul so that the person is faithful or fulfilled? Why...

If a person is followed or guided by his soul, everything serves him/her. Our structuring comes from the way we feed our souls to feel whole...

8 - What does it mean to believe in God and how can this be demonstrated by 3 rules or examples?

To believe that He is ONE and no one deserves to be worshiped except Him. To let the weight of your issues to be supported by Him.

To believe that for everything, the only one that you find after every storm is again Him.

9 - Do you suppose that children are like angels and innocent and why? So how is their suffering explained in God's language and why?

YES, children are innocent and honest. They suffer the mistakes of their parents, but they can also be rewarded in the next life.

10 - Are there two kinds of death: A prewritten one and another that depends on our Actions? If so, how is the child's death explained?

Death exists as a phenomenon. The one that is related to our actions, exists when we die inwardly from the darkness that characterizes us. The child can die from death as a phenomenon that occurs...

11 - Can a human being be filled with love, which comes exclusively from the source within themselves? And from the moment they become aware of that love they do not feel suffering because they are know their purpose and are fulfilled?

YES, if a person finds their own self, they are beneficial in society too. Any love can enwrap us, but the most consolidated is the one that is ours, which keeps us in the right direction. If the person knows their own self, they know their goals, and if they know the goals, they know what they are talking about and trust it.

Q.9: 6 year old female, british

Questions:

1 - Are there three main rules according to the Lord?:
  - Treat others as you would like to be treated.
  - Love yourself as you would like to be loved.
  - Give 100% in everything that you choose.

Yes, ok, if you say so. What? Maybe I am not supposed to say or write that. My main rules are:

1) Love, be kind sweet and friendly. Worship God more than the others.
2) Be loyal to yourself and others.
3) Let your talent express itself and inspire people by your creativity.

2 - Are those 3 rules, all that is required of humans to accomplish in this life? How do you explain the way that these can be applied by a person, born in a family amongst members, who do not comply with those rules?

Yes, but there are more rules:

- be generous to yourself and others.
- love yourself first, then others.
- loyalty makes people feel happy.
- show commitment in your strength.
- do independent work at school.
- be truthful to everyone.
- have compassion as much as you please, but not a little bit.
- follow how your mind says it.
- make hard work in class.
- be faithful to your husband and wife / family.
- don't steal.
- don't just be strong on the outside, be strong on the inside too.
- on someone's birthday if you are their friend, you could kindly give them a present.
- feed hungry ducks, make them strong to swim or fly.
- have love, peace and truth.
- when you find something difficult, think of the kingdom of God.

If you are in a family that does not follow those rules, think about God. But how do we get to think about God? Pray. Listen to God's answer. Pray strongly with all your attention and focus on it. Don't think about anything on the outside, just think about the prayer with all your mind and feel the love when God rises and shines. You will hear the reply from God the great.

3 - For someone to follow the path that makes them happy, do they firstly have to let go of those, who are not happy with themselves, be it even their own family? What is the reason of this?

No! Try and make others follow how they were told, from God. So try and tell them how you did it with God. Pray and God will give you all the important answers. Then you'll try to follow those answers, God gave you. You will hear a sweet and lovely voice.

4 - What is the soul? Where is it located anatomically in humans and what is the role of the soul in this life? Why...

It is easy how to tell the soul. The soul is the house of yourself. It is found in your heart. That's where I feel it. The role of the soul is to keep you in your body, so you can live. That's it. But that's not all. Even, we have to eat food to stay healthy, and be strong and stay alive, but not just food. Do exercise for your bones to get stronger and stronger. The role of the soul is like that because, you need to be you, to be yourself and follow all the rules you have written, trying to follow them, being focused on them, not the other people's business, leave them alone, like a rock. I do not mean rock and roll! I mean to leave them like a muddy looking soil-y rock. That's it.

5 - Can a person live and be guided by their soul? How can this be achieved?

Yes, a person can live and be guided by their soul. It just happens. No one can guide themselves without a soul to guide them.

6 - Does a bad soul exist? The reason why...

Nope, a bad soul does not exist. Because, if a person had a bad soul it would guide them crazy, even punch people without even thinking. If that happened to a person, we would be all injured.

7 - Are the mind, heart and body human utensils, which serve the soul so that the person is faithful or fulfilled? Why...

Yes. Because, they are parts of our body and they are connected. Just some of them are connected sometimes, because some people do not have much connection.

8 - What does it mean to believe in God and how can this be demonstrated by 3 rules or examples?

You just know and believe that God died on the cross and pray and say thank you, not because of the pain, but for rescuing us. Examples:

1 - Pray

2 - Light up a candle and be ready to love.

3 - Shoot fireworks to remember God's pins.

9 - Do you suppose that children are like angels and innocent and why? So how is their suffering explained in God's language and why?

Yes. They are like that because they are kids, they are little, they believe in God. You know why we call them little angels? Because they are small and they have dreams and have wings. Their suffering…you know babies, they are like little angels, but sometimes they like to walk on the pavement or floor, but you know the floor is very dirty, and you know their hands, they walk with their hands, and when they do not know how to wash their hands, when dinner's ready, they put the food on their hands first, and then put it in their mouth o ou! Because they touched the floor, the microbes from the floor go inside their tummy and then they get sick. That's one option.

People die from anything that could cause injury. People die from guns, aeroplanes, cars, bulls with horns, strangers (they might give things with poison, sugar and alcohol, they might add some poison / alcohol to lollipop, then people might die from the poison and alcohol). Children suffer because they sometimes get poor, but then when they are poor and survive they will be called: 'Overcome Bright Angels'!

10 - Are there two kinds of death: A prewritten one and another that depends on our actions? If so, how is the child's death explained?

Yes. So God's rule is that don't steal or you might die, because I am going to show an example of this. If a person steals a bottle / chicken or toys, they (I said 'they' for the shopkeepers) might call the police and then they will be arrested by the police and they might put them into jail and the person still doesn't understand or think about stealing, they will be given one more chance! O ou! If they still think about stealing, they could be sent to death.

11 - Can a human being be filled with love, which comes exclusively from the source within themselves? And from the moment they become aware of that love they do not feel suffering because they know their purpose and are fulfilled?

Yep! Because they might know how to be friendly to themselves and others. They do not suffer because they have that love inside them that helps them get through.

Q.11 psychologist/therapist ABA around 30 year old Albanian

Questions:

1 - Are there three main rules according to the Lord?:
  - Treat others as you would like to be treated.
  - Love yourself as you would like to be loved.
  - Give 100% in everything that you choose.

--- *(no answer)*

2 - Are those 3 rules, all that is required of humans to accomplish in this life? How do you explain the way that these can be applied by a person, born in a family amongst members, who do not comply with those rules?

If you do not help them, at least do not hurt people. This is my motto. Otherwise, there is an imbalance in homeostasis, which needs psychotherapeutic interventions to address this problem.

3 - For someone to follow the path that makes them happy, do they firstly have to let go of those, who are not happy with themselves, be it even their own family? What is the reason of this?

We are the average of the 5 people who we surround ourselves with in our everyday life. Perhaps we should be surrounded by positive people to think positively.

4 - What is the soul? Where is it located anatomically in humans and what is the role of the soul in this life? Why...

The soul can sometimes also be a subject... the soul is where we are or where we are not...

5 - Can a person live and be guided by their soul? How can this be achieved?

I don't know but I think that everything has a soul.

6 - Does a bad soul exist? The reason why…

I do not believe there is a bad spirit. I think that there is a suffering or a sick soul, but not bad.

7 - Are the mind, heart and body human utensils, which serve the soul so that the person is faithful or fulfilled? Why...

I think the "commander" of every organ in the body is the mind. The others are its companions...

8 - What does it mean to believe in God and how can this be demonstrated by 3 rules or examples?

To not judge. To love anyone.

9 - Do you suppose that children are like angels and innocent and why? So how is their suffering explained in God's language and why?

Children are like angels, but for other things it is not for me to speak, but for those who serve the Lord. I cannot talk about things, which do not belong to my field of study.

10 - Are there two kinds of death: A prewritten one and another that depends on our Actions? If so, how is the child's death explained?

I think there are several kinds of death: accidental, from old age, terminal illness…regarding children, except the age- related one, there are many factors leading to death, and unfortunately, we cannot prevent all their deaths.

11 - Can a human being be filled with love, which comes exclusively from the source within themselves? And from the moment they become aware of that love they do not feel suffering because they are know their purpose and are fulfilled?

Everything is, because we think or feel that way, not that we actually are that way... so everything is unique. What may be called fulfilling to me is not so for someone else, and vice versa. And we do not have the same desires to fulfil at a given time. At different times we have different desires and dreams ...'we are slaves of our desires', has said Schopenhauer, the well-known philosopher. 'Man', he said, must come out from the "wheel" of desires to be really happy!!'

Q.12 Albania female., around 20 years old.

Questions:

1 - Are there three main rules according to the Lord?:
  - Treat others as you would like to be treated.
  - Love yourself as you would like to be loved.
  - Give 100% in everything that you choose.

I think not all. Point 2, for example: I cannot love myself as others love me.

2 - Are those 3 rules, all that is required of humans to accomplish in this life? How do you explain the way that these can be applied by a person, born in a family amongst members, who do not comply with those rules?

Life is diverse, and as such, it does not offer the possibility of strict rules. Man grows, increases his knowledge and improves. What is needed, is the will and the desire to change for the better.

3 - For someone to follow the path that makes them happy, do they firstly have to let go of those, who are not happy with themselves, be it even their own family? What is the reason of this?

I believe it is that way because, it avoids the negative energy.

4 - What is the soul? Where is it located anatomically in humans and what is the role of the soul in this life? Why...

Did you ask this question seriously?! For me it is an indefinite notion ... it is a term used to express love to another person...

5 - Can a person live and be guided by their soul? How can this be achieved?

Man is oriented by reason and conscience, not the soul.

6 - Does a bad soul exist? The reason why...

No, there are bad people. The soul is a feeling, not something physical.

7 - Are the mind, heart and body human utensils, which serve the soul so that the person is faithful or fulfilled? Why...

I think yes, in order to be in this life and to have good conscience or positivity we must live ... but these are physical actions that occur in the human body.

8 - What does it mean to believe in God and how can this be demonstrated by 3 rules or examples?

To believe in God means that you are one who respects the moral principles, so you are a just and reasonable person about your actions.

9 - Do you suppose that children are like angels and innocent and why? So how is their suffering explained in God's language and why?

They do not carry vices when they are born, but it is the environment, where they grow, that makes them wear them by transforming into devils.

10 - Are there two kinds of death: A prewritten one and another that depends on our Actions? If so, how is the child's death explained?

Fate is predestined, and so are our actions. This explains the deaths of children.

11 - Can a human being be filled with love, which comes exclusively from the source within themselves? And from the moment they become aware of that love they do not feel suffering because they are know their purpose and are fulfilled?

Yes, when they find peace in themselves and with the others around.

Q.15: around the age of 50. English male.

Questions:

1 - Are there three main rules according to the Lord?:
  - Treat others as you would like to be treated.
  - Love yourself as you would like to be loved.
  - Give 100% in everything that you choose.

Yes.

2 - Are those 3 rules, all that is required of humans to accomplish in this life? How do you explain the way that these can be applied by a person, born in a family amongst members, who do not comply with those rules?

Maybe these are the only 3 rules, or the summary of the other rules.
But if I begin to behave differently to others in my group/family or culture, by following any of these 3 rules, then that will begin to affect their behaviour too.
But it maybe that these 3 rules may already be known naturally in every culture/ family even if on the surface these cultures don't seem to follow or practice the 3 rules.

3 - For someone to follow the path that makes them happy, do they firstly have to let go of those, who are not happy with themselves, be it even their own family? What is the reason of this?

To follow that path, a person may have to let go of their past, their group, their family – Jesus taught that certainly. But to follow the happy path maybe to go on a way that does not make me happy at first. Normally a family says it is happy with the way things are – why do you want to change these things?

Following the 3 rules does not appear to lead to happiness if that is the main goal one is trying to follow.

4 - What is the soul? Where is it located anatomically in humans and what is the role of the soul in this life? Why...

I used to think it was like the heart or to be almost outside the human, but now I understand it to be part of the body, not separate from it.

Soul and body are the same and can be anywhere in the body – but I don't understand this clearly.

5 - Can a person live and be guided by their soul? How can this be achieved?

The hope of a spiritual practice is to find this guidance from within.

We need the silence and some skills to listen for this quality of soul in the body and we need the body to confirm this in our lives, by consolation.

Ultimately finding one's own souls is to find God, who dwells within.

6 - Does a bad soul exist? The reason why… Yes there are bad souls.

There is lostness of the soul.

Some of the great souls feel their lostness.

Some of the bad souls have no inner awareness of their violence to others.

7 - Are the mind, heart and body human utensils, which serve the soul so that the person is faithful or fulfilled? Why...

Mind heart and body are not utensils, or functions or tools to be used by humans, but are aspects of the wholeness of a human.

Becoming whole – in mind body and soul are part of the path to fulfilment and are aspects of faithfulness.

8 - What does it mean to believe in God and how can this be demonstrated by 3 rules or examples?

To believe in God is to acknowledge a higher power and to find the reality of God inside oneself and in all creation and in every speck of dust.

9 - Do you suppose that children are like angels and innocent and why? So how is their suffering explained in God's language and why?

I probably believe now that children are born innocent.

I can't explain the suffering of the world, nor how this happens in the providence of God, through all the wars that go on or how the world can be made right amidst the bad behaviour of the mighty.

10 - Are there two kinds of death: A prewritten one and another that depends on our Actions? If so, how is the child's death explained?

Well we all live and we all die. Some children die too young. Death is a part of life. Some kind of life goes on after death.

11 - Can a human being be filled with love, which comes exclusively from the source within themselves? And from the moment they become aware of that love they do not feel suffering because they are know their purpose and are fulfilled?

Normally we know about this love, through our contact with another, which authenticates that love. I suppose the more deeply we love, the more capacity we have to suffer too. Some with deepest pain, know the deepest joy.

Question.16: 19 years English male/ studding law degree

Questions:

1 - Are there three main rules according to the Lord?:
  - Treat others as you would like to be treated.
  - Love yourself as you would like to be loved.
  - Give 100% in everything that you choose.

Yes.

2 - Are those 3 rules, all that is required of humans to accomplish in this life? How do you explain the way that these can be applied by a person, born in a family amongst members, who do not comply with those rules?

It's about keeping those values close to your heart until you are able to support yourself and then you can implement the rules in your life.

3 - For someone to follow the path that makes them happy, do they firstly have to let go of those, who are not happy with themselves, be it even their own family? What is the reason of this?

No they do not. They love their family for other reasons and must embrace why they love those members, and not be so narrow minded by thinking only those who share your beliefs are worthy of loving.

4 - What is the soul? Where is it located anatomically in humans and what is the role of the soul in this life? Why...

The soul is the balance of the will of the heart and will of the brain.

5 - Can a person live and be guided by their soul? How can this be achieved?

A person can be guided by their heart and brain and the soul will compromise between the two and give an all-round best choice.

6 - Does a bad soul exist? The reason why…

No because the soul is pure, but it may get lost as the brain takes over.

7 - Are the mind, heart and body human utensils, which serve the soul so that the person is faithful or fulfilled? Why...

Yes, because I just believe the soul is in charge of our humans parts and helps us to keep it in balance.

8 - What does it mean to believe in God and how can this be demonstrated by 3 rules or examples?

Treat others as you would like to be treated.
- Love yourself as you would like to be loved.
- Give 100% in everything that you choose.

9 - Do you suppose that children are like angels and innocent and why? So how is their suffering explained in God's language and why?

Children are innocent, as they are a blank slate and are taught what they learn growing up.

10 - Are there two kinds of death: A prewritten one and another that depends on our Actions? If so, how is the child's death explained?

No, only one that is determined by our actions.

11 - Can a human being be filled with love, which comes exclusively from the source within themselves? And from the moment they become aware of that love they do not feel suffering because they are know their purpose and are fulfilled?

No they cannot. They can love themselves but this can cause loneliness if they only love themselves and cannot share or receive love back.

Q.17: Pastor, age around 35 from Nigeria.

Questions:

1 - Are there three main rules according to the Lord?:
  - Treat others as you would like to be treated.
  - Love yourself as you would like to be loved.
  - Give 100% in everything that you choose.

- The Lord said, love the Lord your God first, then love your neighbour as you love yourself.
- Treat others as you would like them to treat you.
- Giving 100% in everything one choses, is a function of faithfulness that is revealed in commitment. Love and Faithfulness are fruits of God's Spirit in the regenerated man.

2 - Are those 3 rules, all that is required of humans to accomplish in this life? How do you explain the way that these can be applied by a person, born in a family amongst members, who do not comply with those rules?

These virtues are not all that is required of humans to accomplish in this life. They rather form the foundation of God's expectation from man. They are not achievable through human ability but by the Grace of God given to any man who has allowed Christ the Saviour to indwell him.
The Graced person in the midst of noncompliant individuals, whether they be family, office colleagues or neighbours, though severely tasked, is to shine as light in thick darkness.

3 - For someone to follow the path that makes them happy, do they firstly have to let go of those, who are not happy with themselves, be it even their own family? What is the reason of this?

It takes hope and faith that works with love to be happy.
So to be happy I do not need to let go of those who are not happy in themselves, rather I should love them and show them the way.

4 - What is the soul? Where is it located anatomically in humans and what is the role of the soul in this life? Why...

The soul is the seat of the human personality.
It is made up of the Mind, Will and Emotion. Naturally it is located in the head region, physically speaking.

5 - Can a person live and be guided by their soul? How can this be achieved?

--- (no answer)

6 - Does a bad soul exist? The reason why…

I think there is a bad soul. That is why a lot of things are happening negatively today on earth.
A lot of factors contribute in making souls bad: first it is endemic as a result of the original sin than runs in every unregenerate human.
Only embracing Christ makes a soul whole, though the transformation of life is the individual's responsibility after the first encounter with Christ.

7 - Are the mind, heart and body human utensils, which serve the soul so that the person is faithful or fulfilled? Why...

The body only showcases what is predominant in in the soul. Christ, Satan or Self.

8 - What does it mean to believe in God and how can this be demonstrated by 3 rules or examples?

To believe in God is to trust the Lord Jesus whom HE HAS sent for the salvation of man since fall of Adam.
That I believe in God should not just be heard from my lips but seen in my actions (love, care, others first, etc.), for faith without works is dead.

9 - Do you suppose that children are like angels and innocent and why? So how is their suffering explained in God's language and why?

Why do innocent people including children suffer? Why is there suffering at all? Why is there so much lack in the midst of plenty? Why are there denials, frustrations, killings and so on?

These are happening for the time being because Satan the evil one is still at large with his demons. Man submitted to him, remember, and he is acting out his ruler-ship of wickedness.

Yet a time will come later when he(Satan) will be removed to his deserved abode, the lake of fire. Then God the Father will restore all things and wipe away all tears. Revelation 21:3 to 5

10 - Are there two kinds of death: A prewritten one and another that depends on our Actions? If so, how is the child's death explained?

There are three kinds of death.

   i.   *Physical transition: This is when someone ceases to breathe physically. This is not actually death, because the person lives on either in paradise or hell.*

   ii.   *Spiritual death: This is a man's separation from God as a result of sin. Returning to God in repentance is a remedy to this.*

   iii.   *Second death: This is as a result of spiritual death. When and individual loses his physical life in the state of spiritual death(ii above) It is the complete and total separation from God forever.*

11 - Can a human being be filled with love, which comes exclusively from the source within themselves? And from the moment they become aware of that love they do not feel suffering because they are know their purpose and are fulfilled?

Yes. This is a height in spirituality.

Q.18 Male age around 50 Albanian

Questions:

1 - Are there three main rules according to the Lord?:
  - Treat others as you would like to be treated.
  - Love yourself as you would like to be loved.
  - Give 100% in everything that you choose.

In the first question, I disagree with the rules, since often the will being influenced by the ego, the lusts and the delights can lead to the wrong way. God, besides giving us freedom, at the same time, he has created us as conscious beings to reason and behave so as not to harm others.

2 - Are those 3 rules, all that is required of humans to accomplish in this life? How do you explain the way that these can be applied by a person, born in a family amongst members, who do not comply with those rules?

Concerning the second question, consider that the rules determined by a family or society are norms and should be respected, but not all people are born the same and diversity develops us by alluding and searching for rules that are acceptable to all - if not, there are sanctions.

3 - For someone to follow the path that makes them happy, do they firstly have to let go of those, who are not happy with themselves, be it even their own family? What is the reason of this?

I would relate the third question to the psychology of self-confidence that in the first preamble has a very clear message: Possibly, do not waste time with those who feed you negative energy.

4 - What is the soul? Where is it located anatomically in humans and what is the role of the soul in this life? Why...

The soul for me is an analogy of the engine in the car - according to my conviction it moves in every cell of the body.

5 - Can a person live and be guided by their soul? How can this be achieved?

The soul expresses a person's identity, and the physical condition is soul-oriented.

6 - Does a bad soul exist? The reason why...

Yes, there is a bad spirit and the reason is that it was born to do evil and to have the bad spirit.

7 - Are the mind, heart and body human utensils, which serve the soul so that the person is faithful or fulfilled? Why...

Consider that any action that is taking place is aided by something - what it is called is of no importance, so what it is important is that we are served, so that the soul can function, so that the firstly the object serves the body and then in the object operate the other vital organs, such as the mind, heart, and others.

8 - What does it mean to believe in God and how can this be demonstrated by 3 rules or examples?

For me, faith in God is the utmost definition, because nothing in this world is without genesis, so the universe is the creator, and the omnipotent. It's omnipotent, it's all the same and for everyone and everything, it has created the circumstances for life.

9 - Do you suppose that children are like angels and innocent and why? So how is their suffering explained in God's language and why?

YES, children are compared to a blank and unwritten letter. Their sufferings are due to society and family.

10 - Are there two kinds of death: A prewritten one and another that depends on our Actions? If so, how is the child's death explained?

Yes, the prewritten death is the partition from this life. Someone can be alive or in life but is not worth as much as the dead one, and the death of a child is God's predestination. Birth and death are very determined by God.

11 - Can a human being be filled with love, which comes exclusively from the source within themselves? And from the moment they become aware of that love they do not feel suffering because they are know their purpose and are fulfilled?

As far as love is concerned, I will define it in love and happiness. Love is pretty much in the broad sense, but if one feels happy, I think he has achieved the goal for himself.

Q.20: 27 years old Albanian…writes poems
I read the book! It gave me nothing! I'm sorry!

Questions:

1 - Are there three main rules according to the Lord?:
  - Treat others as you would like to be treated.
  - Love yourself as you would like to be loved.
  - Give 100% in everything that you choose.

God does not exist. It is a game of a man's imagination, which he invented due to the fear of the unknown!

2 - Are those 3 rules, all that is required of humans to accomplish in this life? How do you explain the way that these can be applied by a person, born in a family amongst members, who do not comply with those rules?

There are no rules in life, because, man is responsible for his own actions in life!

3 - For someone to follow the path that makes them happy, do they firstly have to let go of those, who are not happy with themselves, be it even their own family? What is the reason of this?

I am very happy with the life I do; I read, write, love, kill and continue...

4 - What is the soul? Where is it located anatomically in humans and what is the role of the soul in this life? Why...

The soul is a label for the essence of the human being, but the soul is only a platonic concept that does not, in fact, exist!

5 - Can a person live and be guided by their soul? How can this be achieved?

Man lives on the basis of his (rationality) mind!

6 - Does a bad soul exist? The reason why…

There are people with good and bad behaviour, depending on what they are fed with, during the formation of their personality!

7 - Are the mind, heart and body human utensils, which serve the soul so that the person is faithful or fulfilled? Why...

I do not want to give an answer, because they are very infantile questions, which tell me nothing! And finally, do not dare to mistakenly use my name anywhere in any devious book or magazine with such questionnaires, because I will sue you, if you misuse my name somewhere.

8 - What does it mean to believe in God and how can this be demonstrated by 3 rules or examples?

They are all stupid questions. I wanted to answer, I started... but they are so idiotic and naive that they disgust me, I do.

9 - Do you suppose that children are like angels and innocent and why? So how is their suffering explained in God's language and why?

--- (no answer)

10 - Are there two kinds of death: A prewritten one and another that depends on our Actions? If so, how is the child's death explained?

-- (no answer)

11 - Can a human being be filled with love, which comes exclusively from the source within themselves? And from the moment they become aware of that love they do not feel suffering because they are know their purpose and are fulfilled?

--- *(no answer)*

Q.21 34 years old, British.

Questions:

1 - Are there three main rules according to the Lord?:
  - Treat others as you would like to be treated.
  - Love yourself as you would like to be loved.
  - Give 100% in everything that you choose.

Yes I believe the three rules should apply to everything we do in life. They are like a cure or a solution if we follow those rules. If everyone steps back and thinks of those three rules, the world will be a better place to live.

2 - Are those 3 rules, all that is required of humans to accomplish in this life? How do you explain the way that these can be applied by a person, born in a family amongst members, who do not comply with those rules?

Definitely the three rules can make anyone a better human being. It applies in a family as is the core the base of a good upbringing. As a mum of two I strongly apply those rules to my children. If they believe them, they give the kids better chances to follow them during their adult life.

3 - For someone to follow the path that makes them happy, do they firstly have to let go of those, who are not happy with themselves, be it even their own family? What is the reason of this?

Yes, I do believe that to follow your own path you should cut out negative people. However, if you are strong minded and you believe in yourself fully, you still can manage to help a family member to find their peace and path, while you can still keep track of yours.

4 - What is the soul? Where is it located anatomically in humans and what is the role of the soul in this life? Why...

What is the soul?? Uaaa that's an in-depth question. Well, I'm answering these questions in a spare of moment and writing down what comes to my mind in instinct. However, when I read this question it kind of puts me back a bit. Well, the soul should be located in the middle of everything we do... deep down in us but yet easy to reach when needed. Without a soul we are empty human beings living for nothing - basically like an empty box.

5 - Can a person live and be guided by their soul? How can this be achieved?

Yes a person can be guided and live by the soul.

6 - Does a bad soul exist? The reason why…

Yes, unfortunately there are bad souls out there. This could have been due to the way they have been raised or been through something and lost their way and turned their souls to evil but also I believe every soul can be saved.

7 - Are the mind, heart and body human utensils, which serve the soul so that the person is faithful or fulfilled? Why...

Everything is connected with our body, heart, soul and brain, but for a person to be fulfilled they need to connect all together and make use of all them at all times.

8 - What does it mean to believe in God and how can this be demonstrated by 3 rules or examples?

Believing in God makes a human being a better person. Just by knowing that someone is watching us it's a good feeling, especially when we do something good and you have that feeling that you will be rewarded.

9 - Do you suppose that children are like angels and innocent and why? So how is their suffering explained in God's language and why?

Yes I believe every child born it's an angel until they grow and depends on that family and how loved they are and that shapes them into better adults. Well, children happen to get sick but I believe God gives us life and can take it from us at any time and it doesn't have an age.

10 - Are there two kinds of death: A prewritten one and another that depends on our Actions? If so, how is the child's death explained?

Well, I think our action does play a role, maybe a little but I strongly agree everything it's meant to be and we die when it's our time. That's why believing in God doesn't make death very sad as I know it's a better place up there, and doing good, as I mentioned above, gets you to a better place.

11 - Can a human being be filled with love, which comes exclusively from the source within themselves? And from the moment they become aware of that love they do not feel suffering because they are know their purpose and are fulfilled?

The best love is within our self. There is no better loving than loving ourselves. And it's true if you love yourself, others will love you and respect you.

Q.22 IT student age 19 English

Questions:

1 - Are there three main rules according to the Lord?:
  - Treat others as you would like to be treated.
  - Love yourself as you would like to be loved.
  - Give 100% in everything that you choose.

Yes, I do believe that God expects everyone to respect and treat each-other the same.
Yes, God has created everyone, so people should appreciate themselves in life and their values. No, you cannot always be successful.

2 - Are those 3 rules, all that is required of humans to accomplish in this life? How do you explain the way that these can be applied by a person, born in a family amongst members, who do not comply with those rules?

It is important for people to be able to communicate with each-other and understand the meaning of how life works. Not everyone can follow these rules so it's okay for someone to be different.

3 - For someone to follow the path that makes them happy, do they firstly have to let go of those, who are not happy with themselves, or are becoming obstacles for your journey and will not allow you to achieve your dream's, can be it even their own family? What is the reason of this?

If you feel that someone, is holding you back with achieving your goals, no matter the reason being, avoid that person. If the person is a family member, that decision will be a very difficult decision.

4 - What is the soul? Where is it located anatomically in humans and what is the role of the soul in this life? Why…

A soul is something given by God.

5 - Can a person live and be guided by their soul? How can this be achieved?

-- (no answer)

6 - Does a bad soul exist? The reason why…

No, God has given everyone a soul of their choice, that would benefit people in their own way.

7 - Are the mind, heart and body human utensils, which serve the soul so that the person is faithful or fulfilled? Why…

A person's emotion is controlled with his own mind and heart, not with the soul.

8 - What does it mean to believe in God and how can this be demonstrated by 3 rules or examples?

Everyone has their own way for believing in God and their beliefs. I believe that God intends to lead everyone to the right path in different methods.

9 - Do you suppose that children are like angels and innocent and why? So how is their suffering explained in God's language and why?

No

10 - Are there two kinds of death: A prewritten one and another that depends on our Actions? If so, how is the child's death explained?

I believe that only God knows the exact day and timing and location for your death because has planned your life.

11 - Can a human being be filled with love, which comes exclusively from the source within themselves? And from the moment they become aware of that love they do not feel suffering because they are know their purpose and are fulfilled?

What do you think is the love within? And why do you think that way? No, love simply comes the moment people are able to communicate with each-other and become closer.

Q.23 Female/age35/teacher/trainer/assessor/british

Questions:

1 - Are there three main rules according to the Lord?:
  - Treat others as you would like to be treated.
  - Love yourself as you would like to be loved.
  - Give 100% in everything that you choose.

I think there is more than these rules, to live a happy and well balanced life.

2 - Are those 3 rules, all that is required of humans to accomplish in this life? How do you explain the way that these can be applied by a person, born in a family amongst members, who do not comply with those rules?

I believe that there is more than these rules to feel fully accomplished in life. The ability to learn, enables us to construct our personalities and adapt to different situations. We need to find the purpose motivating our life.

3 - For someone to follow the path that makes them happy, do they firstly have to let go of those, who are not happy with themselves, or are becoming obstacles for your journey and will not allow you to achieve your dream's, can be it even their own family? What is the reason of this?

I would not give up on my decisions although, at the same time persist to stay committed.

4 - What is the soul? Where is it located anatomically in humans and what is the role of the soul in this life? Why...

The ability to feel, rationally think, equal to love. I don't know where but I feel it everywhere.

5 - Can a person live and be guided by their soul? How can this be achieved?

Not sure.

6 - Does a bad soul exist? The reason why...

Not sure.

7 - Are the mind, heart and body human utensils, which serve the soul so that the person is faithful or fulfilled? Why...

Not sure.

8 - What does it mean to believe in God and how can this be demonstrated by 3 rules or examples?

Not sure - treat others fairly, with justice.

9 - Do you suppose that children are like angels and innocent and why? So how is their suffering explained in God's language and why?

Yes, I believe that children are innocent. Children's suffering is mainly explained as a fault of adults egos, their selfishness.

10 - Are there two kinds of death: A prewritten one and another that depends on our Actions? If so, how is the child's death explained?

I don't know.

11 - Can a human being be filled with love, which comes exclusively from the source within themselves? And from the moment they become aware of that love they do not feel suffering because they are know their purpose and are fulfilled?

What do you think is the love within? And why do you think that way? Yes, a human is partially filled with love by loving themselves but this kind of love does not become a sufficient for someone else. loving yourself to the extent to fix the purpose.

Q.30 26 years old/grecce/psychologist/female

Questions:

1 - Are there three main rules according to the Lord?:
  - Treat others as you would like to be treated.
  - Love yourself as you would like to be loved.
  - Give 100% in everything that you choose.

Being fair and by treating others, as we would like to be treated, we attract positive things in our lives. Good things also happen to us also when we know that we love ourselves and we are committed to our goals.

2 - Are those 3 rules, all that is required of humans to accomplish in this life? How do you explain the way that these can be applied by a person, born in a family amongst members, who do not comply with those rules?

I believe that these rules are enough to accomplish someone's life, but when you are positioned or surrounded by people, who do not appreciate these rules, you need more strength and effort to achieve and probably you need a mentor's help.

3 - For someone to follow the path that makes them happy, do they firstly have to let go of those, who are not happy with themselves, or are becoming obstacles for your journey and will not allow you to achieve your dream's, can be it even their own family? What is the reason of this?

I believe that you have to protect yourself from the negative energy, even if it comes from your family or your most beloved ones, and keep a distance from there because they ruin your inner balance and happiness.

4 - What is the soul? Where is it located anatomically in humans and what is the role of the soul in this life? Why...

The soul is our spirit, which is visible only through our attitude and behaviour and maybe in our dreams. It's an energy throughout our whole body.

5 - Can a person live and be guided by their soul? How can this be achieved?

A person can be guided by his/her soul only if they want to do so and feel like the need for it. Some can achieve it on their own, while others need help by a psychologist.

6 - Does a bad soul exist? The reason why…

I don't believe in bad souls, but in badly sharpened ones.

7 - Are the mind, heart and body human utensils, which serve the soul so that the person is faithful or fulfilled? Why...

They are, but it needs a lot of time and effort to achieve it.

8 - What does it mean to believe in God and how can this be demonstrated by 3 rules or examples?

9 - Do you suppose that children are like angels and innocent and why? So how is their suffering explained in God's language and why?

A child that comes in life is innocent, but she is shaped from the very first experiences of their life depending whether they are positive/negative.

10 - Are there two kinds of death: A prewritten one and another that depends on our Actions? If so, how is the child's death explained?

It always depends on our actions, but I will have doubts about prewritten things.

11 - Can a human being be filled with love, which comes exclusively from the source within themselves? And from the moment they become aware of that love they do not feel suffering because they are know their purpose and are fulfilled?

What do you think is the love within? And why do you think that way?

I believe in this possibility though I find it rare to happen. It is finding absolute satisfaction from yourself and making things for yourself to achieve it.

Q.40: 10 years old female, british

Questions:

1 - Are there three main rules according to the Lord?:
   - Treat others as you would like to be treated.
   - Love yourself as you would like to be loved.
   - Give 100% in everything that you choose.

These rules are enough, because for example, loving yourself means that you care about you and that is very good

2 - Are those 3 rules, all that is required of humans to accomplish in this life? How do you explain the way that these can be applied by a person, born in a family amongst members, who do not comply with those rules?

They are all you need. If someone doesn't follow these rules I would treat them and listen to their opinions.

3 - For someone to follow the path that makes them happy, do they firstly have to let go of those, who are not happy with themselves, or are becoming obstacles for your journey and will not allow you to achieve your dream's, can be it even their own family? What is the reason of this?

I would convince them, and tell them 'that is what I love', and then maybe they might let me.

4 - What is the soul? Where is it located anatomically in humans and what is the role of the soul in this life? Why...

- The soul is where the wisdom is held.
- It is located near the heart... I think.
- The soul helps you by telling you to do the right thing.

5 - Can a person live and be guided by their soul? How can this be achieved?

A person can be guided by their soul and it can be achieved by behaving.
--- (no answer)

6 - Does a bad soul exist? The reason why...

A bad soul doesn't exist because everyone is warm an nice inside.

7 - Are the mind, heart and body human utensils, which serve the soul so that the person is faithful or fulfilled? Why...

I think so, because everything they do, is very special but combining them, makes something powerful like the soul.

8 - What does it mean to believe in God and how can this be demonstrated by 3 rules or examples?

- To believe in god means that you believe.
- I communicate with God by talking to him. I can talk to him because he made us and he is a part of me.

9 - Do you suppose that children are like angels and innocent and why? So how is their suffering explained in God's language and why?

Not all of them are, because some suffer and angels are perfect and those kids don't have the right to speak.

10 - Are there two kinds of death: A prewritten one and another that depends on our Actions? If so, how is the child's death explained?

Don't know.

11 - Can a human being be filled with love, which comes exclusively from the source within themselves? And from the moment they become aware of that love they do not feel suffering because they are know their purpose and are fulfilled?

What do you think is the love within? And why do you think that way?

People can still love themselves if they are lonely. The love within is that you are loving yourselves. I think that way because it's what I think.

Q.41 6 years old female/british

Questions:

1 - Are there three main rules according to the Lord?:
  - Treat others as you would like to be treated.
  - Love yourself as you would like to be loved.
  - Give 100% in everything that you choose.

Yes, they are the main rules because my mum, dad and aunty taught me those rules and they are enough. Rule number one helps me because you can treat others kindly. Loving yourself helps me by loving myself and liking my expressions, and if they are not good, I will find a way how to improve them.

2 - Are those 3 rules, all that is required of humans to accomplish in this life? How do you explain the way that these can be applied by a person, born in a family amongst members, who do not comply with those rules?

Yes, these are enough and I will try to make others believe in this too, or I will be a bad person also if they don't learn.

3 - For someone to follow the path that makes them happy, do they firstly have to let go of those, who are not happy with themselves, or are becoming obstacles for your journey and will not allow you to achieve your dream's, can be it even their own family? What is the reason of this?

I would continue on my own and try convince them by listening to me.

4 - What is the soul? Where is it located anatomically in humans and what is the role of the soul in this life? Why...

The soul is all of me, the whole of me. The soul can teach me to be good and gives me advice. Based on my soul, I can respond.

5 - Can a person live and be guided by their soul? How can this be achieved?

Yes, by the soul you can be guided.

6 - Does a bad soul exist? The reason why…

A bad soul doesn't exist.

7 - Are the mind, heart and body human utensils, which serve the soul so that the person is faithful or fulfilled? Why…

The soul is the boss and the rest work for it. The soul is me. The mind, body and heart without soul distract me to be bad.

8 - What does it mean to believe in God and how can this be demonstrated by 3 rules or examples?

He gives advice.
I can listen to him, because he is in my body, and he made me.

9 - Do you suppose that children are like angels and innocent and why? So how is their suffering explained in God's language and why?

Don't know.

10 - Are there two kinds of death: A prewritten one and another that depends on our Actions? If so, how is the child's death explained?

Don't know.

11 - Can a human being be filled with love, which comes exclusively from the source within themselves? And from the moment they become aware of that love they do not feel suffering because they are know their purpose and are fulfilled?

It's not enough, because I still need my mum and dad, but it is: as I care for myself, I will find a way to be fulfilled.

CHAPTER XI

ALL ANSWERS OF QUESTIONERS

Love 🧡 Believe 🧡 Dream 🧡 Visualise 🧡 Act

We deeply appreciate your dedication for taking part in this questionnaire and thank you for your contribution of the opinions and impressions, in order to help in this important charity research. (We would like to emphasize: *Please simply provide the thoughts, which come to you in the moment, not prepared ones*).

Title: Human perceptions: how to bring peace and love to ourselves and around us. How can we know our own self (soul) to guide us? How to nourish the mind with our soul's thoughts for the feelings to be produced as a result of thoughts that come from our own self (soul)?

Purpose: This research is developed to find out the way of people's healing from the past, to enjoy the moment and realise the dreams that they want to achieve by understanding themselves, life and to find their inner source of love.

Hypothesis: 'I believe that once the person finds their inner source of love, they are able to understand themselves and the life around based on peace and love'.

Please answer the following questions as a part of the study: (each participant is named in numbers, example the answers of participant one will be on each question named as answer 1)

Questions:
Q1:

1 - Are there three main rules according to the Lord?:
  - **Treat others as you would like to be treated.**
  - **Love yourself as you would like to be loved.**
  - **Give 100% in everything that you choose.**

Participant 1: Yes! …and I would add one more, which to me is the first rule: Love your God with all your soul, heart, and mind, and with all your strength in prayer and faith.

Participant 2: I have grown atheist - these were my grandmother's and my parents' guidance.

Participant 3: No, The feelings are not predefined by the laws of the nature or according to the Lord. It depends upon the individual to who embodies into oneself.
Treat Others – As far as my experience Sis I tell you that This World is pre- equipped
With different types of people, so everyone has different set of mind make up and deportment. On my personal basis, I tried to tell the people this is the scenario if one comprehends it well and good but for others I leave up to them you are free to make your own stories out of it. So My level of conversation depends upon person to person, as everyone has its own taste and different level of comfort zone so that I can
Converse with them. For Eg, If I tell someone stranger in the market who is typically from my area and is not that much into understanding of Healing process, he possess the simple life get up in the morning & get ready to work and in the evening have some relaxation by watching TV or moving around outside for a while. If I grab his attention and tell about healing oneself you know Sis Simply He will laugh on me or say what are you talking about. As his set of mind is filled from the beginning that the more money one has, has all the powers with him. As with money he can buy anything he wants and do anything – The General Scenario here the common masses one possess and for him this all exists and does look good in books and in the literature. I am telling you the clear picture so as to find the people like me who synchronises with my mind and try to understand me are v rare and Indeed in practical sense these type of people follow some other spiritual healers here like Pundits and all. So my duty was to tell them but how one treats or comprehends depends upon the character and the gamut of the environment he dwells in.
If someone comprehends me well and good, and if someone is going to make a joke of it I just leave it I do not respond or rather that group or gossip. So it depends Sis How people treat me I treat them in their own way. As I cannot change them as they are not at all ready to change or I simply avoid unnecessary arguments.

LOVE - Love oneself that is the better option left as I tell you Sis in present scenario
The value of True Love is lost, The artificial love prevails in this world in the masses now as far as if I am helpful or good to one I am v adorable to him/ her and once the task is over, project is over who cares for whom, nobody. As nobody has time and no
one understands it rather playing games with each other is the motto left, Ego Hatred Jealousy prevails in practical scenario of life. OMG!!! He is earning less than me and look at him He is still smiling and having such an awesome life. What He has inside him that makes him so happy and joyful. this is the feeling left as I see around. Sis, In real life I talk
with v less people with whom I am most comfortable with, not with everyone I open my pages. Rather you can say Its simply the act of formality I do as they do with everyone. So its better to find happiness around is the happiness that lies inside me and Yes I have no friends nobody here Yes all my dear ones are far away and I most of the time live alone and live my life, trying to do best for myself to make me feel happy. So loving oneself is the key and True love lies in Nature paradise, going outside in

the park and having a walk feel closely with the nature by being surrounded by flowers petals trees and autumn leaves falling down. I love all that.
So as a person I myself has set of things I love doing what I do and if I do not like it all
I wont do it at all no one can force me to do that thing which I do not like doing. I am simply like that.

Giving 100% - Yes I give 100% in whatever I do and for me if the task is new and I am liking it I will Google

I will Google it everything and will do everything with passion and 100% determination.

Participant 4: No I dont think they are .

Participant 5: They are not the main one but everyone should be aware of them.

Participant 6: I think that there are no rules set by the lord, or in written and in fact. But I believe that it is the rules that emanate from the inside that the individual decided to follow in order to feel complete.

Participant 7: Yes there are.

Participant 8: Yes.

Participant 9: Yes, ok, if you say so. What? Maybe I am not supposed to say or write that. My main rules are:
1) Love, be kind sweet and friendly. Worship God more than the others.
2) Be loyal to yourself and others.
3) Let your talent express itself and inspire people by your creativity.

Participant 10: Yes I do think they are the main rules by God. Participant 11: Do the 100% in everything you chose to do.

Participant 12: No I dont think all the points , example the point 2 you can not love yourself how others love me.

Participant 13: Yes they are.

Participant 14: Are the three main rules below from God ?: In my opinion, these are the three main rules, as it is normal to love and love the same. Treat others the way you like to be treated. And the determination to make 100% everything is also the key

Participant 15: Yes

Participant 16: Not sure.

Participant 17: The Lord said, love the Lord your God first, then love your neighbour as you love yourself.
- Treat others as you would like them to treat you.
- Giving 100% in everything one choses, is a function of faithfulness that is revealed in commitment. Love and Faithfulness are fruits of God's Spirit in the regenerated man.

Participant 18: In the first question, I disagree with the rules, since often the will being influenced by the ego, the lusts and the delights can lead to the wrong way. God, besides giving us freedom, at the same time, he has created us as conscious beings to reason and behave so as not to harm others.

Participant 19: Yes there are three main rules according to the lord. and if you do the three of them you are an complete being,,,both spiritually and physically.

Participant 20: God does not exist. It is a game of a man's imagination, which he invented due to the fear of the unknown!

Participant 21: Yes I believe the three rules should apply to everything we do in life it's like a cure to or sole of we follow those rules. Of everyone stamps back and thinks of those three rules the world will be a better place to live.

Participant 22: Yes I do believe that god expects everyone top respect and treat each other the same. yes god has created everyone so people should appreciate themselves in life and their values.
no you cannot always be successful

Participant 23: I think there is more than these rules to live a happy and well balanced life.

Participant 24: Those are things which are important in life to have allowing you to be successful and get along with others.

Participant 25: Not sure

Participant 26: I am atheist

Participant 27: Yes

Participant 28: I believe only the first is true according to the lord Participant 29: No, there are 8 commandments.

Participant 30: Being fair and by treating others as we would live to be treated we attract positive things in our lives. good things also happen to us when we wont we love ourselves and we are committed to our goals.

Participant 31: True yes because my mum.

Participant 32: I do agree. it has to do with our life experiences and that our parents has taught us since childhood.

Participant 33: Yes this is my belief, to give love and respect. I would like for myself.

Participant 34: Treat others how you want to be treated. Participant 35: Yes

Participant 36: Yes, through listening to elders and my brother.

Participant 37: love life as a gift and love will have you sali .(not sure of last word)

Participant 38: I believe that these are the main rules because life has teached me and are true.

Participant 39: There are more than those.

Participant 40: These rules are enough because for example loving yourself means that you care about you and that is very good.

Participant 41: Yes, they are the main rules because my mum, dad and aunty taught me those rules and they are enough. Rule number one helps me because you can treat others kindly. Loving yourself helps me by loving myself and liking my expressions and if is there not good I will find away how to improve them.

Participant 42: I agree with the first two rules, but I disagree with the third, I dont believe that everything is certain, and you shouldn't get your hopes up by putting to much effort.

Participant 43: They are great rules to never break for anyone.

Participant 44: No they are not from god, they are from people who hasnt written to bile or people who god has sent.

Participant 45: There are important rules but not more important.

Participant 46: These may be 3 rules according to smart people.

Participant 47: I believe that are the 3 main rules according to the lord.

Participant 48: Three rules -maybe, sometimes, depends on the task, sometimes my 'chosen' thing is not worth putting 100% in.

Participant 49: Not sure.

Participant 50: The will has to come from yourself and with the help of the god everything you decide you should achieve it 100%.

Q2: Are those 3 rules, all that is required of human to accomplish in this life? How do you explain the way that these can be applied by a person, born in a family amongst members, who do not comply with those rules?

Participant 1: Yes, with the addition of the rule number 1 as previously mentioned. The person must have or gain a deeper connection with themselves and develop spiritual intelligence by focusing on their core self – their soul. How this occurs depends on the person's purpose in this life. For instance, some people living in adverse conditions, receive an inner calling, which brings them guidance, love, peace and resilience, so they choose to follow it. As in all human beings there are certainly fluctuating periods of doubt, but getting up again and again and again by seeking God and the righteousness, helps one to achieve the comforts needed. A person's natural passions are also a way of finding and preserving themselves.

Participant 2: In life we learn every day, face challenges and joys, meet with others with whom we exchange our values and experiences, sometimes good sometimes bad, sometimes predicted sometimes unpredicted.

I wish those, who live in a family where the above values are not endorsed, are not affected but create immunity.

Participant 3: Better Life for Better Tomorrow for the Human Race Yes This is most important to achieve and if this is not achieved the hatred jealousy racism egoist and all the dreadful cause is engulfing the whole world. Humanity has to be there and Love is the language we have to understand one day for the better tomorrow. With Fight Arguments and violence nothing is achieved. Killing nowadays is so common that you will be shocked to hear arguments on silly talks and shot the gun on person head right there within seconds game over. This has to have an end and only Love that is the biggest feeling the human is born with is to be embody in everyone heart more deep. The Meaning of true love one has to feel and understand it, quiet playing games with my heart. Dont treat me as an option if someone feels like one can leave. I am not hungry for love I know my ways how I can love myself I have seen the darkest scenario when everything was off for me, I came out from that well, alone and talked to me million times with myself otherwise I would have ended up myself by eating medical pills only. It's nobody did nothing for me it's me my wish to come out from the darkest room and I said Yes to Life and began talking with the people.

HOW THIS CAN BE ACCOMPLISHED WITH THOSE WHO DO NOT COMPLY WITH THE RULES - *Interesting question you asked Sis*

Sis you know the basics of life and the answer is Love oneself and the gamut of the people around and love your family.....The Answer lies in this only. Scenario... I am talking to XYZ and explaining the things which was there in your lovely book woven so beautifully but but but if someone is stick and is not ready at all to change his thinking process, I will become his mirror image I will copy his whole life routine and the way he talks with the people and the types of people he meets I will copy all the mannerism in my mind and scan his brain vibes and I know The Buddy is lacking somewhere in understanding the true meaning of loving oneself and the people around, all he does his activities just to get profit in money making. I will make him understand why the deal is not coming up its because of your temperament or deportment. So Jolly V Sis, It does not matter to me that I will follow anyone rules strictly and exactly enforce other to follow that but rather I will become the mirror image of the buddy and tell Yours Core Values The Basics which you wish to deliver to the masses I will try to explain as per his scenario or the page of the book he is opened with.

Participant 4: There are not everything but there are really difficult.

Participant 5: No, they are not everything, that the individual in life is very demanding. Starting with the smallest things and ending in the most unimaginable but achievable   Everyone can change themselves or do it as it desires itself does not matter to the environment but the logic of the person himself   That person one day it can also change that family, a single person can change a lot just want will and never surrender

Participant 6: Normally, those 3 rules are the basis for you to feel self-fulfilled, but are not everything. They are just an indication to move us to other things, goals and objectives set against ourselves.
-We are human beings with the ability to adapt to any environment, in which we are part of. But since our family does not have a role in our formation, we can normally meet the 3 main rules. In addition, I think it is more difficult for those who are born into a family that does not respect these rules in advance. But, by knowing that the power springs from within, everything is achieved.

Participant 7: If one applies these 3 rules, s/he is able to find a solution for everything. These are not rules for "elected people" but are laid out on any person – it depends on how much that person chooses to live according to them. S/he can apply them, by keeping the distance.

Participant 8: I believe that yes, those three rules are not important but very important in the life of any of us who want to live well and reach where we want. I believe that a person who consists of members of families who do not apply these rules, although I find it difficult to come to observe these rules only when it is enough grown to understand reality and be aware of its actions and above all by putting the intelligence into work.

Participant 9: Yes, but there are more rules:
- be generous to yourself and others.
- love yourself first, then others.
- loyalty makes people feel happy.
- show commitment in your strength.
- do independent work at school.
- be truthful to everyone.
- have compassion as much as you please, but not a little bit.
- follow how your mind says it.
- make hard work in class.
- be faithful to your husband and wife / family.
- don't steal.
- don't just be strong on the outside, be strong on the inside too.
- on someone's birthday if you are their friend, you could kindly give them a present.
- feed hungry ducks, make them strong to swim or fly.
- have love, peace and truth.
- when you find something difficult, think of the kingdom of God.

If you are in a family that does not follow those rules, think about God. But how to we get to think about God? Pray. Listen to God's answer. Pray strongly with all your attention and focus on it. Don't think about anything on the outside, just think about the prayer with all your mind and feel the love when God rises and shines. You will hear the reply from God the great.

Participant 10: Those 3 rules are all that is required of the individual. If a person has family members that he or she applies, I believe I must find the strength to make that person apply to.

Participant 11: If you do not help them, at least do not hurt people. This is my motto. Otherwise, there is an imbalance in homeostasis, which needs psychotherapeutic interventions to address this problem.

Participant 12: Life is diverse, and as such, it does not offer the possibility of strict rules. The person grows, increases his knowledge and improves. What is needed, is the will and the desire to change for the better.

Participant 13: There are not everything. Could be achieved by the individual if they are determent.

Participant 14: To some extent, I think they are principled for everyone and can be somewhat complementary. But for people born in families who do not apply these rules is very difficult. Somewhat implausible, that is, it depends on the strength of the person.

Participant 15: Maybe these are the only 3 rules, or the summary of the other rules
But if I begin behave differently to others in my group/ family or culture by following any of these 3 rules, then that will begin to affect their behaviour too
But it maybe that these 3 rules may already be known naturally in every culture/ family even if on the surface these cultures don't seem to follow or practice the 3 rules.

Participant 16: Its about keeping those values close to your heart until you are able to support yourself and then you can implement the rules in your life.

Participant 17: These virtues are not all that is required of humans to accomplish in this life. They rather form the foundation of God's expectation from man. They are not achievable through human ability but by the Grace of God given to any man who has allowed Christ the Saviour to indwell him.
The Graced person in the midst of noncompliant individuals, whether they be family, office colleagues or neighbours, though severely tasked, is to shine as light in thick darkness.

Participant 18: Concerning the second question, consider that the rules determined by a family or society are norms and should be respected, but not all people are born the same and diversity develops us by alluding and searching for rules that are acceptable to all - if not, there are sanctions.

Participant 19: I think that there may be many other things that a being has to do in this life,,because life itself imples to do so many things ,,I personally think about the positive things to give in this life,,,people are different and many of them do not believe in these three rules and do not apply them,,,but does not mean they can not practice these rules one day,,and that happens when they start to feel spiritually empty that something missing.

Participant 20: There are no rules in life, because, man is responsible for his own actions in life!

Participant 21: Definitely the three rules can make anyone a better human being. It applies in a family as is the core the base of a good upbringing. As a mum of two I strongly apply those rules to my children if they believe it form kids the better chances for them to follow it during the adult life.

Participant 22: It is important for people to be able to communicate with each other and understand the meaning at how life works. not everyone can follow these rules so its okay for someone to be different.

Participant 23: I believe that there is more than these rules to feel fully accomplished in life. the ability to learn enables us to construe our personalities and adapt to different situations. we need to find the purpose motivating your life.

Participant 24: There are many things needed such as being caring, work together and so forth. it would be difficult for them to apply such things as they maybe opposite.

Participant 25: As guidelines.

Participant 26: Someone can choose to follow the rules if they wish.

Participant 27: Yes I think those are the 3 main facts in life you treat others nicely, love yourself and do the best in everything.

Participant 28: A person is nothing but a product of their environment a person likely follow these trends.

Participant 29: No, I dont know

Participant 30: I believe that these rules are enough to accomplish someone's life but when you are positioned or surrounded by people who do not appreciate these rules you need more strength and effort to achieve and probably you need a mentors help.

Participant 31: Leave them behind.

Participant 32: You cant follow these rules anger does not allow you to Participant 33: External factors are also important.

Participant 34: If the life is decided by the board and that power driver each human resistance in this universe.

Participant 35: Yes, keep distance

*Participant 36: No, cant think of anything
distance yourself with love.*

Participant 37: We do not choose our family, still, we choose how we behave…

Participant 38: You need to be you and not listen to negative people even if you are surrounded by negative people.

Participant 39: Following these rules will make your life positive.

Participant 40: They are all you need,
if someone does't follow these rules I would treat them and listen to there opinions.

Participant 41: Yes these are enough and I will try to make others believe in this too or I will be bad person also if they don't learn.

Participant 42: I think that there are many more rules that are required of the human to accomplish in this life, such as , be yourself and never hide yourself or try to be nice others. Some people do not love themselves as they would live to be covered as they may have insecurities.

Participant 43: Not sure

Participant 44: As a start I think they have concluded everything and every person should follow.
I think think the people who are born in a family who dont follow those rules, need to accompany good people Participant 45: I think is more the wish then rules.

Participant 46: Not sure

Participant 47: These three rules are crucial in order to fulfill an accomplished life. I believe that there are also other rules depending on circumstances eg. I would state that to remain healthy is also a rule that is received in order for one to fulfilled a complete life.

Participant 48: I think the ones close to you know how you feel about most things, especially rules- if they don't comply that's fine, you can still be there for them. listen and let them find out in their own way.

Participant 49: No its not necessary to have all three present to be accomplished in life as not everyone is privileged to have all three.

Participant 50: Yes of course those rules everyone wants to achieve in this life. The person who has been born in the family who dont follow those rules then needs to do their best to follow those rules in life.

Q3. For someone to follow the path that makes them happy, do they firstly have to let go of those, who are not happy with themselves, or are becoming obstacles for your journey and will not allow you to achieve your dream's, can be it even their own family? What is the reason of this?

Participant 1: Yes, this would certainly make things easier. Personally, I believe that this is required, for the person to focus and expand on their true identity, and be fully established on their true purpose. However, this action depends on the person's purpose in life. There are cases where the person remained in the family, (because they somehow had already found their inner strength and aim) in order to give a lesson to them and the surrounding community. There are other cases where the person needs distance in order to strengthen and grow spiritually and the time depends on them. Some people keep occasional contact, some cut the family out completely; it depends on the relationship they had, and its functionality.

Participant 2: I do not think that a person should leave, regardless of what circumstances we face or with whom. We need to create opportunities so that our goodness and values can change those around us, not prejudicing anyone.
To believe in the expression: Everything happens for a reason.

Participant 3: Lack of communication and unwilling to understand the basics of life Sis I tell you I do lot of things sometimes not to make myself happy also first
But I do it for you, Yeah Everything or most of thing I do it for you. To make you smile as you smile that makes me smile and you being so precious for me it makes me happy.
Yes Yes For those who are not happy with themselves, Yes I have been in the scenario when I used to feel so down buried deep inside carrying heart of darkness which was so heavy for me.
One cannot dim the light inside ones body its up to one who can dim or turn off the light by themselves. I do not know much, be it family or friends or group of people one is around with it affects the person to a certain percentage but if for scenario taking - Jolly V Sis if you keep on pouring in me brightest light or the pass so powerful positive vibes to me to encourage me to do it anyhow and on the other hand if I turn off the light inside me and I am v much depressed this will not effect me to that extent I will rather feel yeah I will do it Sis but when what will that time I do not know. I know the things but I am not doing but
On the other way if I decide on my own and recall every words you said and turn my light on within myself by reinventing me I will do exactly the way to find the happiness in me.

Participant 4: Yes because when you are alone you could face the reality and can fight.

Participant 5: Absolutely not in my opinion it is not important to leave people who are not satisfied with themselves, each has its own life and do not judge others. Will you be satisfied ?! Do. Will you change it ?! Do. But do not judge others because we are not judging in this life

Participant 6: Being a good and a bad person is something relative, because each one of us sees the good and bad in different dimensions, I believe it is something difficult to do or even to be defined. However, if we refer to the vices, which we do not like, YES we have to leave. As we know, others influence us and people with vices can spoil our style and quality of life. Whoever they are, family or friends, if we cannot help them improve, we will have to leave.

Participant 7: Coping with such people, puts obstacles on our way, but I am also of the idea that by recognizing their obstacles or dealing with them, they always learn.

Participant 8: Often people do not follow the path that makes them happy and that does not make you happy, but I believe that everyone's happiness is of the greatest importance, so I believe that it is worth let go of those that hold you back if it depends my happiness.

Participant 9: No! Try and make others follow how they were told, from God. So try and tell them how you did it with God. Pray and God will give you all the important answers. Then you'll try to follow those answers, God gave you. You will hear a sweet and lovely voice.

Participant 10: No you should not move away from your family because in that way you are not following the rules in question one.

Participant 11: We are the average of the 5 people who we surround ourselves with in our everyday life. Perhaps we should surround our self with positive people to think positively.

Participant 12: I believe Yes because, it avoids the negative energy.

Participant 13: Because need to eliminate the obstacles.

Participant 14: No, I do not think so, we have to accept others as they are. With their weaknesses and strengths. Just as we do not want to change us and others do not have to change.

Participant 15: To follow that path, a person may have to let go of their past, their group, their family — Jesus taught that certainly
But to follow the happy path maybe to go on a way that does not make me happy at first.
Normally a family says it is happy with the way things are — why do you want to change these things. Following the 3 rules does not appear to lead to happiness if that is the main goal one is trying to follow.

Participant 16: No they do not. they love their family for other reasons and must embrace why they love those members, and not be so narrow minded by thinking only those who share your beliefs are worthy of loving.

Participant 17: It takes hope and faith that works with love to be happy.
So to be happy I do not need to let go of those who are not happy in themselves, rather I should love them and show them the way.

Participant 18: I would relate the third question to the psychology of self-confidence that in the first preamble has a very clear message: Possibly, do not waste time with those who feed you negative energy.

Participant 19: To be a happy person there is no formula,,we can not control the situation we are in,,,but we can control our reactions,,,i think that the happiness in life is influenced by quality of thoughts,,motivation to pursue desires and positive thinking,,to feel good about ourselves and to love ourselves,,

Participant 20: I am very happy with the life I do; I read, write, love, kill and continue..

Participant 21: Yes I do believe to follow your own path you should cut out negative people however if you are strong minded and you believe in your self fully you still can manage to help a family member to find their peace and path while you can still keep track of yours.

Participant 22: If you feel that someone is holding you back with achieving your goals no matter the reason being, avoid that person. if the person is a family member, that decision will be very difficult decision.

Participant 23: I would not give up on my decisions although at the same time persist to stay committed.

Participant 24: Depends if they do as long as it keeps them happy and calm. there are many obstacles to overcome including family as they may be in the way of their own happiness.

Participant 25: Noo, other situations shouldn't effect your situation Participant 26: Depends on the situation.

Participant 27: No you dont you can help them on your path.

Participant 28: A persons circumstances are always different this is very subjective on that person.

Participant 29: Yes, their self doubt can stop them from achieving wat they want. others may try and stop them.

Participant 30: I believe that you have to protect yourself from negative energy even if it comes from your family or your most beloved ones and keep a distance from there because they ruin your inner balance and happiness.

Participant 31: Leave them behind.

Participant 32: This is a dilemma for me but I would really appreciate someone who goes for his journey.

Participant 33: Sometimes letting go can be productive.

Participant 34: Happiness is choice if an individual and if will be hard for others to make others happy.

Participant 35: Yes, if they dont understand then ill leave them.

Participant 36: Yes, let go if they dont make you happy or are not happy. Because their negative energy might fight against your energy. Stopping you from becoming the best.

Participant 37: To be happy, you need to feel free, to feel free you need to let loose those who hold you back. Participant 38: Yes I do keep distance because I know what I want and I will get it with any cost.

Participant 39: leave all people that hold you back.

Participant 40: I would convince them and tell them that its what I love and then maybe they might let me.

Participant 41: I would continue on my own and try convince them by listening to me.

Participant 42: Yes I think that even family, in some cases people need to let go of others in order to help themselves achieve and succeed. This is because they might unintentionally be holding you back.

Participant 43: To always take you path of your own and to succeed and achieve it for yourself.

Participant 44: Whoever people are, even the family, if they dont understand me, ill leave them behind and choose my dreams, because they dont dont understand me now and will never understand me, follow your dreams .

Participant 45: To be happy helps when staying with people who feel good about themselves is not everything that makes them happy.

Participant 46: You do not need to go away from those people are not happy with themselves. Just do not be like them.

Participant 47: In order for someone to follow the path that makes them happy they need to let go of any obstacles that restricts them, even if that be family. This is because obstacles hold you back from feeling free and achieving your maximum potential.

Participant 48: Depends on who it is-sometimes it's better to let go. There could be many reasons. If you're pretty happy with your life, you're in a better position to help someone.

Participant 49: No, you dont have to let go of the person because they help in other ways.

Participant 50: To follow the road that makes you happy does not mean to keep distance from people that are not happy but to continue your path. If they become obstacle then you can keep distance from those people that are not happy.

Q4. What is the soul? Where is it located anatomically in humans and what is the role of the soul in this life? Why…

Participant 1: The soul is the very essence or centre of our being that is in the image of God and actively connected to God. It allows us and reminds us to align our personality and actions according to its mission.

Participant 2: For me is the deepest part of our being. A role of awareness, a pure feeling, an inner clock.

Participant 3: The Soul is immortal the body after death decays but the soul comes out and it takes it.

Another form of life, it never dies. The Soul is the immaterial part of human being or the animal. Its located below the stomach and the upper abdomen region near Naval region. Its role is important and it has its vital meaning as It's voice is v soft and v light and it whispers in my ears what's right and what's wrong. It indeed controls my nervous system, the brain and the heart Together it just enlightens me up and zeal up the confidence in me and the enlightenment becomes too strong when some positive vibes strikes it and I learn something new in my life.

Participant 4: The soul is something that is not seen but is felt, without which I have no life. Physically, I think it is found in our feelings close to the heart.

Participant 5: The spirit is our world. is located everywhere and has the role to guide you.

Participant 6: I think and believe that the soul is our existence, which gives life to all organs so that they can work. I do not know where it is found physically in us, but what I believe is that when our biological hour is over, the spirit continues to exist.

Participant 7: I cannot define it on physical terms, but the soul is the key that leads humans. Through the soul the people manage to demonstrate themselves in every dimension of life.

Participant 8: The soul is feeling sleeping within us, the soul is the one that makes us sensible, because only when we touch on the soul I believe we react to the truth as we really feel and we are.

Participant 9: It is easy how to tell the soul. The soul is the house of yourself. It is found in your heart. That's where I feel it. The role of the soul is to keep you in your body, so you can live. That's it. But that's not all. Even we have to eat food to stay healthy, and be strong and stay alive, but not just food. Do exercise for your bones to get stronger and stronger. The role of the soul is like that because, to be you, to be yourself and follow all the rules you have written and trying to follow them, being focused on them, not the other people's business, leave them alone, like a rock. I do not mean rock and roll! I mean to leave them like a muddy looking soil-y rock. That's it.

Participant 10: The soul is the universe inside us.

Participant 11: The soul can sometimes also be a subject... the soul is where we are or where we are not...

Participant 12: Did you ask this question seriously?! For me it is an indefinite notion ... it is a term used to express love to another person...

Participant 13: The soul is in the nervous system, in the brain.

Participant 14: The soul is our core. He has the role to guide us and make us feel. Physically I think it's in the middle of the chest and it's a point everyone believes I know.

Participant 15: I used to think it was like the heart or to be almost outside the human, but now I understand it to be part of the body , not separate from it.
Soul and body are the same and can be anywhere in the body – but I don't understand this clearly.

Participant 16: The soul is the balance of the will of the heart and will of the brain.

Participant 17: The soul is the seat of the human personality. It is made up of the Mind, Will and Emotion. Naturally it is located in the head region, physically speaking.

Participant 18: The soul for me is an analogy of the engine in the car - according to my conviction it moves in every cell of the body.

Participant 19: The soul is the unlucky part of the being…the ability to judge and distinguish between… evil and good…the mind and consciousness… the spirit…the propensity to act…thought…create and perceive…the soul is the inner voice of being.

Participant 20: The soul is a label for the essence of the human being, but the soul is only a platonic concept that does not, in fact, exist!

Participant 21: What is the soul?? Uaaa that's an in-depth question well I'm answering these questions in a spare of moment and writing down what comes to my mind in instinct. However when I read this question it kind of put me back a bit. Well soul should be located In the middle of everything we do… deep down in us but yet easy to reach when need it. Without a sound we are empty human beings living for nothing. Basically like an empty box.

Participant 22: A soul is something given by god.

Participant 23: The ability to feel, rationally think, equal to love. I dont know where but I feel it everywhere.

Participant 24: Soul is you and located deep within yourself, the role us to travel in this world and get knowledge.

Participant 25: Not sure

Participant 26: I am not religious however traditionally I believe its located in the torso area.

Participant 27: Not sure.

Participant 28: I do not believe in souls but we more a persons personality.

Participant 29: The soul isn't a physical thing .

Participant 30: Soul is our spirit which is visible only through our attitude and behaviour and maybe in our dreams, its an energy throughout our whole body.

Participant 31: In the body

Participant 32: I feel it between heart and universe it is for me to love it, to make me love myself and realise my goal in the beginning in this life.

Participant 33: I dont believe the soul to be physiological entity.

Participant 34: It is a physical component of a lords creation.

Participant 35: My mum says that the body is all over the body.

Participant 36: Soul is connection to nature and universe through energy. Located at the bottom of your food (sole) connect you and protect you.

Participant 37: My definition of soul is : our being, our feelings, our emotions, our thoughts, dreams and our inner self

Participant 38: I believe that the soul is the feelings because this the way I feel it.

Participant 39: No idea

Participant 40: The soul is where the wisdom is held,
-the located near the heart… I think
-the soul helps you by telling you to do the right thing

Participant 41: The soul is all of me, whole of me , the soul can teaches me to be good and gives me advise. Based on my soul I can respond.

Participant 42: I believe that the soul is located, not in a specific area but all over the human body. I believe the soul is to guide us.

Participant 43: To automatically take your own risk and your own path of your own.

Participant 44: The soul is a sentence that describes how you take decisions based on emotions.

Participant 45: The soul is our strong breath that is on our human being.

Participant 46: Probably, we call soul the senses of human body including emotional feelings. Which ones make us feel like that is the soul but that's how human body is builded and you can call it whatever you want. All these senses are connected to the brain.

Participant 47: The soul is the part of the body which makes honest decisions, it is not located, it consists of humans as a whole. The soul is what connects us to genuine feelings and decisions.

Participant 48: Not sure, I think the soul is all of you. For me, the soul is about feeling, acting in calmness, passion, anger because you feel it's the right thing to do.

Participant 49: Soul is most probably the heart of the body, located in the forehead. A soul makes you different to other people.

Participant 50: The soul is not something physical, but I think is the breath, heart and mind are essence of the soul. Your emotions, the positive energy, thoughts and actions are fruits of your soul.

Q5 & Q6. Can a person live and be guided by their Soul? How can this be achieved? Does a bad soul exist? The reason why…

Participant 1: Yes, the inner guidance is what should manifest outside. Personally I believe it requires, attention, continuous prayer, inner conversations and expressions through forms of art such as writing, drawing, music etc.

Participant 2: The soul is something surreal. The more the years pass, the more the mind, heart and soul come closer, more and more, and each one feels, that is being led by the soul.
I do not believe so the bad soul exist..

Participant 3: Yes Of course the person can live and guided by their soul as it can be achieved
Through meditation process just concentrating on oneself and inhale and exhale the air out and let the pores of the body open and listen to the instant voice of the soul as
It will guide you in seconds what's right or wrong and its up to the person that follows it. That's why its said the universe lies within you while one is searching for happiness around.

There is no good or bad soul in general, the soul itself is pure its the character of the
Person that makes it good or bad. The Soul is always pure in Human Body even if one talks to the prisoner who committed crime, but its the bad character in him/her that made or force him/her to do crime is lying in the prison, the circumstances may be many why he/she did that but the soul is never bad. We can heal that person and convert him/her to the different opposite good person. For Eg, I heard The Akon group of music industry who has a unique voice committed something crime and was in prison but he changed his image and its through his unique voice today he has a different place in the Music Industry. I am not sure about Akon but I heard this from my senior may be I am wrong but this is the scenario like.

Participant 4: A person without soul has no life, and can only live by following the path of the heart because for me what feels in the soul is true and I have never been mistaken...Does a bad soul exist? The reason why...They say it does, and I believe it... The soul is not created to be bad but the turmoils make it shaken...

Participant 5: Of course, thinking more about yourself and trusting in it I believe that is. I do not know exactly but, from what I see, I believe they happen.

Participant 6: Yes, I believe they can be commanded by their soul, and can achieve it by following the intuition. Because, I believe that there is not a straightforward explanation for the intuition, but only the theories we find ourselves in. I think intuition is our soul.
Does a bad soul exist? The reason why...Yes, as long as there are murders, thefts, incest, etc. I believe this is, because they are people who do not know who they belong to, what they want, and are unable to cope with their fears.

Participant 7: I would call it the competition and recognition of myself and the philosophy of life. If a human were to be directed through their soul, they would achieve it by applying those three comprehensive rules (in question 1).
Does a bad soul exist? The reason why...NO, there is no bad spirit. Evil is the incorrect interpretation that a human does to their soul.

Participant 8: Of course, yes. I believe that this is achieved only by following our internal voice and always doing what makes us happy, for example: to follow our dreams I do not believe it has a bad spirit, I think it has a bad mind to transform it into bad spirits. This is because people think wrong and unconscious, so they do not put themselves in the place of others, do not ask themselves questions how they would react in a particular case.

Participant 9: Yes, a person can live and be guided by their soul. It just happens. No one can guide themselves without a soul to guide them. Nope, a bad soul does not exist. Because, if a person had a bad soul it would guide them crazy, even punch people without even thinking. If that happened to a person we would be all injured.

Participant 10: Yes, there is a bad spirit. Because circumstances and life can make a person get back to that shape but one can live By being oriented according to his spirit.

Participant 11: I don't know but I think that everything has a soul. Does a bad soul exist? The reason why... I do not believe there is a bad spirit. I think that there is a suffering or a sick soul, but not bad.

Participant 12: Man is oriented by reason and conscience, not the soul. Does a bad soul exist? The reason why...No, there are bad people. The soul is a feeling, not something physical.

Participant 13: Hardly, the material world can not be ignored. Yes of course. Genetically evil is planted.

Participant 14: I believe that the individual can be aligned with his soul because I think it's all that the individual has. I do not know how to determine it with certainty, I believe there are evil spirits condemned by situations that have come to the fore.

Participant 15: The hope of a spiritual practice is to find this guidance from within.
We need the silence and some skills to listen for this quality of soul in the body and we need to body to confirm this in our lives, by consolation
Ultimately finding ones own souls is to find God , who dwells within.

Participant 16: A person can be guided by their heart and brain and the soul will compromise between the two and give and all round best choice.

Participant 17: I think there is a bad soul. That is why a lot of things are happening negatively today on earth.
A lot of factors contribute in making souls bad: first it is endemic as a result of the original sin than runs in every unregenerate human.
Only embracing Christ makes a soul whole, though the transformation of life is the individual's responsibility after the first encounter with Christ.

Participant 18: The soul expresses a person's identity, and the physical condition is soul-oriented. Does a bad soul exist?
The reason why…Yes, there is a bad spirit and the reason is that it was born to do evil and to have the bad spirit.

Participant 19: Of course it can, but if the mind is one with the soul,,and about the bad soul I do not believe that exist,,i think that there are ignorant minds that guides you in wrong way.

Participant 20: Individual lives on the basis of his (rationality) mind! Does a bad soul exist? The reason why…There are people with good and bad behaviour, depending on what they are fed with, during the formation of their personality!

Participant 21: Yes a person can be guided and live by a soul and yes unfortunately there are bad souls out there. This could of been if they way they have been raised or been through something and lost their way and turn their souls to evil but also I believe every soul can be saved.

Participant 22: No, God has given everyone a soul of his choice that would benefit people in their own way. Participant 23: Not sure

Participant 24: People are how they are and live how they see fit and it depends on environments and personalities.

Participant 25: Not sure if one exists.

Participant 26: I believe not. this is because I'm not religious .

Participant 27: I think there is no bad soul because everyone is good in there own way no one is bad. Participant 28: No, people can always change .

Participant 29: No, I dont think they can be guided by their soul because their choices came from their brainbad souls and everywhere because people are complicated.

Participant 30: A person can be guided by his/her soul only if they wants to do so and he feels like need for it. some can achieve it on their own while others need help by a psychologist. I dont believe in bad souls, but in bad sharpened ones.

Participant 31: By listening to the soul.

Participant 32: There is no bad soul, its human kind. everything around you should not come between you and your soul. think with your soul and just listen to your intuition.

Participant 33: Yes, by listening to your heart. no a persons circumstances can often make a person make bad choices.

Participant 34: Yes! it is hard to practice that in this modern world. where you give up love for existence you can do it.

Participant 35: Yes, it can and this can be achieved by relaxing and thinking and believing in god.

Yes it does exist bad soul because people born that way.

Participant 36: Yes you can be guided by your soul and yes it does exist bed soul. depends on what energy the soul is fed by connecting with your self and the source.

Participant 37: Now adays is giving guided by the soul is almost impossible , society imposes ...(not sure what it says) and there are good and bad souls

Participant 38: Yes, by believing in yourself . yes and the reason is that does exist negative people that they don't want to see others better then themselves.

Participant 39: Bad souls come with negative violence.

Participant 40: A person can be guided by their soul and it can be achieved by behaving.
   - a bad soul doesn't exist because everyone is warm an nice inside

Participant 41: Yes by the soul you you can be guided
   - and a bad soul doesn't exist

Participant 42: I believe that a person can live and be guided by their soul. the reason to this is because I think that someone's soul is something that defines you as a person. I do not believe that a bad soul exists.

Participant 43: They follow their own soul, they are stuff.

Participant 44: I think a person shouldn't be guided by their soul because you might love something that isn't good for you, no one can be born with a bad soul, but taking the wrong decisions in life can turn in to a bad soul

Participant 45: I think it is not only the soul who can guide you because is need it the heart and mind. Yes it does have bad soul but I don't know the reason why.

Participant 46: I don't be guided by my soul but by my mind and thoughts.
A bad "soul" can exist and it may do because or inherited variation from the parents or it can change to bad through the life.

Participant 47: Yes I believe a person can be guided by their soul, if they choose to connect with their genuine belief. A bad soul doesn't exist in my opinion, circumstances and situations can change individuals.

Participant 48: Possibly- I call it intuition-following your 'gut feeling'
I don't think so. Evil behaviour is more about a persons hold on their emotions- or a release of their emotions, in other words, 'control.

Participant 49: Yes, their soul is like direction. Perhaps bad souls do exist.

Participant 50: Of course can be guided by your soul.

I think so, could be lots of reason why do bad soul exist: 1-because of lots of unerring, 2-peverty , 3-could me genetics.

Q7. Are the mind, heart and body human utensils, which serve the soul so that the person is faithful or fulfilled? Why...

Participant 1: There are simply good souls because they are created on the image of God.

Participant 2: As above. The closer they are, the easier life is, the more fulfilled it is, the more meaningful it is.

Participant 3: It depends upon the person to person and the character one plays.
One who knows the value of soul knows the reinvention or reprogramming process
Nobody is perfect Yeah One needs to rinse away the dust from the body and the mind and listen to the deep soft sound of soul and concentrate more on oneself by giving time to oneself.

Participant 4: It is true, everything starts with the feelings you have in your soul. If I check them I will be satisfied. Without them I'm not what I want to be.

Participant 5: Of course, you should be grateful to God for everything.

Participant 6: Yes, as long as there are murders, thefts, incest, etc. I believe this is, because they are people who do not know who they belong to, what they want, and are unable to cope with their fears.

Participant 7: If a person is followed or guided by his soul, everything serves him/her. Our structuring comes from the way we feed our souls to feel whole...

Participant 8: Yes I think so.

Participant 9: Yes. Because, they are parts of our body and they are connected. Just some of them are connected sometimes, because some people do not have much connection.

Participant 10: Yes, mind, heart, and body are the tools of the soul, because in some ways the soul does a mini-balance between them.

Participant 11: I think the "commander" of every organ in the body is the mind. The others are its companions...

Participant 12: I think yes, in order to be in this life and to have good conscience or positivity we must live ... but these are physical actions that occur in the human body.

Participant 13: Yes there are because with out them the soul and the body can not be function.

Participant 14: Yes, they are the "human tools" that must be in the service of the soul and to be true believers. Because when a individual submits to the creator .

Participant 15: Mind heart and body are not utensils , or functions or tools to be used by humans, but are aspects of the wholeness of a human
Becoming whole – in mind body and soul are part of the path to fulfilment and are aspects of faithfulness

Participant 16: Yes, because I just believe the soul is in charge of our humans parts and helps us to keep it in balance.

Participant 17: The body only showcases what is predominant in in the soul. Christ, Satan or Self.

Participant 18: Consider that any action that is taking place is aided by something - what it is called is of no importance, so what it is important is that we are served, so that the soul can function, so that the firstly the object serves the body and then in the object operate the other vital organs, such as the mind, heart, and others.

Participant 19: I think if all three are in cooperation with one another... and a being it feels faithful and fulfilled.

Participant 20: Everything is connected with our body heart, soul brain, but for a person to be fulfilled they need to connect all together and make use of all them at all times.

Participant 21: A persons emotion is controlled with his own mind and heart not with the soul *Participant 22:* Not sure

Participant 23: Not sure

Participant 24: I see them as necessities which are needed in this world.

Participant 25: Not sure

Participant 26: A good healthy brain should allow someone to achieve their goals and become fullfeed.

Participant 27: I think the heart and mind serve the soul

Participant 28: No

Participant 29: The person want to use their mind to make those decisions that make them faithful or faithful. the soul doesn't do anything.

Participant 30: They are, but it need a lot of time and effort to achieve it. Participant 31: No its difficult

Participant 32: They serve the soul. soul mates decisions. because I do things not according to my mind but my soul.

Participant 33: Mind, heart, and body are the tools we have to achieve our potential.

Participant 34: If the mind reaches the spirituality level then the soul become faithful Participant 35: No because the heart and soul don't work in same level with mind. Participant 36: Yes there are physical aspects that work for you spiritual side of you.

Participant 37: I perceive mind and heart as part of soul and body just a tool

Participant 38: No, the reason is that soul and heart are one and do not coordinate with mind.

Participant 39: Dont understand

Participant 40: I think so because everything they do is very special but combining them makes something powerful like the soul.

Participant 41: The soul is the boss and the rest work for it. The soul is me. The mind , body and heart with out soul distract me to be bad.

Participant 42: Not sure

Participant 43: Sometimes people take horrible risks, bad, they probably would take both.

Participant 44: Yes because one soul without mind cannot take decisions in life and how to believe things. ones soul without heart cannot function and of course the body follows the soul differently the others.

Participant 45: I dont know the answer because it needs lot of thinking and carful consideration.

Participant 46: They're just human utensils which ones you cant live without. They are just to make your body function. For example someone uses artificial heart but that doesn't mean that his old personality changed because he got a different heart.

Participant 47: Yes, the mind, heart and body are utensils which serve the soul so that one is fulfilled. They allow an individual to obtain life of their own in their own way.

Participant 48: Can be fulfilled, not sure about being faithful.

Participant 49: Yes , perhaps.

Participant 50: Yes the heart, mind and body are tools to serve your soul. The individual should believe and be determent to achieve it.

Q8. What does it mean to believe in God and how can this be demonstrated by 3 rules or examples?

Participant 1: Yes. The whole being should serve the mission of the soul. When the mind, heart and body are aligned to the soul's purpose, the person feels inner peace, fullness and harmony. If they are not in alignment with the soul, the person feels disintegrated, disconnected and hollow inside - which is sometimes further exploited by numbing the feeling in various addictions, - or in some cases the person accepts the hurt of this brokenness and takes healing steps in accordance to the soul's liberation and external manifestation.

Participant 2: I believe in values, not in God.

Participant 3: Yes I do believe in God

> *Miracle do happen and Its His Almighty power that does that.*
> *When the world is against you or the time is like that everything happening is*
> *Not correct one after the other the problems are rising its head and their is no way out in spite of everything we do so at last its said God helps those those who helps themselves and His call is the supreme one and his blessings too. When it was no one of my acquaintance as a Healer I used to believe that God is the only one that can help me out if I am facing some problems and Yes On Daily basis, I do pray and their is supreme power in that if one started believing in that. Yeah I know there are many people who do not believe in worship but I do believe in that and I worship daily if its a good or bad or anytime.*

Participant 4: Believing in God is a new beginning with the truth alongside.
1 - Treat others as they deserve it, love yourself and others for God's sake.
2 - Be patient because miracles exist, and those who endure are the ones who gain.
3 - Be pious, respect the family, the society, the relatives.
4 - Always SMILE.

Participant 5: It means that there is a shelter to be supported. 1) God is present in our lives, believe me. 2) God created us, for the sake of all the good that he has …….

Participant 6: Personally, I believe that there is one God and that he exists everywhere and his presence is seen and is very easy to prove it to those who have eyes to see, and ears to hear. God is present by giving us so many good things that we have every day, He is present by making us possessors of ourselves but, when we forget, He is there to remind us that we are the ones, who need Him. And I believe that God has created the best habitat for all of us: the FAMILY.

Participant 7: To believe that He is ONE and no one deserves to be worshiped except Him.
To let the weight of your issues to be supported by Him.
To believe that for everything, the only one that you find after every storm is again Him.

Participant 8: Trusting in God means believing in the almighty that gives us strength to live every day, to walk, to talk, to see, to hear, to talk, to reason and above all to make good use of all the good that he has forgiven us, and we thank him as much as possible as he created us and to him we will return inshallah. Trust in God means not to lose hope, to believe in justice, to strive to add to the good in the midst of very bad things, such a force.

Participant 9: You just know and believe that God died on the cross and pray and say thank you, not because of the pain, but for rescuing us. Examples:
1 - Pray
2 - Light up a candle and be ready to love.
3 - Shoot fireworks to remember God's pins.

Participant 10: To believe in God means to thank you for everything you have. For the life you have given. 3 tips: The good things you do they come back to you in one way or other soon or later. Pray to God for family members and for loved ones. We should take care of ourselves and others.

Participant 11: To not judge. To love anyone.

Participant 12: To believe in God means that you are one who respects the moral principles, so you are a just and reasonable person about your actions.

Participant 13: I believe in God because: When I asked for help, He helped me; Warning 1 day before 3 days before someone's death dies, During the prayer and during Ramadan I feel strong ...

Participant 14: Trust in god I think that's all. 3 advices according to me
1) Believe in god
2) Follow the relevant rituals
3) Be devout believer

Participant 15: To believe in God is to acknowledge a higher power and to find the reality of God in side oneself and in all creation and in every speck of dust

Participant 16: Treat others as you would like to be treated.
- Love yourself as you would like to be loved.
- Give 100% in everything that you choose.

Participant 17: To believe in God is to trust the Lord Jesus whom HE HAS sent for the salvation of man since fall of Adam. That I believe in God should not just be heard from my lips but seen in my actions (love, care, others first, etc.), for faith without works is dead.

Participant 18: For me belief in gods is the maximum definition, because nothing in this world is not without genes, so even the universe has its creation and it has overwhelmed it. It is plenipotentiary, it is for all individuals and persecils and always has created the circumstances for life

Participant 19: Life has put me in front of losses and successes,,in both cases I have only asked for the help of lord,,,because I believe in his existence and I felt realized by what I asked,,
1 - you have to believe
2 - you have to ask
3 - you have to act Participant 20: Not sure

Participant 21: Believing in God makes a human being a better person,, just knowing that someone is watching us it's a good feeling especially when we do something good and you have that feeling that you will be rewarded.

Participant 22: Everyone has their own way for believing in god and their beliefs. I believe that god intends to lead everyone to the right path in different methods.

Participant 23: Not sure - treat other fairly, justice.

Participant 24: Beliefs depend on person and how they see things in the world.

Participant 25: It means something different for everyone

Participant 26: Considering the lack of evidence for the existence of god then for me to believe in god would mean I believe in something I have no evidence for. I accept that there is a less than 0000.1% chance that god exists simply because humanity hasn't literally everything however if there a chance god exists then there are a billion other things existing as well of instead.

Participant 27: I think believing in god means that you have guidance and you have a more brighter past.

Participant 28: control
segregation
hypocrisy

Participant 29: It means you believe in a higher power. demonstrated by following bible, believing in it, shaming the word of god.

Participant 30: Believing in god means believing in a superpower which can be described in different ways depending on the religion and the beliefs of somebody. personally, I dont believe in god so I dont knowhow it might be demonstrated.

Participant 31: To follow the lord by example and do righteous thing.

Participant 32: I know something above us exists, I dont know whether it is god but great creates people, and greats this world go around.

Participant 33: I dont know.

Participant 34: We are god, but the modernism of the human life style does not allow us to become god.

Participant 35: God bought us into the world and my heart says to believe on him.

Participant 36:   God means everything to me, talk to myself a lot. I try to do good to others and appreciate even the smallest things

.

Participant 37: I believe in some power above us that is the centre of the energy of the existence… some call god…. Some call it zot… some call it by different name.

Participant 38: God has created us and everything in this life we have it because of him.

Participant 39: Go to church, believe in him, obey his commands.

Participant 40: To believe in god means that you believe.
- I communicate to god by talking to him, I can talk to him because he made us and he is a part of me.

Participant 41: He gives advice
- I can listen to him because he is in my body and he made me .

Participant 42: To believe in god is to believe in something powerful watching over you and guiding you, I believe that you must not sin and if you done , then you must respect for those sins. There are different ways of sinning, three of them being: do not kill, do not hurt others in any way and do not hurt yourself.

Participant 43: Better to believe in god always.

Participant 44: To believe in god means,it means to believe in peace, that has created everything.

Participant 45: To believe on God it means a greater force with out being replaced that inspires.

Participant 46: There are no facts that god exists. Innocent people get killed everyday ones who believe and who don't believe in god. Probably someone clever came up with God when back in time was no security and polices so that helped to decrease the crimes and make people behave better as they would be scared believing that god will see them if they do anything wrong and will punish them. I believe in science.

Participant 47: To believe in god means to :
-do not harm anyone,
-listen to your intuition,
-thank god for all the good things that occur.

Participant 48: For me, the belief in God is about your own private world- what you perceive as being good, the goodness in people and the goodness in self.

Participant 49: It brings you peace and sense of direction.

Participant 50: To believe, to dedicate to God with your soul, heart and mind. Not to do bad to no one , to have a big heart and pure, not to think bad about no one.

Q9. Do you suppose that children are like angels and innocent and why? So how is their suffering explained in God's language and why?

Participant 1: I have to accept the limitation of not being able to explain this, but I have faith that somehow, God knows.

Participant 2: I believe that death is one. The causes are various.

Participant 3: Yes Children are the embodiment of God's Image I believe in that way and ofcourse they are the most innocent version the human will ever have as they are neutral in their way and they do what they feel like doing. Yes Of course I love kids. They are innocent one as they are unaware of feeling like hatred, racism, ego problems to a certain age. After a certain age when they grow up they see the society and the behaviour of the people around the scenario changes and they adopt themselves which is best suited for them.

Yes There are many mythological epics and stories that depict the existence of God in form of a small kids and various hardships the kid goes through as he grows up, it is shown to us so that from his early childhood days one inculcate the good qualities and in spite of lots of hardships one should never choose the wrong path as the building blocks of being good is deeply rooted in the childhood era. The Growing child catches and copies the good things around v quickly as at that time the brain and the eyes sees it for first time.

Participant 4: Children are angels and innocent. I have seen little of those children who suffer because of poverty, or because they are killed or harassed by others.

Participant 5: Of course they are, their purity demonstrates this. I do not believe that God brings suffering.

Participant 6: I do not know how to explain this exactly. But, I believe in karma. What you have done, will be returned to you. And I often believe that children suffer the consequences for the mistakes of adults.

Participant 7: YES, children are innocent and honest. They suffer the mistakes of their parents, but they can also be rewarded in the next life.

Participant 8: All children are born innocent, coping with insecure people, transmitting their culture makes them suffer example: they made them grow before their time, they do not allow them to grow in the right stages, and deny the most beautiful age of the individual, their childhood. I believe because we are all selected in some way or another, we are destined to suffer or to be happy.

Participant 9: Yes. They are like that because they are kids, they are small, they believe in God. You know why we call them little angels? Because they are small and they have dreams and have wings. Their suffering…you know babies, they are like little angels, but sometimes they like to walk on the pavement or floor, but you know the floor is very dirty, and you know their hands, they walk with their hands, and when they do not know how to wash their hands, when dinner's ready they put the food on their hand first, and put it in their mouthTho ou! Because they touched the floor, the microbes from the floor go inside their tummy and then they get sick. That's one option.
People die from anything that could cause injury. People die from guns, aeroplanes, cars, bulls with horns, strangers (they might give things with poison, sugar and alcohol, they might add some poison / alcohol to lollipop, then people might die from the poison and alcohol). Children suffer because they sometimes get poor, but then when they are poor and survive they will be called: Overcome Bright Angels!

Participant 10: The children are innocent angels. Because there are full of purity, their delicacy it made you to treat them like most pressures thing on this life.

Participant 11: Children are like angels, but for other things it is not for me to speak, but for those who serve the Lord. I cannot talk about things, which do not belong to my field of study.

Participant 12: They do not carry vices when they are born, but it is the environment, where they grow, that makes them wear them by transforming into devils.

Participant 13: Children are innocent but not angels, because they do not know how to plan evil!

Participant 14: I believe that children are innocent angels because they are creatures full of love. And I believe their suffering does not come from the Lord.

Participant 15: I probably believe now that children are born innocent
I cant explain the suffering of the world, nor how this happens in the providence of God, through all the wars that go on or how the world can be made right amidst the bad behaviour of the mighty.

Participant 16: Children are innocent as they are a blank slate and are taught what they learn growing up.

Participant 17: Why do innocent people including children suffer? Why is there suffering at all? Why is there so much lack in the midst of plenty? Why are there denials, frustrations, killings and so on?
These are happening for the time being because Satan the evil one is still at large with his demons. Man submitted to him, remember, and he is acting out his ruler-ship of wickedness.
Yet a time will come later when he(satan) will be removed to his deserved abode, the lake of fire. Then God the Father will restore all things and wipe away all tears. Revelation 21:3 to 5

Participant 18: YES, children are compared to a blank and unwritten letter. Their sufferings are due to society and family.

Participant 19: Children are the purest and most affluent thing that God brings in this life, and in the earth, they continue to be anything from zero, they have no evil minds and they don't think to hurt others, they give away the infinite love and great energy, I believe that the God does not give his angels suffering but he prepares them slowly for the unexpected life.

Participant 20: Don't know.

Participant 21: Yes I believe every child born it's an angel until they grow and depends I what family and how loved they are and that shapes them into a better adults. Well children so get sick but I believe God gives us lives and can take it from us at anytime and doesn't have an age.

Participant 22: No

Participant 23: Not sure - treat other fairly, justice.

Participant 24: Children are innocent

Participant 25: I dont think they are as there's no proof as angels.

Participant 26: Children are not agents or messengers of god in my opinion and if they are what does that say about god? the fact there is suggesting and poverty amongst children.

Participant 27: I think god made us in there own. everyone is an angel Participant 28: No I believe children are too hide to know good from bad.

Participant 29: In a way, there are innocent at first but its environmental circumstances that make them corrupt.

Participant 30: *A child that comes in life is innocent but she is shaped from the very first experiences of their life depending whether they are positive/negative.*

Participant 31: *Not sure*

Participant 32: *Yes, children are like angels. suffering is a revenge, good makes in name of love. people come into life by love and then they enter this world in a bad place.*

Participant 33: *I dont know, I'm not religious .*

Participant 34: *Until you became adult yours status is closer to god there for they suffer from then.*

Participant 35: *Children are angels and pain becomes from people and adults.*

Participant 36: *Yes, because their mind, body and soul has not been corrupted.*
Because perants and people in general are constantly learning and experiencing. Suffering is just a part of that.

Participant 37: *No*

Participant 38: *Children are angels and adults couses their pain.*

Participant 39: *Even if they suffer they will still go heaven.*

Participant 40: *Not all are because some suffer and angels are perfect and those kids don't have the right to speak.*

Participant 41: *Dont know.*

Participant 42: *I believe that they are angels to a certain extent, due to their innocence. however angels are perfect and no one is perfect.*

Participant 43: *Its like every spring a baby borns and all cute.*

Participant 44: *I agree that children are angels, because kids can make mistakes but are forgiven, I think their struggles are explained that it is not in gods hands to decide what happens to the kids, but in the hand of humans.*

Participant 45: Of course that children are innocent and other part I can not explain.

Participant 46: Children, adult or old people are the same being same thing we just look at them in a different way.

Participant 47: Yes children are angels, god creates kids as innocent humans circumstances and situations can change how a child acts or behaves. Suffering is explained as an obstacle, it may lead to a better outcome in the end.

Participant 48: Children are product of their genes, environment and their families. Not sure children as angels…….

Participant 49: Children are innocent because they have not gone through the ego where they can make decisions.

Participant 50: Of course the children are innocent and angels. God has decided our path and everyone should do the maximum to achieve the purpose.

Q10. Are there two kinds of death: A prewritten one and another that depends on our Actions? If so, how is the child's death explained?

Participant 1: Death means when the soul feels lost: This can be in this life (i.e. when the person is out of touch with who they are) or after it departs from the body.

I have faith there must be an explanation, to this occurrence in human beings including children.

Participant 2: Children are human beings, who are being formed. I wish that just like the body creates antibodies for self-defence, the children were also formed.

Participant 3: Yes of course, there are two kinds of death.
The child's death in real sense the death might occurred medically or in psychological terms everybody has a child inside the body and that part of child is played with the company of those with whom we are v close to. May be A man of 40 yrs can act as a small child in front of Her Mom and make her smile as for Mom how old a person is He is a son after all.
Psychologically in terms the child death occurs when there is a lot of pressure in professional and personal life and there is only in tension the person lives and there is no way out so ironically its the dead end of the child the person was having inside him/her. Though Healing process one can retain the same way of life and Yes Everything is possible today its up to one how much priority one gives to the things.

Participant 4: Dont know.

Participant 5: Yes. The death of children is explained to be mostly due to our actions.

Participant 6: Death is one of the unrecognized mysteries, so I do not know what to think and consequently what answer to give to this question.

Participant 7: Death exists as a phenomenon. The one that is related to our actions, exists when we die inwardly from the darkness that characterizes us. The child can die from death as a phenomenon that occurs...

Participant 8: I believe that yes, the child's death I think is a trial for the parents and my personal opinion is that the child being a pure coming from God wants to take with him the children as they may be happier, this thought that I have also encouraged my soul not to feel bad about their deaths.

Participant 9: Yes. So God's rule is that don't steal or you might die, because I am going to show an example of this. If a person steals a bottle / chicken or toys, they (I said 'they' for the shopkeepers) might call the police and then they will be arrested by the police and they might put them into jail and the person still doesn't understand or think about stealing, they will be given one more chance! O ou! If they still think about stealing, they could be sent to death.

Participant 10: We have Two Deaths. The first part of the death of the children I can explain with the fact that it can be anticipated.

Participant 11: I think there are several kinds of death: accidental, from old age, terminal illness...regarding children, except the age-related one, there are many factors leading to death, and unfortunately, we cannot prevent all their deaths.

Participant 12: Fate is predestined, and so are our actions. This explains the deaths of children.

Participant 13: No two, only one exist, the one predicted and the childs death is already written.

Participant 14: Yes, we have two types of death, and the children do not always die unpredictably. After a few moments have happened that they have died as a result of the actions of other people. But even when God gets them. As I think their mission is to be angels.

Participant 15: Well we all live and we all die. Some children die too young. Death is a part of life. Some kind of life goes on after death

Participant 16: No, only one that is determined by our actions.

Participant 17: There are three kinds of death.

    i.   Physical transition: This is when someone ceases to breathe physically. This is not actually death, because the person lives on either in paradise or hell.

    ii. Spiritual death: This is a man's separation from God as a result of sin. Returning to God in repentance is a remedy to this.

    iii. Second death: This is as a result of spiritual death. When and individual loses his physical life in the state of spiritual death(ii above) It is the complete and total separation from God forever.

Participant 18: Yes, the prewritten death is the partition from this life. Someone can be alive or in life but is not worth as much as the dead one, and the death of a child is God's predestination. Birth and death are very determined by God.

Participant 19: I believe that God has given the individual one kind of death, though some people say in certain situations that their death come as a cause of their actions but I do not believe that is so, I believe that god has written everyones the way of the death, an accident, a disease, or many other ways, while the child's death I think is because the god brings angels to the ground as well, and he thinks this is a test for the parents and he wants to see how much confidence they still have in him.

Participant 20: Dont know.

Participant 21: Well I thing our action does play a role maybe a little but I strongly agree everything it's meant to be and we die when we it's our time that's why believing in God doesn't make death very said as I know it's a better place up there and doing good as I mentioned above gets you a better place.

Participant 22: I believe that only god knows the exact day and timing and location for your death because has planned your life.

Participant 23: I dont know

Participant 24: Indeed I think it depends on ones actions and prewritten one.

Participant 25: There isn't there is only one type of reality

Participant 26: I wouldn't know

Participant 27: No there are one does whether someone kills you or you die

Participant 28: The death of anyone is a loss. no death is prewritten. the death of a child is tragic

Participant 29: No only one. depends on our action. the child death in explained by what they were doing and where they were at the time.

Participant 30: It always depends on our actions but I will have doubts about prewritten things.

Participant 31: People either go to hell or heaven depending on their actions.

Participant 32: There are 2 kinds of death. not sure about the second.

Participant 33: I dont believe in prewritten children die for many reasons.

Participant 34: If the death is determine by the god, then the god plan accordingly.

Participant 35: Up to age 7 the children don't happen anything and after age 7 child start to feel pain which is caused by adults.

Participant 36: Yes, just a lesson to someone.

Participant 37: Death is death, it just happens.

Participant 38: I dont' know, I don't know how to answer.

Participant 39: No one is sure of what is going to happen in life after death.

Participant 40: I don't know.

Participant 41: I don't know.

Participant 42: Yes , I believe so , in my opinion, a child death is prewritten and very unfortunate.

Participant 43: Mostly a murderer would kill them.

Participant 44: The death of children is on the hand of faith, of luck, and if the person kills a child he will suffer after.

Participant 45: I think we have only one death. The death of children can not explain nor accept with out feeling much pain.

Participant 46: There's no prewritten death. Anything depends on people's actions including children's death.

Participant 47: Death is prewritten as god has written life. Those who die young are to precious to be living on this earth. God wants these humans closer to him (discussed this yesterday night with my 15 year old sis)

Participant 48: Don't know….death can reveal …reseackness process.

Participant 49: Not sure.

Participant 50: Yes we do have to kind of deaths, one prewritten and other one depending on our actions. The death of the child is written by God.

Q11. Can a human being be filled with love, which comes exclusively from the source within themselves? And from the moment they become aware of that love they do not feel suffering because they are know their purpose and are fulfilled?

What do you think is the love within? And why do you think that way?

Participant 1: Yes, and this kind of humans are called saints.

Participant 2: I do not know. It seems a bit more complicated than that. The human being learns to manage the feelings they experience, channel any kind of energy towards them, into positive energy.

Participant 3: Yes Of course The Universe lies within oneself and Love do exists in human heart and one who recognizes it to what level it depends upon the person to person, how strong the ignition of love is inside him/her it depends upon the person to person.
Yes Without love one cannot do anything and if one never develops the passion and the zeal inside one will never do the task complete and this one cannot force anyone to love that thing or love anything its the person own choice so that they can achieve their purpose. When I talk about love I mean true love not artificial love.

Participant 4: Totally true, and it is exactly why I know this, that I often cannot be happy. The cause is the external factors.

Participant 5: Of course we must be filled with love to feel fulfilled. But love does not relieve our suffering.

Participant 6: I've heard a lot about love - that is considered to be one of the most beautiful sensations in the world, that fulfils and equates to life. I personally have not tried all the kinds of love, but, I am fulfilled with the love of family and friends. I cannot say that being filled with love, one does not look at the sufferings - they certainly look at them because, they are there with you, but these are the people who love to donate things, to ease things and dress their eyes with positivity and optimism.

Participant 7: YES, if a person finds their own self, they are beneficial in society too. Any love can enwrap us, but the most consolidated is the one that is ours, which keeps us in the right direction. If the person knows their own self, they know their goals, and if they know the goals, they know what they are talking about and trust it.

Participant 8: I think yes, when a person has a love in the soul I believe it is fulfilled on all sides.

Participant 9: Yep! Because they might know how to be friendly to themselves and others. They do not suffer because they have that love inside them that helps them get through.

Participant 10: The individual could not be fulfilled and loved in this kind of life.

Participant 11: Everything is, because we think or feel that way, not that we actually are that way... so everything is unique. What may be called fulfilling to me is not so for someone else, and vice versa. And we do not have the same desires to fulfil at a given time. At different times we have different desires and dreams ...'we are slaves of our desires', has said Schopenhauer, the well-known philosopher. 'Man', he said, must come out from the "wheel" of desires to be really happy!!"

Participant 12: Yes, when they find peace in themselves and with the others around.

Participant 13: Can be filled with love but suffering knows and have everybody! I am fulfilled but I suffer when others suffer.

Participant 14: Love in my opinion the love is the saviour of all. If you are surrounded with love. Everything has a solution.

Participant 15: Normally we know about this love, through our contact with another , which authenticates that love I suppose the more deeply we love, the more capacity we have to suffer too. Some with deepest pain know deepest joy

Participant 16: No they cannot. they can love themselves but this can cause loneliness if they only love themselves and cannot share or receive love back.

Participant 17: Yes. This is a height in spirituality.

Participant 18: As far as love is concerned, I will define it in love and happiness. Love is pretty much in the broad sense, but if one feels happy, I think he has achieved the goal for himself.

Participant 19: The love is a name that makes you love more then your self, "love is the key that opens the doors of happiness," if you take it away the land where you live will go to chaos, is a motive, the motive of hope, , sacrifice and happiness at the same time, so if inside the individual there is love then the key that he keeps open every door.

Participant 20: Don't know.

Participant 21: The best love it is within our self. There is no better loving than loving ourself. And it's true you live yourself others will love you and respect you.

Participant 22: No love simply comes the moment people one able to communicate with each other and become closer.

Participant 23: Yes, a human is partially filled with love by loving themselves but this kind of love does not become a succent for someone else. loving yourself to the extent to fix the purpose.

Participant 24: Indeed they can but it also depends on the surrounding and others reactions towards the person.

Participant 25: I think people can be happy without the need for any external factors e.g god.

Participant 26: Chemical reactions within the brain I think this due to scientific research.

Participant 27: You can love yourself but need to love others to.

Participant 28: Yes, there is no problem with a person having love. however this will not solve suffering.

Participant 29: The love within in how happy you are with yourself and your achievements.

Participant 30: I believe in disposability though I find it rare to happen it is finding absolute satisfaction from yourself and making things for yourself to achieve it.

Participant 31: Yes because we have to be kind.

Participant 32: It can be filled with love but needs people to help with offering trust. sometimes you offer love and dont get it. so you change to fit it.

Participant 33: I think everyone should feel love.

Participant 34: If you do not love yourself, you comfort love anyone else in the world.

Participant 35: Yes, god is filled with love because of vetbelieve and wisdom the things comes.

Participant 36: It is possible Love within is love off all, if you love everything within, you will then love everything without.

Participant 37: Yes , I strongly believe that our happens lays within us. If we feel unhappy, angry, sad is because we chose to….we choose our we feel through our emotions.

Participant 38: Yes, because the person who does not have self believe is lost in this life.

Participant 39: It depends on the situation, people are to live happy ever after.

Participant 40: People can still love themselves if they are lonely. The love within is that your loving yourself. I think that way because its what I think.

Participant 41: It's not enough because I still need my mum and dad but is as I care for myself and I will find a way to be fulfilled.

Participant 42: Yes, I believe that the love of oneself is extremely important and once you love yourself you can start loving others around you and become confident with yourself. I also agree with , once you become couse of what love, you feel no suffering.

Participant 43: love is the one to help you win and succeed your achievement.

Participant 44: I think the person can not be too happy because the person thinks about others happiness not only for themselves.

Participant 45: It is possible for a person to be filled with love and inspiration from his own self. Whoever the sufferings are never-ending but transitory.

Participant 46: I don't think so.

Participant 47: It an individual has no self love, other source of love are not genuine experienced.

Ove within is the admiration for yourself which then allows you to love others. I believe this because this is what I experience.

Participant 48: Yes can be doing the right thing because when you care is alloys evidence of those receiving in the end is results in love.

Participant 49: Yes definitely.

Participant 50: Yes it has to have self-love.

Note: We assure you that in this research your identity will remain confidential. The personal contact details are required exclusively to verify that the information and impressions given belong to real participants.

Name Surname: _____

Age and your profession: _____

Contact (telephone number, address, email):

_____

REFERENCES

1) Huss. B. (2014). Spirituality: The Emergence of a New Cultural Category and its Challenge to the Religious and the Secular. Journal of Contemporary Religion. Volume 29, Issue 1. P47-60.

2) Albaugh, J.A. (2003)'Spirituality and life-threatening illness: a phenomenological study',Oncology Nursing Forum, 30: 4. P:593-598.

3) Kotsos, T. (2017). Self-love the greatest love of all. Mind Your Reality. Change the Invisible and the Visible will Follow. Available online at: <http. http://www.mind-your-reality.com/self_love.html>

4) Department of Health. (2011). Spiritual care at the end of life: a systematic review of the literature. Available Online at: <http://www.dh.gov.uk/publications>

5) Jones, R.A., Taylor, A.G., Bourgignon, C., Steeves, R. Fraser, G. Lippert, M. Theodorescu, D., Matthews, H & Kilbridge, K.L. (2007). Complementary and alternative medicine modality use and beliefs among African American Prostate Cancer survivors. Oncology Nursing Forum, 34: 2, 359-364

6) Marie Curie (2009). Liverpool Care Pathway for the dying patient (LCP) Pocket Guide. Liverpool: Marie Curie Palliative Care Institute.

7) Department of Health (2009) End of Life Care Strategy First annual report, London: DH Publications.

8) Nardella, N. (2014). Why Self-Love is the Most Important form of Love. Available Online at: < https://www.elephantjournal.com/2014/10/why-self-love-is-the-most-important-form-of-love-natalie-nardella/>

9) Koenig, H.G., McCulough, M.E. & Larson, S.S. (2001) Handbook of Religion and Health Oxford: Oxford University Press.

10) NICE. (2015) New guidelines on end of life care. National Institute for Health Care and Excellence. Available online at: <https://www.nhs.uk/news/medical-practice/new-guidelines-on-end-of-life-care-published-by-nice/>

11) Coyte, M.E., Gilbert, P. & Nicholls, V. (2007) Spirituality, Values and Mental Health: Jewels for the Journey, London: Jessica Kingsley.

12) Elliot D. Cohen Ph.D (2012). *What Would Aristotle Do? Are You Your Own Person? Take the Self-Determination Inventory to Find Out.* Available online at https://www.psychologytoday.com/blog/what-would-aristotle-do/201202/are-you-your-own-person

13) Adamson M (2017). *Connecting with the Divine. The major world religions and their beliefs about God. Hinduism, Buddhism, Islam, Christianity, and New Age.* Available online at < https://www.everystudent.com/features/connecting.html>

14) Frater J. (2007). *Top 10 Organized Religions and their Core Beliefs.* Available online at < http://listverse.com/2007/07/31/top-10-organized-religions-and-their-core-beliefs/ >

15) Rich T. (2011). *What Do Jews Believe? Level: Basic.* Available online at http://www.jewfaq.org/beliefs.htm

16) Steinberg M. (1965). *Basic Judaism. The essential book for Jews and non-Jews eager to know more about one of the world's great religions.* P:6.

17) *Views on Heaven and Hell.* Available online at: https://christianity.org.uk/index.php/a/views-on-heaven- and-hell.php

18) Moberg D. (1984). *Subjective Measures of Spiritual Well Being.* Review of Religious Research. Religious Research Association. New York.

19) Steiger N. & Lipson J. (1985). *Self Care Nursing: Theory and Practice.* Brady Communications, Bowie, Maryland.

20) Freeman. J (2014). *7 levels of consciousness: The path of enlightenment.* Transcendental Meditation. Available online at: < https://tmhome.com/books-videos/7-states-of-consciousness-video-interview/ >

21) Stoll R. (1979). *Guidelines for spiritual assessment.* American Journal of Nursing. 79(9),1574-1577.

22) Howden J.W. (1992). *Development and psychometric characteristics of the spirituality assessment scale.* Unpublished doctoral dissertation, Texas Woman's University, Denton, Texas.

23) Frankl V.E. (1959). *Man's Search for Meaning.* Washington Square Press. Washington.

24) Oldnall A. (1996). *Meeting the spiritual needs of patients.* Journal of Advanced Nursing. 23:138.

25) *Burkhardt M. (1989) Spirituality: an analysis of the concept. Holistic Nursing Practice 3(3), 69–77.*

26) *Culliford. L. (2017). Spirituality and Art. A priceless living bridge between mind and spirit. Spiritual wisdom for secular times. Available online at: https://www.psychologytoday.com/blog/spiritual-wisdom-secular-times/201712/spirituality-and-art*

27) *Camic PM. Playing in the mud: health psychology, the arts and creative approaches to health care. J Health Psychol 2008;13(2):287–298*

28) *Stuckey. H.L. and Nobel. J. (2010). The Connection Between Art, Healing, and Public Health: A Review of Current Literature. American Journal of Public Health. 100(2): 254–263.*

29) *Jusino. T. (2017). Mayim Bialik Explains How Science and Religion Can Co-Exist. Available online at: https://www.themarysue.com/mayim-biyalik-science-religion-co-exist/*

30) *Dietrich. E. (2017). Is Science a Religion? Available online at: https://www.psychologytoday.com/blog/excellent-beauty/201710/is-science-religion*

31) *Lovgren. S. (2004). Evolution and Religion Can Coexist, Scientists Say. Available online at: https://news.nationalgeographic.com/news/2004/10/1018_041018_science_religion.htm*

32) *Greene. B. (2005). The Fabric of the Cosmos: Space, Time, and the Texture of Reality. Penguin Press.*

33) *Mastin. (2011). Arguments for Atheism. Living without religion with a clear conscience. Available online at: < http://www.argumentsforatheism.com/what.html>*

34) *www.oxforddictionaries.com*

35) *Kipp. M. (2014). Daily Love. Growing into Grace.*

36) *Merritt, Anna Lea. Love Locked Out: The Memoirs of Anna Lea Merritt with a Checklist of Her Works. Boston: Museum of Fine Arts, 1981.*

37) *Bandura, A. (1986). Social foundations of thought and action: A social cognitive theory. Englewood Cliffs, NJ: Prentice Hall.*

38) *Schunk, D. H. (1999). Social self-interaction and achievement behavior. Educational Psychologist, 34, 219-227.*

39) *Hardy, D. (2012). A Seven-Step Prescription for Self-Love. Self-love is an action, not a state of feeling good*

www.ingramcontent.com/pod-product-compliance
Lightning Source LLC
Chambersburg PA
CBHW041646120626
46551CB00016B/2332